Ursu... University, befor... ...al Horticultural Soc... ...isley and the Royal Botanic Gardens, Kew. For more than twenty-five years, she wrote a gardening column for a succession of national newspapers, including the *Observer*, *Sunday Telegraph* and *Daily Telegraph*, as well as the *Spectator*. She has won three major writing awards from the Garden Media Guild. In 2011 she was named the Garden Media Guild's Gardening Columnist of the Year.

Praise for *A Green and Pleasant Land*

'A compelling account . . . It also unearths some unexpected facts – such as the liberal use of cyanide as a pesticide.'

House & Garden

'An intriguing glimpse of horticultural life in war conditions . . . Buchan's excellent book, both touching and informative . . . could also, perhaps, offer a blueprint for a much-needed overhaul of the 21st-century lifestyle.'

The Lady

'A well-researched and evocative account of how Britain's gardeners fought the Second World War.'

The Countryman

'Buchan's keen eye for the bonkers often has you laughing out loud [but] she will also set you hunting for your hanky.'

Hortus magazine

'This year's most stimulating work of Horticultural History . . . an exhaustively researched, possibly definitive, and occasionally myth-dispelling account of the role of gardeners in World War II.'

Morning Star

ALSO BY URSULA BUCHAN

A Green and Pleasant Land

How England's Gardeners Fought the Second World War

Ursula Buchan

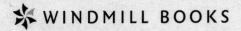

Published by Windmill Books 2014

2 4 6 8 10 9 7 5 3 1

Copyright © Ursula Buchan 2013

Ursula Buchan has asserted her right under the Copyright, Designs and
Patents Act, 1988, to be identified as the author of this work.

This book is a work of non-fiction.

First published in Great Britain in 2013 by Hutchinson

Windmill Books
The Random House Group Limited
20 Vauxhall Bridge Road, London SW1V 2SA

Addresses for companies within The Random House Group Limited
can be found at: www.randomhouse.co.uk/offices.htm

The Random House Group Limited Reg. No. 954009

www.randomhouse.co.uk

A CIP catalogue record for this book
is available from the British Library

ISBN 9780099558668

The Random House Group Limited supports the Forest Stewardship
Council® (FSC®), the leading international forest-certification organisation.
Our books carrying the FSC label are printed on FSC®-certified paper. FSC is
the only forest-certification scheme supported by the leading environmental
organisations, including Greenpeace. Our paper procurement policy can be
found at: www.randomhouse.co.uk/environment

Typeset in Perpetua by Palimpsest Book Production Ltd, Falkirk, Stirlingshire
Printed and bound by CPI Group (UK) Ltd, Croydon, CR0 4YY

TO H.W.E.T.,
WITH LOVE

CONTENTS

LIST OF ILLUSTRATIONS

WEIGHTS, MEASURES AND MONEY

Imperial weights

1 ounce (oz) is the equivalent of approximately 28 grams
16 ounces in a pound (lb)
2 lbs 3 ounces in a kilo
14 lbs in a stone
112 lbs in a hundredweight (cwt)
20 cwt in a ton

Imperial volumes

1 pint is the equivalent of 568 ml
2 pints in a quart
4 quarts in a gallon

Imperial measures of length

One inch (") is the equivalent of 2.5 centimetres
12 inches in a foot (ft)
3 feet in a yard (yd)
1760 yds in a mile, the equivalent of 1.6 kilometres
The rod (syns. perch and pole) is equivalent to 5.5 yards. In the case of allotments, a rod usually denotes a square measurement.

Money

Decimalisation was not introduced until 1971. In 1939, the smallest unit of coinage was a farthing (a quarter of a penny), followed by a ha'penny, then penny (1d), threepenny bit, sixpence, shilling (1/- or 12 pence), florin (2/-) and half a crown (2/6d). Ten shillings (10/-), a pound (£1 or 20 shillings) and five pounds (£5) were notes. A guinea was 21 shillings.

Prices rose substantially during the war, but to get some idea of the value of money during this time, £40 of today's money would be the rough equivalent of £1 in 1942.

'War is the normal occupation of man – war and gardening,' Winston Churchill told the poet Siegfried Sassoon in 1918. This provocative remark contains more truth than you might at first think. War and gardening are what people have done since the earliest times. These occupations are truly antithetical: the one profoundly destructive, disruptive, uncivilised and ugly, the other constructive, orderly, civilised and both useful and capable of promoting beauty. Between 1939 and 1945 in Britain, war and gardening were very different-coloured strands of national life, which surprisingly often became entwined.

As it turned out, gardening proved to be one way that civilians as well as service personnel and prisoners of war mitigated the shocks and griefs, as well as the food shortages, that they were forced to endure. Gardening also served as a reminder to Britons – at times comforting, at others invigorating – that their green and pleasant land, as well as its more innocent and insular pursuits, was worth fighting and dying for.

Over time, 'the soil' has developed a symbolic meaning and acquired a resonance far removed from the dirt in garden or field. The soil equates to the country itself; we use the words interchangeably. In the mid twentieth century, people were proud of the fact that there had been no fighting on British soil since the Battle of Culloden in 1746, and no successful foreign invasion since 1066. Despite so many changes and convulsions in the first decades of the twentieth century, they retained their highly romantic view of the countryside and their nostalgia for a past rural innocence, which had been fostered by nineteenth- and twentieth-century Romantic writers, artists and composers. The land, especially the countryside, was sacrosanct, inviolable and infinitely precious.

The land even had the capacity to make Britons better people, or so G. W. Giles, the secretary of the National Allotments Society – a man who never shrank from the high-flown sentiment – remarked in 1939: 'it is generally agreed that the closer association of man with Mother Earth the better citizen he becomes. As a nation our roots strike deep into the soil and some of the finest traits of British character derive their origin from it.'[1]

Most people might have hesitated to express their indebtedness to their land in quite that way, but the sentiment would have resonated nevertheless. Love of the soil sharpened a sense of nationhood; this was deeply felt, although people were understandably resistant to officialdom articulating that love on their behalf and in a heavy-footed manner.

Of course patriotic feeling breeds myths, and the wartime generations were certainly inveterate mythmakers. A number of the more potent wartime myths have survived to this day, despite the gallant efforts of social historians to explode them. In our sphere, the most enduring are the enormous 'success' of both the Dig for Victory campaign and the jam-making of the Women's Institute. We shall see whether the facts actually bear out the extravagant claims still made for them.

Undoubtedly justified was the widely held, if rarely explicitly expressed belief, that gardening was stitched into the tapestries of both national and private life, which could not easily be unpicked even when the nation stood on the edge of catastrophe. For many centuries, Britain's stupendously rich and varied gardening tradition, a tradition of remarkable endeavour and achievement, had markedly influenced society and culture. British people were notably proud of that fact, and the policy-makers were quick to perceive this and to trade upon it when the time came to wake the sleeping behemoth to attend to its wartime duties.

This book is an attempt to examine the Second World War and its legacy, as refracted through the prism of public and private horticulture. Although care must be taken when drawing conclusions about the general in the light of the particular, a study of gardening in wartime is very revealing. It may be one relatively small area of human activity, yet a close examination of it during the war years casts light on many broader themes and preoccupations: propaganda and the role of the media, women's changing aspirations and status, the capacity of people to live normal lives in abnormal circumstances, class and hierarchies, the inter-action between government and people, the role of voluntary organisa-tions and 'community', the march of science and technology, the reach of money, the power of myth.

In peacetime, gardening is an activity that is pursued by millions of people, more or less willingly, sometimes to the exclusion of much else. It has practical, aesthetic and spiritual dimensions; it is both earthily satisfying and emotionally recuperative. As all keen gardeners know, gardening is a potent consolation in bad times or circumstances; so it is small wonder that in wartime people often strove very hard to tend a garden, sometimes in extremely unpromising circumstances. Small wonder, too, that the way they tackled gardening in all its forms during the war years turned out to be emblematic of the way they dealt with many of the difficulties and constraints imposed on them: with thrifty ingenuity, a keen scepticism and invincible humour.

This is the story of how the government encouraged and exhorted the nation's civilians to contribute to the war effort by growing or rearing some of its own fresh food and cooking it properly, and of how ordinary people, as well as gardening experts, responded to the challenge. It is the story of how gardening promoted good morale and later helped reconcile the population to the shabby austerities of peacetime. It is also the story of how, by the end of the war, gardens and gardening had changed profoundly and permanently.

When reading contemporary archives*, I am often struck by how different from me are those people who read bombastic posters and dour leaflets, laughed at *Punch* cartoons and *ITMA* wireless broadcasts, dug holes for Anderson shelters in their lawns, filled pig-swill bins, counted their 'points', stood bored in queues, sang in pubs, refrained

---

* I have restricted myself to consulting English sources in order to keep the work within reasonable bounds. Of course, the government was concerned with the whole United Kingdom, even if there were some national variations, but the differences on the ground in Wales, Scotland and Northern Ireland remain a worthwhile subject for future research.

Numbered references are designed to be helpful to future researchers, but the endnotes are also for the benefit of the general reader: the facts contained in them do not justify a place in the main text but nevertheless add colour and depth to the story.

from swearing in front of a lady, made casual racist comments, wrote weekly letters to their loved ones, wrung the necks of their chickens, risked their lives putting out fires or rescuing their neighbours, looked for their possessions in the ruins of bombed-out houses, deferred to their 'betters', and made do and mended. I may have the coffee mug, but I have little experience of what it is to 'Keep Calm and Carry On' when it really matters. I was born only eight years after the war ended, yet I scarcely recognise myself in these forebears of mine, with their quiet courage, dogged stoicism, restraint and impressive reserves of often baseless optimism.

Only in the gardening sphere can I discern an unbroken thread stretching back to the 1940s, and truly empathise with all the difficulties gardeners experienced in dealing with slugs or providing palatable vegetables for the kitchen in early spring, as well as sharing their fascination with the changing seasons, and pleasure in a blowsy dahlia flower, an apple tree in blossom, a ripe greengage or a larder shelf of bottled tomatoes. Like them, I can appreciate the way that gardening offers the possibility of putting away past failures as one season ends and another beckons – the fact that there is always next year. It is in the garden that I can most closely connect with those who went before me, since the essence of a garden is timeless.

CHAPTER ONE

THE SCENE IS SET

Engdland in the 1930s was a very different place physically from the country we know today. If transported back in time, we might scarcely recognise some parts of it. Agriculture and market gardening were in deep trouble, mainly as a result of freely imported cheap food, and the visible signs of this were many derelict orchards and much neglected scrubland on the less fertile soils. Horses still pulled the ploughs in many arable fields. Great tracts of 'unimproved pasture', parcelled into fields by hedges planted in the eighteenth century, were bright with wild flowers, birds and butterflies, and sustained a large livestock population. The biggest gardens were to be found on the large country estates with houses at their heart, of which there were many more than there are now. Villages were well supplied with good-sized gardens although, curiously, a tenth of rural households had no garden at all.[1]

Cities were not well provided with gardens, as housing density was high, especially in the slums which disfigured many urban landscapes. In inner London, for example, a quarter of residential buildings were without gardens and the situation was similar in the great industrial centres in the north. Allotment provision in both town and country was patchy.

There were no motorways, nor many trunk roads, and traffic jams were common in the centre of towns, since there were few bypasses. Unbridled ribbon development had begun to run out from the big cities, especially London. The post-First World War housing boom had provided four million more dwellings, mainly built on what we now call greenfield sites; many of these were on the outskirts of cities and towns, creating suburbs. It was the age of 'Metroland'. These houses often had gardens, at least partly as a result of the nineteenth-century 'leisure garden'[2] movement, the ideals of which had heavily influenced post-war planners. Nevertheless, by the beginning of the Second World War, it was estimated that there were only 3,500,000 private gardens in Britain, a comparatively modest figure in a country with a population of about 45 million.[3]

For most garden owners in those years, fruit and vegetable growing was not the top priority. The 'typical' 1930s back garden encompassed a well-kept lawn of fine grasses, cut by a push cylinder mower, together with colourful flower beds containing a mixture of perennials and hardy annuals, a separate rose bed and shrub borders, a rockery, serpentine 'crazy paving' paths, a small vegetable plot and possibly a sunken pond. The flower beds might be circular and cut out of the lawn, but they were more often lined up against the garden wall or fence. The rockery might possibly be made of real stone, leaning back slightly in strata, in approved Alpine Garden Society manner, but was more likely to be composed of a mixture of clinker and concrete, and therefore only home to the most amenable rock plants, such as purple aubretia and rampaging 'snow in summer'. The 1930s garden was partly influenced by the 'Gardenesque', a style that emphasised the individual beauty of plants, so that trees and shrubs were often scattered about, which had been advocated by John Loudon a hundred years earlier. The other influence was the Arts and Crafts movement, and in particular its early twentieth-century exponents, Sir Edwin Lutyens and Gertrude Jekyll. The better-off middle-class householder might have paid a general nursery to design and lay out his garden, but only the wealthy employed 'garden architects', and there were comparatively few of those.

There was little discussion of garden planning in newspapers or practical gardening books. One exception was A. G. Hellyer's *Your New Garden* (1937), which featured a number of designs for the standard British garden, though these were really only refined versions of the kinds of rectilinear plans that most gardeners instinctively adopted anyway. Hellyer wrote that:

Garden planning is another immensely important task that looms large at the outset. No matter how thoroughly you prepare the soil or how cleverly you cultivate plants, your garden will never be thoroughly satisfactory if it is badly designed. It is a little ironical that the trained garden architect is usually left to demonstrate his skill on comparatively large and therefore easy plots of ground, whereas the small town garden, which fairly bristles with problems, is planned by an amateur, or, worse still, a careless and unimaginative jobbing gardener.

All well and good, but he rather spoiled it in the next paragraph by remarking:

You may even need to become quite a proficient carpenter during the first few years in your new surroundings. It is always useful to be able to wield saw, chisel and plane in a workman-like manner, but never more so than when one is starting a new garden and must equip oneself with tools and potting sheds, frames, greenhouses, arches, pergolas and many other items calling for at least an elementary knowledge of woodworking.[4]

So, early on in the book he seems to be addressing an exclusively male readership, and implying that garden planning has as much to do with carpentry as artistry.[5]

One contemporary gardening writer, J. Coutts, MBE, VMH,[6] broached the design of a new garden in the *Journal of the Royal Horticultural Society* early on in the Second World War: 'When laying out a small garden it is important to keep it as simple as possible, for such gardens are usually rectangular in shape . . . From this it follows that the correct thing to do is to lay out the garden in straight lines.'[7]

The interwar spirit of Modernism, with its belief that 'traditional' forms of art, architecture, literature, even daily life were becoming outdated in the contemporary, fully industrialised world, had made remarkably little impact on garden owners of any kind. Even those who had heard of the garden designer Christopher Tunnard were rarely impressed, since he seemed to advocate dull gardens of grass, trees and concrete, with little emphasis on the flowers that Britons loved so well and which they were so good at growing. On the whole, rationality and functionalism seemed to gardeners poor substitutes for colour and life. Tunnard's book, *Gardens in the Modern Landscape*, made an impact in rarefied architectural circles, thanks to his emphasis on design which avoided 'the extremes of both the sentimental expression of the wild garden and the intellectual classicism of the "formal" garden; it embodies rather a spirit of rationalism'.[8] However, with these words he risked offending pretty well everybody who called themselves a garden lover. Tunnard certainly had a valid point in wishing to turn garden designers away from that Jekyllian nostalgia for a more innocent age – which must have seemed particularly inappropriate the far side of the 'war to end all wars' – but he probably reckoned without humankind's inability to bear too much reality.

In any event, when Tunnard departed for the United States in 1939, there were few left to keep the Modernist flame alive. Even those landscape architects with Modernist tendencies, like Geoffrey Jellicoe and Sylvia Crowe, were careful not to frighten away their aristocratic clients with over-adventurous schemes.

Just as the majority of ordinary British gardens were remarkably similar in their design and maintenance regime, so, in another way, were the large mansion gardens owned by the rich or well-to-do. The spaces immediately around a big house were almost always laid out on geometric lines, and were bounded by walls and hedges. Parterres were expensively bedded out each year with half-hardy annuals in summer and hardy biennials in winter, while other beds were planted with roses or perennials. Sweeping expanses of well-kept grass sward provided an attractive surface for *al fresco* meals and games. Further away from the house, across the ha-ha, was a less tended, more natural parkland landscape, which had probably not altered much since the eighteenth century except that the trees were now mature. There was usually a large walled garden or gardens, often a fair walk from the house, with elaborate lengths of glasshouse for both ornamental and productive plants. These walled gardens were intensively cultivated by a dozen or more professional gardeners, providing enough fruit and vegetables, as well as pot and cut flowers, to ensure a sufficiency for the house and its occupants at all seasons.

About a quarter of agricultural land (and the houses that went with it) changed hands in the year after the First World War ended, as a direct result of both the threat of increased death duties in the 1919 Budget and the premature death of many sons of the house. A substantial number of large country houses – perhaps as many as 400 – were pulled down. However, in those that remained, even if in different ownership, the 'old ways' were carried on wherever possible. There was no strong imperative to simplify the country-house style of gardening, since labour during the 1920s and 30s was still cheap and plentiful.

'Private service' gardening, as it was called, had developed during the nineteenth century into an intensely hierarchical system, which had similarities to the guild system of apprenticeship, even using some of the same language, such as 'journeyman'.[9] As late as the 1930s, and despite the generally low wages, it was still the wish of many country dwellers that when a son left school at fourteen, he should be taken on as a garden boy at 'the big house'. Often he would not be paid more than a shilling a day for a few months until he had proved his staying power, and the tasks he was set were probably the worst he would ever have to accomplish: steeping new clay pots or cleaning old ones in a cold water tank whilst standing on a stone floor, sweeping floors, cleaning out the heating boiler's stokehole or digging out weeds from the gravel drive with a broken knife. He wore a gardener's apron, with a pocket for knife and 'bast' (raffia), and strong boots. There was no college training involved; everything was learned on the job.

A bright and ambitious boy would keep his eyes and ears open and eventually be promoted to improver journeyman, then journeyman or sub-foreman, then foreman of a particular gardens department, then under-gardener and, finally, head gardener. In gardens with large staffs, the head gardener was a very considerable person, the outdoors equivalent of the butler, often on terms of mutual respect with his employer and definitely paid a salary, rather than a weekly wage, which he could augment by selling surplus produce.

However, to achieve that career progression, the lad would almost certainly have to move from one garden to another 'to improve himself', hence the many small advertisements which appeared in the weekly periodical *The Gardeners' Chronicle*. Until a man was appointed a senior gardener, it was impossible for him to marry, since he would be lodged in the all-male 'bothy', usually next to the extensive range of potting and tool sheds which gave access to the glasshouses on one side of the walled garden. The proximity of the bothy was at least partly to ensure that the young gardeners could stoke the boilers late at night and early in the morning, and be on hand for weekend glasshouse duties. Once married, a gardener would move to a tied cottage owned by his employer. The head gardener's house was often to be found in one corner of the walled garden, so that he only had to open his door and walk out into his domain each morning.

At its best, private service on a large country estate ensured the finest examples of productive horticulture that this country has ever seen, thanks both to the amount of money that house owners were prepared to expend on it and to this rigid but rigorous apprenticeship system. In particular, the quality of fruit – figs, grapes, peaches, nectarines and apricots – grown under glass was exceptionally high. Percy Thrower, who became the first really successful television gardener after the war, recalled of his time working at the royal gardens in Windsor in the early 1930s:

> The training I had in the fruit houses at Windsor was of a kind that, since those days, it has been almost impossible for a young gardener to obtain. For to grow fruit under glass is an art in itself. In all things we were taught to do the right thing, at the right time: no half measures . . . We had to do our work properly; if we didn't we were out, and if one were sacked from a private estate in those days it meant leaving without a

reference and consequently having little chance of getting a similar position anywhere else in private service.'[10]

As it turned out, the spirit of perfectionism which this system promoted was to prove unhelpful to both employer and employee in wartime.

An example of particularly lavish pre-war estate gardening was to be found at Ditchley Park in Oxfordshire. Designed by James Gibbs, with an interior by William Kent, this large mansion was bought by a very rich Anglo-American couple, Ronald and Nancy Tree, in the early 1930s. House, garden and parkland had been neglected by an ancient but declining family, but the Trees brought the estate back to life and Ditchley became a byword for grand but comfortable and stylish country living; it was the scene of many large and smart house parties throughout the decade.

Nancy Tree was a Southern belle from Virginia with a salty sense of humour, a penetrating intelligence and great taste. She was probably the most talented interior decorator of her time, founding the English interior decorating firm, Colefax and Fowler, after the war. Not surprisingly, she was also an inspired garden maker. She and Ronnie Tree, who had been elected MP for Market Harborough in 1933 and was a political ally of Winston Churchill, made a handsome and charismatic couple.

At Ditchley, six professional gardeners lived in the bothy, working under the head gardener, Mr Williams, who resided in the larger house that came with the job. There were seventeen indoor and outdoor servants in all, as well as farm workers, gamekeepers and grooms; all of them seemingly necessary to keep the 3,000-acre estate working well.

On one side of the house was a cricket pitch, laid out and tended by the gardeners; on the other a sunken Italianate parterre designed by the young landscape architect, Geoffrey Jellicoe, using stone from Wrest Park in Bedfordshire, which had recently been sold. Before the war, this parterre was bedded out with red dahlias, pelargoniums and begonias, which sounds very striking, although during hostilities the more restful and easier-to-maintain lavender, rosemary and box replaced them. There was also a beautiful herb garden designed by Jellicoe's business partner,

Russell Page.[11] A four-acre kitchen garden, with a range of glasshouses and a 'cutting' garden, provided most of the fruit and vegetables, as well as floral decorations for the house.

Ditchley became one of the most fêted houses in England, the scene of a ball for a thousand guests in June 1937. The women all wore red and white; among them were Mrs Winston (Clementine) Churchill, Lady Diana Cooper, the wife of MP and author Duff Cooper, and Merle Oberon, the American actress. As Geoffrey and Susan Jellicoe drove away at the end of this dazzlingly elegant evening, they wondered to each other, perhaps with a shiver of foreboding, whether they would ever see the like again.[12]

Ditchley apart, times were already changing even for some of the greatest houses, and by extension for the outdoor staff who worked for them. Percy Thrower, the son of a head gardener, saw that the future for an ambitious young horticulturist was to be found not in the country houses but in the public parks. He left Windsor in 1935 to go to work for Leeds Parks Department.

In the 1920s and 30s, substantial provision was being made for public parks and recreation facilities, such as playing fields, to accompany the enormous surge in house building in towns and suburbs. In 1925, the National Playing Fields Association was founded; this organisation lobbied the government of the day for five acres of open space per 1,000 head of population, of which one acre would be for parks and four for playgrounds and playing fields. The following year, the Institute of Park Administration came into being; this was the professional body that represented park superintendents.

In the 1930s, Parliament passed a number of helpful measures, including the Physical Training and Recreation Act, which enabled grants to be made for the purchase and development of land for these purposes. Crucially, the London County Council Green Belt Scheme was introduced in April 1935, to protect the countryside around London from unfettered and undesirable development. After King George V died in 1936, the public donated money to a fund to boost the provision of memorial gardens, playing fields, tennis courts and the like.

Many of the new suburban parks were designed by their superintendents, although often in conjunction with landscape architects. In 1926, the celebrated landscape architect and town planner Thomas Mawson, working on Stanley Park in Blackpool, incorporated a rose garden and Italian garden amongst the many different types of sports pitches in an innovative design.

Mawson also did some work with one of the best-known park superintendents, Captain A. Sandys-Winch, who laid out no fewer than seven parks in Norwich in the 1920s and early 1930s, including Waterloo Park, which boasted an impressive 300-yard-long herbaceous border.[13] As was frequently the case elsewhere, much of the work was done by labourers on unemployment relief schemes.

In the interwar years, park superintendents tried very hard to please local residents, especially in the way of colourful bedding displays, carpet bedding and floral clocks, using many of the same horticultural techniques as estate gardeners employed. Most bedding was grown in glasshouses on site. This required a twice-yearly explosion of activity, firstly in May when the spring bedding of biennials and bulbs was pulled up and replaced with half-hardy annuals – especially the reliable pelargoniums and begonias – and in autumn when the reverse happened. It was a very labour-intensive process, but the results were extremely popular with the public and had the practical advantage that no plant stayed in the ground long enough to be adversely affected by the smoky atmosphere which choked all industrial cities until the Clean Air Acts of the 1950s. Public parks, then as now, were for leisure and relaxation in pleasant surroundings; parks superintendents did not concern themselves with food production.

Paid relief schemes for unemployed men, such as those which provided labour in the public parks, were commonplace in the early 1930s. Unemployment amongst working-class men was very high, particularly in the heavy industry centres, and the dole was simply not enough for families to live on without considerable hardship. January 1933[14] saw the nadir of the country's economic fortunes, with 2,955,000 people out of work, a quarter of the workforce. Enforced idleness turned a fair few of them to allotment gardening, in order to help feed their families.

An allotment was a piece of ground usually, but not exclusively, ten square rods in area, which was 302.5 square yards or one sixteenth of an acre. This parcel of ground could be rented for a modest sum – usually one shilling a rod – from a landowner, a charity or a local council. The allotment, as a means whereby those without gardens could grow edible produce, dates from the huge upheaval created after 1750 by the Enclosure Movement, which effectively took away common grazing rights from landless rural labourers. For a variety of reasons – some paternalistically philanthropic, others self-interested – landowners began to make land in small parcels available to labourers who had lost their common rights. The first Enclosure Act to stipulate that some land be set aside for 'poor gardens' was that for Great Somerford in Wiltshire in 1806.[15]

Agitation for better and more reliable allotment provision, especially in the towns, led to the Allotments Act of 1887, which gave local authorities powers to acquire land for allotments. The Smallholding and Allotments Acts of 1907 and 1908 required councils to look for suitable land, both in country and town, and to provide allotments where there was a demand for them.

During the First World War, the progressive shortage of food at home prompted the government in December 1916 to give local authorities power to take over unoccupied land for allotments. By the end of 1917, there were one and a half million plots, producing, it was said, two million tons of vegetables a year.[16] After the war ended, more than 50,000 acres of requisitioned land were taken back out of cultivation by local authorities, and mainly used for residential developments. By 1929, the number of allotments had sunk below one million; the numbers had slid further, down to 819,000 by 1939. Of these, many were 'statutory allotments'[17], in other words they were on land specifically bought by the authorities for use as allotments, and which could not be sold for building, say, without the permission of the Minister of Agriculture. Others included railway allotments, of which there were a great many. The railway companies had a tradition of leasing land on each side of railway lines as allotments; indeed the four main railway companies were important landlords in this respect. That said, the allotment had come to be seen as the preserve of the urban and rural poor, and the interest in allotment gardening of the early years of the century was long gone.

However, allotments did have a champion in the shape of the National Allotments Society (NAS), which had originally been founded as a small co-operative in 1901, but had grown substantially by the 1930s to represent many local allotment societies. Indeed, affiliation fees were the Society's main source of income. The NAS mediated with landlords and government departments on behalf of local societies, acted as an information bureau, helped recover compensation for damage on allotments, ran a fire insurance scheme, and also provided publicity and advice material.

The extreme danger and uncertainty of the international situation, culminating in the Munich crisis of September 1938,[18] concentrated the minds of the officers of the National Allotments Society on the possible forthcoming conflict. Its annual report averred that:

It [the Society] still holds steadfastly to the opinion that allotments are of immense service to the nation in times of peace, and are indispensable in times of war; and that the contribution which they make to personal and public health are immeasurable, and it believes that no other spare-time occupation combines so many recreative and economic advantages.[19]

In 1939, the NAS was largely run by two energetic individuals, the Secretary, G. W. Giles, and the Treasurer, Henry Berry, who was also a member of the London County Council. There were regional committees of the NAS in the provinces. The President, Sir Francis Acland MP, died in June 1939 and was succeeded by Lord Trent, who was the son of Jesse Boot, the philanthropically inclined son of the founder of Boots the Chemist. Both Acland and Trent were high-minded, public-spirited men and helpful advisers to the secretariat.

In the early months of 1939, with war threatening once more, the NAS voiced anxieties that the government was not preparing sufficiently to increase domestic food production and would not do so until the crisis actually arrived:

For many years it [the allotment movement] has made an important contribution to food supply, public health, useful employment and national well-being. In the last war it admittedly made a most notable contribution to our country's needs. It is, of course, now prepared to undertake with all its strength any national service asked of it and as, in spite of all the difficulties against which it has to contend, it is in a finer state of organisation and loyalty than a generation ago the contribution which it could make to the nation's strength if a special call came would be considerable.[20]

It was the local allotment associations, in tandem with those authorities which took their duties under the Allotments Acts seriously, who would prove to be the engines for allotment growth as the war threat intensified, as well as relentless prickers of the consciences of those not doing their utmost to provide the necessary land.

During the 1930s, the NAS became closely allied with the Friends'[21] Allotments Committee, chaired by Dr Joan Fry,[22] which raised funds by public subscription to provide half-price fertilisers, seeds and tools for unemployed allotmenteers. This scheme had operated initially in the mining valleys of South Wales during the 1920s but expanded its range elsewhere during the Depression. By 1931, the Ministry of Agriculture was sufficiently impressed with what it had achieved to match public donations pound for pound. The scheme was popular, with 102,000 applicants in 1938. The NAS had representatives on this committee, and local affiliated allotment associations organised bulk buying and distribution for it, as they did for their own members. At the outbreak of war this scheme was extended to include indigent old-age pensioners, widows of servicemen, and wives of men serving in the armed forces.

The interwar housing boom was the main reason for the decline in numbers of urban allotments after the 1914–18 conflict. In many localities, houses had been built on old allotment sites, much to the sorrow of the NAS, since hard-won soil fertility was lost forever beneath concrete and brick. The Society regarded the precipitous fall in the number of allotments as a national misfortune and in 1939 pressed the issue of security of tenure with the Minister of Agriculture, Sir Reginald Dorman-Smith, receiving nothing more substantial than fine words in reply. Dorman-Smith refused to promise central government funds to help local authorities in this regard, nor would he give assurances concerning security of tenure beyond the growing season. This issue would become even more prominent in the war years, when much land was taken in by local authorities for 'wartime' allotments, without there being any guarantee of security of tenure when the war was over. All the Minister would agree to do was to send a strongly worded appeal to the local authorities, reminding them of their statutory responsibilities.

Allotment holders, garden owners and estate gardeners all depended on commercial concerns to provide them with seeds and plants. There were hundreds of plant nurseries and dozens of seed businesses, either serving a local customer base or sending their goods across the country by rail or road. Nurseries either offered an extensive range of hardy plants, or specialised in particular types of plant: hardy nursery stock (that is, trees and shrubs); herbaceous perennials; alpines or greenhouse plants. Vegetable plants could be bought in the spring at many country nurseries, or at their shop outlets in towns. Most perennial plants were 'sent for' – that is, ordered from a catalogue and delivered to the house-holder in the dormant season, between November and March, having been dug up from fields. Only tender greenhouse plants were sold out of pots; the rest were 'bare-rooted'. Many nurseries were small in extent, perhaps only an acre or two. There were no garden centres as we know them. Seeds were also bought mail-order, although Cuthbert's did sell a selection of cheap packets through the high street chain Woolworth's. Bare-rooted roses and soft fruit could also be acquired there.

In the late 1930s, market gardening in Britain was not in very good shape, thanks to the ease with which cheaper hardy vegetables could be imported from northern Europe, and tender vegetables and fruit from colonial dependencies or the Dominions (Canada, South Africa, Australia and New Zealand.) The value of imports of fresh fruit and vegetables was a very substantial £33.8 million in 1939. For example, nearly 250,000 tons of onions were imported that year, mainly from Holland and Belgium,[23] and 80 per cent of the country's fruit came from overseas.[24] As a result, there had been little investment in horticultural infrastructure or mechanisation in the years before the war, so processes were labour-intensive. (In that regard, commercial horticulture was similar to agriculture.)

There was one particular type of market gardening operation which was to prove very useful during the war. The Land Settlement Association was a co-operative set up by the government in 1934. Its aim was to settle unemployed industrial workers – especially miners – from the north-east of England as well as Wales in communities of smallholdings. These men would grow market garden produce, which would then be sold through the co-operative.

By the time war broke out, there were 1,100 smallholdings in twenty-six settlements with a total acreage of 11,000, of which 3,000 were used for growing horticultural produce while the rest were for small-scale livestock and arable farming. Each smallholding consisted of an area of five acres, with a cottage; the smallholder was provided with suitable livestock by the Association. By 1939, more than 1,200 glass-houses had been erected and there were 80,000 'Dutch lights'[25] in use.

A public-spirited inhabitant of Worthing, Joan Strange, wrote in her diary on 2 July 1939:

. . . went to Sydenham and discussed the Land Settlement Association's scheme there. Each family has a house – four [sic] acres of land, one greenhouse, one pigsty and one hennery.

There are 159 families, all are unemployed miners from the North. It works well in the majority of cases but some of the wives are discontented and prefer a husband on the dole plus near neighbours, cinema, pub, fried-fish shop and Woolworths![26]

Market gardeners were not notably progressive in their methods, partly because money for capital investment was scarce but also because they had surprisingly little to do with the horticultural research institutes, and vice versa. As we shall see, the war would provide the impetus for closer contact, to their mutual benefit. The important institutes with a horticultural remit were Long Ashton, near Bristol, East Malling in the fruit-growing area of Kent, and the John Innes Horticultural Institution at Merton, in south-west London.

In the years before the war, scientists in these institutions were working on a variety of research projects: the development of F1 hybrids[27], virus-free soft fruit, dwarfing rootstocks for fruit trees, plant hormones and hormone rooting powders, reliable seed and potting composts, effective treatments for a variety of pests and diseases, the impact of pesticide residues and vitamin-C-rich fruit syrups.

Amateur gardeners looked to the Royal Horticultural Society, since it was the one organisation concerned with research into the specific problems that they encountered. In 1939, the RHS was an important source of expert gardening advice for ordinary gardeners, and had been so, despite vicissitudes, since its foundation in 1804. Established to advance horticulture in all its branches, the RHS held a unique position in the gardening life of the country; or in England, at least, since that was where most of its members lived. It was a self-confident, learned and philanthropic organisation, but also Anglocentric, conservative and sometimes unimaginative. Its membership was predominantly upper middle class, its leading officials patrician. It catered primarily for well-heeled gardeners in the south-east of England, among them many amateur experts, ranging from landowners with vast woodland gardens to old ladies with pocket-handkerchief gardens full of rare plants.

The membership was divided into Fellows and Associates. Prospective

Fellows had to be nominated by an existing Fellow and pay an annual subscription of between one and four guineas, while Associates were men who were employed in horticulture and who paid a subscription of 10/6d. It was a matter of Gentlemen and Players. The membership rose during the 1930s to 36,500 in 1939, but still consisted of only a tiny fraction of those who pursued gardening seriously. No doubt the necessity of finding a Fellow to put your name forward, as well as the substantial cost, restricted membership to the better-off and horticultur-ally well-connected. Nevertheless, the RHS did have a formal relationship with a great number of affiliated societies – local horticultural clubs that paid a small fee, and received some group benefits in return – and these both helped to disseminate information from the RHS and also, to a limited extent, informed the Society of local concerns.

The RHS held flower shows and meetings at fortnightly intervals throughout the year in the New Hall, opened in 1928, in Greycoat Street in Westminster. Those staged between February and October lasted for two days, while the rest were for one day only. These shows were known, not surprisingly, as 'Fortnightlies', a name that stuck, long after the shows ceased to be held so frequently. The biggest events spilled over into what became the Old Hall in nearby Vincent Square, where also were accommodated the Society's offices and meeting rooms and the Lindley Library, with its 20,000 volumes. Some of the shows were given a title: for example, the Daffodil Show, the Early Market Produce Show, the Fruit and Vegetable Show and, of course, the Great Spring Show. The Great Spring Show was held in the last week of May – to suit the many large-garden owners who grew rhododendrons – not in Vincent Square but in the grounds of the Chelsea Hospital.[28] The show had been there since 1912, after it outgrew its space in the Temple Gardens. No plants were sold at any of the shows.

Fellows of the RHS benefited from a monthly journal, mainly written by the Society's officers or Fellows, for which they received no fee. The Society owned one garden, at Wisley in Surrey, which it had been given in 1911. Here a number of scientific officers were employed, both to pursue research projects useful to amateurs and to give written advice to Fellows, provided that the latter sent in specimens according to very strict prescriptions. There was even a garden inspector, who would look at Fellows' gardens and give advice for a daily fee of three guineas.

The gardens at Wisley were open to the public, except for Good Friday and Christmas Day. On Sundays, only Fellows and their guests were admitted. Garden visitors could reach Wisley by trains of the Southern Railway, although then, as now, it meant an expensive taxi ride from West Byfleet or Weybridge stations. The National Fruit Trials were based at Wisley,[29] although this was an unsatisfactory situation, since – strangely – the trees were planted in a frost pocket, and suffered from damaging spring frosts two years out of three. The flower trials were relatively modest; certainly much less extensive than they are today. Each March, the Society held a distribution of surplus seeds and plants. Everything had to be requested in writing; this was the era of the post-card, sent one day and arriving the next, and costing 1d in stamps.

The Royal Horticultural Society was governed by a council of fifteen members, composed of the good and great in the horticultural world: scientists, nurserymen, professional gardeners, and knowledgeable amateurs who owned large gardens. Like most learned societies at the time, it was run predominantly by men. In 1939, a number of eminent public figures sat on RHS committees, including the artist John Nash; Lt Col. Leonard Messel, OBE, who owned the world-renowned garden of Nymans in Sussex, and after whom a beautiful pink magnolia is named; E. A. Bowles of Myddelton House, Enfield, one of the great plantsman luminaries of the first half of the twentieth century, who sat on both the Scientific and the Narcissus and Tulip committees; and E. A. Bunyard, a Kent nurseryman and self-confessed epicure, who presided over the Fruit and Vegetable Committee.

During the early years of the twentieth century, the RHS had a good relationship with government, at least partly because of its multifarious and helpful activities during the First World War. During that time, it had raised money for the Red Cross, established a horticultural War Relief Fund, allowed the Horticultural Hall to be used as a billet for Australian troops and organised the dispatch of plants to army field hospitals in France, as well as seeds and flower show rules to the civilian internment and prisoner-of-war camp at Ruhleben. This camp, based at a racetrack outside Berlin, was highly organised by the mainly British inmates and even boasted a Ruhleben Horticultural Society, affiliated to the RHS and with almost a thousand members. This society put together flower show competitions, and also held botany classes, where all the plants studied came from the pond in the middle of the racecourse. A glasshouse was made from tobacco boxes, and cold frames were constructed to nurture flowering bulbs. Much ground was dug and thousands of vegetable seedlings planted.

Crucially, the RHS was also involved, from 1917 onwards, in promoting food production in gardens and allotments, organising expert lectures and making demonstration gardens. It also encouraged jam-making and fruit-bottling – to make good use of surplus fruit – and campaigned for the government to release more sugar supplies so that gardeners could make their own preserves.

In the interwar period, the Society lobbied the government on a number of issues, in particular trade descriptions of insecticides and the importance of controlling the burgeoning grey squirrel population.[30] In 1932, the president, Henry McLaren, the second Baron Aberconway (who owned Bodnant Garden in north Wales and was chairman of the Glasgow shipyard John Brown and Co.), wrote a letter to *The Times* encouraging gardeners to continue to buy and plant nursery stock, despite the economic difficulties that the country was facing during the Depression. The Society was certainly the nurseryman's friend.

As war threatened, during the Munich crisis, it was natural that the War Office should turn to the Society again to requisition what was now the Old Hall, this time for the training of the Territorial Army.

The RHS catered for all enthusiastic gardeners, but there were also a number of specialist plant societies in existence before the outbreak of the Second World War. The National Rose Society was one of the earliest to be founded (1876), but dahlias (1881) and chrysanthemums (1884) followed closely behind. They survived the Great War intact, and were joined by the Iris Society in 1922 and the Alpine Garden Society in 1929. Rock gardening had become increasingly popular as plant enthusiasts journeyed to the Alps, with plant hunter Reginald Farrer's overheated prose ringing in their ears.[31] Curiously, there was no national society for promoting the amateur growing of vegetables.[32] That work fell to the National Allotments Society.

During the early 1920s, gardening and gardens as subjects for media attention were confined almost entirely to daily newspapers and magazines, of which *Amateur Gardening*, *Popular Gardening*, *Garden Work for Amateurs* and *My Garden* were prominent. Professional gardeners read *The Gardeners' Chronicle*.

However, in March 1924, less than two years after the British Broadcasting Company was founded,[33] the first practical gardening bulletins were broadcast on the radio. These were provided to the BBC by the Royal Horticultural Society, and mostly written by Frederick Chittenden, director of Wisley Gardens. At the end of 1924, the RHS also supplied a separate bulletin for the north of England. From time to time, well-known gardeners, such as Vita Sackville-West and Marion Cran,[34] provided more elevated contributions. In 1931, the BBC asked the Society to recommend gardeners who might be approached as speakers. One of the names – others were Sackville-West and Dr H. V. Taylor[35] – was that of C. H. Middleton.

Mr Middleton's[36] first broadcast, on 9 May 1931, began: 'Good afternoon. Well, it's not much of a day for gardening, is it?' It was immediately obvious that he had what it took to shine in this new medium. However, for the first three years, he was just one of several broadcasters under RHS direction. It was not until September 1934 that he was given his own weekly series, *In the Garden,* which soon changed to *In Your Garden.* The programme was a great success – and, as we shall see, the obvious vehicle for publicising a wartime gardening campaign – and he continued broadcasting regularly until his untimely death in 1945.

The wireless was well set up before 1939 to be *the* medium for mass communication to the British people during the war. There were only 25,000 television sets, and in any event, the television was turned off on 1 September 1939 during a Mickey Mouse cartoon 'for the duration'.

Radios were not expensive, and most people in the country could get wireless reception. It was estimated that thirty-four million people listened in, although radio licence evasion was so rife that the numbers may have been substantially higher than that. There were two services, National and Regional. Before the war, programmes were broadcast from 10.15 a.m. to midnight. The output was a mixture of news, talks, drama, variety and comedy, dance music, classical music and schools broadcasts. Outside broadcasting was possible, but it was in its infancy. Sir John (later Lord) Reith, the Director General of the BBC, was notably high-minded, so there was an overtly educational slant to much of the programming. Garden talks were, therefore, meant to be as informative as they were entertaining. 'By 1939 the BBC had, by virtue of both its monopoly position and its broadcasting achievements, created a new social focus for the British people, a common source of information and entertainment that neither the press nor the cinema could rival.'[37]

One of the starkest differences between the early and late years of the 1930s was the intensification of government intrusion into people's private lives, culminating in the Emergency Powers (Defence) Act passed on 24 August 1939. In effect, the Act turned the government of the United Kingdom into a benign dictatorship and allowed for the enacting of a great many Defence Regulations. These were divided into five parts: security of the state, public safety and order, ships and aircraft, essential supplies and work, and general and supplementary provisions. Defence Regulation 62 – under the heading of Essential Supplies and Work – was concerned with the control of cultivation and termination of agricultural tenancies, and 62A referred specifically to giving powers to local authorities to release land for wartime allotments.

A second Emergency Powers (Defence) Act was passed on 22 May 1940, when the risk of invasion was at its height. As the historian E. R. Chamberlin put it:

Passed in a single day, instantaneously it turned the United Kingdom into a military camp whose sole objective was military survival. Civil rights gained over a millennium of bitter struggle

were suspended 'for the duration', for the Act thereafter allowed
the government to issue, without further recourse to
Parliament, what orders and regulations it considered necessary
to prosecute the war.[38]

During the course of the next year, 2,000 separate orders were made,
ranging from the taking down of road signs to specifying what crops
farmers were allowed to grow.

As the international situation grew darker and darker in the summer
of 1939, especially after the Nazi–Soviet Non-Aggression Pact was signed
on 23 August, civilians became extremely unsettled. They sometimes
tried to allay their anxieties by solid toil in the garden. A journalist,
Maggie Joy Blunt, who lived in a cottage in Burnham Beeches,
Buckinghamshire, wrote in her diary that when she heard the news of
the Nazi–Soviet Pact, 'I returned to my cottage, believing wishfully that
threatening clouds would pass. I began to prune ramblers.[39] All that
week I seemed to be perched on the top of wobbly steps in the late
summer sun wrestling with dead rosewood and wavering crimson-tipped
new shoots, waiting for news, waiting for news.'[40] As it turned out, she
had only ten days to wait for the news that she, and so many others,
dreaded.

CHAPTER TWO

WHAT HAPPENS NOW?

The day war was declared, 3 September 1939, was a sunny, warm Sunday. Some people recalled going out into their gardens to try to come to terms with what had happened and to make solemn resolutions. Margery Allingham, the detective novelist, who lived in Tolleshunt D'Arcy, close to the Essex coast, described her feelings:

> 'I went down to the end [of the garden] and sat under the laburnum and the fancy red oaks. I could smell the sea, and I watched the sky over the rookery in the Vicarage elms, more than half expecting that I should suddenly see the warplanes coming like starlings in the spring, making the sky black. If the boys were right, they were just about due.[1]

The following day, Harold Nicolson, husband of Vita Sackville-West and owner of Sissinghurst Castle in Kent, wrote in his diary:

> I get up early. It is a perfect day and I bathe in the peace of the lake. Two things impress themselves on me. 1. Time. It seems three weeks since yesterday morning . . . 2. Nature. Even as when someone dies, one is amazed that the poplars should still be standing quite unaware of one's own disaster, so when I walked down to the lake to bathe, I could scarcely believe that the swans were being sincere in their indifference to the Second German War.[2]

It is hard to overstate just how anxious was the civilian population in those very early days of the war, and how convinced they were that the invasion of Britain was imminent. It seems rather obvious to us now that Germany, under its Chancellor, Adolf Hitler, and his National Socialist party, could not risk an invasion until it had subdued western Europe – in particular, France, with its five million soldiers or reservists – but that is with the benefit of hindsight and our knowledge of the larger picture. As far as the ordinary Briton was concerned, once the country had entered into the war on behalf of Poland, all hell would break loose.

The memory of the deaths of nearly 1,500 British civilians on home soil from bombs dropped by Zeppelins in the First World War, the founding of an Air Raid Wardens' Service in 1937, the false alarm before Munich in 1938 and the evacuation of thousands of children and mothers from cities on 2 September all fed this extremely twitchy mood. At the very least, the population feared a ferocious attack by as many as 30,000 German bomber planes.[3] False alarms did not help the nerves: people in many places remember hearing a siren sound just after the prime minister, Neville Chamberlain, finished speaking to the nation at 11.15 a.m. on 3 September. The population was perfectly aware that they would be targets for the enemy. They knew that major cities could be destroyed, however brave and skilful the pilots of RAF fighter planes. In 1932, Stanley Baldwin – former prime minister and well-known pessimist – pronounced his depressing but unarguable opinion that 'the bomber will always get through'. The actions of the Italian air force against Abyssinian armies in 1935–6, the devastating bombing of Shanghai, Nanking and Canton by the Japanese in the summer of 1937, and of Barcelona and Guernica by German and Italian bombers in the same year, showed just what was horrifyingly possible. Indeed, the British government was of the opinion that Germany might strike even before war was declared. As Baldwin predicted in Parliament: 'tens of thousands of mangled people – men, women and children – before a single soldier or sailor suffered a scratch'.[4] Fear of the bomber was no idle or neurotic anxiety.

In 1937, the Committee of Imperial Defence – the forerunner of the wartime Ministry of Information – calculated that, on the evidence of what had happened to Barcelona, there might be 1,800,000 home casualties, a third of them fatal, in the first two months of the war.[5] So seriously did the government take the airborne threat that in early 1939 it issued one million burial forms to local authorities and began to stockpile collapsible cardboard coffins.[6] Moreover, it was expected that German aeroplanes would also drop poisonous gas, hence the manufacture and distribution of gas masks to every member of the population at the time of the Munich crisis.[7] An intensely gloomy report by a group of eminent psychiatrists from the London teaching hospitals and clinics, submitted to the Ministry of Health in October 1938, suggested that serious bouts of hysteria and incidences of nervous breakdown were a distinct possibility, with psychiatric casualties exceeding physical ones by as much as three to one. That would have meant at least four million people suffering from acute panic and other nervous conditions in the first six months of bombardment. These doctors envisaged the necessity for a network of treatment centres in bombed cities, clinics on the outskirts and mobile teams of psychiatrists.[8]

Plans were drawn up for the evacuation of some government departments to seaside towns, and for the taking over of country houses to be used as army camps and hospitals. The government had an obvious duty to do everything it could to protect the civilian population from the worst effects of German bombing, so public surface shelters were built, basements of steel-framed buildings allocated, and in February 1939 local councils began to deliver Anderson shelters for erection in back gardens. These shelters for up to six people, capable of withstanding flying shrapnel although not a direct hit from a bomb, were named after Sir John Anderson, then Home Secretary, who instigated their development and oversaw manufacture from 1938 onwards. Families with an annual income below £250 were given a shelter for free, while richer households paid £7. By September 1939, one and a half million Anderson shelters had been distributed, and more than two million were erected in the course of the war.

The Anderson shelter was designed by an engineer called William Patterson and consisted of six corrugated-steel sheets, bolted together to form a rounded arch, which had to be half dug into a trench in the garden. Fifteen inches of soil was to be piled on top and patted down, to help mitigate the effects of bomb blast, and to make the shelter look less obvious from above. Their very presence in so many suburban and urban gardens underlined daily to civilians how serious things had become. And as it turned out, by no means all families found them congenial places to be during alerts and raids, especially since they tended to flood in wet weather. Civilians continued to worry that the shelters were conspicuous from the air, so many householders made them more appealing and less obtrusive by growing shallow-rooted rock plants, nasturtiums, marigolds, lettuces or marrows on the top, and rambling roses around the entrance. Some even grew rhubarb or mushrooms inside. But no one ever came to love them. Sir John Anderson, who was not known for his lively sense of humour, when complimented on the marrows growing on shelters, replied tight-lipped, 'I had not intended the shelters for the cultivation of vegetables.'[9]

The threat of immediate aerial bombing and the resulting casualties were worries enough for the government to deal with, but it also had reasons to doubt the stout-heartedness of civilians. There had been war-weariness in the general population during the last year of the First World War, exacerbated by extensive food shortages. In 1917 and 1918, a number of European countries, including Russia, had been radically destabilised by revolutionary mass movements. The Russian, German and Austro-Hungarian monarchies had been abolished. In Great Britain, there was a distinct mood of pacifism abroad in the 1920s and 1930s. This was exemplified by the success of the Peace Pledge Union, founded in 1934, which had more than 100,000 members by 1939. The Labour Party opposed rearmament until 1937 and voted against the introduction of conscription in April 1939. Even after the Munich crisis in September 1938, there were plenty of 'appeasers', calling for negotiations with Hitler. In the same years, the economic Depression and associated unemployment had widened the gap between the 'haves' and 'have-nots'. Urban slums shocked liberal social commentators but little was done about them. Class-consciousness and snobbery were endemic. There was a gaping chasm between the Jarrow Marchers and the Bright Young Things.

What is more, before the conflict, civilians had become increasingly vocal in their criticisms of government policies. There were a number of reasons for this, including a certain erosion of deference after the convulsions of the First World War, coupled with the fact that women of property over thirty had the vote from 1918, and were given it on equal terms with men from 1928. Ordinary people had begun to expect politicians to listen to them. The obvious result of increased participation in the democratic process was a growth in knowledge and interest in national affairs amongst the middle classes (although less discernibly amongst workers), and a more sceptical attitude towards their political masters.

Taking all these factors into account, the government was pessimistic about how united and stalwart the civilian population could be relied upon to be in the circumstances of a new war. 'For those planners, often of military background and somewhat contemptuous of anyone not in uniform, the average civilian was less the British bulldog than the pampered poodle: lacking in moral fibre, easily demoralised, neurotic under pressure and as likely to snap at its owner as at the latter's assailant.'[10]

Yet because the country needed to be put on a complete war footing, it was vital that those civilians co-operated fully and did not buckle. A breakdown in consensus at the beginning of the war would obviously have been disastrous. In order to avoid such a breakdown, the government thought it helpful, even imperative, for civilians to see themselves as front-line troops, with victory depending on them just as much as their brothers in the services. Much of the propaganda aimed at civilians during the war reflects this, as the widely-used expression 'Home Front' indicates.

Right from the beginning, the policymakers worried over the very ticklish question of civilian morale. 'Morale' has always been a difficult word to define, although everyone knows it when they see it. A

Cambridge psychologist employed by the Ministry of Information defined it as a lively and not too serious spirit of adventure which met emergencies clear-eyed and calmly. That is inadequate, since morale is also intimately connected with optimism. A better definition came from the social research organisation, Mass-Observation,[11] in 1941:

> By morale, we mean primarily not only determination to carry on, but also determination to carry on with the utmost energy, a determination based on a realization of the facts of life and with it a readiness for many minor and some major sacrifices, including, if necessary, the sacrifice of life itself. Good morale means hard and persistent work, means optimum production, maximum unity, reasonable awareness of the true situation, and absence of complacency and confidence which are not based on fact.[12]

That is certainly setting the bar very high, but it does at least include all the elements likely to promote good morale.

Tom Harrisson, founder of Mass-Observation, wrote in 1940:

> British people can stand a tremendous amount of pain. Many (e.g. the unemployed) have been trained to intellectual pain for years. There is no danger whatever that morale on the home front will crack up, so long as morale is not treated as an ephemeral word, but is regarded as the attribute of human minds. And so long as these human minds are not regarded as uniform and just so many mathematical units, but are treated as variable and delicate human characters.[13]

That surely was the key.

If the reaction of Nella Last, a housewife from Barrow-in-Furness who wrote a diary throughout the war for Mass-Observation, was representative of the majority of civilians, the exact nature of morale worried them as well. On 27 April 1941, at the height of the so-called Barrow Blitz, she wrote: 'What *is* "morale" – and have I got any, or how much? And how much more could I call on in need, and where does it come from and what is it composed of?'[14]

The government's anxiety to foster high morale meant that it sometimes fell into the trap of too much *de haut en bas* exhortation. As Margery Allingham put it: 'Addressing the nation became a mania like diabolo,[15] or so it seemed to us who were addressed. We were addressed like billy-o and, knowing just how important we were and how unnecessary it was to convince us that we had anything to do but fight, we were often dismayed.'[16]

Reflections on how to maintain high morale led to a lively and long-lasting debate at the Ministry of Information, whose Directors during the war were Lord Macmillan, then Sir John Reith, followed by Duff Cooper and, finally, Brendan Bracken from 1941.[17] One thing on which all were agreed was that the civilian population needed to be kept busy: ensuring people were occupied, in order that they did not have too much time to reflect on dangers or deprivations, was an important strand of thinking to be found in government circles, and definitely influenced their attitude towards the population growing some of its own food.

Over the vexed question of whether to tell 'the people' the truth about the progress of the war, senior figures in the Ministry were divided. Some held the view that they could endure anything, provided that they did not think they were being hoodwinked or taken for fools. However, even if the MoI had been consistent about this, it was often thwarted by the service Ministries withholding all but the most anodyne facts about the prosecution of the war.

In practice, during the first eight months of the conflict the civilian population was generally told very little about how the war was progressing, which was why the overrunning of neutral Norway by the Germans in April 1940 proved such a paralysing shock after the truth of the situation was finally revealed. Two months later, after the retreat of the British Expeditionary Force from Dunkirk – a far more serious reverse than Norway – the country was taken into the government's confidence by Winston Churchill, and his popular support did not suffer as a result. Indeed, quite the reverse.

In the summer of 1941, Churchill remarked in Parliament, during a speech about the defence of Crete, that 'the British nation is unique in this respect. They are the only people who like to be told how bad things are, who like to be told the worst, and like to be told that they are very likely to get much worse in the future and must prepare themselves for further reverses.'[18] Understandably, people prided themselves on being so perverse.

The day before war broke out, wireless broadcasting became restricted entirely to the newly named Home Service, which came on air at 7 a.m. on 2 September and broadcast usually from 7 a.m. until just after midnight throughout the war. In June 1940, the Home Service was augmented by a Forces Programme. Both the government and the BBC's bosses expected the Corporation to play a very important role in raising, or at least sustaining, civilian morale, although it took time before the Corporation's broadcasts settled down to perform adequately the dual, and often contradictory, roles of informing and uplifting the people without giving any useful information to the enemy. As the historian of the BBC, Siân Nicholas, put it:

As far as the government was concerned, the BBC's most important wartime function was the swift dissemination of official information to the general public. War would disrupt virtually every aspect of normal life, and the general public would need to be advised how to cope. More than this, they had to be encouraged to identify their day-to-day hardships with the wider national endeavour . . . Radio's immediacy, its directness, its sheer ubiquity, marked it out for this task.[19]

The fear of helping the Germans, even tangentially, led to the suspension of broadcast weather reports on 5 September, much to the particular irritation of farmers and gardeners. These were not reinstated until 2 April 1945.

High morale also depends partly on getting enough to eat and in sufficient variety; a hungry population is likely, by its nature, to be demoralised. This was the major challenge to the Ministry of Agriculture, under Sir Reginald Dorman-Smith, as well as the Ministry of Food, after it was set up on 8 September 1939 with William S. Morrison as Minister.[20] (The first Ministry was principally concerned with producing food, while the second had the equally vital task of distributing it, via a rationing system if necessary.)[21] It is against the background of the government's desire to keep morale high that we must view its attitude to civilians becoming engaged in domestic food production.

The experience of the Great War had convinced most people who lived through it that there would be food shortages, and associated rationing, and that growing more food in Great Britain was absolutely vital. They also expected the threat from German submarines to feature prominently once again, preventing or disrupting the import of a great many staples such as coal, but also tropical and subtropical fruits – bananas, pineapples, oranges and lemons – as well as hardy vegetables like carrots and onions, which had mainly been imported into Britain from western Europe during the 1930s. In 1939, at a time when central planning was frequently muddled and incoherent, there was no doubting official determination to feed the embattled nation.

From 1938 onwards, as war looked increasingly likely, there had been public debate on the morality of rationing food. Many politicians, especially on the Left, maintained that in the last six months of the First World War it had been the fairest means of distributing vital foodstuffs in short supply. There were some dissenting voices: according to the *Daily Express*, 'The public should revolt against the food rationing system, that dreadful and terrible iniquity . . . There is no necessity for the trouble and expense of rationing.'[22] Nevertheless, by the time war broke out, the population in general seemed to have accepted that rationing was inevitable and were grimly resigned. Indeed, in November a British Institute of Public Opinion poll found that 60 per cent of those questioned thought rationing necessary. Some shopkeepers had already started to conduct their own rationing, keeping back basic supplies for their regular customers.

After war broke out, there was a flurry of intense activity by the government to ensure that every British citizen was counted. Not only did ration books need to be issued, but an accurate census was necessary for the purpose of conscription and in order to keep tabs on potential enemies of the state. 29 September 1939 was National Registration Day, after which every adult and child received a unique identity card.

Forthcoming rationing was announced on 1 November 1939, and came into force on 8 January 1940. Each household had to register with a supplier for the rationed items, which initially consisted of bacon, butter and cheese, but later included sugar, tea, eggs, meat and sweets. Vegetarians were issued with a special ration book, which entitled them to more cheese and eggs as substitutes for meat. Unlike other items, meat was rationed by price rather than by weight. (From 23 September 1939, petrol – for the 10 per cent of the population who owned a car – was severely rationed to seven gallons a month, allowing for journeys of no more than 200 miles.)

Rationing was just one part of the answer to the problem of providing enough nutritious food for everyone; increasing home food production was the other. On 2 September 1939, the first task for Mr W. Gavin – Agricultural Adviser at the Ministry of Agriculture – was to organise the setting-up of War Agricultural Executive Committees for each county in the United Kingdom under the Cultivation of Lands Order, 1939. This order authorised the 'War Ags', as they became universally known, to exercise on the Minister of Agriculture's behalf 'certain powers conferred on him by the Defence Regulations for the purpose of increasing home food production in time of war'.[23] The Minister sent a circular letter to these county committees, outlining their immediate task: to bring into tillage another one and a half million acres of land in England and Wales. In order to achieve this, he promised them as free a hand as possible.

The War Ags became the main engines for the official dissemination of information and expertise to farmers and commercial gardeners during wartime. Ministry officials, landowners, farmers, gardeners and scientists sat on these committees; their tasks ranged from compelling (often reluctant) farmers to put their grass pasture under the plough to organising lecturers to speak to village Women's Institutes. In counties where there were a lot of commercial horticultural operations, a horticulture subcommittee was established, which employed paid advisers. By mid April 1940, 10,000 square miles or 1,900,000 acres of pasture had been ploughed up to provide wheat that before the war had mainly been imported from Canada, as well as other foods like potatoes and cabbages.[24]

But British agriculture could not produce everything required, especially vitamin-rich lemons and bananas. By 1939, nutritionists were already well aware of the vitamins required for health, both in adults and children. They knew which diseases and conditions were the result of deficiencies, rickets in children being the most common and harmful of these. They also knew that the British were not as healthy as they should have been. In 1938, it was estimated by Sir John Boyd Orr, who later won a Nobel Prize for his work on the science of nutrition, that half of the population had a diet deficient in some nutrients, while a third (primarily the urban working classes) had a 'seriously inadequate diet'.[25] Just as the imminent prospect of food rationing naturally increased the collective desire of keen gardeners to grow their own food, by definition unrationed, so the realisation that the population needed both health-giving vitamins and morale-boosting variety in their diets meant that the government was keen to encourage them to do so.

It was obvious, to the home Ministries at least, that gardeners had an important part to play in providing vitamin-rich green leaf vegetables, salads, onions, carrots and tomatoes, to take the place of imported fruit and vegetables. And the authorities knew this had to get under way quickly, since they had learned important lessons from the experience of the First World War, when shortages were already extremely acute before production by gardeners finally achieved substantial proportions in 1917. They were particularly keen on increasing the number of allotments under cultivation, since this would give the millions of urban dwellers without gardens the opportunity to grow their own vegetables.

Early on, the Ministry of Agriculture and Fisheries estimated that productive home gardens and allotments together could produce as much as a quarter of non-cereal supplies. This was just one of the many unprovable and often highly optimistic statistics that issued from the Ministry during the war years, but it had a marked influence on policy – and public attitudes.

Interestingly, MAF officials did not consider the cultivation of allotments as purely for the production of extra fruit and vegetables. In an internal minute dated 8 September 1939, a Mr Sanders is reported as saying: 'Stress should be laid on the need for as large an increase as possible in the number of allotments, not only on account of the importance of augmenting the quantity of health giving foodstuffs, but also because of the *steadying effect* [my italics] of work on plots on the large body of persons who will be concerned with allotment work.'[26] Three days earlier, G.W. Giles, the Secretary of the National Allotments Society, had told the Minister of Agriculture in a letter that one of the latter's predecessors, Lord Ernle, had said that during the First World War, allotments did more than anything else to 'steady the nation's nerves'.[27] Giles also reminded Dorman-Smith that the latter had once said that the 'recreational and health-giving properties of allotments were probably of more importance than the produce grown upon them'. It was Giles's opinion that they were of equal value and importance. Whenever the subject of home-grown produce was brought up in Parliament, legislators would line up to praise the advantages – economic, recreational and even spiritual – of kitchen gardening. For example, in the House of Lords, the Marquess of Crewe referred to 'the moral advantage, which the people derive from their [allotment's] existence'.[28] These assumptions informed what soon became known as the 'Dig for Victory' campaign (see Chapter Three).

The period between 3 September 1939 and 10 May 1940, when the Germans invaded the Low Countries, was known as the 'Phoney War' or 'Bore War' because, despite the dire forecasts, and the presence of a large British Expeditionary Force in France, there was little fighting.[29] During this time, although not physically threatened as feared, British civilians had to get used to many unpleasant or dreary restrictions. The restriction they loathed most was the necessity to darken their homes at dusk, using blackout curtain and blind material, boards or shutters. Instantly, houses were cast into a Stygian gloom, which depressed their occupants, even though they accepted the necessity of it.[30] ARP[31] wardens patrolled nightly to see that the blackout was strictly enforced and 'Put that light out!' became a common refrain: many perfectly respectable people found themselves summonsed to the magistrates' court to be fined because of an evening's carelessness. The headlamps of cars also had to be covered, except for a narrow strip which cast a thin, dim light on the road ahead; small wonder that the blackout was a major contributory factor in the record-breaking numbers of deaths, particularly of pedestrians, on the roads during the war. Torches had to be treated in the same way as headlights, with the result that people bumped into each other or lamp posts in the dark, and women were often frightened to go out at night. And any gardener who had once relied on street lights to provide enough illumination to dig his vegetable plot after tea in the winter would now have to depend on moonlight instead.

Meanwhile, the Royal Horticultural Society, like many other voluntary organisations, was preparing itself for the challenges ahead. From July 1939 onwards, the council had been discussing emergency plans, in particular for the evacuation of staff from Wisley, since it might have been in the invasion path to London – although in the event that did not happen. The rarest books in the Lindley Library were moved to a safe haven in Aberystwyth in west Wales. Oddly, once the Blitz began, many other books were taken from the Lindley Library to Wisley, obviously no longer considered in danger. The offices there already housed collections from the John Innes Horticultural Institution, particularly vulnerable to bomb damage at Merton, which was nearer to London. As early as October 1938, E. A. Bunyard, a Kentish fruit and rose nurseryman and stalwart RHS supporter (of whom we shall hear more in Chapter Eight), had produced a report for the RHS on the organisation of emergency food growing for wartime, a report which was to strongly influence government thinking.[32] In it he advocated a planned approach, suggested that increased amounts of seed that might become scarce should be obtained, that there should be vegetable trials in various parts of the country, and that those vegetables with high protein levels such as haricot beans should be tested for their suitability. As for fruit, he thought that maximising production was of the essence; this could best be achieved by good pruning and hygiene in orchards. He recommended that instructional information and pamphlets be devised, and to this end he chaired a committee to develop them.

As a result of Bunyard's recommendations, in September 1939 the Society initiated a programme of lectures and demonstrations for the general public. It later became a member of the Domestic Food Producers Council and willing expert adviser to the nascent Dig for Victory campaign.

At the same time, Bunyard stressed in the RHS *Journal* how important it was that people should not assume that, with the suspension of the flower shows, there remained little point to the Society. In his opinion, Fellows would need the expert advice and encouragement that they received from the *Journal*, in all branches of horticulture. Receiving the *Journal* was the principal privilege of being an RHS Fellow, and the best way of keeping in touch with the Society's work. He suggested to the Council that it continue monthly with a quarter or a third devoted to wartime gardening. As a result, the *Journal* was published throughout the war, even if, by necessity, it did become a shadow of its pre-war size in the middle years.

Inevitably, however, the war did clip the wings of the Society. Initially, the fortnightly shows at Vincent Square were cancelled,[33] as was the Chelsea Flower Show; no yearbooks were published; the RHS ceased to give money to subsidise plant-hunting expeditions, since these had been thwarted by the uncertainties of the international situation; and the trials at Wisley were truncated, with those remaining being mainly of vegetable varieties. The numbers of Fellows and Associates steadily declined during the war to 26,492 at the end of 1941 and 24,772 in 1942.[34] This decline was to prove a headache for the Society, as it needed the revenue from subscriptions and advertising in order to carry out its work on the food production programme and the useful trials at Wisley.

In the summer of 1939, E. A. Bunyard, in some financial difficulty, resigned from the Council and the other committees on which he had served voluntarily in order to take up a paid position as Keeper of the Library and editor of the RHS publications. The vacancy on the Council was filled by Dr H. V. Taylor. Taylor became an important link between the Society and the Ministry of Agriculture throughout the war, in particular on matters concerning the Dig for Victory campaign.

The RHS could only influence its own members, in the main. But in September 1939, millions of ordinary people needed to achieve a mental transition from peace to war, in gardening quite as much as other spheres of domestic life. Helping people to change course radically required a concentrated effort by the print and broadcast media. Newspapers were understandably a little slow off the mark; peacetime theorising about war is a very different matter from the fact itself. *The Gardeners' Chronicle*, for example, was still concerned with peaceful matters even on the day before war broke out. There were, for example, descriptive reports on the late August Southport Show. However, on the subject of the last RHS show, it commented: 'In all the circumstances a large show could not be expected at this fortnightly meeting of the RHS . . .'[35] And there was an advertisement in the Situations Vacant section for 'Experienced gardener, good all-round man, in case of War, SINGLE-HANDED. Wife as Laundress . . .'[36] These particulars show a clear appreciation that many gardeners, especially the youngsters, would not be able to avoid the imminent call-up.

By the following Saturday, the *Chronicle* was up to speed, or rather its advertisers were, with insertions such as: 'Circumstances prevent the holding of our Annual Vegetable Show by seedsmen, Dickson and Robinson' and 'Owing to the International Situation, Stokesley Show for September 21st has been cancelled'. The Dahlia Society did not hold its annual exhibition, which must have been a great disappointment to gardeners who had striven all season to get these pampered darlings of the tender flower world to as near unblemished perfection as possible.

Most interesting is the editorial on wartime gardening, which appeared in that issue, the first of the war:

> Everybody whose whole time is not engaged in other forms of national defence, and who has a garden or garden plot or allotment, can render good service to the community by cultivating it to the fullest possible extent. By that is meant not only getting the largest amount of produce from the soil, but also in keeping the ground in good heart, for the war upon which we have entered may last a long time and therefore next year must be considered as well as this year.[37]

No one was deluded into thinking it would all be over by Christmas this time. The editorial went on to advise on the importance of not letting pests spoil produce, 'as so much is so often damaged and wasted in the kindlier days of peace'.

As early as this issue, professional gardeners, as represented by the contributors and editor, also put down a marker regarding flowers: 'Subject always to the great needs of food production imposed by wartime conditions, flowers of all kinds may play their part by brightening parks and gardens and bringing cheerfulness into homes, hospitals and sick rooms.' And the editor offered the hope that autumn orders for bulbs would not be cancelled, 'as springtime will come as certainly as summer and winter, and we may need the beauty of flowers when there may be so much that is unbeautiful, pitiful and painful. Moreover, flowers inspire faith, hope, cheerfulness and courage, and these we may need in large measure until brighter and more peaceful conditions are reached.'[38] This hope must also have been based on the fact that the *Chronicle* numbered amongst its readers and advertisers many ornamental plant nurserymen, who were understandably extremely anxious to see that the bottom did not fall precipitately out of their market on the declaration of war.

The *Gardeners' Chronicle* editorial on 16 September, while acknowledging the many very knowledgeable amateurs in the country, opined that there were innumerable gardens where neglect was rife and whose vegetable and fruit crops were far smaller than they should be. It was hoped that a garden committee of the older gardeners and skilled amateurs would be formed in every parish, to advise people on how to make their gardens more productive.

In the same issue, there was also a heartfelt plea from the President of the Horticultural Trades Association – the organisation for the nursery trade, both then and now – for people not to cancel their plant orders, since nurserymen needed to sell their existing stocks of plants – bare-rooted trees, shrubs and fruit bushes, as well as herbaceous plants – before moving over to food production.[39]

Nurserymen such as R. Tucker and Sons of Faringdon couched their appeals for custom in patriotic terms: 'Together with all nurserymen we have offered our entire resources to the government and are doing everything in our power to produce more food. However, unless we can clear large quantities of our stock during the next six months we shall not be able to carry out our obligations. We therefore appeal to our customers to plant as usual.'[40] They also played on the gardener's natural anxiety about shortages, saying that the need to increase acreage for food production would lead to depleted stocks – and inflated prices – in the future.

The Gardeners' Chronicle initially advised readers against digging up lawns to grow vegetables, since it was thought they would be needed for grazing small animals, such as rabbits and Indian Runner ducks, which would provide manure to promote soil fertility in vegetable gardens. On 30 September, the editorial leader suggested that gardeners grow 'the more handsome' vegetables in herbaceous borders, in a move that anticipated the 'integrated gardening' trend of the 1980s. Suggestions included 'Painted Lady' runner beans, cardoons, beetroot, even potatoes, as well as immortelles (everlastings), for displaying in the house in winter. The periodical was also beginning to warn against 'early forcing' of fruit and vegetables, because of the heating required to do it, and recommended instead the use of glass cloches as a way of extending the growing season at both ends of the year. 'Cloches against Hitler' soon became the catchy, if rather fatuously grandiose, slogan for promoting the inexpensive protection and gentle forcing of crops in the garden.

As with the rest of the gardening press in the days before war broke out, the RHS *Journal* for September 1939 gave few hints of the trouble ahead, because it was printed in August. But the next monthly edition was very different. In October's issue, notice was given that future flower shows would be cancelled, although the Society did subsequently hold a special Autumn Show at the end of October. In the December issue, this was pronounced 'a great success, coming as it did after a stand-still period of several weeks. The support given by the trade exhibitors and by the Fellows themselves showed the advisability of maintaining the usual practice of the Society in holding Fortnightly Shows.'[41] And, as was noted in the December *Journal*, 'It is perhaps fortunate, if anything about war could be so described, that the outbreak of hostilities happened at the season of preparation; this has made it possible to increase the area available for the cultivation of vegetable crops without the loss, or partial loss, of a growing season.'[42] Fortunate indeed.

CHAPTER THREE

DIG FOR VICTORY!

Ask any British adult what comes to mind when they hear the words 'gardening during the war', and a pound to a penny they will immediately mention the phrase 'Dig for Victory'. It is a slogan embedded in our national consciousness, which in its terse simplicity embodies an important strand of the story of the Home Front. As such, it is emblematic of our collective sense of satisfaction and pride in the way our forebears conducted themselves in the darkest of days. However, it is right that we should examine the validity of the extravagant claims for its success – both at the time and ever afterwards – both in providing healthy foodstuffs and in fostering cohesion and high morale in the national community. To do this, it is first necessary to understand the origins and development of the campaign.

The phrase 'Dig for Victory' was almost certainly coined by Michael Foot[1], later a leader of the Labour Party in the 1980s but at the beginning of the war a young, intellectual socialist journalist working for the London *Evening Standard*. In two unsigned editorial leaders, one published on 6 September 1939 and the next almost a week later, he proclaimed a patriotic, encouraging message:

> Every spare half acre from the Shetlands to the Scillies must feel the shear of the spade. The Minister of Agriculture has plans to increase the area under cultivation by a million and a half acres before next spring. He aims to do in one year what we did last time in four. A fine idea. But with the aid of individual citizens we can double that figure. Turn up each square foot of turf.

Root out bulbs and plant potatoes. Spend your Sunday
afternoons with a hoe instead of in the hammock. Take a last
look at your tennis lawn and then hand it over to the gardener.
And if you meet any poor fool attempting to beat his
ploughshare into a sword, tell him that this war may be won in
the farms as well as on the battlefields . . .

You are proud of Britain's Navy. You sleep safer in your bed
at the thought of these proud steel hulls sweeping the seas as
surely as they have done in days past. But the allotmenteers,
too, are playing their part in keeping our naval power supreme.
More food grown here will relieve ships from convoy duty. We
have four million more mouths to fill than in 1914 and fewer
merchant ships to feed them. More food from our own fields
can thwart the Nazi raiders who will search for our food ships
beneath the seas. Remember, therefore, that food wins victories
as surely as gunpowder.[2]

It was stirring stuff, and intended to be.

The newspaper returned to the subject on 12 September, reminding
readers that the military historian, Basil Liddell Hart, had written that
'The Great War was lost by the letters from home.' In other words, that
tales of food shortages in the German Empire sapped the morale of
German fighting men in 1918. It continued:

The Germans remember 1918. Hence their U Boat campaign,
by which they have sunk some 70,000 tons of British shipping in
the first week of war. The figure is not alarming, for in April
1917 the weekly toll averaged more than 100,000 tons.[3] Our
Navy will fight back and reduce the total, just as it did in that
earlier contest. But the submarine can be defeated on every
square foot of British soil as well as on the high seas. So the
order which the Evening Standard gave a week ago must be
rammed home. DIG FOR VICTORY.'[4]

It is doubtful whether Michael Foot himself had ever done much vegetable gardening, having been born in Plymouth of a middle-class professional family, who almost certainly employed a gardener and owned a tennis lawn. He was educated at Oxford University and became for a short time a shipping clerk in Liverpool, before moving to Fleet Street. As an undergraduate he had developed skills as a politician and orator, and his polemical writings suited the sombre, self-dedicatory mood of the time.

On 3 October 1939, not long after Foot's inspiring words were published, Sir Reginald Dorman-Smith, the Minister of Agriculture, introduced the first 'Grow More Food' campaign, aimed at the civilian population, with a broadcast on the Home Service. He made some implausible claims about the vigour of the agricultural industry, and how British farms produced nearly half the food the nation required. However, he did go on to warn that, although of course the Navy could be relied upon to keep trade routes open and the Dominions and other countries would still supply food,

those supplies may not always be unlimited. It is clearly our duty, just as it is a matter of elementary wisdom, to try to make doubly and trebly sure that we will fight and win this war on full stomachs.

To do this we want not only the big man with the plough but also the little man with the spade to get busy this autumn . . . Half a million more allotments properly worked will provide potatoes and vegetables that will feed another million adults and 1½ million children for eight months out of 12.

The matter is not one that can wait. So – let's get going. Let 'Dig for Victory' be the motto of everyone with a garden and of every able-bodied man and woman capable of digging an allotment in their spare time.[5]

And so, just a matter of weeks after the war began, Dorman-Smith gave government approval to the exhortatory phrase that would appear on millions of leaflets and thousands of posters and come to embody so much toil, sweat, disappointment and satisfaction through the war years.[6] It was deliberately quasi-military, lining up civilians – and the part they could play – alongside the armed forces.

The Minister's subordinates had already been very busy. On 18 September, a letter from MAF went out to all the local councils in England and Wales, giving them power, under the Defence Regulations, to take possession of unoccupied land without the owner's consent, as well as occupied land with the permission of the owner and occupier, for use as allotments. Even common land could be commandeered with the permission of the Minister.[7] Councils were also asked to arrange for expert help to be given to gardeners and allotmenteers.[8] The following day, a letter was sent to all county councils asking them to set up horticultural committees in towns and cities with populations of more than 20,000 in order to organise the campaign. These committees would be helped by the Ministry's employed horticultural inspectors.

On 21 September, the county War Ags received a letter giving them instructions on how to manage the changeover of orchards and large gardens to food production, while retaining essential plant stocks until after the war was over. On the 28th, Lord Denham, the newly appointed Parliamentary Secretary at the Ministry of Agriculture, spoke in the House of Lords on the subject of allotments and gardens. He declared that the government's aim was to produce another half a million allotments in order to bring the figure up to 1,330,000, which had been the peak figure in 1920. This would be achieved, he maintained, as with increased agricultural production, through decentralisation and with education. He ended with the words: 'I do claim that those plans have been well and truly laid and prepared, and I only hope that a successful result will be their reward.'[9]

The fact could not be denied that by 1939 many First World War allotments were badly neglected. If such a target was to be reached, these would have to be brought back into production, together with mansion gardens, prospective building sites, wasteland and fields in the suburbs.

The National Allotments Society should have been the natural expert link between government and allotmenteers in all this, but in truth, it took MAF some time to recognise this, and there were mutterings from the Society throughout the autumn of 1939 and into 1940. Dorman-Smith tried to mend his fences at an NAS conference on 3 February 1940, in a speech in which he praised the Society's work. He also said that there would be no famine in fresh vegetables, but the professional growers' very efficient production could with advantage be augmented on allotments and in private gardens. The Minister was in something of a bind: he could not openly say that there could be acute shortages, yet he had to give people a pressing reason for taking up their spades.

When MAF set up the Domestic Food Producers' Council in 1940, under Lord Bingley's chairmanship, Councillor Berry of the NAS was made vice-chairman, as well as chairman of its Allotments and Gardens Committee. However, when Giles and Berry discovered that there was only to be one NAS member on the latter, while there were four from the poultry industry, they nearly asked for a deputation to the Minister himself. Their mood was made darker still because MAF was initially reluctant to give them any money for their work in supporting local associations – on the grounds that the Society received affiliation fees so did not need government help. Berry complained about the 'total lack of goodwill'[10] towards the National Allotments Society shown by the Ministry. Mercifully, a tactful senior civil servant called Dr Wilkins soothed their hurt feelings, and the NAS eventually received a grant of £1,500 a year. After this initial muddle, the Society and the Ministry seem to have worked well. Certainly, in the NAS's wartime annual reports, G. W. Giles was always fulsome in his praise of the Ministry officials.

The brief of the Domestic Food Producers' Council was to co-ordinate the efforts of the various organisations with an interest in the domestic food production campaign, in particular to advise on how to promote production in allotments and private gardens and to organise supplies of seed, fertilisers and equipment, 'as well as to suggest how to use any surplus produce'.[11] The Council would report to the Ministry of Agriculture and the Ministry of Food, since both had an interest in the results.

The Ministry of Agriculture was also banking on the owners of the three and a half million private gardens using their million or more acres to provide health-giving vegetables, even at the expense of flowers. Thanks to the between-the-wars housing boom, the suburbs of cities had increased substantially, with houses typically built at twelve to the acre, so that many suburbanites possessed gardens of around allotment size. Older houses might have a quarter of an acre or even more, especially in country districts, and these were often in good heart, as far as fertility was concerned, having been worked for decades or even centuries.

Despite mutterings from professional gardeners about the pointlessness of doing so, many householders dutifully dug up their lawns to grow potatoes, sowed runner beans to climb pergolas, planted tomato plants in flower beds once brightly cheerful with lobelia, geraniums or dahlias, and made prodigious compost heaps. Nella Last, patriotic housewife that she was, converted her back garden into a vegetable plot and chicken run soon after the war started – as well as cutting her hair short 'for the duration'.[12]

A well-known gardening writer, Stephen Cheveley, wrote a book about his experiences in *A Garden Goes to War*, published in January 1940. His aim, using a combination of personal experience and straightforward vegetable-and-fruit-growing information, was to 'write something that will really help people who want to help themselves'.[13] He told the story of how he and his small son set to work on a Saturday afternoon early in September 1939 to turn much of the two thirds of an acre of terraced flower garden – or all except his much-loved rose beds at least – into a productive vegetable plot. 'We cut off all the flowers worth taking into the house; whole plants of chrysanthemums were executed, and they made a glorious bunch in a huge bowl in the hall. After the first unhappy twinges of regret we became keen on the job, and once the flowers were out of the way it didn't seem nearly so bad.'[14] At least some amateur gardeners must have followed his lead.

49

Even the armed services were enlisted to help, and vegetables began to be grown on spare ground in military camps, RAF stations, onshore naval bases and around anti-aircraft batteries. For example, potatoes and carrots grew next to the runway at Manchester Ringway, then a parachute base, now Manchester airport. The services reaped the benefit of having in their ranks called-up professional gardeners, even specialist tomato growers. A 'soldier-gardener' scheme was instituted which identified trained gardeners in units who could be detailed to work in the gardens of requisitioned mansion houses to provide food for the canteens; there were several thousand of these gardeners by the end of the war.

Of course, many personnel who volunteered to help out in their spare time never tasted the fruits of their labours, since they were always subject to sudden mobilisations. This does not seem to have deterred everyone. Perhaps they were influenced by the words of Lt Col. W. L. Julyan, who wrote sternly that 'a unit leaving a site without passing over a good garden when there has been opportunity to make one ought to feel the disgrace of it just as much as they would in passing over untidy billets'.[15]

The necessity for an urgent campaign was brought home to all those civil servants and politicians privy to the information on losses at sea. In 1939, 800 tons of fruit and vegetables were destroyed, but in 1940 the figure had risen exponentially to 22,000 tons. Although 1940 was the worst year by far, 2,000 tons were lost in 1942, when far less was imported overall. Nor were losses on the high seas the only problem, since onion imports for example declined sharply because they had come from territories by then occupied by the Nazis. In 1939, out of every 100 onions eaten, only nine were grown in Britain.[16] The imported tonnage slumped year on year until 1943, when only 100 tons made it through. Fortunately, imports rose to 27,900 tons the next year. At times, onions were so scarce that single ones were given as birthday presents or as raffle prizes at community events. They even appeared in cartoons, such as the one depicting a grand lady with a string of onions round her neck and the caption: 'They're real, my dear!'

Tomatoes were, if anything, even more badly affected. In 1939,

142,000 tons came into the country but by 1941 this had dwindled to a mere 1,800 tons. Not one tomato was landed in 1942, 1943 or 1944. Small wonder that mansion gardens and market garden operations were strongly encouraged to grow this vegetable in wartime.

As for fruit, imports of bananas were in much the same position as tomatoes. In 1939, 287,600 tons were imported; this figure plummeted to 100 tons in 1941 and to nothing in 1942, 1943 and 1944. Unfortunately, unlike the tomato, the banana could not be grown even in glasshouses in Britain. It is not surprising that there should be such an enduring folk memory concerning the first bananas to arrive back in the grocers' shops in 1945. When they did, the Ministry of Food decided that, as there were so few of them, children should get priority, and they were rationed to just one each.[17]

Oranges, on the other hand, continued to be imported throughout the war, although at just one tenth of the pre-war figure in 1943. Apples were also hard hit: 234,200 tons imported in 1939, down to a mere 8,000 tons in 1943 and only 30,300 tons in 1945.

Clearly there was a pressing need to increase domestic food production; the question was, how to achieve it successfully with a population for whom this was entirely new ground, so to speak. From the beginning, the officials were only too aware that people would have to be taught and guided to become useful, productive kitchen gardeners. Despite the populist nature of the Dig for Victory slogan, the initial campaign by the Ministry of Agriculture and Fisheries was high-mindedly educational. Senior civil servants, many of whom would have themselves employed gardeners, were inclined to take a paternalistic view. They believed that they had to inform and educate, as well as encourage, a vast, amorphous, willing but ignorant crowd of beginners, many of whom had never held a garden fork before and so would need everything spelled out for them. These people included those living in flats and houses in cities, who mostly had no garden at all and so had to be encouraged to take up the challenge of renting a wartime allotment, as well as the many women, in town and countryside, who had traditionally left this task to their menfolk. In search of expert help, the

Ministry of Agriculture turned to those who already earned a living from horticulture – professional gardeners, rural science teachers, commercial nurserymen, county advisers, research scientists – to help the campaign by giving lectures and demonstrations and writing leaflets and instructional books.

The Ministry's efforts throughout the war were characterised by a blizzard of information pamphlets and bulletins, as well as Dig for Victory exhibitions – 400 of them around the country in 1942 and 1943 alone.[18] The BBC was early enlisted to ensure generous wireless coverage, there was a vigorous poster campaign, and the Ministry of Information Crown Film Unit[19] produced instructional films to be shown in cinemas. All essentially carried the same upbeat message: if you cannot fight, you can help your country in another, just as valuable, way.

Through these media, the populace was told or shown how to rotate crops, improve their soil, make a successful compost heap and, most importantly, grow vegetables for picking or using through the winter, when they were scarcest and most expensive in the shops.

The first wartime gardening bulletin to emanate from MAF was 'Food from the Garden', 'Growmore' Bulletin No. 1. Costing 3d, it was published by His Majesty's Stationery Office in September 1939, having been prepared during the previous spring and summer. It was one fruit of E. A. Bunyard's report. Its production committee consisted of representatives from the Royal Horticultural Society, together with the horticultural research stations such as Long Ashton and East Malling, the Horticultural Education Association, the National Allotments Society and the MAF Inspectorate.

'Food from the Garden' was a thin booklet, very much aimed at novices rather than experienced gardeners, and containing a detailed all-year cropping and rotation plan, a table of crop harvest periods, lists of fertilisers and their alternatives, readily obtainable varieties of vegetables and indications of the amount of seed required. There were notes on digging, manuring and how to grow individual vegetable sorts. It sold 400,000 copies in all.

The booklet, however, became the subject of a sustained attack in the specialist press by gardening experts and experienced allotmenteers, throughout 1939 and into 1940. The chorus of criticism from professional gardeners, especially in the north of England and Scotland, was deafening. They complained that too little space in the cropping plan was given to potatoes, that plant spacings were too tight, that the varieties chosen were not the most suitable, that there were ridiculous typographical errors, that the booklet was published at a time of year when few seeds could be sown outside – although that was something that should have been laid at the door of Adolf Hitler rather than the Minister of Agriculture – and that not enough regard was given to conditions and requirements in colder areas, particularly the north of England and Scotland.[20]

A Mr Pearl, who had helped write the booklet, replied robustly to the critics in early January 1940:

Obviously the official cropping plan differs widely from the peace-time cropping of many allotments, but if examined fairly it will be found to provide the basis for the production of those vegetables especially needed in war-time. For instance, there will be an increased need for leafy, green vegetables and salads to take the place of imported Oranges and other fruits of protective food value, particularly in the early months of the year. There is need here for an appetizing range of foods to supplement the eternal Cabbage. Broad Beans and similar protein-yielding seed vegetables may have to replace restricted meat and fish supplies . . . Continuous heavy production from every available inch of ground is necessary, and the importance of the thorough rotation and cultivation implied in the three-year cropping plan will be obvious.[21]

Despite this spirited defence, MAF bowed to pressure and a revised bulletin was published in January 1941, retitled a month later as 'Dig for Victory Leaflet No. 1'. According to Robert Hudson, Dorman-Smith's successor, who wrote the foreword: 'It has now been carefully revised in the light of experience and changes in the general situation . . .'[22], which was one way of putting it. Like Mr Pearl, Hudson emphasised that the preponderance of green leaf vegetables in the plan was the consequence of the need to replace vitamins normally found in imported fruit, a factor of great importance to the nutritionists who advised the Minister. The area designated for potatoes was increased to please northern gardeners in particular.

Three further 'Growmore' bulletins were published in 1939 and 1940: 'Pests and Diseases in the Vegetable Garden', 'Preserves from the Garden' and 'Fruit from the Garden'. Twenty-one free 'Dig for Victory' leaflets would follow, with subjects ranging from how to make a compost heap to how to store vegetables for the winter.

However, the immediate call to action in late 1939 had disappointing results, at least partly because the first winter of the war was so harsh. The weather was abnormally cold and snowy, so that hardy vegetables like cabbages froze in the ground, and the all-important digging was delayed, with the result that the uncertainty of the new 'army' of diggers increased. At the time when the Ministry was negotiating for a 'propaganda broadcast' in late February 1940 consisting of a discussion between a parks superintendent, an enthusiastic allotment holder and a man in the street, John Green, head of the Talks Department at the BBC, wrote: 'The situation at the moment is apparently critical because the Minister's appeal has only met with local success and the national response is below expectation.'[23]

With this comparative failure as a spur, the government publicity campaign, launched in the autumn of 1940, was better thought-out and organised, and it enjoyed rather greater success than its predecessor. The press had taken up the expression 'Dig for Victory' so enthusiastically, and used it so widely, that the Ministry of Agriculture employed the slogan for all its publicity banners and its posters, introducing a photographic image of a magnified left boot on a spade. The foot may or may not have belonged to a Mr W. H. McKie of Acton (see Chapter Six). This foot and spade logo, printed small or large, as either a photograph or a drawing from the photograph, appeared on all the subsequent campaign posters, and became one of the most instantly recognisable images of wartime government publicity. It came to exemplify the idea of the honest-to-goodness, down-to-earth yet highly purposeful effort of amateur gardeners which the Ministry was so keen to promote.[24]

Unfortunately, the 1940 campaign launch proved rather too dramatic for anyone's liking. The Lord Mayor of London had invited mayors from all over the country to meet at the Mansion House in the City of London on 10 September to hear Robert Hudson's Dig for Victory appeal. But, as Roy Hay, a gardening journalist working for the Ministry of Agriculture on the Dig for Victory campaign, recalled:

'Everything would have been all right if Hitler had not had the idea of wiping out London's Dockland.[25] We set off that morning for the Mansion House full of doubts whether we would ever get there or, even if we did, whether the Mayoral kitchens would have any gas or electricity to warm up the turtle soup. Buses were running as far as Holborn Viaduct, but Cheapside was a tangle of fire engines and demolition gangs. Great clouds of black smoke swirled round the Bank of England, and rivers of filthy water ran in the gutters. By devious routes we reached the Mansion House, tripping over miles of hosepipes and dodging barriers, ignoring the shouts of the City police . . . Would the Mayors risk coming to London when the bombs were falling as thick as coconuts in a hurricane on a South Sea Island? Some did and some did not . . . There were as many empty places as guests when we finally sat down at the table. With the turtle soup came an air raid warning. All the speeches were punctuated by the clanging of fire and ambulance bells. Even the Ministry's publicity department could scarcely have staged a more dramatic setting for the Minister's appeal. Mr Hudson was direct and forceful – as always. He told the Mayors to go home and see to it that the allotments committee was made the most important committee of their Council instead of being the Cinderella of them all. With the warehouses burning all along the river, everybody was impressed.[26]

Hudson requested that there be another 500,000 allotments by the spring of 1941, to make two million in total, and continued: 'if we could get the number of allotments in this country to three million [in fact, something never remotely achieved in wartime] we could be certain that six hundred thousand adults and nine million children would be amply supplied with green vegetables during the greater part of the year'.[27] He also exhorted homeowners to put at least some of their borders down to vegetables. That evening, he broadcast a shortened version of his speech on the wireless. A month later, on 6 October, an allotment church service held at St Martin-in-the-Fields in Trafalgar Square was also broadcast. Mr Middleton, the radio gardener, read the lesson.

The following September, Robert Hudson spoke again at the Mansion House, where he exulted in the fact that more new allotments had been marked out than he had asked for in 1940 – some 600,000 in total. He praised the parks superintendents for all their work, but hinted that some local councils were still not doing all they could to take over vacant land for allotments in their districts, singling out Leeds as a shining example of what could be achieved. He encouraged employers to find vacant land for their employees or to lease it to councils for allotments. He was careful to praise broadcasters and journalists, as well as the National Allotments Society and the RHS for their support. And he finished off with an exhortation to 'crop wisely' so that there were enough vegetables, stored or green, to eat in wintertime. That evening he broadcast on the wireless: 'we can't afford to rest on our spades . . . I want you to look on yourself and your garden as a production unit on active service.'[28]

Crucial to what success the educational campaign enjoyed were the horticultural committees, consisting of professional gardeners, parks superintendents and keen amateurs, in every town and some villages, who gave advice to individuals or provided speakers for public lectures and practical demonstrations. The Ministry of Agriculture supplied lantern slides to speakers, without charge. The Royal Horticultural Society drew up a nationwide list of experienced lecturers who would talk to groups for free, especially in the countryside, and also lent out slides. 'Brains Trust' panels were put together to provide education and entertainment on similar lines to the modern *Gardeners' Question Time*, with the wireless presenter F. H. Grisewood in strong demand as a chairman. Energetic parks superintendents laid out model allotments, following Ministry leaflet guidelines, in parks and open spaces, and staged public lectures and demonstrations in the evenings and at weekends.

Public show plots were also created in botanic gardens, the best remembered one being that laid out according to the Ministry's 'Food from the Garden' bulletin in front of Kew Palace at the Royal Botanic Gardens. Here the gardeners instructed visitors on basic cultivation techniques. The most photogenic demonstration plots were dug in front of the Albert Memorial in Kensington Gardens, as well as on the Park Lane side of Hyde Park. London Zoo also laid out two model allotments on the Fellows' Lawn, presided over by a professional gardener called William Strang. Strang, according to *The Times*, had 'a great gift of explanation and illustration, much appreciated by those who inquire how best to dig for victory: when asked why he had never written a book about gardening, he replied that he was not much of a scribe and that writing with a spade was more effective than writing with a pen. Certainly his gardens at the Zoo are worth reading.'[29]

A survey of the Dig for Victory campaign during 1941 convinced the Publicity Branch of the Ministry of Agriculture that one of the best ways of spurring public interest in a town was to hold a Dig for Victory week or 'drive'. Dorothy Hinchcliffe, an inspector with the Ministry of Agriculture when war broke out, found herself deeply involved in the campaign in Westmorland and north Lancashire.[30] With the help of the local town council and parks superintendent, she organised these events throughout her area, putting up displays and stalls in the town hall and arranging for gardening experts to be on hand, as well as people experienced in the care of pigs, poultry and rabbits. There was usually a produce show, and prizes for the best exhibits. The Ministry headquarters provided her with publicity material and a panel of speakers, and sometimes she would lure Freddie Grisewood (who must have had a very busy war), Joseph McLeod, Donald McCullough or other national figures to talk at an evening meeting.

By May 1942, nearly a million people had attended the exhibitions and demonstrations connected with these 'drives' around the country. After one was held in Yorkshire, Sheffield council received over 500 applications for allotments and Leeds council 400. 'The efforts made during the past three months represent the most vigorous attempt yet to arouse gardening interest, and to disseminate gardening lore among the residents of urban districts,' according to The Gardeners' Chronicle.[31] All in all, there was no shortage of expert help, if the new gardeners were prepared to ask for it.

The efforts of experts were not without effect. Newspapers often told heartwarming stories of how enterprising individuals had taken over factory surrounds, village greens, derelict gardens or bomb sites in places where council-owned allotments were not available. For example, it was reported that workers at Wolseley Motors in Birmingham reclaimed the car factory's scrap heap for an allotment and made cold frames from old windscreens. Only camping sites and sports recreation fields were likely to remain inviolate, since there was a strong feeling that open-air sport remained important for the nation's health. However, even these were in places made over to allotments, much to the displeasure of the National Playing Fields Association, who maintained that it was economically unsound to break up ground prepared so carefully for sport in this way.

The Gardeners' Chronicle ran a column each week of allotment news, and as the newspaper was very dependent on parks superintendents and allotment association secretaries for information, these items were usually upbeat. The newspaper enumerated in commendable, if rather mind-numbing, detail the success of particular local authorities in increasing the number of wartime and permanent allotments in their district – in the spring of 1941, 9,000 in Sheffield, 6,000 in the London parks, 2,000 in Kettering and so on.

They were also keen on estimating the value of the food produced on these allotments. According to *The Gardeners' Chronicle*, in December 1944 the average annual value of produce was, apparently, £17,250,000.[32] This cannot possibly have been accurately calculated, but it must have impressed their readers no end.

Some boroughs were definitely more active and enthusiastic than others. For example, Tottenham in north London had almost 3,000 allotments in 150 acres, as well as a very successful pig club set up by the council dustmen. Another proactive suburban area was Yiewsley and West Drayton, a recently industrialised part of west Middlesex, with a population of 17,000. Every second household rented an allotment, with 2,200 plots in all. Indeed, the Yiewsley allotments featured in a Dig for Victory film made by the Ministry of Information. As W. G. Evans, a horticultural expert from the district, reported in a talk given on the Home Service in early June 1942: 'Our school children carried out the first campaign and made a great success of it: there were 380 applications for plots. This was the start of our snowball.'[33] He went on to recount how professional gardeners in the local area had formed an advisory committee, and emphasised that the 'press, libraries, gardening shows and films, Brains Trust meetings, free gardening leaflets, advisory bureaux, and house-to-house canvass are valuable contributions in our plan of campaign. We get a great deal of encouragement for our work, if only to see butchers, bakers, wardens, policemen, shopkeepers, and soldiers, sailors and airmen on leave . . . all working on the same piece of land.'[34]

Like many others, Mr Evans liked to boast of how much was grown. The National Fire Service Social Committee was cultivating about four acres of ground, including crops in greenhouses, and had provided 26,200 meals in 1941. There was much communal gardening, with Women's Institutes, boys' clubs, and Girl Guides gardening together. The town even had a 'Women's Allotment Week', which encouraged more than 200 women to take up plots. 'One event during the week's campaign which excited the admiration of everyone was a procession in which men and women shouldered their gardening tools and marched through the main streets of our town.'[35] In 1941, ninety-nine people in the district had won the Ministry of Agriculture's certificate of merit, which had been instituted for allotment gardeners who had been deemed by their local society to be particularly proficient. Taking into account the 4,000 home gardens, which approximated in size to 2,000 ten-pole allotments, Mr Evans believed that the district would be self-sufficient – a source of great pride to the urban horticultural committee, and not something that many other places could boast. So enduringly enthusiastic were the townspeople that they won the Bledisloe Cup for the best performance in the 1943 Dig for Victory campaign.

One of the most inspiring of all local Dig for Victory stories was that of the Bethnal Green Bombed Sites Producers' Association. Bethnal Green in east London was very badly bombed during the Blitz. Yet the locals were not daunted and turned bombed-out buildings into garden plots. Gardening in places where houses had once stood must have taken considerable dedication; not only would there have been thousands of glass shards, but brick dust is not a good medium in which to grow vegetables. At times, the members of this association were forced to sieve soil with pierced dustbin lids to remove the debris. In August 1942, there were 300 adults growing vegetables on thirty bombed sites in the district.

On 20 September 1941, the Duke of Norfolk visited the allotments, as well as a vegetable show in Bethnal Green, even going into back yards to inspect hens and rabbits. This visit was promoted by Roy Hay, who managed to persuade the BBC to broadcast an item about it that evening:

Bethnal Green has always been one of my pet places and before any question of a Ministerial visit was raised I had in mind trying to get something over about these people, mainly because I feel that thousands of shirkers in Torquay, Gleneagles and other hideouts might feel a little ashamed of themselves if they could see or realise what the people in Bethnal Green are doing.[36]

The Queen also visited the borough, on 17 June 1943. Wherever she went, crowds gathered, and she finished her tour at the combined allotment and model farm, where she saw pigs, rabbits, chickens, geese, a goat and a pony, all housed in buildings made from scrap. The goat ate the Dig for Victory leaflets. She was accompanied on the tour by the chairman of the Bethnal Green Bombed Sites Producers' Association, Sir Wyndham Deedes, a distinguished retired career soldier and devout Christian, who lived in a house in the borough throughout the war with his nephew, Bill.[37] Sir Wyndham was a local councillor, chief air raid warden and vice-chairman of the National Council for Social Services. A few days after the royal visit he wrote to The Times to enlarge on what the inhabitants of Bethnal Green had achieved. On one bombed site, where once had stood houses, shops and a pub, seventeen people now tended allotments. In some places they had to dig down six feet through solid foundations, and fifty tons of hardcore had been carried away by the lorries of the Heavy Rescue Service. Deedes included a lengthy litany of vegetables grown, at a cost of £4, which included creosoting the fence and 37s. 6d a year charged by the Water Board. He finished the letter:

Thus this experiment shows . . . that with hard work and relatively little expense of money, even Bethnal Greeners can make their contribution to food production. It has also shown – and let us remember it when the war is over – that the desire for an allotment is almost universal and, I may add, passionate.[38]

The rather more salubrious Hurlingham Polo Ground was turned into allotments, and vegetables grew even in the deep silt of the dry moat around the Tower of London, a most symbolic site of last-ditch national defence. The incendiary-bomb-damaged roof garden of Selfridge's department store was turned into a plot, which produced vegetables for the restaurant. There were vegetables growing in the Twickenham stadium, appropriately enough since the home of English rugby football was colloquially known as the Cabbage Patch, it having been a market garden until 1907. Tomatoes grew in ornamental pots flanking the doors of gentlemen's clubs in St James's as well as in boxes in front of humble high street shops.

The ancient universities played their part, with the lawns of some Cambridge courts and Oxford quads turned over to vegetables.[39] A notable success was Girton College in Cambridge, thanks to its energetic Garden Steward, Chrystabel Proctor, whose motto was: 'We *may* be bombed, we *must* be fed.'[40] She introduced pigs and poultry to the college grounds and cut the lawns for hay, which she traded with the university farm across the road for modern fertilisers and manure. Their sheep grazed the college's tennis lawns.

Undergraduates were encouraged to lend a hand in their college gardens, as one girl at Lady Margaret Hall in Oxford loftily recalled:

Some of the lawns were sacrificed for the 'Dig for Victory' campaign. I remember one year when we were invited to volunteer to help bring in the potato harvest. By and large the students did not come from the horny-handed classes, and the response was poor. They were gently prodded in the right direction by two successive dinners featuring boiled rice as a vegetable followed by rice pudding as a dessert. Next day there was a rush of volunteers to wield the garden forks.[41]

Digging for Victory was never going to be without its contentious issues and problems. One of these was how to dispose of surpluses by gardeners and allotmenteers, and whether that disposal might compete with commercial retailing of fresh vegetables. The Ministry of Agriculture was ambivalent on the subject, sometimes encouraging amateurs to grow more than their households needed and at other times definitely not. In February 1940, Sir Reginald Dorman-Smith told a conference of the NAS: 'The new allotment drive does not aim at competing with the market gardening industry, which must be maintained for the national service. *It is not intended that allotments should grow produce for sale* [my italics].'[42] This was substantially to underestimate the capacity of those gardeners with large gardens or allotments, especially in the countryside, to grow more than their families required. In the eyes of MAF, there seemed no easy answer to the potential waste involved, if small commercial retailers were not to be threatened financially, and in the light of substantial transport difficulties.

In May 1940, this hot potato was handed over to Lord Woolton and his Ministry of Food, to try to deal with without burning their fingers. In characteristic manner Woolton made clear in a letter to Robert Hudson at MAF that vested interests should not get in the way of greater consumption of fresh vegetables and that gardeners should be encouraged to grow as much as they could and any surpluses be redistributed. As a result, that summer County Garden Produce Committees[43] were set up throughout England and Wales, under the auspices of a central committee chaired by Lord Bingley, since it was thought that surpluses were most likely to occur in the countryside. These committees oversaw local Village Produce Associations, whose members were garden owners, allotmenteers, beekeepers, and keepers of domestic livestock.[44] One of the tasks of the VPAs was to deal with the distribution of surpluses, where they occurred, by giving or selling them to local schools, hospitals, army NAAFIs, communal feeding centres, works canteens, market stalls and so on. VPAs were enjoined to work very closely with Women's Institute Produce Guilds, where these existed; in reality, they often consisted of the same *dramatis personae*.

However, people bombarded Hudson with complaints about how difficult it was to get rid of surpluses, which may be the reason why, in March 1941, he pronounced:

The policy I advocate for the amateur grower is one of orderly cropping, with the cropping so planned that a succession of vegetables is obtained all the year round, that over-production of summer vegetables is avoided, and that any production surplus to the grower's own requirements is of non-perishable vegetables which can be stored for use during the winter months. I have commended this policy to the organisations concerned in advising amateur growers throughout the country. Should it prove that surpluses of storable vegetables are in fact produced, I am satisfied that the machinery of committees now established is sufficient to carry out any arrangements for collection which may be decided upon.[45]

Whatever had been said in 1940, by 1941 the Ministry was only keen to promote surpluses of winter-storage vegetables. The problem was that in the nature of things there was always much less risk of a surplus in these than in perishable summer vegetables.

It was at this moment that the responsibility for the work of the County Garden Produce Committees reverted to the Ministry of Agriculture, since Lord Woolton was not keen on being associated with a policy that potentially restricted food production. It is possible to discern a certain squirming by politicians when questioned in Parliament on the issue. For example, in July 1941 Lord Davies put the Duke of Norfolk, Joint Parliamentary Secretary at the Ministry of Agriculture, thoroughly on the spot when he asked him whether the policy of the Ministry of Agriculture was to encourage or discourage the growing of vegetables. In essence, the Duke replied that only the collection and storage of non-perishable amateur-grown produce would be possible. In other words, parsnips yes, lettuces no. But parsnips were not the problem.[46]

Although politicians continued to fret, the situation was sorted out in the end by the good sense of the Women's Institutes, who combined with the National Allotments Society and the County Garden Produce Committees to estimate the scale of surplus produce and put together plans to collect it, grade it at collection centres and distribute it to wholesalers, retailers or WI market stalls. The National Allotments Society also organised the collection and disposal of surplus food produce in towns and cities, via the local allotment associations. These systems worked better in some places than in others; as with many aspects of Home Front endeavour, success often depended on the calibre and determination of particular individuals on the ground. Certainly the Ministry of Agriculture never completely found the best way to encourage the public to grow just the right amount of their own food.

A surplus to which no one could object was that of young plants provided by philanthropic garden owners to their local Victory Diggers. Sir Jeremiah Colman, an august figure in the upper echelons of the RHS, who lived at Gatton Park in Surrey, wrote to *The Times* in late 1941, using a Biblical analogy with which his readers would have been thoroughly familiar:

> The importance of helping those who 'dig for victory' to furnish their plots would appear to have received too little attention. A serious shortage of suitable seed is reported, besides which smallholders are at a disadvantage in not having facilities for raising plants before the arrival of spring, and as a consequence their crop reaches maturity two or three months late. In private gardens where plants are raised under glass there is always a waste of surplus plants. A distribution of such crumbs as fall from the rich man's table proves a great boon to the smallholder.
>
> I have put the theory to the test. The first distribution from my gardens, which consisted of some 20,000 plants, led to a scramble for participation by some 85 'diggers' and proved such a success that I have given directions for special raisings to be made for distribution next season. Such favourites as onions, tomatoes, marrows &c., can only be brought to early maturity by being started under glass.[47]

In fact a number of parks departments also grew vegetable plants in their greenhouses and nurseries, which they sold to local gardeners and allotmenteers at a competitive price.

The officers of the National Allotments Society fought hard on the ministerial committees to bring to the attention of the politicians the needs of allotmenteers, in particular for assurances on security of tenure. The politicians were adept at sidestepping the issue, since they knew that, in peace time, wartime allotments would either revert to their pre-war use or, in many instances, be built over. All that the Ministry of Agriculture was prepared to concede was that allotment holders would be compensated if the land were taken away during the cropping season.

Other persistent problems associated with wartime allotments included widespread thieving and malicious or inadvertent damage. These were difficult to solve when there was usually no spare fencing or wire for making allotment gardens secure against trespassers and stray dogs. It was a matter that exercised allotmenteers, who were not slow to report their grievances to the Ministry. Robert Hudson received many letters from disheartened and disgruntled gardeners. Defence Regulation 62 provided that any unauthorised person on agricultural land would be guilty of trespass, and on 20 May 1943, an Order in Council decreed that trespass notices were not obligatory at allotment sites. One of the reasons for this was that they were often defaced or torn down. Conservative backbenchers opposed this measure, on the ground that it violated civil liberties. But the mood of the House was generally with the Minister of Agriculture, who explained:

Before the war, in the overwhelming majority of cases, allotments were fenced, and therefore they were to some extent protected, and before the war the police had more leisure than they have to-day. Since the war we have been conducting an intensive 'Dig for Victory' campaign, and we have been urging everyone who possibly could to make themselves and their families self-supporting in vegetables as a contribution to the war effort in order to save shipping and in order to release farmers for producing other crops. The result of that has been very striking. The number of allotments has risen from 930,000 to 1,675,000. The number of private gardens being cultivated for the growing of vegetables has risen from 3,000,000 to 5,000,000 [an astonishing statement, since there were only 3,500,000 private gardens at the start of the war and there was little house building during it]. Therefore the fact that that has been done has definitely made an invaluable – I use that word advisedly – contribution to our total war effort. But at the same time, as some Hon. Members have said, it is a regrettable fact that pilfering and damage, both malicious and involuntary, have been on the upgrade, and I have been receiving letters from all over the country in increasing numbers.

After all, as part of this 'Dig for Victory' campaign, we have taken vacant building plots scattered throughout towns and turned them into allotments. There is no fencing or anything, but everyone must know and recognise when a piece of ground is being cultivated. It may not be easy to define what an allotment is, but it is like an elephant – you recognise it when you see it. We want to make it abundantly clear to the public at large that for the period of the emergency, that ground is the property of the man who works it. The object of this is to serve with a notice all and sundry that an allotment belongs to the person who is working the land and also to his family . . . It is distasteful to us to have to bring in Regulations creating new offences, but we have been extremely patient; we have applied every possible alternative remedy we could think of.[48]

It is significant that, in a debate about trespass, Hudson should have taken the opportunity to praise the contribution amateur gardeners made to the war effort and to boast of the success of the Dig for Victory campaign, however dubious the statistics he employed. It is also significant that, despite the many and various assaults on civil liberties that had already occurred since the war began, the Minister should still feel he had to explain to the House why he had added one more, very minor one.

So serious was the problem of pilfering, however, that many allotment societies recruited 'plot watchers' to keep an eye on produce and materials, especially at night. Some were paid and others were public-spirited volunteers. In September 1941, a man from Penryn in Cornwall was sentenced to two months' hard labour in prison for stealing onions and potatoes from a railway allotment, which shows just how sternly the authorities viewed the matter. In 1942, in St Helen's in Lancashire, a man who stole 8d worth of onions was saved from a prison sentence only because he was seventy-three years old, while in Hampstead two women were fined £1 each for stealing runner beans.

Humans were a nuisance to dedicated allotmenteers, but so were a whole range of domesticated and wild stock, from dogs (their owners were fined £5 if they were found running loose on an allotment site), sheep, rats, mice, cats and wild rabbits. In places, would-be growers cited the lack of netting and fencing as a serious deterrent to cultivating an allotment.

The peaceful nature of allotments could be rudely shattered by far worse than wild or domestic livestock, however. Those allotments situated in or on the outskirts of British cities were no more immune from bomb attack than were houses. The admirably phlegmatic Mass-Observation diarist Herbert Brush, a retired Electricity Board Inspector from Sydenham, put down his thoughts in October 1940 after a particularly bad night of bombing, which he had spent mainly in the dugout in his garden, except when he was extinguishing a fire ignited by an 'oil bomb'.

3 p.m. W. and I went round to look at the allotment, but it was a case of looking for the allotment. Four perches[49] out of the five are one enormous hole and all my potatoes and cabbages have vanished. Apparently the bomb fell on the footpath between two allotments and when it exploded had preference for mine, although I must say that there is not much left of Hardy's and the plot on the other side of mine has a huge pile of my earth on it. The result is that all my work there has been wasted, absolutely wasted, and the potatoes at Christmas certainly will not come off my allotment, though if I have sufficient energy for some deep excavations I may find a potato or two somewhere in the mountain on each side of the ten-foot hole. When I went there the other day I noticed that there were several nice cabbages nearly ready to eat, and I meant to dig potatoes this weekend. Now I should have some difficulty in finding the place where they stood.[50]

Only in the phrase 'wasted, absolutely wasted' can one catch a glimpse of his bitter disappointment.

Late in the war, when London and its environs were plagued by V-1 and V-2 bombs, the school yard near Brush's allotment was also hit:

> Thursday, 11th [January, 1945] W. and I went to the plot this afternoon to get some green food if possible. Deep snow lies on the allotments and it was not easy to find anything worth bringing home but I cut a couple of miserable-looking cabbages and managed to dig up a couple of roots of celery. Then we went to look at the bomb-hole [made by an unmanned V-2 rocket launched from northern France], which is about 60 yards away in the school playground.
>
> Huge boulders of clay are scattered all round the crater, which is the largest hole I have seen for a long time. I don't like to guess at the size as it's difficult to estimate with so much snow around, but when standing on the edge, the far side seemed to me more than 20 yards away and looking down the bottom of the hole might be 20 feet below . . .
>
> I think that if I had been working on the plot I should have stood very little chance of escape, as huge lumps of clay have been scattered far and wide, and I noticed several snow-covered lumps on my plot which I did not investigate, but feel sure they are lumps of clay from the bomb crater. The wooden fence between the plots and the playground has been swept away and some of the large trees have been smashed and twisted about as though they were small branches in the hands of a mischievous boy.'[51]

Despite all the difficulties, there is no doubt that renting and working an allotment had a beneficial effect on town and city dwellers. There are countless testimonies to the relaxing and peaceful nature of many of the tasks, and the satisfaction that could be derived from the exercise, the camaraderie and the healthy produce. It is true that it could be harmful to the health, when overdone. One Mass-Observation diarist wrote of her husband in April 1940: 'He is all over aches and pains. Every time he gets up he groans and groans something chronic . . . It's them allotments as gets him.'[52] However, provided people did not crock themselves by digging too much in one go, many began to enjoy what the allotment had to offer them.

That did not necessarily mean that they were good at vegetable gardening, even well into the war. In the summer of 1942, the Ministry of Agriculture was concerned that the average production of vegetables in small gardens and allotments was only half of what it should have been. In particular, the problem of feast and famine – too much in the summer, little or nothing in the winter – was still an issue; hence the continuing poster campaign to get gardeners growing the workaday but vital winter vegetables like cabbages, kale and leeks. After the 1942–3 season, a gardening paper calculated that almost 1,000,000 tons of vegetables[53] had been produced on allotments, which is rather more than half a ton per allotment. In the light of the Ministry's findings, this seems unlikely.

The experience of Brighton stands as a representative example of how the Dig for Victory campaign played out in practice. Just before the war started, there were 2,600 allotments in Brighton and 150 smallholdings. In the summer of 1939, MAF had sent out a circular to all town clerks in England and Wales explaining the benefits of allotments, in case they needed to be told, and making clear the powers that local councils now possessed to requisition land for wartime allotments. After the September circular from MAF, advising that town councils should form a horticultural committee and appoint full-time technical instructors, the Brighton Allotment Subcommittee compiled a survey to discover just how many allotments existed, which ones were neglected or had tenants in arrears, and where there might be suitable land that could be requisitioned. Demand was strong and the council took over parcels of land in many parts of the town. By the end of February 1940, land amounting to 157 ten-rod allotments had been found, together with 129 rods that had not been used for many years. Schoolchildren became involved in allotment cultivation as well.

The Allotment Subcommittee bought bulk fertilisers and seed and sold them at cost price to gardeners. In 1941, a model allotment was laid out in the grounds of the eighteenth-century Brighton Pavilion – which considering that its builder had been the sybaritic Prince Regent is a delicious collision of ideas – and overseen by the parks superintendent. It remained there until October 1944.

At nearby Hove, however, there was opposition to an alderman's suggestion that part of the town's parks be ploughed up; since the beaches were off limits to civilians, parks were vital for leisure. People were allowed to sunbathe in the parks, with the deckchairs provided, and beach huts were moved and became allotment sheds.

However, the civic organisation did not always run smoothly. On 22 February 1942, the *Brighton and Hove Herald* reported a spat in the Brighton council chamber over allegations from the Allotment Sub-committee about the efficiency of the volunteer Horticultural Committee. 'It was further marked by the threat of a painful scene when Mr Ingram, having made some remark about Alderman Galliers which elicited a swift retort, crossed the council chamber, squared his shoulders, threw out his fists and adopted a fighting attitude. Alderman Galliers, undaunted, stood ready for anything – but fortunately restraining hands prevented "anything" happening.'[54] The upshot of this contretemps was that a Food Production Committee was formed to take over the functions and responsibilities of the two committees. In March the following year, this committee was merged with the Wartime Meals Committee and the Kitchen Waste Committee and reconstituted as the Wartime Food Committee. It would seem that bureaucratic impulses and vain self-regard were features of the campaign quite as much as selfless patriotic action.

Security of tenure, especially into the post-war world, seems always to have been a lively issue for those who took up wartime allotments in Brighton. Another was the lack of piped water in many allotment gardens; this mattered particularly for the cultivation of the many leafy vegetables that gardeners were urged to grow. Where water was available, 2d was added to the general rent of a shilling a rod. In late 1941, Brighton applied for a loan from the Ministry of Health to get water piped to allotments, and the improvements were made in due course.

Brighton and Hove had problems with pilfering and wilful damage; so bad was it that volunteer special constables patrolled the worst-affected allotments. At one point, the Brighton magistrates warned that theft and damage would be severely dealt with, after two teenage girls were fined 2s.6d for taking fruit to the value of £2, with additional damages and costs.

The two council nurseries produced vegetable seedlings for sale but the local traders muttered that they undercut them by selling seedlings to allotmenteers at just about cost price (two shillings per hundred); to which the answer came that there were so many new gardeners that the trade could not possibly have supplied them all. After all, by March 1941 the number of allotments in Brighton and Hove had more than doubled, from the pre-war figure of 2,750 to 6,000. As well as council allotments, another thousand plots were either privately owned and rented out, or leased from the Southern Railway.[55] In December 1941, it was estimated that altogether these allotments had produced 10,000 tons of food, although that is a figure that would have been impossible to verify. As late as 1942, the council was still pegging out new allotments: in October, the Food Production Committee reported that there were 3,634 permanent allotments and 2,250 wartime allotments.

Flower shows, such as the Brighton Police Horticultural Society Annual Show in August 1942, and the Brighton Horticultural Show in October of that year, showed the gardeners' mettle. The latter included a Brains Trust in the evening, starring – inevitably – C.H. Middleton and Freddie Grisewood. The money raised at the show went to the Royal Sussex County Hospital in Brighton. The show was opened by no less a personage than Lord Woolton, who spoke of his 'fearful responsibility' and how he had to 'run the risk of sacrificing the nation's appetite in order to preserve the nation's health'. Replying, Dr Donald Hall, JP, claimed that 'apart from our peerless Prime Minister' he did not know of any Minister of the Crown to whom so much was owed as Lord Woolton.[56]

In February 1943, at the national launch of that year's Dig for Victory

campaign, Robert Hudson told his audience that the number of allotments now stood at 1,750,000 and four million families were growing
their own vegetables, but that more were needed since the farmers
were finding labour very difficult to get and needed to be able to
concentrate on producing grain, potatoes, milk and sugar. Schools and
hospitals in particular were urged to make themselves self-supporting
in vegetables. A new slogan was coined: 'Better Planning – Better
Cropping', because the authorities continued to be concerned that the
quality of garden planning was not good enough for maximum
production.

Hudson was keen that year that gardeners should lay much less
emphasis on growing potatoes. How much of a garden or allotment to
give over to potatoes was a point for discussion and disagreement
throughout the war, since commercial supplies fluctuated so wildly – one
year a glut and the next a shortage – and with them fluctuated the advice
from the Ministry, much to the exasperation of gardeners. This aspect
of the campaign was only one of many examples of micro-management
by government during the war, when bossiness had an official imprimatur,
under the guise of promoting efficiency and productivity. However, *The
Gardeners' Chronicle* was inclined to the view that cottage and allotment
gardeners would cling tenaciously to their potato patch, and no amount
of government assurance about the availability of potatoes in shops would
make them give up growing them.

A *Times* leader of the time computed that 1,750,000 allotments
amounted to 100,000 acres, or the size of Rutland, England's smallest
county, and mused on the power of the spade that it could dig a whole
county. It went on to calculate that if private vegetable gardens were
taken into account, that would mean Huntingdonshire had been dug as
well.

However, despite all this upbeat rhetoric, there were definite signs
of fatigue amongst both gardeners and those whose job it was to help
promote amateur food production, in particular the BBC. The Director
of the Campaigns Division at the Ministry of Information, E. M. I.
Buxton, sent out a preliminary memorandum to interested parties on

14 August 1943, which is very revealing about how government publicity worked:

> As a result of discussion between Campaigns Division and [the Ministry of] Agriculture it is agreed that the problem is to maintain the present number of Victory diggers and to raise the standard of cultivation in order to secure a bigger output with emphasis on winter vegetables. As the problem is one of maintaining existing enthusiasm rather than creating it, Campaigns Division believe that it will be possible to cut down some forms of publicity without detriment to the campaign as a whole.[57]

Buxton outlined how the Ministry of Information intended to continue to insert regular weekly gardening items in national Sunday papers, as well as selected provincial papers, but they would omit the coldest weeks of the year when gardening operations were suspended, so that there would probably be forty-four insertions rather than the fifty-two taken the year before. The technical press, such as *The Gardeners' Chronicle*, however, would get the same information as before, as would women's magazines and the *Radio Times*, which were targeted in the spring and summer months.

There would be no sixteen-sheet posters for display on hoardings, but supplies of double-crown posters, blanks and banners for use in local drives would continue as before. The Ministry of Information also intended to print a four-page leaflet in two colours designed to convince waverers that however near the end of the war seemed, food rationing and restrictions would continue for several years afterwards, and that 'Digging for Victory' was still necessary. This leaflet was to be distributed at local shows.

Buxton hoped that the BBC would continue the support that it was already giving to the campaign, and that the Films Division would maintain the supply of trailers and instructional films. As for exhibitions, the Ministry was intending to refurbish the existing displays, which told the Dig for Victory story, to save money: the last initiative had cost about £156,000[58], but Buxton was hopeful that this one would be about £100,000. He was trying to avoid saying that things were winding down, but they plainly were.

Nevertheless, the Dig for Victory campaign lasted throughout the war: there were always more people, it seemed, who needed encouragement to start digging their gardens as well as advice on growing vegetables. And there were plenty of allotment gardeners who had given up after a while, disheartened by the inherent difficulties and – often – lack of very concrete rewards, or just plain exhausted, who needed to be invigorated once more.

In December 1944, Robert Hudson appealed to gardeners not to rest on their spades, again emphasising that shortages would last beyond the end of the war. And in January 1945, the Ministry issued the first of twelve monthly 'Allotment and Garden' guides. These were aimed at new gardeners, were illustrated with line drawings, and were heavily reliant on existing 'Dig for Victory' leaflets. Each month's guide begins with a folksy or poetic quotation, such as: 'April, April, Laugh thy girlish laughter; Then the moment after, Weep thy girlish tears.' However, there was plenty of common sense along with the whimsy, such as: 'Good Friday is the traditional day for potato planting; but the wise gardener knows that it's risky to stick to traditions: he pays more attention to soil and weather conditions.'[59] The last guide was published in December 1945. By then everyone had had quite enough.

Separating fact from myth when considering the efficacy of the Dig for Victory campaign, both for shoring up morale and for the provision of otherwise scarce nutritious foodstuffs, is not an easy matter. The campaign's success has become one of the enduring 'facts' of the war. The slogan has echoed to us down the years, and is facilely invoked by any modern politician wishing to give themselves 'green' credentials, or to inspire in their audience a sense of the value of working for a common purpose and a common good – even if the comparison makes them look ridiculous in the process.

Wartime newspapers and magazines were certainly full of anecdotal evidence that the campaign was a huge success, as we have seen, but this evidence was naturally selective. After all, editors had to be careful not to print anything that might possibly be construed as unpatriotic if they did not wish to risk drawing down the government's wrath, or the criticism of their readers. It is certainly possible that they were never told fully the results of the surveys conducted by the Ministry of Agriculture to try to discover how successful the Dig for Victory publicity campaigns had been, to count the number of wartime allotments that were occupied, or to find out how much produce was generated in gardens and allotments.

In August and September 1942, the Ministry of Agriculture carried out 'An Inquiry into the Effects of the "Dig for Victory" Campaign'. This was a survey of nearly 3,000 gardeners and allotment holders.[60] Its results are surprising to us and would perhaps also have surprised wartime gardeners. For example, the proportion of households that were growing vegetables was only just above half, at 55.2 per cent. Although 91 per cent of households in rural areas were growing vegetables (i.e. practically all with gardens), the number barely reached 50 per cent in urban areas. The figures in the north were particularly low: 39 per cent of households in the north of England and 41.4 per cent in Scotland.[61] Although, generally speaking, gardeners had increased vegetable production at the expense of flowers, the surveyors also discovered that town dwellers with gardens were more likely to continue to concentrate only or mainly on flowers.

Depressingly for the Ministry, only 16 per cent of those questioned attributed their lease of an allotment to its publicity campaign. Indeed, the report expressed disappointment at the relative failure of their information, especially about the all-important cropping plan.[62] But there was satisfaction that the emphasis on the importance of growing green-leaved vegetables in the winter was having some effect. In 1941, 14 per cent of the sample was not growing brassicas, while the figure had gone down to 4.5 per cent in 1942.

One of the signal successes of the campaign appeared to be the fact that 75 per cent of the sample had compost heaps, while about two thirds understood that they should not spray for potato blight in polluted industrial districts (because of the risk of cumulative chemical damage to plants).

The surveyors were, understandably, keen to discover how enthusiastic women were as vegetable gardeners, but had problems finding enough female allotment holders to interview, which in itself is indicative. However, the report concluded that those women who did take allotments seemed to manage about as well as the men, although they could usually call on more assistance, especially with the digging.

It is likely that the report's authors may also have been rather surprised by the findings; they were certainly not very pleased. They could not resist criticising new allotment holders for the quality of their cultivations: 'Almost everywhere local authorities commented to us upon the failure of many gardeners to adopt the best methods for success . . . We had numerous examples shown to us of crop failure through the omission of elementary precautions.'[63]

On the subject of publicity, the report concluded that 'in this respect there remains a very considerable amount to be done before the Ministry of Agriculture really has gardening habits in this country under anything like complete control'.[64] It is a wonder that they ever thought they would – or could.

However upbeat Robert Hudson might have appeared in his public utterances, it is certain that his Ministry officials were not happy with the impact of the Dig for Victory campaign on new gardeners & allotment holders, which they concluded 'has been fairly satisfactory throughout the war'.[65] 'Fairly satisfactory' is scarcely a rip-roaring success, although no one was going to tell the public that.

At just the time when this survey was being collated, C. H. Middleton wrote in his *Daily Express* column:

We can turn our gardens into munitions factories, for potatoes and other vegetables are munitions of war as surely as shells and bullets are . . . Do not think of your allotment as an ordeal or wartime sacrifice. Regard it as your pleasant and profitable recreation . . . And what can be said of the campaign so far? We have shouted 'Dig for Victory!' from screen, platform and poster. Has it produced the expected results? Broadly speaking, I think so. The country is definitely garden minded, but we still have a long way to go.'[66]

In his perspicacious way, Middleton had reached the nub of the matter. The country had become 'garden minded', which was a significant result, but that did not mean everyone by any means wanted to put their shoulders to the wheel.

Similarly telling was the survey on garden and allotment produce, dated 30 December 1944, produced by the Surveys Branch of the Reconstruction Division of MAF.[67] This survey would have had modern market researchers scratching their heads, for it excluded rural areas completely, on the dubious grounds that most vegetables and fruits that were consumed in country districts would have come from gardens and allotments, an assumption which should never have been made. Nevertheless, the findings certainly undermine the rosy picture of the urban population continuing to spend its spare time cheerfully acquiring blisters on their hands, and triumphantly carrying home enormous cabbages in string bags.

By June 1944, less than half of urban households could be persuaded to cultivate vegetables and fruit: when all households were added together, 34.4 per cent grew vegetables and fruit in their gardens, 6.5 per cent grew them in allotments, 4.4 per cent grew them in both gardens and allotments, and 54.7 per cent did not grow them at all. 10.9 per cent of households cultivated an allotment: what a lot of publicity effort had gone into achieving even *that* modest figure.[68]

The regional statistics were even more stark. The north-west of England turned in the worst figures, with 28 per cent of households growing vegetables, which means that nearly three quarters of urban and suburban households in that region had either failed to buy into the campaign, had been unable to satisfy their desire to do so, or had had enough of it and stopped. The north-east fared only a little better with

32 per cent and Scotland 38 per cent, while the most enthusiastic growers were in the south, in particular the south-west (58 per cent) and south-east, with 68 per cent in the latter region cultivating a garden or allotment. Inner London did as badly as the north-west, although the suburbs turned in better figures, not surprisingly, since 50 per cent of households in the suburbs had gardens, while that number dropped to 23 per cent in inner London. The highest take-up of allotments was in the south-west of England, followed by the south-east, then the Midlands.[69]

Also remarkable were the statistics concerned with class: 58 per cent of urban or suburban working-class households and 31 per cent of middle-class ones had neither a garden nor an allotment in the summer of 1944.

One of the findings that overtly surprised the civil servants was that garden and allotment cultivation did not have the marked effect on the purchases of commercial fruit and vegetables by working-class households that they had either expected or hoped.[70] The surveyors measured the number of ounces of various vegetables eaten by each person in a week. With the exception of potatoes, cabbages and rhubarb, there was no very great difference in the amount that gardeners and non-gardeners bought in the shops. Even in the summer months, when garden produce formed the largest proportion of consumption, it only represented 20–30 per cent in value. Working-class households in towns, in particular, were nowhere near becoming self-sufficient in vegetables.

Much of the propaganda about the importance of growing vegetables at home in order to release agricultural land for growing other crops, like wheat, must therefore have fallen on deaf ears. You can sense the disappointment behind the carefully worded official report, which pronounced that 'the difference in purchases between those with and those without gardens and allotments was not always of significant dimensions'.[71]

When considering these results, it is important to set them against the backdrop of a generally public-spirited population who, though they might have grumbled, were in no doubt of the importance of 'doing their bit'.[72] So it was not lack of a desire to contribute that led to the unimpressive figures.

There are a number of factors that may help to explain the lack of enthusiasm. Most able-bodied adults under sixty-five had many other burdens imposed on them; the men were either in the services or had Home Guard, ARP or fire-watching duties. Women were conscripted for the first time from late 1941, when single women and childless widows between the ages of twenty and thirty became liable for national service of some kind. By 1943, the lower limit was nineteen and the upper limit forty.

Another possible explanation might be that emergency provision of spare land for allotments did not satisfy demand in the large, densely populated conurbations in the north-west and north-east. However, the fact that many local councils at different times reported that not all their available allotments had been taken up seems to suggest apathy rather than lack of provision.

Certainly, climatic differences between the north and the south meant that kitchen gardening was likely to be more rewarding in the south; that is what the Ministry officials concluded at least. They also assumed, probably rightly, that ownership of a garden tended to mean a higher economic status, and therefore increased consumption, especially of the more expensive vegetables, such as peas and lettuces, which was why garden owners still bought quantities of vegetables in the shops.[73]

However, it is impossible to avoid the general conclusion that many town-dwellers – for reasons of old age, infirmity, lack of time or even inclination – were impervious to the blandishments of Ministry propaganda throughout the entire war. In mitigation, much of the gardening that they were being encouraged to take up was of the dreariest and least rewarding kind. Picking sun-warm greenhouse tomatoes to add to a salad is a pleasure; weeding round shot-holed brassicas on a windswept allotment is not. It is surely permissible to infer that at least some civilians hated that kind of gardening so much that no higher authority could persuade them that it was worth their while, when there was so much else to occupy their scarce leisure hours. However, it would have been distinctly unpatriotic to say so out loud.

Keen gardeners certainly noticed their contemporaries' lack of enthusiasm, and reported it to the gardening papers. In October 1941, a correspondent to *The Gardeners' Chronicle* opined: 'There is reluctance on the part of many to do anything towards the conversion of even a part of their garden . . . but they should realize the issue at stake justifiably demands that a portion at least should be made productive . . . There seems no way of getting at these people, unfortunately . . .'[74] And nor indeed was there, however hard the government tried.

It can be no surprise that the Dig for Victory campaign came in for a fair bit of gentle ribbing, both from ordinary citizens and from journalists – although not gardening writers, who appear to have been generally 'on side' and to whom levity was foreign. The earnestness with which the Ministry of Agriculture approached a matter that, for many private citizens, was peripheral to their wartime experience was bound to find expression in humorous scepticism. There were always some people, especially amongst the educated classes, who mocked the publicity campaigns for the humourless piety of their tone, their confected enthusiasm, their naked appeals to blind patriotism, or even their futility. And the professional humorists joined in.

According to Peter Ender, a contributor to the weekly periodical *Punch*, who wrote and illustrated a slim volume, *Up the Garden Path*, published in 1944:

There are several types of gardens. There are front gardens, kitchen gardens, bedroom gardens, back gardens, halfback gardens, inside-forward gardens, zoological gardens, hanging gardens and swinging gardens.

But for the purpose of supplementing the government's Dig-for-Dear-Life campaign, to which this book is dedicated, we shall confine ourselves principally to a discussion directed around back gardens.

The back garden is often situated at the rear of the house,

and is easily discerned as facing the door, which has no knocker. It is generally in the open air although, in colder districts, many back gardens are rolled up and taken indoors at night.[75]

This mildly satirical take-off of the campaign seems tame and innocent nonsense by modern standards. It's not very funny either: 'The Ministry of Agriculture has announced that if every citizen begins cultivation of his garden to the fullest possible extent, there will be enough melons alone to keep eleven million garage doors open.'

There is a running gag in the book, consisting of a succession of cartoons in which the author depicts a ship sinking, a condemned man about to be hanged, even a missionary in a cannibal's cooking pot, with one character saying to another: 'Grand planting weather.' You obviously needed to be there. And you have to wonder how the following joke went down, even at a time in England when casual anti-Semitism was endemic: 'Jerusalem Artichokes are still popular in England although on the Continent they grow mainly in concentration camps.'[76]

In *Punch*, Lady Addle, Mary Dunn's fictional *grande dame*, had helpful horticultural experience to relate for the good of her readers:

The beautiful clock golf course at Coot's Balder . . . is now given over to groundsel for the estate canaries, the Duke of Quorn's fernery is a beetery, while Lord Sealyham's famous eighteenth century maze was sacrificed to make asparagus beds for his evacuees; an extremely difficult task, involving endless labour digging the beds in all the tortuous twists and turns of the maze. The sad thing is that the labour was in vain, as it transpired afterwards that the evacuees would only eat asparagus if it had first been tinned . . .

As for our garden at Bengers, we have of course tried to do our bit for the garden front, but I fear that it has not been altogether successful. I sacrificed my water garden to aubergines, only to find that they would not grow in a damp place, or in fact in England at all. I installed tomato plants in the weeping

willow walk, thinking their gay colour would light up the
avenue, which gets practically no sun during the day (nor at
night of course), but the tiresome things just would *not* ripen. I
also tried, unsuccessfully, to grow mustard and cress, on old
pieces of Addle's shirts, on the statuary along the terrace. Then
we have been very unfortunate with pests. All our radishes have
suffered from slut weevil, and an entire crop of early parsley
was devoured by the fell sod fly. In fact, so ill-fated did we
appear to be in this direction, that at one time I thought it
might be best to yield to Dame Nature's stern decrees, and so
made all plans for encouraging the woolly aphis in our orchards,
as I felt sure there must be some method of gathering and
spinning their product in order to save shipping space for
imported wool.[77]

Even the most committed and cheerful of Victory Diggers will have
felt something of Lady Addle's despair from time to time. Considering
the abnormal and difficult circumstances, perhaps the wonder is that
half of all households actually did grow their own vegetables, rather
than that the other half did not.

CHAPTER FOUR

WOMEN AND CHILDREN GO TO IT

As young men left home and their retired fathers or grandfathers returned to work in their old occupations, or signed up for onerous civil defence duties, much additional work inevitably fell on the shoulders of the millions of women still at home. The Ministry of Agriculture tried to persuade them that vegetable gardening was one of the important tasks that they could and should do, and that they were perfectly capable of managing a home vegetable plot or an allotment successfully. Unfortunately for MAF, there were very few female role models amongst professional gardeners, and most people of both sexes believed that the kitchen garden was men's rightful domain. Women would require a substantial shift in mindset if they were to play a useful part both as producers of their own fresh vegetables and as employed market gardeners.

Altering this mindset would not be straightforward. In the early days of the war, there was undoubtedly a widespread, if mild, prejudice against women as gardeners. They were not thought to be 'up to it'. This letter to the gardening press was typical:

A photograph of . . . nurses digging up Tavistock Square must
have caused some amusement to practical men. What a picture!
Dutch hoes were being used, and the nurses wore low shoes.
Probably an enthusiastic press photographer tried to score a
'bull' but only got an 'outer'. Another illustration I saw was of a
girl demonstrating spring Cabbage planting, also in low shoes –
not to mention silk stockings.[1]

The male correspondent had realised that these were propaganda photographs – probably using models or women called off the street – but he betrayed an attitude about women as gardeners that was commonplace. Incidents of prejudice against women allotmenteers might be expressed in nothing worse than a patronising jocularity, but even that must have been thoroughly off-putting to any woman new to the task. True, by February 1940, the gardening magazine *Garden Work for Amateurs* was commenting: 'Reports from various sources indicate that women gardeners are making a splendid response to the Minister of Agriculture's "Dig for Victory" Appeal. Local authorities have already received numerous applications from women for allotments.' But words like 'splendid' and 'numerous', which appeared frequently in press accounts, are too nebulous to be trustworthy. The writer went on to say: 'Provided that the initial digging and trenching is carried out by the sterner sex, I can see no reason at all why a woman cannot run an allotment with the greatest success.'[2]

The redoubtable members of the Women's Institute at least had no patience with leaving the heavy work to the sterner sex. The same magazine ran this story the following month:

> The National Federation of Women's Institutes plans to make a survey of all village allotments and derelict gardens with a view to putting them to the best possible use in growing foodstuffs and feeding material for pigs and poultry [with the permission of the owner]. A scheme has also been evolved where Institute members will, where necessary, carry on all the work of cultivation of plots owned by men called to the services.[3]

This is just one amongst many examples of concerted wartime action by the Women's Institute, the only organisation in England and Wales that consisted entirely of rural women. The idea of countrywomen joining together for companionship, education and to promote the public good had spread from rural Canada to the British Isles during the First World War, and the first village-based Institute in Britain was founded in

Llanfairpwyll on Anglesey in 1915.[4] This Institute's first resolution set the tone for future endeavours: 'We, the members of the Llanfair Women's Institute, pledge ourselves to do our utmost to make the Institute the centre of good in our neighbourhood.'[5] It is salutary to remember that, until the foundation of Women's Institutes, there was no community focus for village women, apart from the church or chapel, since they were not welcomed in pubs and usually denied the chance to share masculine leisure pursuits such as cricket and football.[6]

Many more Institutes came into being during the war. Their formation was in part a response to the dire shortage of food, as a result of the tightening of the German U-boat blockade in 1917. But only in part: there were growing numbers of educated people in England and Wales who considered that countrywomen deserved the kind of opportunities for social interaction and education that many of their urban sisters enjoyed, rather than simply having to bring up large families in cramped, often insanitary conditions. In this regard, countrywomen were the tangential beneficiaries of the (mainly) urban-based suffragette movement.

Of these educated women, the most influential was Lady (Trudie) Denman. The success of the Women's Institute movement owed a great deal to her drive, vision, humanity, tact and genius for organisation. Her name is only remembered now by those members of the WI who enrol on courses at Denman College in Oxfordshire, which was opened by the National Federation of Women's Institutes soon after the war; yet she played an exceptionally valuable and significant role in our story, both as Chairman of the NFWI – right from its inception in 1917 until 1946 – and as Director, chief organiser and moving spirit behind the Women's Land Army from 1938 until the end of the war.

Gertrude Denman was the daughter of Sir Weetman Pearson, a rich and powerful businessman with interests in many enterprises, in particular oil, large-scale construction projects and newspapers. He had been made the first Viscount Cowdray in 1910. He was a prominent Liberal and inculcated his daughter with many of his high-minded beliefs. In 1905 he gave her a country house, Balcombe Place, in Sussex, along with 3,000 acres, for her twenty-first birthday, a gift which was to prove extremely useful for her war work.

Two years earlier, she had married Thomas, the 3rd Baron Denman, who was a Liberal peer. As a young married woman, Lady Denman was active in the women's suffrage movement, serving on the National Executive of the Women's Liberal Foundation. During the First World War she busied herself with charity work – including organising morale-boosting 'smokes' for the Forces and encouraging people to keep poultry – until she was elected Chairman of the NFWI. She also helped to found the Women's Land Army, and was therefore well known to the Ministry of Agriculture.

From the beginning, the organisation of the Women's Institutes was purposely decentralised. The individual village Institutes were affiliated to county federations, which themselves looked to the National Federation. The small size and geographical limits of village Institutes meant that they were well placed to foster local community spirit. The fact that few members had transport of their own, beyond a bicycle, did not matter. The women who joined the Institutes in their thousands in the 1920s and 1930s were motivated partly by an urge to improve their skills and widen their outlook, and partly by a desire for a social life outside the home, at least for one evening or afternoon a month.[7] The motto of the organisation was 'For Home and Country', a rallying cry likely to appeal strongly to women, some of whom had acquired the vote in 1918.[8]

One of the more interesting features of the WI movement was how many well-to-do and often cultivated women felt moved to help found local Institutes or to join the committees of those already in existence. This was probably the first time that countrywomen had come together socially, without significant class barriers to divide them, and the experience boded well for co-operation in wartime. The fact that ladies of wealth and standing were involved favourably predisposed politicians and Whitehall mandarins towards the organisation. How could it not be so when Queen Mary agreed to be the first President of the Sandringham WI? The story goes that she sent a lady-in-waiting to give the treasurer one pound as her membership fee, and the woman returned with eighteen shillings change, since all members paid the same subscription.

The WI – together with many other voluntary organisations in wartime, such as the Women's Voluntary Service – could depend particularly on public-spirited women who were unmarried or childless. In 1939, those approaching middle age were of the generation that had lost husbands, sweethearts or the chance to find one at Passchendaele or on the Somme. Miss Grace Hadow, Vice-Chairman of the NFWI, Miss Frances Farrer, National Secretary, and Miss Edith Walker, Agricultural Secretary, were unencumbered women of energy, enterprise and intellect, with the skills to manage the NFWI in the different, and potentially difficult, conditions of wartime.

From the start, the WI movement was both apolitical and interdenominational, and it was this last feature that influenced the directions that it took during the Second World War. The decision was made very early on that WIs would not become involved in civilian war work, since that might challenge the consciences of those members who were Quakers and *ipso facto* pacifist. Civil defence was, Lady Denman insisted, more fittingly carried out by local authorities or delegated bodies, which represented both men and women. And, of course, the recently formed Women's Voluntary Service[9] positively embraced Home Front defence activities and so was the obvious organisation for any public-spirited woman to join, whether she lived in town or country.

The WI's refusal to become involved in anything that actively promoted the prosecution of the war was criticised both inside and outside the organisation, and was one of the reasons why membership dropped to 291,000 in 1940. But Lady Denman stood firm, pointing out that there was nothing to stop WI members actively helping civil defence as individuals. And no one objected to them assisting in the organisation of billets for evacuees, as well as personally providing homes for them, which they did with great promptitude in the early days of the war.

WI members, at both local and national level, were conspicuously whole-hearted, once they decided on a course of action. Tasks were done with determination, thoroughness and good organisational skills, often in the face of considerable difficulties, such as petrol and food rationing, the blackout and other tiresome wartime restrictions. Monthly meetings carried on as normally as possible – although in the day rather than the evening because of the blackout – 'thus providing for the members a centre of tranquillity and cheerfulness in a sadly troubled world'.[10] WIs also held out the hand of friendship to female evacuees and Land Girls, inviting them to join their local groups, or at least attend the meetings at a cost of 2d or 3d a time. In places, this must have taken considerable diplomatic effort, since relations between adult evacuees and countrywomen were often strained.

Just before the outbreak of war, the Ministry of Information wrote to the heads of a number of voluntary organisations, including Lady Denman:

> The functions of the Ministry will include . . . the distribution
> of information concerning the progress of events; and the
> dissemination of instructions, appeals and advice. A very
> important function would be that of keeping the public in good
> heart by insistence on the truth, by prompt countering of enemy
> propaganda and the many mischievous rumours which are bound
> to arise, more especially if communications are interrupted.[11]

The Ministry wanted to enlist the assistance of voluntary organisations in distributing propaganda material and providing poster sites. Lady Denman replied saying that the WIs were happy to help. A letter later in the month encouraged the WIs to continue their normal activities, and promised that the Ministry would arrange a panel of lecturers so that the women might have the opportunity of understanding the origins and causes of the war. In other words, the MoI felt that morale would be enhanced by appropriately filtered information to the grass roots.

Interestingly, in June 1940, at the time of maximum peril for the country after the precipitate retreat of the BEF from France, the WI National Secretary, Miss Frances Farrer, received a letter from the Ministry of Information saying that 'the Women's Institutes can be more valuable than any other Institutes in the world in creating confidence in Government pronouncements, in the BBC and in our leaders, and in conducting a constant campaign against the chatterbugs who undermine morale'.[12] At the lowest point of Britain's fortunes, the MoI saw both how important countrywomen would be in keeping everyone's spirits up, and also how compliant they were likely to be.

At the start of the war, the WIs had a number of other things on their minds besides morale. In 1926, Lady Denman had chaired the Denman Committee on the Practical Education of Women in Rural Life, the report from which emphasised the need for the improvement of skills in home food production and use. As a consequence, the number of WI produce and flower shows increased markedly. During the 1930s, the NFWI trained local cookery demonstrators, and Long Ashton Research Station and the Royal Agricultural College at Cirencester provided courses on fruit and vegetable preservation for WI members. In 1939, the WIs were ready to play their part in the optimum production and use of food during the war, as well as in all the others things for which they had an aptitude: knitting for the troops, organising salvage collections, gathering local contributions to National Savings, and collecting native plants for medicines. Indeed, the decision to step away from active civil defence had a paradoxically beneficent effect, since it left the WI movement free to concentrate on those aspects of the Home Front battle for which no one else had much free time. During the course of the war, the Women's Institutes became known beyond the countryside for their fruit preservation centres (see Chapter Twelve) and market stalls in large villages and small towns, as well as their lectures and demonstrations on cooking and nutrition, the organisation of shows and exhibitions, the promotion of livestock keeping, the making of fur clothing using rabbit skins – and kitchen gardening.

In 1938, thanks to a Ministry of Agriculture grant of £500 from its Development Fund, a professional horticulturist, Miss Elizabeth Hess, was recruited as an Agricultural Organiser, attached to the NFWI, with the aim of helping to promote food production amongst its members. Her job was to travel all over England and Wales to talk to large WI gatherings and encourage them to grow more of their own food. That year, she helped establish the Produce Guild, for those WI women who were keen gardeners and cooks or anxious to become so, and by the end of 1938 there were forty-eight county branches of the Guild in the two countries. Those who joined paid an annual subscription of one shilling, but that was suspended after the war began. Generally, the level of interest from members was satisfactory.

The Produce Guild instituted vegetable competitions, and recruited and trained judges and demonstrators. Women learned basic skills, either at meetings with Miss Hess or local experts, or at regional agricultural colleges, if they had the means of travelling there: 'Please bring your gum boots and a spade' was the invitation to its members from the Isle of Wight Federation when Miss Hess visited the island on 10 November 1939.[13] The same month, the West Suffolk County Federation announced a comprehensive list of talks which included 'Mother Earth and How to Take Care of Her' as well as 'Compost Making' by Mrs Bond, 'Preservation without Sugar' by Mr Grange FRHS[14] and 'Goat Keeping' by Mrs Jenkins.

Miss Hess considered herself a pragmatist, and taught members that double-digging was 'quite good enough', as opposed to the 'trenching' – triple-digging – that she had been taught as a student. This must have come as a relief to the women she was instructing. She also taught them how to store vegetables through the winter in clamps, how to blanch winter salads like chicory, how to harvest their crops most efficiently and how to use derris powder on vegetable pests. 'I got hold of a new handgun duster [used to puff the powder onto plants],' she recalled later. 'You could see insects dying in front of your eyes.'[15] She wrote, and oversaw the publication of, a variety of explanatory bulletins, including a fruit tree pruning chart, which cost 1d.

Miss Hess also came to an arrangement with the 'Sutton boys'[16] – the four members of the Sutton family, who owned the pre-eminent seed company, Suttons Seeds of Reading – that they provide bulk orders of discounted vegetable seeds for WI members. Together they devised a list of suitable varieties, the seeds of which were sealed in square brown packets and put in a box, which cost 2s.6d.[17] There was also a smaller collection of winter vegetables, priced at a shilling, which contained hardy lettuce, August-sown onion, prickly spinach and stump-rooted carrot. These boxes were distributed via the VCOs – the WI county organisers – at the members' monthly meetings. The regional organisation of the WIs made it relatively easy to reach them. During the war, 140,000 fruit bushes, as well as 134,000 packets of seed, were bulk-ordered by the NFWI and sold, cheaply, through the Produce Guild to WI members. Women's Institutes were also encouraged to liaise with local horticultural societies and to arrange educational meetings at a time when their men could also attend.

Local institutes found innovative ways to involve their members in produce growing. In April 1940, Blisworth Women's Institute in Northamptonshire issued three potato tubers to each of its members at a cost of 1d each, for a competition to discover which member could grow the most weight of potatoes from them. This was judged the following October, when the potatoes were dug up. In 1941, Miss Stockley won the competition with an impressive 34 lb.

By 1942, there were thirteen Blisworth WI members – out of seventy – in the Produce Guild. These keen gardeners also planted blackcurrant bushes, since these were considered both the easiest soft fruit to grow (birds don't eat them) and the best garden fruit source of vitamin C. In that year, Blisworth also received vegetable seeds from the 'women of America', as well as from the WI organisation in Ontario, Canada. In January 1943, the Blisworth Produce Guild put on an exhibit of root vegetables grown from 'Institute' seed. Unfortunately, however, 'owing to transport difficulties', very few members managed to attend the gardening classes held at Moulton Farm School, near Northampton, a common difficulty for country-dwellers throughout the war.

On a national scale, Miss Hess was helped in her endeavours by the existence of WI market stalls, established in the 1930s and organised by Miss Vera Cox from the London headquarters. These stalls provided opportunities for Women's Institute members to sell surplus produce from their gardens and kitchens, in the process keeping all but a penny in the shilling for themselves.

By the end of 1939 there were thirty registered market stalls around the country and the success of the Produce Guilds, coupled with the exigencies of war, meant that many more opened as the years went on. By the end of 1944 there were 319. Care was taken not to undercut local traders; indeed, when interviewed some years later, Miss Hess could not recall any overt resentment from retailers, which just shows that the Ministry of Agriculture probably worried too much about the problem of surpluses.

If Marguerite Patten's experience was typical, women in the countryside and leafy suburbs who embraced gardening found it a powerful source of contentment and relaxation. This well-known cookery expert lived with her mother in a house in High Barnet while her husband was in the RAF. She recalled for the BBC's *People's War* what it was like to work in a large, fruitful garden:

Fortunately, I shared her [mother's] love of gardening, so we worked happily together. Both of us were busy women – my mother was still teaching and I was one of the Food Advisors in the Ministry of Food. In winter we worked at weekends, but in summer we were out in the garden during the light evenings to weed and harvest fruits and the vegetables that were mature.

The garden was large with green fields at the end of it. A flower garden and lawn adjoined the house but beyond that was an abundance of produce. There were apple and plum trees plus a small pear tree, a long line of black, red and white currants (delicious raw), with gooseberry bushes, raspberries and loganberries. The Royal Sovereign strawberries were our pride and joy. Beans were great favourites so through the months we picked the broad, French and runner varieties, also lots of peas.

There were plentiful supplies of onions to give flavour to wartime dishes, leeks, potatoes, carrots, turnips (delicious when young and small) and parsnips. For some reason we did not grow swedes. Throughout the months there were various green vegetables – kale and spinach being favourites, plus a good range of herbs. The cos lettuce and tomatoes were so plentiful we could present some to friends. When it got dark we retired to the kitchen to bottle fruits – including tomatoes – and make jam and chutney when we had saved sufficient sugar from our rations. War-time gardening was hard work but very satisfying and productive.[18]

That was all well and good for country dwellers or those with large gardens, but the vast majority of women lived in towns, and most had little pre-war experience of kitchen gardening. From 1941 onwards, the government began to aim posters and leaflets specifically at women, particularly urban women, who they referred to, coyly, as the 'New Victory Diggers'. Even two years into the war, these publications did not avoid entirely a patronising tone, since they usually depicted a woman being shown how to do the job by an experienced male neighbour leaning nonchalantly over the fence while smoking a pipe, accompanied by the caption 'See that the beginners start right.' This campaign was renewed in 1942, but by that time, all women aged thirty and under without small children were required to take a job. A year later, as the shortage of labour became really acute, most women of fifty-one and below, unless heavily involved with family responsibilities, were required to work at least part-time. Hours to spend on the allotment, especially when it was a distance from home, were inevitably harder and harder to find.

In all, only about 10,000 allotments were rented specifically by women in the years 1942 to 1944. More, no doubt, will have been listed under a husband's name but exclusively cultivated by his wife. Nevertheless, there is no escaping the fact that the vast majority of women never became enthusiastic allotmenteers. Nor did they listen very hard to the advice so painstakingly prepared for them. In this matter, women turned out to be more resistant to propaganda appeals. The Ministry inquiry into the effects of the Dig for Victory campaign, in the summer of 1942, revealed that, although a rather higher proportion of women than men had taken up allotments since the war started, female gardeners were less influenced by the publicity. Only 36 per cent had sent away for Dig for Victory leaflets, as opposed to 44 per cent of men. They read fewer gardening articles in newspapers as well.[19]

Editors and advertisers will have been disappointed by that, since they certainly did their best to encourage women to spend time gardening. In women's magazines, advertisements for soap and beauty products were aimed at women who were growing vegetables but who did not want their hands to show the effects of rough work. Dungarees were advertised for sale as being more suitable wear than a sensible skirt for the allotment. Predictably, women's magazines also carried gardening columns specifically aimed at women, although they often contained as much cooking as gardening information.

There was at least some anecdotal evidence from around the country that women were actively engaged in allotment gardening. For example, in June 1944, the manager of the shop run by the Dewsbury Allotments Association reported that women were doing more gardening than men that year, with the result that the demand for 'chemical manures' had fallen off, although it is hard to see exactly where the connection lay. At the same time, two allotments associations in Chesterfield boasted female secretaries.[20] Preston had its own Women's Allotment Association, which must have been an encouragement for those women fearful of drawing forth the scorn of their male allotment neighbours.

One woman who definitely took to allotment gardening was Joan Strange, a middle-aged, middle-class physiotherapist living in Worthing. She kept a diary through the war years and in it detailed her positive experience of tending an allotment. As she wrote on 19 March 1941: 'Help! I've not written this old diary for nearly a week. It's the allotment's fault! The weather has been so good that I have gone up most evenings and got too tired digging to write this diary. The two oldish men on the next plot have helped me a bit . . . There is a very friendly spirit up there and I hope to learn a lot.'[21] It wasn't always good news: at one point 'digging for victory', as she called it, gave her acute neuritis in her arm, and a friend had to plant her potatoes for her. On the other hand, she picked 20 lb of peas that summer, grown from a 6d packet of seed, which gave her enormous satisfaction. By July she had the confidence to plant leeks and thin carrots on her sister's allotment in Battersea Park in London. And in August she had contributed several kinds of vegetables from her allotment to the 'bring and buy sale' in aid of the Mayor's Rest Centre.

A letter to *Woman* magazine from a Miss J. W. of Horsham will also have warmed the hearts of the Ministry publicists.

> We live in the country and have a large rambling garden and orchard, but nobody but my mother ever took much interest in either. Consequently, for years, it looked wild and desolate. You should see it now though! We have all gone back to the land and are now digging for victory with a vengeance. The boys have taken a nice slice off the coal bill by chopping down some old half-dead trees, and we have all dug and weeded and pruned and planted till our backs felt like breaking. But the results have been worth it. Mother laughs and says it takes Hitler to do in a few months what she's been trying to do for years.[22]

Dig for Victory information was not just targeted at adult gardeners. The authorities were also keen to get children involved. The notably garden-minded King and Queen allowed their daughters, the wonderfully photogenic teenage princesses Elizabeth and Margaret Rose, to pose for photographs pushing wheelbarrows and carrying garden tools. In 1942, the Ministry of Information also issued a number of photographs and film newsreels which showed children wielding forks and spades in school grounds, in their own gardens or on bomb sites, in a conscious effort to promote gardening amongst the young. They were often pushing at an open door, since children were notably patriotic and willing to help, especially if gardening got them away from a stuffy classroom. As a result, many were inspired not only to take up gardening but also to look after livestock.

Gardening had been part of the curriculum in some schools, particularly rural ones, before the war, but it became almost universal in 1940, replacing games on one afternoon a week (which was just as well, since school pitches were often at least partially dug up). If there was no room on school premises for a vegetable plot, local garden owners were asked to provide space, and often willingly did so. The vicar of Oving in West Sussex, for example, invited pupils from the Parochial School to cultivate twelve plots in his garden. A number of city or seaside-town boarding schools were evacuated to country houses where there was usually plenty of space in which to grow vegetables in the walled gardens abandoned by male staff now serving in the Forces. In May 1942, *The Gardeners' Chronicle* reported that in the West Riding of Yorkshire elementary schoolchildren were cultivating more than 400 acres of ground, when they had managed only ninety acres before the war. It has to be said, however, that it was almost always the boys who tended the school crops.

The produce cultivated was often used in the school kitchens and sometimes even sold to local shops. In Knighton-on-Teme, in Worcestershire, for example, 130 meals a day were cooked using vegetables raised by schoolchildren in the village. These children – a mixture of local-born and evacuees – were so successful that they were the subjects of a Ministry of Information official photography session in 1943.

Sensibly, those who organised these school work parties tended to concentrate on staples such as potatoes, onions and carrots, which required little active cultivation in the summer holidays and would store through the winter. Where there were particularly enthusiastic and committed teachers, it was not uncommon for schoolchildren to rear goats, sheep, pigs and hens as well.

Jean McCredie Forster, the rural studies organiser for Wiltshire Education Committee, spent her time advising children and schools how to increase food production, how to make compost and how to look after livestock. She made a demonstration garden in Palmer Gardens in Trowbridge, a plot of land owned by the council, and ran courses for teachers there; it also served as a seedling nursery for the school gardens, especially for 'onions galore'.[23]

Preston in Lancashire boasted a children's allotment association, inspired and encouraged by Mr A. Walmsley, the town's allotments supervisor, and his wife. The local council gave the association a field to rent, and the children, aged from eleven to eighteen, worked in pairs, each sharing a five-rod plot. They formed a committee and kept proper accounts, and their parents bought the vegetables from them at prices that were slightly lower than those in the shops, giving the children a very useful source of pocket money. They even made their own paths, with hardcore dumped for them by the council. Roy Hay, who visited this model enterprise, noted that there was not a weed to be seen anywhere.

The boys of Westcliff High School, near Southend-on-Sea in Essex, showed themselves particularly stalwart. By June 1940 they were already cultivating an acre of playing field, only to find themselves evacuated to the Midlands, leaving the fruits of their labours to be enjoyed by the army. By the autumn of 1941 they had double-dug, sown, then harvested two hundredweight each of carrots, parsnips, beetroot and runner beans for themselves and their foster families. The following year they had to leave 1,200 Savoy cabbage plants behind when they were precipitately sent back to Westcliff. However, during their time in the Midlands, they had earned £20 for their 'seeds fund' so could begin once more growing vegetables in their old school playing fields.

Although the authorities believed that all this activity was a good in itself, they were also hopeful that the children's interest would have a salutary effect on their parents, particularly those who were resisting all appeals to take up an allotment. For example, in 1941 in Newcastle-upon-Tyne, 700 new allotments were made available by the city council, but remained empty and so had to be offered to schools in the area instead.

Children were generally so amenable that a number spent their holidays working outdoors for the war effort. Helping with the potato harvest was familiar to country children, but they were called on in wartime also to pick fruit and collect medicinal herbs and nettles (see Chapter Twelve). The local education authority often co-ordinated these activities. For example, Devon County Education Committee planned a 'children's holiday campaign' for the summer of 1940, which involved children helping with harvesting, trench digging on golf courses and commons, allotment work, hedge cleaning, the clearing of nettles and docks, bracken pulling, leaf mould collecting, wood collecting and chipping, cone collecting, fruit picking, salvage of all kinds, mending, sewing, knitting for the Red Cross, collecting for hospitals and looking after small children. The idea was that the work should be made as pleasant as possible by breaking it up with games, singing and picnics, as well as by a combined treat at the end of the week. The Committee considered that some of the work was not very attractive, but they anticipated that if the children could sense that they were voluntarily co-operating in a big scheme and doing their bit, there would be a good response. No child can ever have been bored in Devon in the summer holidays, but they must have sometimes felt a little put upon.

Of course, the country needed professional gardeners rather more than amateurs or children, and the war was to provide novel opportunities for young women to become trained in food production, and also to be promoted swiftly – at least while it lasted. For girls of conscription age, in particular, gardening offered an attractive alternative to factory work, nursing or the women's services. Factory work, especially engineering or the making of munitions, was comparatively well-paid but could be hard and unpleasant, while nursing was seen by many as a vocation rather than a temporary wartime job. The women's services were thought to be very strict and disciplinarian, although they did have the advantage to girls of throwing them into the path of eligible young men.

Most aspirant women gardeners joined the Women's Land Army, which had been founded in 1917 under the auspices of the Board of Agriculture. This had been a crisis measure, prompted by the fact that there was only three weeks' food supply in the country, as a result of the German submarine blockade.[24] The first Director was Miss (later Dame) Meriel Talbot, with Lady Denman honorary Assistant Director, and by the end of the 1914–18 war, 23,000 women had signed up to work on farms and in gardens.

The organisation was disbanded after the war, but in the spring of 1938, the Ministry of Agriculture approached Lady Denman to take charge of its Women's Branch, which would oversee the remobilisation of the Women's Land Army. Lady Denman took up her post on 1 June; by the time war broke out, 1,000 women had already volunteered, and this grew to 4,500 by the end of the year. Most were girls in their late teens or early twenties from London or the industrial cities of the north.

Although the WLA was called an 'Army' and the women had to promise to go wherever they were sent, they were not under military discipline, and were paid by their employers, not by the state. Lady Denman ran the entire organisation with consummate skill and good sense from her home, Balcombe Place. 'Imagine a baronial hall thus transformed,' wrote Vita Sackville-West in 1944. 'The red velvet curtains still hang heavily in their place, the oak panelling still makes a rich and sombre background, but the splendid rooms are now filled with office-desks and trestle tables, piled with card-indexes and stationery, type-writers and telephones, pots and paste and Stickphast . . .'[25] The reception-rooms became offices, the staff slept in dormitory bedrooms, and the girls' new uniforms were warehoused in the stables and squash court. Almost everyone employed was female, so there was much of an earnest girls' boarding school atmosphere about the place. Lady Denman's assistant was Mrs Inez Jenkins, whom she had recruited from NFWI headquarters. The office staff members were salaried, as were those who manned each county office, but everyone else, from the Director to the local Representatives, gave their time voluntarily. Many were already WI stalwarts.

The regional organisers, or Representatives, were often upper-class contemporaries or friends of Lady Denman. The County Rep kept an eye on the girls placed locally, and tried to ensure that they were not mistreated, lonely, bored or overworked, or suffering unduly from the shortage of suitable uniform, especially rubber boots and mackintoshes. In 1944, when Vita Sackville-West published a history of the Women's Land Army up to that date, she not surprisingly dwelled on the difficul-ties faced by Representatives like herself. But she also wrote admiringly of the young women from towns who laboured so hard to prevent the country running short of food, almost always well out of any limelight and often in filthy weather and uncomfortable conditions. She was moved to write, when describing one of the periodic London conferences, at which Lady Denman and senior officials of the WLA met County Representatives, 'I felt how much, how very much, I liked the English; how much, how very much, how painfully much, I loved England.'[26]

By December 1943, the Women's Land Army numbered some 80,300, the highest figure it would attain during the war. The majority worked on farms, but there were also some rat-catchers, excavation digger drivers and 'lumber Jills' in the Timber Corps. A sizeable minority worked in market gardens and smallholdings, as well as in mansion gardens geared up for food production.

It took a while before a regular and reliable supply of women gardeners could be found for this work. Would-be horticulturists often turned to another organisation, the Women's Farm and Garden Association, which acted as an employment bureau. Formerly the Women's Agricultural and Horticultural Union, it had been founded in 1899 by philanthropic women, mainly farmers or landowners, who were interested in promoting gardening and farming as an occupation for well-bred ladies. The organisation had played a part in the recruiting of women for land work during the latter half of the First World War. At the end of that war, it had combined with the Women's National Land Service Corps to become the Women's Farm and Garden Association. The WFGA was also a conduit for information about training and a source of good-quality work clothing. It produced a journal, kept up a lending library and even owned a hostel in London, run on club lines. The women's horticultural schools, like Swanley and Waterperry, were affiliated to it.

In 1940, the WFGA helped negotiate and secure a national agricultural minimum rate of pay for women land workers. This was fixed at 28s. a week for women over eighteen, and 22s. 6d for those under eighteen, with board and lodging deducted at 14s. or 12s. 6d respectively. In the same year, it also founded a much-needed Garden Apprenticeship Scheme. The organisation realised that for many girls there was neither the time nor the money for the stately progress of training in the women's horticultural colleges or universities; gardens needed these women immediately. One of the people involved in shaping this scheme was the highly regarded landscape designer Brenda Colvin. In October 1940 she wrote to a colleague:

I have taken on a job for the Women's Farm and Garden Association – organising a training scheme for women gardeners in wartime. It is being tried out in this neighbourhood first [she was staying near Salisbury at the time, so she meant Woodyates Manor] but one hopes that it will extend soon to a much wider area, as I think it is really needed . . . the WFGA is flooded with demands for women gardeners to replace men called up.[27]

Lady Lucas of Woodyates Manor was the driving force behind the Garden Apprenticeship Scheme, which aimed to give girls a six-month grounding in practical work and, in particular, food production. The WFGA managed to persuade twenty county councils to agree to help individual students with grants – since many of the County Farm Institutes had closed their doors to students – provided that the trainees were given a 'sound training in food production with a view to semi-skilled women replacing men'.[28] By the following winter, about a hundred girls were in training and there was no difficulty in finding them suitable jobs at the end of it. Indeed, demand far outstripped supply. In 1942–3, employers requested 1,237 workers, two thirds of them for horticulture, from the WFGA but the employment department could only supply 117 gardeners.

One of these WFGA-trained gardeners was Muriel Green, a rural Norfolk girl, who wrote a diary for Mass-Observation throughout the war years. She made no bones about why she wanted to become a gardener; it was in order to place herself in a reserved occupation, so that she could avoid compulsory conscription after she turned twenty in early 1941. In March that year, she wrote to the Women's Farm and Garden Association and offered herself as a gardening student. She confessed to her diary that she hated gardening 'and had never done a stroke before the war, but thought the scheme for 6 months in a garden would be at least a change and play for time. Then the winter will be near and gardening will not suit my constitution I foresee.'[29]

Muriel Green wrote in her diary of her arrival at Woodyates Manor just after Easter 1941. She had never been so far from Norfolk before.

> Met off bus by Lady L, owner of manor house where I am to work and Hon Anne, daughter . . . a charming old house and garden. There are five girls here and head lady gardener quite young and very nice . . . We live in a charming 'ideal home' old cottage and sweet bedroom each and bathroom (h & c)[30], kitchen where we share washing-up and lounge common room. All delightful. I can see I shall be quite happy for a month here. Food is sent in ready cooked from Manor House and is plentiful. We had high tea when we arrived . . . 6.30–7.30 the lady gardener who lives with us gave a lecture on pests and spraying.

Her diary for Saturday 19 April reads: 'Spent morning sweeping paths ready for weekend visitors and return of the colonel, the master of the manor. Then we pollinated the peach trees by tickling them with rabbit's tails on canes. We finish at 12 on Saturdays.'

There was great excitement the following week because the girls were told that they were to be photographed for *Picture Post* planting onions. 'We hurried lunch and then were told to do our hair etc and pose ourselves artistically in the sitting room ready for being taken "at leisure".' All afternoon the students were photographed 'in unnatural gardening poses with tools and wheelbarrows, and doing things we never do or [are] ever likely to do and we had a lot of laughing.'[31]

Despite her early misgivings, Muriel took to the training, since she spent it all in mansion gardens where the work was very varied. She was also taught well by the head gardeners. About her contemporaries at Woodyates she wrote: 'All the girls here are like me avoiding factories etc. One is a conscientious objector and the others just taking care of themselves like me.'[32] A year later, having endured scrubbing down greenhouses and picking Brussels sprouts during frosty January weather ('the coldest job in the world'), she reflected on whether she would have been better off in the ATS[33] after all, and decided that she would not, since the pay as a gardener was higher and the living accommodation better. 'It is true our working uniform is not shattering and we get no privileges (or not so many) as an ATS girl and have to face the elements more but I think we get more admiration and are just as useful to the war effort.'[34]

At the beginning, male head gardeners found female workers a novelty, and not a particularly welcome one, but they were forced to get used to them very quickly, since women were the main replacements in gardens that had switched to commercial food production. The anecdotal evidence about the treatment of women gardeners by their male colleagues is mixed. There was certainly some prejudice against them, particularly in the early days and especially in remote country districts. There were men who found the presence of girls unsettling and took it out on them in a myriad mildly bullying ways. When Muriel Green moved to a large estate in Gloucestershire, where the house had been made into a hospital, the adjoining nursery was staffed by Land Girls and their foreman told his men not to lend a hand to these girls when asked. He said the men would lose money if they spent time helping the women. But that kind of approach was not as common as initially feared, and many employers and senior staff were quickly won over by the hardiness, determination and willingness to learn of most Land Girls and female gardeners.

One WLA recruit, who was sent to work at a traditional private estate garden, was Sibyl van Praet. She joined up in 1940, and after spending a brief month training at Rodbaston Agricultural College, in Staffordshire, found herself working at Broughton Hall. This was a fifty-room Jacobean house, the wartime home for an evacuated preparatory school, which had extensive grounds and a four-acre walled garden. Before the war there had been sixteen gardeners, but now Mr Lowe, the head gardener, together with the elderly under-gardener, Mr Sawyer, and Sibyl had to provide enough vegetables for 120 people, staff and children. Despite the shortage of labour, they dug the entire walled garden by hand, and 'cultivation was our watch-word . . . in short HOEING . . . we hoed a great deal! The results were quite startling – our cabbages were so large that four were sufficient to supply "greens" for the whole school and staff.'[35]

Mr Lowe, like most conservative head gardeners of the time, had his own recipe for potting compost. He would send Sibyl to the woods to bring back sacks of leaf mould, and to the disused tennis courts for lime gravel, which he would mix with garden soil and sand to make a 'wonderful loamy mixture'. She attributed the success of the tomatoes to this special compost – they were 'magnificent in size and flavour'. So expert were the three gardeners at growing vegetables that, despite the large numbers of people in the house, surpluses of tomatoes, cucumbers and lettuces were sent for sale to Stafford market.

It must be said that not all Land Girls could stand the life. Jean Barker, later Baroness Trumpington and a Minister of State at the Ministry of Agriculture (ironically), was sent to work on former Prime Minister Lloyd George's fruit farm in Sussex in 1940. Many years later she recalled: 'I hated being a land girl. There were only old men there. The young ones had joined up. And it was all apples. No animals, which I love.'[36] She soon left the WLA to help break German secret codes at Bletchley Park. All in all, however, it is remarkable what a high percentage of Land Girls stuck it out, and usually retained intensely happy memories of their war work in later life.

Nearly 11,000 Land Girls were involved in horticultural employment during the war. Unlike on farms, where they never quite equalled a man's work output (except when looking after poultry), gardeners proved that in some instances they could outperform a man: they scored better in cutting, bunching and packing flowers, and pulling peas and runner beans; and they equalled men in their small-fruit-picking capacities (and were paid only two thirds of a man's wages for doing it). However, in 1943, most Land Girls working in private gardens were withdrawn from work on food production when the need for labourers on farms became too pressing.

More than 600 Land Girls studied horticulture by correspondence course, and some even sat the RHS exams, since the Land Army hierarchy encouraged self-advancement. Moreover, eighteen out of the thirty-nine agricultural and horticultural colleges in England and Wales remained open in wartime, providing everything from university degree courses – at Reading and Nottingham – to short practical ones. Most of the students were women, who were accepted on equal terms with men; demand for places on the courses was high. There was some 'telescoping' of training, with Reading University, for example, adding a fourth term during the summer vacation. A few of the county agricultural schools, like Houghall in Durham, also taught some basic horticulture.

There were several horticultural colleges specifically for women, most notably Swanley College in Kent, Studley College in Warwickshire and Waterperry School of Horticulture for Women in Oxfordshire. Unfortunately, Swanley College was bombed in 1943, when one student was killed, so the rest of the girls were evacuated to Wisley for a short time, before moving on to Wye College in Kent in 1946.

On the other hand, Studley College performed strongly throughout the war. Founded in 1898 by Daisy, Countess of Warwick, as the Warwick Hostel in Reading for women agriculture students, it had moved to Studley Castle in Warwickshire in 1903, and was renamed the Studley Horticultural and Agricultural College. In the early twentieth century there was steady demand for a women's gardening college, since head gardeners of private establishments were not enthusiastic about training women – as much from the difficulties of providing suitable accommodation as from any ingrained misogyny. Studley College catered for both those who wanted to be workers and those who would be employers. The objects of the training were many and varied: to run or own a farm, obtain a post on one, prepare for colonial life (if your future husband was a tea planter, say), run a market garden or private garden, become a head or under-gardener, teach in a school or prepare for further scientific work at a university. The expressed aim was 'to turn out capable, resourceful, intelligent, keen, reliable workers, physically fit and mentally alert, ready to make use of new knowledge and opportunities'.[37] The training was a mixture of the theoretical and practical, and the only important subject that does not seem to have been taught was garden design. The sixty or so students studied for the RHS examinations, in which they were conspicuously successful. In June 1941, for example, Studley girls came top in each of the three types of RHS examination. About twenty Land Army girls were trained separately at Studley, receiving rather more practical than theoretical teaching.

Of all the training establishments open to women, however, Waterperry School of Horticulture for Women in Oxfordshire was probably the best-known and most distinctive. It had been founded by two women, Miss Beatrix Havergal and Miss Avice Sanders, when a gardening school that they ran at Pusey in Berkshire proved too small for the demand. In 1932 they leased from Magdalen College a large eighteenth-century mansion, Waterperry House, with fifty bedrooms and sixty-three acres of agricultural land, as well as an ornamental garden, several glasshouses and a walled kitchen garden. Here, in a small, picturesque village near Oxford, the two spinsters ran a two-year practical and theoretical gardening course for young upper-middle-class women. Thanks to the extraordinary personality of Miss Havergal[38] – famous far and wide for her felt hats, collar and tie, stout shoes and masculine manner – and the rigorous, but kindly and Christian, regime which she and her partner, Miss Sanders, instituted, these girls were remarkably well taught. The 1937 prospectus included the following aspiration:

> It is the object of the School to provide the theoretical foundation, the practical knowledge of Horticulture and the specialized skill required to make a first-class gardener, and in addition to this, the development of the qualities of organization necessary for the management of a small or large staff of under-gardeners . . .
>
> There is, in these days, scope for the Jobbing gardener, the Market gardener, and for the highly qualified Landscape gardener, and the training at Waterperry includes all that is

necessary to enable a girl to take up any of these careers, or any other specific branch of horticultural work.[39]

That was some aspiration, but Miss Havergal had high ambitions for her students. It is significant that in 1938 she wrote to Professor Osborn, Sherardian Professor of Botany and Agriculture at Oxford, encouraging him and the Oxford authorities to consider instituting a BSc in horticulture at the university, with the practical tuition to be provided at Waterperry, since university courses in horticulture were generally theoretical. Miss Havergal appreciated how mutually beneficial this would have been, and how it would have raised the status of women gardeners. But it was not to be.

Nevertheless, when war broke out, the Waterperry School was well placed to turn much of its land over to food production, while still providing training not only for its own students but for a number of Land Girls, the presence of whom undoubtedly expanded the social mix. This change of circumstances also alleviated the financial difficulties which were a leitmotif running through the life of Waterperry during the 1930s, at least partly because Miss Havergal was no businesswoman; the understanding and sympathy of the Magdalen bursar, Mark van Oss, was required at those times when the rent was not paid on time or in full.

Food production, especially of potatoes, onions, tomatoes and cabbages, turned out to be very successful at Waterperry, partly because there was good fertile ground in the fields surrounding the mansion and garden, but also because the girls were trained well and worked extremely hard. There was no such thing as overtime; they simply worked until the job was done. The county War Ag gave the school a Fordson tractor and a two-furrow plough – there were already two carthorses – as well as a machine that speeded up cabbage planting. After a visit to East Malling Research Station in Kent, Miss Havergal instituted a programme of fruit bush propagation, in particular of virus-free raspberry canes and strawberry plants. These, with much of the other produce, were sold at Oxford market (see Chapter Seven). All in all, it was a conspicuously successful operation.

On the whole, women who worked in market gardens, nurseries or mansion gardens appear to have been content with their lot. They worked hard and long hours[40] for less money than their factory contemporaries, and sometimes in very isolated places, but they were at least in the fresh air, mainly away from the bombing – except in the coastal regions of the south of England – and were often able to mix with servicemen socially, especially after the Americans arrived in the countryside in 1942. They were also spared the kind of rigid discipline expected of women who went into the women's services yet were able to say truthfully that their efforts made a real difference. For some women, their wartime experience was the beginning of a lifelong fascination with gardening, and for still more it was a strange, almost dream-like interlude that they would remember with gratitude and a brisk nostalgia all their lives.

GROUNDWORK

Without ceremony, ordinary people were pitched into the business of growing edible produce. Almost overnight, gardening had become a patriotic duty, to add to all the others that must not be shirked if the war was to be won. There was no question of gardeners being gently persuaded, even wooed, as would have been the case in peacetime. They were given leaflets, sold booklets, shown films as a captive audience in cinemas, and lectured earnestly and incessantly in newspapers and on the wireless. With exhortations ringing in their ears, they had somehow to muddle their way into proficiency.

It was to the credit of the Ministry of Agriculture that the bulletins, leaflets and notes produced were, with the possible exception of the first, of high quality, even on matters about which experts might disagree, such as how to make a compost heap. They were clearly illustrated and carefully written, their authors obviously sensitive to the difficulties caused to novices by lack of education, resources, money or time. In fact, they were models of their kind, for they managed to avoid burdening the beginner with a lot of knowledge that he or she might not need but addressed all the important issues: how to plan for optimum cropping, how to feed the garden, what seeds to sow, how to perform the important practical operations, and how to protect growing crops from pests and diseases. That said, they must still have made dull reading for the disengaged.[1]

The modern reader cannot help but be forcibly struck by how familiar is so much of the information on offer. Descriptions of how to rotate crops, take out drills, sow seed, thin seedlings, weed beds and harvest produce all ring true today. Although fashions in kitchen gardening change, and technological and scientific advances eventually find their way into the cultivation of private plots, there were still the eternal verities of plant biology, growth dynamic, weather, soil profile, nutrients and pest attack. Even the tools used were much the same.

The types of vegetables and fruits that were available for the home gardener to grow as seeds or plants in wartime were surprisingly extensive and even included 'luxury' produce such as mushrooms, asparagus and melons. Of course, available varieties of each type decreased as the war wore on, since imports of seeds declined markedly, but early on there was reasonable choice. 'Food from the Garden', 'Growmore' Bulletin No. 1, contained, as an appendix, a list of suitable varieties of vegetables for cropping which could be generally obtained – or so its authors hoped. In this list were a number that had been in continuous cultivation since Victorian times, having proved their value in a variety of soils and regions of the country. Amongst them were 'Egyptian Turnip-rooted' beetroot, 'Painted Lady' runner beans, 'Flower of Spring' cabbage, 'Arctic King' lettuce, 'Musselburgh' leeks, 'Kelvedon Wonder' peas and 'White Lisbon' onions. These are varieties that can still be found in seed catalogues today.

Anyone who faithfully followed the bulletin's instructions should have produced enough for a family of five for two thirds of the year. In order to achieve that, however, they would need to concentrate on growing the brassica family and root vegetables, together with lettuce, spinach, beans and peas to give variety to meals in the summer.

As it turned out, however, there was considerable popular resistance to growing brassicas, since they were prone to clubroot on acidic soils, were miserably affected by a range of dispiriting pests, from caterpillars to wood pigeons, and were traditionally cooked so badly that they were scarcely edible, let alone nutritious. And even the experts did not bother to promote the cauliflower, since it is notoriously difficult to grow successfully, needing both good soil and a benign climate to thrive.

The two Ministries, of Agriculture and Food, were not

in the business of changing tastes, but rather making sure that the population had a basic understanding of what well-known vegetables could provide in the way of minerals and vitamins, and that there should be a steady and regular supply of these. Particularly valuable, in their opinion, were crops that would survive winter weather, such as leeks and brussels sprouts, and those that could be stored, such as potatoes, parsnips and carrots. Emphasis was laid on the importance of these throughout the war, until sensitive people must have been ready to scream.

The types of vegetable recommended for sowing were almost without exception long-established elements of the British diet. Continental influences were practically non-existent. Kitchen gardeners, except possibly in mansion gardens, were most unlikely to grow courgettes, aubergines, salsify, kohlrabi or chillies, while garlic was uncommon and widely viewed with suspicion because it was thought to taint the breath. The most generally grown herbs were mint, parsley, rosemary and thyme; dill, coriander, basil and tarragon were uncommon.

The scarcity of imported onions meant that these were high on the government's recommended list, despite the fact that novices were thought to find them difficult to grow, especially if working newly dug land. 'Bedfordshire Champion' was the variety for storing, while 'White Lisbon' was the popular spring onion. Onions were grown from seed; 'sets', that is small onion bulbs, which take much of the guesswork out of onion cultivation, were not readily available in those days. The experts very sensibly promoted shallots, which were easier to grow and could be stored for a long time without spoiling. Winter-hardy leeks, like 'The Lyon', were recommended as a substitute for onions, partly because they kept well.

Gardeners had always liked growing peas, such as 'Onward' and 'Kelvedon Wonder', together with broad beans, like 'Seville Long Pod' and 'Broad Windsor'. Runner beans ('Scarlet Emperor') enjoyed considerable success during the war since they were relatively simple to cultivate, produced good crops, and were amenable to being grown up pergolas or fences. Gardeners could also put the beans in jars with salt to preserve them through the winter, although few people remember the result with much sentimental feeling.

At the beginning, the government did not encourage the growing of large quantities of potatoes, but that changed from 1940, after it was discovered that people found them simple to grow, and easy and versatile to cook. Potatoes were both a source of vitamin C and also what Lord Woolton called a 'filler'. Moreover, they have to be lifted and stored before the winter, so there was no risk of bad weather destroying them. Popular varieties included a number with the prefix 'Arran', as well as the blight-prone 'King Edward VII' and the patriotically-named 'Home Guard'. The other important root vegetables were beetroot, like 'Crimson Globe', turnips, such as 'Early Milan', carrots ('Chantenay'), and parsnips ('Tender and True'). These could all be easily stored.

Much emphasis was placed on these in the campaigns, although gardeners themselves undoubtedly preferred to grow the tastier summer vegetables, like early carrots ('Early Horn'), lettuces ('Tom Thumb' and 'Wonderful'), tomatoes ('Sutton's Abundance'), rhubarb ('Timperley Early'), marrows ('Green Bush') and even cucumbers ('Telegraph').[2]

Everyone agreed that the frost-tender tomato had an important part to play in replacing scarce fruit, since it was high in vitamins A, B1, B2 and C, as well as being versatile in cookery.[3] Those amateur gardeners who owned greenhouses usually grew tomatoes, such as 'Ailsa Craig', in them. People without the means to heat glass, however, bought plants from nurserymen, hardened them off in frames and then planted them against a south-facing wall or fence. Varieties such as 'Evesham Wonder' and 'Best of All' were specifically recommended for growing outdoors, but they required hot, dry summers to do well, otherwise they were prone to the same blight that could strike potatoes in wet summers.

The only non-traditional vegetable to be heavily promoted by Ministry publicists, and backed up by gardening journalists, was the haricot bean. It had never before enjoyed popularity, probably because it was thought to be 'foreign'. But the Ministry considered it very useful because the seed could be dried and stored for use in the winter. Cultivars included 'Dutch Brown', 'Comtesse de Chambord' and 'White Leviathan'. As it turned out, haricot beans were often a failure in gardens and on allotments, unless gardeners recognised that they needed a lot of sun, space, and plenty of sulphate of ammonia and phosphates. Their popularity never took off in the way that the experts hoped.

Because of the increasing shortage of imported vegetable seed, gardeners were urged to save their own, which was possible to do in those days, before the advent of F1 hybrid seeds.[4] The seed of peas, beans, tomatoes, onions, lettuce and marrows could all be stored for the following year, if a few plants were left to grow on and set seed. It might make the kitchen garden look scruffy, and hold up the autumn digging, but gardeners found it a useful stratagem, especially in the case of seed that became very scarce, such as onion.

In the publicity campaigns, far less emphasis was placed on tree fruits than on vegetables, since it was considered that these were very wasteful of space, and took some years to come into good bearing after planting. The government did not go so far as to advise gardeners to grub up existing orchards, but it certainly expected them to grow vegetable crops between the rows. Gardening writers advocated that apples be grown on small 'cordons'; these trees were grafted on to 'dwarfing' East Malling-selected 'Paradise' rootstocks and came into fruit in only two or three years, taking up much less space than traditional 'standard' trees. Pears could be grown this way too, if they were grafted on to quince 'A' and 'C' rootstocks.

More enthusiastically encouraged was the growing of soft bush fruit, particularly blackcurrants, since they were productive and easy to grow, even if the fruits did require sugar to make them palatable. Recommended varieties included 'Baldwin' and 'Boskoop Giant', which were both good for making jam. Strawberries were viewed as an unnecessary luxury and the growing of them was rarely actively encouraged, although 'Dig for Victory' Leaflet No. 22 does give some cultivation details and mentions suitable varieties, such as 'Royal Sovereign' and 'Cambridge Early', both still grown today. More emphasis was placed on redcurrants ('Laxton's No. 1'), gooseberries ('Careless', 'Whinham's Industry' and 'Leveller'), summer-fruiting raspberries like 'Brockett Hall' – autumn-fruiting varieties did not exist – and blackberries, such as 'Himalayan Giant' and 'Merton Early'. The leaflet advised that brambles be grown in odd corners, against sheds or trained over a pergola as a productive alternative to rambling roses.

The real problem for a new gardener lay not in choosing the right varieties but in learning a wide assortment of practical techniques, some of which had fallen out of fashion in the years before the war. For example, they had to learn how to store vegetables through the 'hungry gap' in winter using outdoor 'clamps'. The instructional leaflets were heavy with detail. Gardeners were told to pile up root vegetables no higher than two and a half feet, and cover them with straw to keep them in the dark and protect them against frost. If the clamp was built outside, it needed four inches of soil placed over the straw, with ventilation holes every five inches, located by tufts of straw. Ideally, the clamps were to be four feet wide and as long as necessary.

Other storage stratagems would be more familiar to us: onions were to be laid on wooden slats or hung, plaited on strings, in dry sheds, while parsnips and late carrots were to be left in the ground in winter until needed.[5]

Even Mrs Clara Milburn, a well-to-do middle-class housewife living in Balsall, near Coventry, who was a very keen and accomplished home gardener, had problems with her potato clamp. On 8 June 1942 she wrote in her diary:

A really chilly wind has persisted all day . . . This is too great a change to be pleasant, but it was nice for hard work in the garden and I managed to get in a row of purple sprouting broccoli, which was a great satisfaction. Jack stuck peas. Later we had a great blow when we found our potato clamp was growing great sprouts, great shoots pushing forth. Will they be eatable now, we wonder?[6]

The authorities also stressed the importance of storing fruit correctly, because of the pressing need for fresh fruit in winter and the prevention of waste. In the most precise terms, the Wiltshire Federation of the Women's Institute advised its members what to do when preparing fruit for sale on a market stall. This was necessary because, if wrapped correctly, apples could be put in boxes that could be piled on top of each other. Fruit was to be wrapped inside a square of oiled paper, between eight and eleven inches in size, with possible alternatives being newspaper or tissue paper.

1. Pick up square of paper with the left hand so that the paper is flat against palm. 2. Take the apple in right hand and throw it against left hand with sufficient force to make the paper form a holder . . . the cheek of the apple should be against the paper. 3. Partially close the left hand, turning the corners of the paper upwards. 4. Gather the corners together with the right hand and turn neatly under, forming a pad (not a twist). Apples should be packed in [the] box with the pad downwards for protection.[7]

It can only be a matter of conjecture as to whether zealous WI members went through the same process for their home-stored fruit.

Choosing the right seeds and storing produce correctly exercised novice gardeners, but so did the practicalities of vegetable gardening, and none more so than digging. Of all the well-known garden tasks that Michael Foot might have emphasised in his *Evening Standard* leaders, surely digging was the most unfortunate. It is the one aspect of gardening of which everybody has heard, but it is also a job that can be thoroughly overdone. Certainly, digging the ground and burying the turf was necessary when turning a lawn into a vegetable garden – since the soil would be low in organic matter and probably compacted as well – or when renovating a thoroughly neglected allotment. However, digging was unnecessary in an already established and fertile kitchen garden where there was organic matter, such as garden compost, available to spread on the soil or just fork in lightly in autumn. In these circumstances, more harm than good is achieved by digging since it disrupts beneficial mycorrhizal relationships in the soil. Double-digging risks burying nutriments too deeply in the soil to be useful for shallow-rooted vegetables.

For women and older children especially, deep digging and turning over of soil – particularly a heavy clay one – every winter would have been a soul-destroying task, causing soft hands to blister like old paintwork. It is painful to reflect on the many hours of hard, unpleasant grind these tired and harassed civilians endured which they could have partly avoided had 'no-dig' techniques been accepted before the war. 'No-dig' cultivation methods consist of covering a patch of soil in a thick blanket of compost or manure, which is then left for the worms to pull down into the soil over winter. Seeds can then be sown into what remains of the compost in the spring. Of course, in many wartime gardens it was not possible to acquire sufficient organic matter to make the soil humus-rich, so digging was the only way to ensure that the soil was properly aerated each year. Nevertheless, where gardeners were assiduous compost makers or had access to straw or hay, much of the really heavy work might have been avoided. Even now, seventy years later, British gardeners are still suffering from the backwash of this almost obsessive interest in digging, and we have those wartime horticultural experts and Ministry copywriters at least partly to blame for it.

That said, one cannot help admiring the toughness and commitment of 'Victory Diggers', if sixty-year-old Marjorie Williams of Lamledra in Cornwall was at all representative. She wrote in her diary in February 1940: 'Ray [the gardener] and I dig steadily on the new ¾ of an acre, trenching [triple-digging] day after day, often in fog and wind so cold that my hands can hardly hold the fork tight enough. The ground is breaking up well and it's good exercise . . . We have only been held up for three days by ground frozen too hard to work.'[8]

For most amateur gardeners, the prospect of digging up their lawns the hard way was understandably daunting. In March 1940, Mr Frederick Poke of Parkside, Wimbledon, south London made the newspapers by cultivating his lawn for vegetables using a Swiss machine called a Rototiller. This machine did the work in two hours rather than the fortnight it would have taken to dig by hand. The mayor of Wimbledon and his councillors came along to see the demonstration, with a view to buying one and hiring it out to private gardeners, and they 'watched girls using the Rototiller without difficulty'.[9] This was a nice idea but will have almost certainly foundered later in the war when the basic ration of petrol for ordinary citizens was abolished.

The emphasis on vigorous and deep digging highlighted one of the major limiting factors in wartime kitchen gardening, namely the shortage of suitable soil conditioners and fertilisers. Rotted farmyard manure, which was such a staple of pre-war gardening, especially in the countryside, rapidly dwindled in quantity; this was not just because farmers needed it for fertilising their fields but also because so much grazing pasture had been ploughed up for arable crops and there were far fewer cows as a consequence.

Much thought was expended, by both experts and amateurs, in finding ways round these shortages. Recommended alternative soil conditioners and fertilisers included seaweed in coastal areas, bone manures, feathers, hair, 'shoddy' – a by-product of the wool textile industry obtainable in towns in the north – 'spent' hops, available from breweries, and 'night soil', available anywhere in the country where there was no indoor sanitation. This commodity came highly recommended by E. Graham in his *Gardening in War-time*:

> One of the richest of all natural substitutes is night soil. It is excellent for practically all garden purposes and is suitable to all soils. As the night soil is removed it should be mixed with an equal quantity of earth and sprinkled with gypsum. Gypsum prevents the ammonia evaporating and it acts as a complete deodoriser. The heap should be covered to prevent the rain washing any of the nutriment away. It should be used sparingly – about a spadeful to each square yard.[10]

It was a good thing that gypsum was quarried in Britain.

Some local authorities sold treated sewage sludge. Plymouth

Corporation, for example, offered it at 1s. 6d a ton. It was said that tomato seedlings would germinate in it in the spring. Coir or coconut waste is mentioned in gardening books as an alternative, although it must be assumed that, as this came all the way from India and Ceylon, its import would have been highly restricted once Japan entered the war.

Some of the soil conditioners available were decidedly makeshift. Mrs Bridget Andrew, a student at Swanley College, remembered that they dug 'London dung' into the soil, which arrived by lorry, 'had a peculiar smell and included old pieces of corset, and a lot of paper'.[11]

Wood ash from domestic fireplaces was a soil conditioner but was also surprisingly high in potash: a bushel – that is four pecks or eight gallons – contained between four and five pounds. It was therefore carefully hoarded, covered if stored outside so that rain did not wash the nutrients away, and often mixed with soot – quite rich in nitrogen – that was begged from the sweep when the house chimneys were swept in the summer. Wood ash also came from garden bonfires, although gardeners had to tend these very carefully because of the blackout regulations; bonfires had to be either covered with sheets of corrugated iron before dark, or raked out in the afternoon while there was still light.

The authorities were quick to see that, with the increasing scarcity of farmyard manures, they must vigorously promote the composting of garden and kitchen waste as the most efficient substitute for manure to be used in vegetable gardens. So gardeners were taught how to make compost pits or heaps for creating 'manure from garden rubbish', a skill they have never since forgotten. It was dinned into them by posters, wireless talks and cinema films, and there was even a 'Dig for Victory' leaflet on the subject.

The great expert on composting was Sir Albert Howard, an agricultural chemist and botanist, who had spent much time working in India and had perfected a method based on Far Eastern agricultural practices. He called it 'the Indore process', after the city where he carried out the research between 1924 and 1931. His influential book, *An Agricultural*

Testament, was published in 1940. Howard's central idea was that soil fertility was the key both to yield and to minimising attacks from pests and diseases, anticipating the philosophy of the post-war 'organic' movement. The Indore composting process used both vegetable rubbish and animal wastes, which were put in either a pit or a large heap, kept moist but not saturated, and protected from wind. He was most insistent on the necessity in the process for urine – what he rather charmingly called 'bedroom slops', well-known to a substantial minority of the population who still used outdoor privies – but reassured his readers that the smell disappeared immediately on contact with soil, which was also a necessary ingredient for a successful compost heap. Generally speaking, a simplified version of his methods was adopted by gardening writers and Ministry officials and formed the basis of the advice they passed on to amateurs – although they were less adventurous in the list of suitable ingredients and in particular there was no mention of 'bedroom slops'.

Howard's ideas also had a profound effect on the young 'organic' movement, especially its leading light, Lady Eve Balfour, who owned an experimental farm in Suffolk, where she pursued Howard's methods and published a popular book, *The Living Soil*, in 1943. The concept of organic, sustainable agriculture and horticulture, as we know them today, was considered eccentric by most farmers and gardeners in the 1930s. But during the war years there were sufficient stirrings of interest to lead to the founding of the Soil Association in May 1946.

The year that *An Agricultural Testament* was published, Howard moved to Milnthorpe in Westmorland, and came into contact with F. C. King, the head gardener at nearby Levens Hall.[12] King was a well-known local figure who worked hard lecturing and advising on gardening to local groups. He had become so enamoured of the Indore process that he even published a practical and thoughtful book in 1943, entitled *A Compost Gardener*, which included an Afterword by Sir Albert. King showed the same wariness about the value of chemical fertilisers that Howard exhibited; he considered that they often promoted the wrong kind of growth and also put nothing of value in the way of humus into the soil. King was also an early advocate of the 'no-digging' method, publishing a book in 1946 entitled *Is Digging Necessary?*.

On the whole, gardening commentators thought of organic manures more as soil improvers than as plant feeders, and were keen on the use of chemical fertilisers for the latter purpose.[13] This was to prove difficult since conventional potash fertilisers, such as sulphate of potash, were almost all imported – from France, Germany and Poland – and supplies dried up rapidly after war broke out. Although the stocks were reasonably high in 1939, they had fallen to 50 per cent of their pre-war level by the summer of 1940. The dearth of potash fertilisers became a major headache for gardeners, since potash was a necessary nutrient for promoting good fruiting and flowering, especially of fruit-type vegetables like tomatoes. A certain amount of potash had also been imported from the USSR, Palestine and Spain before the war and a limited quantity continued to arrive. Allotmenteers were allowed to buy a maximum of 3.5 lb of muriate of potash (potassium chloride) a year, which was scarcely sufficient. In any event, the chloride ion made this fertiliser toxic to some plants, including potatoes and fruit.

Nitrogenous fertilisers such as nitrate of soda were easier to come by, and seed merchants like Suttons sold a range of such well-known pre-war fertilisers as well as bizarre-sounding substitutes, including Ichthemic Guano, Poultmure (which was treated chicken manure), and Garotta, which was essentially sulphate of ammonia and was used to accelerate decomposition in compost heaps. Even these chemical fertilisers were in such limited supply that the customer had to promise faithfully to use them only in the vegetable garden. If a gardener could get a small quantity of manure – perhaps the droppings from the milk-float horse in the road outside – he could make a nitrogenous liquid fertiliser by putting it in a hessian sack and suspending it in a large container of water.

So concerned were the authorities with maximising home-based food production and allotment gardening, and so dubious were they about the amateur gardener's scientific knowledge of soil nutrients that they launched, in a blaze of publicity in 1942, a standard 'compound' granular fertiliser called National Growmore. The chemical constituents of this feed were in the ratio 7:7:7 NPK, in other words, 7 per cent nitrogen, 7 per cent potassium and 7 per cent phosphorus. National Growmore proved popular because of its general applicability and the ease with which it could be used, and that is why it still sells well today. For many gardeners and allotmenteers it finally took the guesswork out of feeding their plots; provided that the soil was already reasonably fertile, National Growmore would help produce satisfactory crops.

Horticultural experts put great emphasis on the importance of the right pH for the soil, in order to ensure that clubroot of brassicas was kept at bay, as well as to maximise the effectiveness of other nutrient elements. However, assessing whether your soil needed lime to raise the pH, and if so, how much, was hardly straightforward, since testing the pH had to be done with hydrochloric acid ('spirits of salt') bought from the chemist. Alternatively, if the soil tasted 'sweet' it was alkaline, if 'sour' it was acid. Most people probably asked their neighbours whether they had trouble from clubroot, and acted accordingly, or made a rough guess.

There were many sources of lime that could be used to raise a soil's pH: gypsum, basic slag, slaked lime, quicklime, spent carbide and ground limestone – the latter still popular today. A substantial 30 lb per rod was recommended triennially. Whether those gardeners working chalk soils fruitlessly obeyed these recommendations is a matter for conjecture, but unless gardeners badgered their local expert advisers, no one seems to have bothered to tell them that alkaline soils do not need liming.

Of course chemical fertilisers were only one element in the struggle to achieve high productivity; gardeners also needed a range of equipment, some of it just as difficult to come by. If, for example, they were moved to propagate their own tomato or other vegetable plants – or garden flowers come to that – they would need to make some wooden boxes, traditionally fifteen inches long, ten inches wide and, variously, three, four or five inches deep, depending on the size of seed to be sown. If a propagating case – a mini cold frame – was not available in which to put these boxes, gardeners put a sheet of glass over the box, and a sheet of newspaper over that.

Once germinated in these boxes, seedlings then had to be potted on into pots, which were made of clay, terracotta in colour, and hand-thrown. These came in a variety of sizes between 'thimbles' or 'thumbs', which were 2″ in diameter, right up to 'ones', which were 20″ across. In between were 'twos', 'fours', 'sixes', 'eights', 'twelves' 'sixteens', 'twenty-fours', 'thirty-twos', 'forty-eights', 'fifty-fours' and 'sixties'. Alternatively, they were classified by diameter: 2½″, 3″, 3½″, 4″, 5″ and so on.[14] Before clay pots could be used for the first time, they had to be 'steeped' in a tank of water for several hours; this was to ensure that the porous clay took up sufficient moisture so that it did not steal it from the compost into which the plant had been potted.

Also important for the wartime garden was the glass cloche or dome. Their greatest value resided in their capacity to protect against the cold and damp, rather than actively 'forcing' plants into precocious growth. They could also be used to warm up the soil in late winter or spring, prior to seed sowing. Cloches were particularly useful in extending the growing season at both ends of the year. In fact, with careful planning, it was possible to grow three vegetable crops on the same bit of ground in the course of the year using cloches: say, early lettuce, then peas, then quick-maturing carrots.

There were 'bell' or 'lantern' cloches, which protected individual plants, or 'barn' cloches, which could be butted up against each other to cover a whole row of winter lettuce, for example. These came in a variety of shapes and sizes: long tent, small tent, medium tent, long barn, small barn, low barn, large barn and tomato 'T'. The 'T' cloche had one side that was removable, so that the gardener could pinch out the tomato plant sideshoots easily.

There was a definite knack to assembling barn cloches, but once this was achieved, they proved very useful; their major disadvantage was that the glass broke all too easily when they were being stacked away for the summer or were accidentally kicked by a clumsy gardener wearing big boots. And horticultural glass became very scarce as the war wore on.

A permanent fixture in many gardens was the cold frame, which was really a cloche writ large. Ideally, it had a brick base, was taller at the back than the front, and was covered by a 'Dutch light' placed on the slope. The 'Dutch light' was a large glass panel in a wooden frame with a metal handle, with which it could be moved or lifted. If fresh manure was put in a cold frame in late winter or early spring and covered with a thin layer of soil and then the Dutch light was closed, the activity of microbes would ensure that the soil warmed up sufficiently for seed to germinate in it. This was called a 'hot bed'. Lettuce and other low-growing hardy vegetables were good candidates for hot beds early in the season. Cloches, hot beds and cold frames went at least some way towards making up for the fact that most amateur greenhouses were unheated during the war, because fuel for greenhouse boilers was at first rationed and then unobtainable. As the war went on, timber also became hard to find, so asbestos was used for making frames instead.

Those bits of equipment were for the experienced gardener, who had gained some confidence over the years. For the complete novice, sowing seed under cover was far less a preoccupation than how to identify annual weeds in the vegetable patch, particularly when small. Beginners also needed to learn how to recognise and get rid of deep-rooted peren-nial weeds, usually the biggest problem when first taking over a neglected garden or allotment. Gardeners had only the border fork, small hand fork and hoe in their armoury, since chemical weedkillers were either unavailable or else lamentably indiscriminate. Sodium chlorate, for instance, killed everything it touched, was highly flammable, and was demonstrably less effective on alkaline soils than acid ones.

However, despite the dearth of suitable weedkillers, the authorities were very firm about the importance of keeping vegetable gardens well weeded, not only so that weeds did not take nutriments needed by crops,[15] but also so that neighbouring gardens would not be plagued by perennial weeds coming through under the fence or hedge. Even owners who had evacuated their premises were not exempt from the duty of keeping their gardens 'clean'. Puzzlingly, though there were 'Dig for Victory' leaflets on everything from the use of cloches to saving seeds, there was never one on weeds and weeding, although these were aspects of vegetable growing that will have preoccupied Victory Diggers more than most.

Gardeners, then as now, would have been hard pressed to decide which were the greater enemies to their vegetables and fruit – weeds or pests and diseases. In 1926, Vita Sackville-West had published a long poem called *The Land*, which included a stanza about the ills to which fruit trees are heir:

'Look, too, to your orchards in the early spring.
The blossom-weevil bores into the sheath,
Grubs tunnel in the pith of promising shoots,
The root-louse spends his winter tucked beneath
Rough bark of trunks or chinks of tangled roots;
Canker, rot, scab, and mildew blight the tree;
There seems an enemy in everything.'[16]

As an accomplished and experienced gardener and small farmer, Sackville-West knew perfectly well how hopes of a fine fruit harvest could be dashed in many diverse ways. And it was true of vegetable crops as well. It is small wonder that the Ministry of Agriculture's pamphlets and posters seemed so concerned about pests and diseases. Cabbage white butterfly caterpillars, slugs, wireworms, leatherjackets, greenfly, whitefly, potato blight, onion fly: they made up a seemingly endless litany of ills that needed instant attention, and usually dispatch by the use of some noxious chemical or time-honoured, time-consuming folksy remedy. The second 'Growmore' bulletin was entitled 'Pests and Diseases in the Vegetable Garden', and on the front was an illustration of a man with a knapsack sprayer, carrying a lance in his hand and spraying cabbages. The message was clear: if you wanted to be successful, you needed to use chemical pesticides.

Information about pests and diseases was very often couched in militaristic language: it was a war out there, and either you killed the pests or they blitzed all your efforts. Because the pendulum has swung so far the other way in the last thirty years, and gardeners refrain from using pesticides unless driven to distraction, and sometimes not even then, it is hard for us to imagine how necessary, if dreary, all this sounded. Gardeners then did not know what we know now: that many of the pesticides they used so blithely, often without any kind of protective clothing, were potentially harmful not only to wild and domesticated creatures but to the user as well. The way the gardening press welcomed DDT when it came on the market in 1944 strikes fear into our hearts now. Nor must we forget that, in the intervening period, much work has been done to breed vegetable cultivars with at least some resistance to damage by pests and diseases, so that many are not as vulnerable as varieties available in the 1940s.

The war accelerated the introduction of a number of synthetic chemical pesticides, as well as DDT, in particular dieldrin, aldrin and malathion. Interestingly, so effective was dieldrin against glasshouse whitefly that the biological control *Encarsia formosa*, which had been introduced to both amateur and professional greenhouses in the 1920s and 30s, was widely abandoned in wartime.[17] The flower decorator Constance Spry had been an enthusiastic devotee, but she was not typical. In 1942 she wrote:

> Most people who grow tomatoes under glass know all about the
> white fly scourge. We were very badly attacked by this and tried
> a good many remedies without great success until we used a
> white fly parasite, which we got from the Experimental and
> Research Station at Cheshunt, Herts. I must say when the little
> bunches of dried-up leaves arrived, I looked at them with a
> doubting eye, and it was some time before I could appreciate
> the potency of their work.'[18]

The efficacy of *Encarsia* was rediscovered in the 1970s, and the parasite is now widely used as a benign biological control in both commercial and amateur glasshouses.

William Lawrence, who was Gardens Curator at the horticultural science establishment, the John Innes Horticultural Institution, wrote on the subject of available pesticides in wartime:

The most fearsome of our weapons was cyanide. Bowls of sulphuric acid would be placed along the length of the [green] house and weighed amounts of potassium cyanide in screws of tissue paper dropped into the acid, one by one, while the operator beat a hasty retreat before the acid ate through the paper! The cyanide fumes of course were deadly to humans and doors had to be tied up so that no one could enter the house before next day.'[19]

Lawrence's cyanide was almost certainly only available to professional gardeners, but the experts recommended plenty of other toxic chemicals for amateur gardeners to use. Against clubroot, for example, they advised 'corrosive sublimate', in other words 4 per cent calomel dust or mercuric chloride. This had once been a treatment for syphilis. Even *The Gardeners' Chronicle* admitted that 'It is a deadly poison to man and beast as well as to the pest [clubroot] and, if used, gloves should be worn, and an earthenware pot or jug used to mix it in. A very weak solution[20] will suffice.'[21] It is a relief to know that gardeners were encouraged to wear gloves at least. Even C.H. Middleton, who seems to modern readers shockingly cavalier in his attitude to poisonous chemicals, advised his listeners to be careful with it.

Lead arsenate paste was used to kill sucking insects on fruit trees, despite the fact that it was poisonous to honeybees, as indeed were a number of other insecticides. When buying lead arsenate in the chemist's shop, customers had to sign a poisons book, or a special form if ordering from a sundries catalogue. That was also true of nicotine products.

Wartime gardeners were lucky that tar oil winter washes had appeared on the market in the 1930s, for, when sprayed on fruit trees, these effectively 'spring-cleaned' them of pests. Derived from creosote, this chemical was not particularly toxic to humans, but care had to be taken not to splash it on the grass below, because it killed green growth so effectively. Mortegg was the proprietary brand, which everybody used. It was advertised in the newspapers as if it were a government announcement: 'Ministry of Mortegg Information. Mortegg tar oil winter wash is your Maginot Line against insect pests on fruit trees.'

The most commonly used glasshouse pesticide in the 1940s was nicotine, derived from the tobacco plant. Nicotine was particularly effective against greenfly and whitefly. It could be bought as a powder, added to water in a bucket and sprayed on to plants using the household stirrup pump kept as a precaution for use against incendiary bombs. Professional gardeners, with larger areas to spray, used heavy metal knapsack sprayers. Those gardeners who did not want to pay for proprietary nicotine simply soaked old cigarette butts in water with a little soft soap, and then sprayed the resulting dark brown liquid.

Outside the greenhouse, the great enemy of promise in the vegetable garden was the slug, especially destructive on salad plants. At the beginning of the war they were poisoned with metaldehyde, although the increasing shortage of bran – in which it was mixed – meant that supplies became progressively harder to find. Instead, the full panoply of traditional remedies was employed, from sunken containers with a little beer in the bottom, to upside-down eaten halves of oranges – when they were available – to planks smeared with jam and laid on the soil.

As for cabbage caterpillars, derris powder, from the derris root, was the great standby for anyone who did not want the laborious and horrible job of picking them off the leaves by hand and drowning them. Derris also dispatched flea beetles, which chewed pieces out of seedlings, especially those of brassicas. Unfortunately, the supply dried up after the Japanese invaded Malaya. Even more unfortunately, its place was taken by a newly developed, highly toxic organochlorine called HCH, marketed as Lindane.

The very common pest, carrot fly, was discouraged by stringing a line painted with creosote above the carrot row, on the basis that the smell would mask the scent of carrot leaf and the flies would not land

and lay their eggs. This stratagem relied on an accurate knowledge of the ways of this insect, but it made up for the fact that there was no suitable soil insecticide available.

Underground, the eelworm or nematode, a microscopic soil-dwelling organism, was particularly troublesome to vegetable gardeners. Few of them had the space to rotate their crops sufficiently for nematodes to die out for want of a suitable host. Nematodes, especially potato eelworm, spread through allotment sites very quickly, as a result of the allotmenteer's habit of saving a few tubers from year to year rather than buying fresh 'seed', since it was so scarce. The government encouraged gardeners to buy 'certificated' seed potatoes, but these were not always easy to acquire in wartime. Almost all potato 'seed' was grown in Scotland because the cooler climate there discouraged aphids, which carried virus diseases. However, long-distance transport difficulties meant that seed potatoes were often unavailable in late winter when gardeners wanted them for 'chitting'. This was particularly the case in early 1941.

Potatoes could also be ravaged by wireworms, which, along with leatherjackets, were the two most serious pests of newly dug lawn or grassland, of which there was a great deal early in the war. The former is the larval stage of the click beetle, the latter of the crane fly or 'daddy-long-legs'. Wireworms burrow into potato tubers and carrot roots, and also attack tomato plants, while leatherjackets eat the stems of lettuces and other leaf vegetables at ground level, causing them to wilt and die. The chemist's remedy for wireworms was 'whizzed' or powdered naphthalene, which is the active ingredient in old-fashioned mothballs. C. H. Middleton himself recommended it as a remedy in both columns and advertisements that appeared in the *Daily Express*.

In the 1940s, the non-chemical way of dealing with these pests was to sow a mustard crop and then dig it in. The mustard smelled unpleasant to wireworms, and the leafy crop helped feed the soil. Alternatively, if the gardener did not mind an arduous task, he could bury half a potato stuck on a stick in the ground. Every few days he would have to pull up the stick and dispatch any wireworms. Equally laborious was the remedy for getting rid of leatherjackets: if they killed a plant, a gardener would have to stab the ground in a circle around the plant with a sharp knife.

One imported pest about which most people had heard, but which they were not adept at identifying, was the Colorado beetle. These aliens unnerved farmers and gardeners alike, since they could completely destroy a potato crop in very quick time, and they had become well established in northern France. After the war, a story emerged of how the Germans dropped boxes filled with Colorado beetles over the Isle of Wight. According to a retired British Museum entomologist, Richard Ford, who told the story to the newspapers in the 1970s, the Germans had first dropped these beetles near the village of Chale in 1943. This fact had been kept 'hush-hush' at the time so as not to alarm the public. Ford recruited bands of evacuated schoolchildren, swore them to secrecy and sent them out into the fields to catch the beetles.

It was my duty to destroy them immediately, so I plunged them into boiling water. I still possess a few dried-up specimens as souvenirs.

The bombs were, in fact, rather crude cardboard containers, and I believe the Germans, because of their Teutonic precision, made a big practical error in their approach. We discovered that they dropped the beetles in groups of either 100 or 50, so our beetle hunters knew how many they had to seek out and destroy to overcome any particular attack.[22]

How those children must have enjoyed themselves.

As far as plant diseases were concerned, potato blight was the one that most frightened gardeners, whether they had studied Irish history or not. Potato blight affects first the leaves and then the tubers of potatoes in late summer, especially if the weather is warm and wet. Blight also infects tomatoes, since they are closely related to potatoes. So important was the control of potato blight on allotments that the Ministry produced a 'Dig for Victory'[23] leaflet specifically to teach gardeners how to make Bordeaux mixture and Burgundy mixture, sprays that could be used as prophylactics. These fungicides had originally been developed in France for use on grapevines: the first is copper sulphate mixed with water and dissolved hydrated lime, and the second is copper sulphate mixed with dissolved washing soda. These sprays had to be made up in a bucket and the strength tested by dipping a knife blade in the solution. If the blade darkened in colour, more quicklime or washing soda solution was required.

Not so harmful to humans or wildlife as many of the recommended chemical solutions, but nevertheless unpleasant if you were allergic to it, was 'flowers of sulphur', a powder that was the most common remedy against the fungal disease powdery mildew. Dorothy Pembridge, a land girl working at Madresfield[24] for the Earl and Countess Beauchamp, developed a rash on her neck from cleaning the grapevine in winter because she had to untie the treated rods and lay them against her neck as she worked on them.[25]

Assiduous readers of government information, and those who both- ered to attend talks or Brains Trusts given by professional gardeners, would have been left with the distinct impression that gardening was a very hard grind, resulting after much labour in the production of some pretty dull vegetables. Let us hope that at least some of them read the writings of Constance Spry, for these would surely have lifted their spirits:

There are scoffers who find truly comic eccentricity in the consideration of beauty in what they call common vegetables. These are suffering from blindness caused by familiarity. Even the most hilarious mocker would have been compelled to stop laughing to admire a certain long border of dark green curly kale that I saw lately in a grey-walled garden. I came on it suddenly and stopped dead; the plants were more imposing than Victorian funeral plumes, and as covered with delicate bloom as a bunch of hothouse grapes. The bloom and curl of the leaves gave an illusion of softest velvet.'[26]

Not many people could have expressed themselves like that, but those who persevered in vegetable gardening at least found that the practice was often a great deal more pleasant than the theory. Indeed, there are many accounts of gardeners finding the process surprisingly fun and companionable and the results of their labours satisfying and nearly always a source of pride. A female allotmenteer from Bedfordshire recalled after the war that 'I was so proud of my achievement when I cycled home with baskets of fresh vegetables and fruit and occasional bunches of flowers.'[27]

CHAPTER SIX

TALKING OF SCARLET-VEINÈD BEET

> *On a Wireless Set*
> Who is this coming to the microphone?
>   Is it the man again to cast his jest
> New-minted on the garrulous unknown?
> What sailor comes to answer our request?
>   What fair economist? What little street
> Is emptied of its Joad[1] this brain-sick hour
>   To prate of Plato old or Socrates?
> What gardener talks of scarlet-veinèd beet,
>   Of onions, or the clotted cauliflower,
> Or sounds the praise of upward-climbing peas?[2]

The answer, of course, to the last question was Mr Middleton, presenter of the weekly radio programme *In Your Garden*, and the most famous wartime broadcaster on gardening.

Cecil Henry Middleton was born in 1886, at Weston-by-Weedon in Northamptonshire, the son of Sir George Sitwell's head gardener at Weston Hall. He was much of an age with Sitwell's three extraordinary children, Edith, Osbert and Sacheverell, and almost certainly played with them as a boy, since his father, although an employee, would have enjoyed a considerable status on the estate. Sir George Sitwell was an avid garden maker, both in England and Italy, and published a well-regarded book on design, *On the Making of Gardens*, in 1909.[3]

Middleton began his working life, aged thirteen, as a garden boy in the Weston Hall garden, but at seventeen, with only fifty shillings in his pocket, he left home for London. He found work with a seed firm, then took up a place as a student gardener at Kew. By 1912, he was married and already working as a teacher of horticulture. During the First World War, he worked in the horticultural division of the Board of Agriculture and Fisheries, the forerunner of the Ministry of Agriculture. He gained the National Diploma of Horticulture, the highest RHS qualification, and then joined Surrey County Council as an instructor. It is certain that the Director of Wisley, Frederick Chittenden, who wrote gardening bulletins for the BBC, would have known him personally, since they lived and worked in the same county. As we saw in Chapter One, it was Chittenden who recommended Middleton to the BBC in 1931 as a potential presenter of gardening programmes.

In Your Garden was originally broadcast at ten past seven on a Friday evening, but when, in October 1936, a move to two o'clock on Sunday afternoons was mooted, Middleton asked the listeners themselves what was best: 'There does not seem a better way of finding out what your wishes are, whether you regard me as a stimulation for the weekend's gardening, or to send you off to sleep after Sunday lunch. The BBC want to please you and I am quite prepared to do what I'm told as far as I can and to give you what you want.'[4] The answer from the listeners, who wrote in their thousands, was more than two to one in favour of Sunday, and he did what he was told.

The show consisted principally of Middleton talking to the audience, although he would sometimes invite in another gardening expert for a conversation. People began to think of him as their kindly, knowledgeable, understanding gardening friend from the rural Midlands, in much the same way that a later generation considered Geoff Hamilton. In 1935, the critic Wilfrid Rooke Ley wrote: 'It is the art of Mr Middleton to address himself to the lowest common denominator of horticultural intelligence without the faintest hint of superiority or condescension. He will assume that your soil is poor, and your pocket poor. All he asks is that your hopes are high and your Saturday afternoons at his service . . . He has the prettiest humour. He stands for common sense and has the gift of consolation.'[5]

Such a valuable gift was to prove very attractive to his listeners in wartime.

The Ministry of Agriculture was keen that *In Your Garden* should survive the outbreak of hostilities, and wrote to the BBC asking for assurances on that score. In March 1940 the BBC replied in reasonably enthusiastic fashion: '. . . his [Middleton's] talks are inherently better value than any alternatives that could be found. From the point of view of propaganda or practical advice it is unlikely that we could find speakers who could rise above his level. On the other hand, they might easily fall below it and would not be likely ever to rise to the heights to which he can aspire on occasions.'[6]

Certainly, for a specialist broadcast, Middleton's programme was extremely popular, with an average audience in late 1940 of 2,950,000, which was more than the Daily Service or the Wednesday Symphony Concert, but substantially less, not surprisingly, than *The Kitchen Front*.[7] These talks were sufficiently highly regarded by the BBC to be reproduced in its weekly periodical, *The Listener*.

His appeal lay partly in his pleasant manner, rural accent and simple, even homespun language, which proved to be the best way to strike a chord with millions of novice gardeners. At the end of 1939, he declared:

We are all going to be kitchen gardeners next year, but I hope that doesn't mean that we are going to neglect the flowers too much. At times like these we need our flowers more than ever: they help to turn our minds to the better side of Nature occasionally. We are all gardeners at heart, and I believe if we were all gardeners in fact there wouldn't be any wars. But perhaps the fact that most of us are gardeners or garden lovers will help us to live cheerfully through these dark days, and build a sweeter and better world when the nightmare is over. I am sure it will, because the very essence of gardening consists of rooting out and destroying all the evil things,[8] and cultivating and developing all that is good and beautiful in life. So let us put forward all our efforts to make 1940 a record gardening year in every way.'[9]

In a broadcast later that month, while talking about seed catalogues, he said: 'I thought this afternoon I would get you to come and look over my shoulder, and that we would go through this catalogue together. Shall we begin with the flowers?'[10] To which no doubt many listeners replied to the wireless set: 'Yes, please.'

He was plainly a romantic, something which must also have gone down well with many listeners: 'In these days of strife and anxiety, I often let my mind wander back to the old country village, where the orchards and gardens were humming and buzzing with bees, and our old lime-tree in June sounded like the deep diapason note of a great organ.'[11] He was also quietly religious. When talking about gardeners in a broadcast in 1935, he was describing himself:

> Generally speaking they're very much as other men are –
> perhaps a little better in many ways: wholesome, decent-living
> people who love their work – usually straight and often deeply
> religious people, perhaps without knowing it, and certainly
> without shouting about it. They work hand in hand with Nature
> and they know their work is under the direct supervision of the
> Great Architect.[12]

Though mild-mannered, Middleton did not shrink from the kind of controversy which shook up even his gentle world from time to time. For example, in early 1940, when there were comments in the press about how allotmenteers might undermine the profits of market gardeners, he fought back. 'Allotment holders, at the best, are only a small percentage of the population,[13] so let us put forth all our efforts to avoid a shortage, and not listen to unfounded theories about surplus.'[14] Nor was he going to be pushed around by tricky correspondents. He answered a few queries in *The Listener* each week, and when one person questioned his advice to strip ivy off other people's trees, he replied: 'I should think it might easily lead to a thick ear if I were foolish enough to give such advice, but I never did.'[15]

The BBC realised very early on that they had found a natural radio broadcaster in Middleton. He was so fluent and dependable that, within a short space of time, he was granted the unusual dispensation of no longer having to submit manuscripts of his projected talks, since it was thought that he was more than capable of extemporising from notes, even though the broadcast was 'live'. Once the war began, however, and broadcasters became extremely careful about what they said,[16] Middleton did provide scripts and even submitted to a 'run-through'.

This precaution did not always prevent him from ad-libbing. He rounded off one broadcast early in the war with the words: 'Now a last word about carnations. Some of you find them difficult subjects, but it's because they like lots of lime, so cheer up, the way things are going at the moment there will soon be plenty of mortar rubble about. Just have another go.'[17] Generally, though, the Talks Department was tolerant of his minor departures from the script.

He was treated reasonably well by the BBC, although it is hard to escape the conclusion that he was patronised, at least behind his back, because his subject was gardening rather than anything they considered more elevated.[18] That said, in 1940, BBC Talks producers bemoaned the fact that they couldn't find the right presenter for a literature programme, someone they said who would be a 'Middleton of books'.[19]

He was paid twelve guineas a programme – and five guineas for the weekly reproduction of his script in The Listener – and if he had to travel, his expenses allowed him to go First Class, which must have been a relief on those overcrowded wartime trains. His duties were a sore trial at times, especially from the autumn of 1940, when he and his wife were bombed out of their house in Surbiton and they had to camp with relatives in Northamptonshire for eighteen months until they could return to Surrey. During that period he no longer recorded In Your Garden in a garden in Cavendish Place, but instead at a BBC station at Wood Norton Hall, outside Evesham, which had been established at the beginning of the war just in case Broadcasting House was bombed.[20] His other commitments made these journeys difficult, and his BBC bosses were not very sympathetic when he asked them to arrange extra petrol coupons, calling him 'grabbing'.[21]

However, he was protected by powerful allies in the upper echelons of the Ministry of Agriculture who, right from the start of the war, were keen that he should spread the official message that they were taking such pains to develop.[22] And even the BBC considered him sufficiently important to be invited to the Corporation's twenty-first birthday lunch in December 1943, an event at which Brendan Bracken, the Minister of Information, spoke.

After war broke out, there was initially a marked falling-off in Middleton's audience ratings, but the BBC sensibly assumed that this had more to do with war conditions than disenchantment, although John Green, his boss in the Talks Department, did point out that the decline might have something to do with the fact that gardening was no longer a hobby and so his 'soporific appeal' had diminished.[23]

Nevertheless, Middleton's air time was extended during the war. Every so often he broadcast to the forces, and he also spoke on *Ack-Ack, Beer-Beer*, a Forces Programme series aimed at personnel manning observation posts or working anti-aircraft guns and searchlights. These listeners had many weary hours to kill when nothing was happening, and often made gardens around their installations.

Each year Middleton took a leave of absence from the programme for several months in the summer and early autumn, and his place was taken by Roy Hay, an able, but less charismatic, gardening journalist who was already working on the Dig for Victory campaign for the Ministry of Agriculture and so was well versed in what was required of him.

On the back of his undoubted national celebrity, Middleton was much in demand, promoting the Dig for Victory campaign at exhibitions, talking to gardening clubs and at flower shows all over the country, and writing a weekly column in the Saturday edition of the *Daily Express*. He was the horticultural consultant to Boots the Chemist, which at that time sold fertilisers and pesticides.

He was the first gardener to become a household name, and was sufficiently famous to be 'sent up' by comedians. The music hall trio Vine, More and Nevard wrote and performed a witty comedic song in 1938 with the refrain 'Mr Middleton says it's right'. In 1943, he was Roy Plomley's guest on *Desert Island Discs*. He even appeared, as himself (as did Michael Standing, head of Outside Broadcasting), in Arthur Askey's madcap film of 1940, *Band Waggon*. Despite the strong discouragement of John Green, he occasionally appeared on non-gardening programmes: for example, he was the 'Mystery Voice' on *Tonight at Eight* in February 1944, and took part in *Victory Night at Eight*, which was transmitted on 14 May 1945, a few days after VE Day. He also participated in three *Brains Trust*[24] radio broadcasts in 1944, much to Green's disapproval, since he did not consider that Middleton was a 'brain'.[25] Even more worthy was his contribution about country churches, which was broadcast on Christmas Day 1943, as part of a programme entitled *What Else Do They Do?*.

Historian of the BBC, Asa Briggs, paid the radio gardener this compliment: 'A man like Middleton, who had established his reputation as a broadcaster before the war, was an artist in his own right – easy in manner, on occasion acid in humour, always capable of improvising, always conscious of his vast, if strictly limited, authority.'[26] Those who knew the country house gardening system well would have recognised Middleton as a type: a supreme professional, hard-working and conscientious, who had generations of substantial standing behind him. His pleasant, outgoing personality and natural empathy saved him from pomposity but then anyone who, as a boy, played with the Sitwell children must have grown up with a lively sense of the endearing eccentricities of human nature.

C. H. Middleton died suddenly of a heart attack outside his house in Surbiton on 18 September 1945. He was only fifty-nine. His funeral was filmed for a Pathé newsreel that was shown in cinemas. His coffin was carried in a hearse crammed with the dahlias that he loved so much. It cannot be unreasonable to conclude that his punishing wartime schedule hastened his end. It was a cruel irony that a man who cared for flowers so much more than vegetables should not have lived to enjoy a retirement growing them.

George Barnes, Director of Talks at the BBC, wrote to Mrs Middleton on the day of her husband's death:

We turned to him on many important and critical occasions and he never failed us; I shall long remember, for instance, the talk he recorded in [*sic*] the first day of September 1939.[27] But the two qualities of his which are ineffaceable are his modesty and his integrity: he never allowed the insistent demand for his services which fame brought, to lower the standards he had set or to divert him from his task of inspiring and teaching gardening.[28]

In 1940, Middleton had introduced Fred Streeter, the head gardener at Petworth House, to listeners during an episode of *In Your Garden*, talking about fruit and vegetables. By 1945, Streeter was filling in for him in the summer months,[29] and after Middleton died, the BBC decided that he would simply carry on doing so. Despite the criticism that Streeter's scripts were more suitable for the country house gardener than the suburban housewife, he retained the job and successfully made the switch to television, presenting *Television Garden* from 1951, the garden in question being one laid out in the grounds of Alexandra Palace in north London.

Dominant as Middleton was, *In Your Garden* was not the only programme on gardening during the war. Roy Hay explained in a memoir how *Radio Allotment* came about:

One day in December, 1941, Michael [Standing, of the Outside Broadcasting Department and later Director of it] became inspired, I like to think, by the Ministry of Agriculture's suggestion that those who had no time to cultivate an allotment individually might combine with two or three friends and take a plot collectively . . . After consulting one or two members of the Outside Broadcasting Department, he asked me if there was any chance of obtaining an allotment within reasonable distance of the BBC headquarters . . . he hit on the idea of making regular broadcasts from the plot-side to let listeners know how the communal allotment was proceeding, and to share the joys and sorrows common to all gardening tyros.[30]

Standing wrote to the then Director of Talks, Sir Richard Maconachie, as well as to John Green about the idea, ending with the words: 'I'd be glad to have your views without too much mockery!'[31] But his bosses did not mock, and Roy Hay soon found a piece of ground, ten rods in size, in Park Crescent, a residential square near to Broadcasting House. He also managed to get some money from the Ministry to pay for tools and seeds, since this endeavour was seen as excellent publicity for the Dig for Victory campaign. Hay became the expert advising a group of people who were novice gardeners but professional broadcasters, amongst them Raymond Glendenning, who commentated on the Derby and other major sporting events, and his secretary Sheilagh Millar, as well as Wynford Vaughan-Thomas, who was to become a well-known commentator and a highly regarded war correspondent, and Gilbert Harding, a very famous radio and television presenter after the war. All learned how to grow vegetables under Hay's tutelage.[32] There were even a few broadcasts from Roy Hay's kitchen in Baron's Court, when preserving produce or cooking vegetables was discussed, to the accompanying clatter of saucepans.

The live programmes went out for ten minutes every other Wednesday lunchtime, starting on 18 February 1942. They boxed and coxed with a feature on salvage or a classical music concert. They were repeated either on Friday evenings or Sunday mornings. Inevitably, the first programme was on the subject of double-digging. It is hard to imagine how the BBC personnel managed to make it sound interesting, but the programme called forth praise from an unlikely quarter, namely R. G. C. Nisbet of the Department of Agriculture for Scotland, who wrote to Roy Hay at the Ministry of Agriculture to congratulate him. The letter was sent on to Michael Standing with the note: 'The Scottish Department are well known grumblers and critics so you can imagine the receipt of this letter was heralded with cries of amazement from the Department here.'[33]

Other broadcasters who became involved in the programme from time to time included Stewart MacPherson, Frank More O'Ferrall and John Wynn Jones. They were always referred to as 'this amateur team', and the location was never identified beyond 'a London residential square'. Every fortnight throughout the growing season, these BBC employees could be found sowing broad beans, staking tomatoes or planting spring cabbages. It was all intensely practical, although there were opportunities for what we would now call banter.[34] As the plot was so close to Broadcasting House, it naturally attracted notice from other BBC people: 'advice, exhortation, criticism, admiration or contemptuous derision were hurled quite unsolicited by passing announcers, programme assistants, engineers and messengers . . . This friendly attention we accepted joyfully as a sign that the allotment was regarded with a degree of proprietary affection that we had never antici-pated.'[35] It is amusing to think of those clever, ambitious young people – careful not to be too flippant, on air at least – taking pleasure in the germination of the first peas, and developing their powers of description by talking about the taste of a radish or the precision of a well-hoed row; powers that they would later use, in Vaughan-Thomas's case, to commentate on a Lancaster night bombing raid and Princess Elizabeth's wedding, and in Michael Standing's case, to speak from the Normandy beaches on D-Day.

In 1943, Roy Hay left the Ministry of Agriculture and went to Malta to advise on food production. His place on *Radio Allotment* was taken by his father, Tom Hay, the retired Superintendent of the Royal Parks. Hay senior seems to have managed quite well, despite having a thick Scots accent and a tendency to mumble. In the summer of 1943, the BBC's Listener Research Department produced a report on the programme, which concluded that gardeners in Scotland, the north of England and the extreme south-west had such different growing conditions that much of the value of the programme was lost for them. Listeners were more likely to describe *Radio Allotment* as 'very helpful' than 'very entertaining', which in the context of vegetable gardening that has to be described rather than seen is scarcely surprising. Listener Research found that the programme was most helpful to novice gardeners, again not surprisingly, and that some people thought that the allotment was 'phoney'.[36] But it would be a remarkable programme that won universal praise.

In 1944, the Radio Allotmenteers even ventured a hook-up with the north of England, talking live to a Yorkshire allotment gardener in Leeds. This temporarily quietened the justifiable criticism that English gardening programmes mostly benefited listeners in the south. The programme was discontinued in 1945 because the BBC personnel became too busy to cultivate the allotment. But it says much for their commitment that they saw through the 1944 season, when there was so much happening in the war to take them away from London.

Although *In Your Garden* and *Radio Allotment* were the most popular gardening programmes, there were others, such as the five-minute *Over the Border* – which featured panels of experts in both Edinburgh and London – and *Backs to the Land,* which was broadcast every fortnight at lunchtime on Saturday, alternating with features such as 'Discussion on Rabbits', 'Talk for Beekeepers' and 'Pig Clubs'.

There were also some one-off transmissions: Roy Hay, for example, recorded a *Saturday Afternoon* programme in January 1942, entitled 'Digging for Victory in the East End', which was about Bethnal Green (see Chapter Three). There was even a humorous radio play, entitled *Digging for Victory*, by Lawrence du Garde Peach, which was scarcely disguised propaganda for government information leaflets and must have made for pretty unexciting listening. The immortal last lines were: 'Back to the land – and if you are able, contribute a sprout to the national table.'

The BBC broadcast one regular and high-quality schools programme, *Science and Gardening*. It was aimed at children of about thirteen years old and was hosted by two horticultural scientists called Keen and Lawrence. The programme mixed botany, plant physiology and practical horticulture. Since most schools cultivated gardens during the war, the audience was no doubt substantial, especially as it presented an opportunity to bunk off formal lessons.

Of course, broadcasters and gardening writers were no more free agents during the Second World War than anyone else, and their output was both dictated and circumscribed by the fact that at least three Ministries were extremely interested in conveying particular messages to the population. For reasons of circulation and ratings figures as well as for fear of censorship, they were also keen to accentuate the positive, or at least steer clear of the negative. It is small wonder, therefore, that worthy stories concerning blind people taking on allotments, children winning prizes at flower shows, or old age pensioners bicycling twenty miles to their allotment three times a week were often used as a counterbalance to dismal or downright alarming stories from home and abroad. The business of public relations was less sophisticated than it is now, but at least the Ministries could confidently expect the contents of their press releases to find their way into print and on to the wireless.

Nothing gives modern gardeners a keener sense of the gulf between then and now than reading gardening books and periodicals from this period. The advice on offer was severely practical and often couched in a homespun yet, at the same time, curiously pretentious style. Irony, which runs through modern journalism like a name through a stick of rock, is almost absent from these doggedly high-minded publications. That said, the information was clear and unequivocal and, most importantly, accurate, for almost all the writers had started life as professional gardeners, having trained at Kew or another horticultural establishment before becoming full-time writers.

Magazines included *Garden Work for Amateurs*, which was firmly aimed at beginners, *The Smallholder* ('The war food-growing weekly'), the very popular *Amateur Gardening* and *My Garden*. *My Garden* was the most upmarket publication, appealing especially to those garden owners who had employed gardening staff before the war. It was owned and edited by a well-known journalist, Theo A. Stephens, and was a small-format magazine with excellent black and white illustrations and sometimes even colour pictures. A number of first-rate amateur gardeners contributed to it, including Beverley Nichols, Eleanour Sinclair Rohde,[37] and even Captain W. E. Johns, author of the 'Biggles' books. Stephens recalled that the *My Garden* offices were next to those of *Popular Flying*, a magazine of which Johns was editor. When asked by Stephens whether he had ever written about his gardening experiences, Johns told him that he was tired of writing about flying and that it would be a pleasant recreation.[38] He wrote for *My Garden* from 1937 until the magazine folded in 1951, under the title 'The Passing Show'. *My Garden* could be rather whimsical and overwritten at times, but it supplied an otherwise unsatisfied need, since it catered for an educated readership of garden owners who had no intention of giving up their entire gardens to vegetables; indeed, the kitchen garden scarcely ever got a mention. Considering how bombarded on the subject gardeners generally were, this must have been something of a relief.

Expert amateurs as well as many professionals read the *Journal of the Royal Horticultural Society* and *The Gardeners' Chronicle*. However, these publications had a very small impact on ordinary gardeners, especially novices, who gleaned almost all their information either from listening to wireless programmes or from reading gardening columns in the popular press.[39] Of these, the most popular were those delivered or written by C. H. Middleton. According to a Ministry of Agriculture inquiry in 1942, 72 per cent of the sampled owners of wireless sets listened to gardening radio programmes; of these, 79 per cent tuned in to Middleton's programme *In Your Garden*, while 13 per cent listened to *Radio Allotment*, but only 4 per cent to Roy Hay's other programmes.[40]

What is more, of the 77 per cent of the sample who derived knowledge from newspaper columns, 21 per cent read Middleton in the *Daily Express*, which made him the most popular newspaper columnist as well. This is not at all surprising, since he was undoubtedly the best at it. He wrote as he spoke, naturally and without affectation, deploying a fund of hard-won knowledge and an attractive, self-deprecating humour. Unlike some of his contemporaries, he never assumed that he was always right, nor did everything go smoothly for him. He plainly did not mind being thought of as a 'character' – what man of head gardener stock would? – shown by the fact that a line drawing caricature of him, with his trademark curly-brimmed felt hat, detachable round collar and round spectacles, appeared on the page, together with a facsimile signature. Here are two examples of his approach:

Watched a man sowing peas the other day, and felt tempted to tell him he was doing it the wrong way, but I didn't. I did once venture a word of friendly advice to a stranger who was planting gladiolus corms upside down, but he said he preferred them that way and told me to mind my own business, so now I pass by and hold my peace. But about these peas . . .[41]

Reproducing a letter he had received, which ran, 'You tell me to dig up my lawn and grow food, the government shouts "Dig for Victory", but why should I, if it is only to put fat profits into the pockets of seed merchants? Do you think I am a perfect fool?' he replied: 'Well, no, I wouldn't go as far as that but I do think it is rather foolish to write such piffle without a little knowledge.'[42]

The *Daily Express* gave big money prizes to its readers: £1,000 in 1939 to the best allotment holder, who was then taken on to give tips every Saturday in the newspaper, and £5,200 in 1940 to the winner of the 'Grow More Food' competition. That strongly suggests that Lord Beaverbrook considered that Middleton's column sold newspapers.

Middleton also published a number of books, some of which were collections of his broadcast talks, such as *Mr Middleton Talks About Gardening*, which appeared in 1935, *Your Garden in War-Time* (1941) and *Digging for Victory* (1942). He also wrote *Colour All the Year in my Garden* (1938), and an encyclopaedia of gardening, *Mr Middleton Suggests* (1939).

Next in popularity for its gardening output was the *Sunday Express*, which disseminated information via a comic strip, although there was nothing remotely comic in the single-minded dedication with which 'Adam the Gardener' went about his tasks. 'Adam the Gardener' was written by Morley Adams, a man better known for his books of crosswords. Cyril Cowell, who illustrated the strip, made Adam consciously old-fashioned, even for the 1940s, by giving him a wraparound beard, a felt hat, and corduroy trousers 'yorked up' below the knee. This was presumably to reassure readers that he was experienced and knew that what he was doing was the right thing. Morley Adams was a journalist, and must have had some good sources amongst professional gardeners of the old school, for the practical information imparted so tersely by the illustrations and text was accurate, if sometimes dispiritingly perfectionist. On 5 May 1940, as German tanks rolled towards the Low Countries, the strip was entitled 'Beetroot, Bark-Ringing and Marrow'. In a few frames, Adam dealt with sowing maincrop long beetroot for use in the autumn, checking the rate of sap rise on apple and pear trees if they were growing too vigorously, and planting marrow seedlings on a compost heap.

Sometimes, the juxtaposition of his comic strip with national events was startling: on 23 June 1940, Adam the Gardener was blanching salad crops; on the same page, the government was appealing to the Empire 'to fight on to the final victory', just a few days after Winston Churchill's 'Finest Hour' speech.

Most of the other newspapers carried their own column of practical gardening advice: Albert Gurie in the *News Chronicle*, Richard Sudell in the *Daily Herald* and Percy Izzard in the *Daily Mail*. Although forgotten now, H. H. Thomas, the *Daily Telegraph* columnist, was a tremendous swell, since he was the son of Queen Victoria's head gardener, trained at Kew, and wrote thirty-two books, including *Making Love to Mother Earth* (1946), a title which did not immediately encourage the reader to conclude that it was an account of laying out a two-acre garden in Buckinghamshire.

Raymond Keene used humour in his approach to the subject in the *Sunday Pictorial*. He took on the persona of an 'old-timer' talking over the garden fence to a young neighbour called Robinson, and used excruciating puns to embed practical information in the minds of the readers: 'It is true he [Robinson] has dug trenches in Britain, planted mines in North Africa, and raised hell in the Ruhr, but back home again phlox to him were what shepherds watched at night; asters were merely millionaires.'[43]

There were also a number of unsigned columns in the Sunday national papers and the larger regional ones; these were written by people working in the MAF publicity division, who issued them weekly during the growing season. They were studiedly earnest, practical in content and often highly compressed. This unsigned comment in the *News of the World* in spring 1940 was almost certainly provided by the Ministry: 'Soot is fine stimulant for strawberry bed; also deters slugs.' Deathless prose it was not.

What was entirely missing in wartime was the kind of inspiring and intriguing gardening column by an established writer that was made popular by Vita Sackville-West[44] and Beverley Nichols in the decade after the war. And the range of topics covered by wartime writers was also rather narrow: there was little written about the design of gardens, about visiting those that had been designed or indeed about garden history.

Quite often, a gardening-orientated cartoon would appear in one or another of the newspapers, as for example that by Wyndham Robinson published in the *Sunday Express* on 19 May 1940, which depicted a little man in Home Guard uniform towered over by an enormous, menacing wife in a dress, next to a spade. The caption read: 'I'm off to Parashoot dear, YOU can dig for victory'.

Newspapers and magazines were very good at propagating gardening campaigns of a charitable nature; there was never any shortage of coverage of Red Cross initiatives, for example. In 1943, the Horticultural Committee of the Red Cross Agricultural Fund developed a scheme to increase the supply of onions to the armed services at home, the demand for which the Ministry of Food simply could not meet. The committee proposed that Onion Clubs be set up, and the scheme was well publicised in the RHS *Journal* and elsewhere.

It is suggested that each club should consist of 12 to 20 members who should aim at cultivating between them a quarter of an acre of Onions for sale to the NAAFI[45] or the contractors to the Admiralty, the proceeds going to the Red Cross. In some cases, instead of taking over new ground, a number of garden-owners may undertake to grow more onions than they need, and arrange for the surplus to be collected at a convenient centre in due course.'[46]

The Secretary of the National Allotments Society wrote to *The Times*, adding the Society's weight behind the campaign and suggesting that certificates or small prizes should be given by local allotment associations to the person who grew the most. 'If every allotment-holder in the country gave only 7 lb, 5,000 tons would be available for this worthy cause.'[47] These estimates of productivity were always unverifiable, but they were uncritically published and no doubt impressed the readers.

Like newspapers and magazines, books suffered seriously from paper and ink restrictions during the war, and they contracted in size as a result. Nevertheless, the innovative *Practical Gardening and Food Production in Pictures* (1940) by Richard Sudell contained a great number of black-and-white photographs as well as line drawings; it sold very well, both during the war and after it. Equally popular was *The Vegetable Garden Displayed*, which was to prove one of the greatest contributions that the Royal Horticultural Society made to the dissemination of information during the war. Published in 1941 and priced at a modest one shilling, this was the Society's most successful publication to date. Like Sudell's book, it had monochrome pictures, providing a step-by-step illustrated account of the tasks a conscientious vegetable gardener should undertake. The murky pictures, shot at the RHS gardens at Wisley, showed a variety of male gardeners, all wearing cloth caps and waistcoats, taking great pains to dig a straight celery trench, make a carrot clamp or sow peas in a drill. The important monthly tasks were enumerated, and there was a copy of the plan from the 'Growmore' Bulletin No. 1, to which RHS experts had of course contributed. Emphasis was laid on maximum productivity, using crop rotation, catch crops[48] and successional sowings. There were forewords by both Robert Hudson and Lord Woolton, setting the food Ministries' seal on the project. This publication went through eight impressions in the course of the war.

What is more, in an admirable and public sign of reconciliation, the book was translated into German and published in September 1947 under the title *Frisches Gemüse im ganzen Jahr* (*Fresh Vegetables All Year Round*). The German version contained the same photographs as the original one; the only changes concerned the varieties of vegetable recommended.

Wartime gardening books often started with a patriotic clarion call to arms, and then returned to their default position – a series of complex disquisitions on exactly how to double-dig, and all the remedies that should be employed in the battle against the garden's enemies. The prose was didactic and sometimes dour; substance mostly won over style. But at a time when most people acquired knowledge of new skills through the printed word and had little leisure, such books were invaluable.

A typical example was *War-time Gardening* by John Reed Wade, published in 1940. In the Foreword the author wrote: 'The effort of each individual gardener may be small; but when you think of the millions of gardens there are all over the country which could be changed over from the production of flowers to the much more practical production of vegetables and fruits, it will be understood how great and magnificent an effort for victory on the home front lies within the hands of those who own a garden.'[49] If garden owners felt reluctant or uncertain, it was not from want of expert encouragement.

Two female writers who added a definite sparkle to garden writing were Constance Spry and Eleanour Sinclair Rohde. Constance Spry had become famous in the 1930s for her innovative, relaxed style of flower arranging. However, her 'war work' was a cookery book aimed at garden-minded housewives who wanted to do interesting things with vegetables and make their rations go further; it was called *Come into the Garden, Cook*. This book had the signal virtues of being witty, well-written and original. It was almost certainly read in the main by middle-class house-wives trying to manage without the cooks they had employed in peacetime.

Eleanour Sinclair Rohde was an Oxford-educated historian, and her interest in kitchen produce was antiquarian as well as practical. She had been trained in the cultivation of medicinal herbs during the First World War, when there was the same shortage of drugs which was to dog the Ministry of Health in the Second World War (see Chapter Twelve). Mrs Rohde set up a nursery in Surrey and, during the war, employed Land Girls and prisoners of war to grow herbs and unusual plants. She was a prolific journalist and had also published a number of books on herbs and vegetables before the war, which were still in print. She continued to write books, including *Hay Box Cookery* (1939), *The Wartime Vegetable Garden* (1940), *Culinary and Salad Herbs* (1940) and *Uncommon Vegetables and Fruits* (1943). Although there is little evidence to suggest, as her *Times* obituarist did in 1950, that the mantle of Miss Gertrude Jekyll had fallen upon her, she was certainly influential, in particular reviving the idea of the herb garden, and raising the profile of vegetables and herbs amongst an educated readership. She was more of a practical and practising gardener than Constance Spry, and correspondingly less forth-right in her remarks. Like Mrs Spry, she had a very ready appreciation of what foods were good for you.

The Dig for Victory campaign would not have had much impact without the enthusiastic co-operation of the print and wireless media, but nor would it have reached such a wide audience were it not for the black-and-white Pathé Pictorial newsreels and short educational films made for the Ministry of Information by the Crown Film Unit and shown in cinemas.[50]

These films featured vegetable gardening, often with the message that gardeners should plan ahead if there was not to be 'want', especially in winter. There were longer films, too, such as the Ministry of Information's 'Dig for Victory', made in 1941 in conjunction with the RHS and featuring a commentary by Roy Hay, who had a pleasant, neutral speaking voice. 'Food is just as much a weapon of war as guns,' he told the audi-ence. This film was most informative on the subject of necessary practical operations, like planting leeks and lifting cabbages. It finished with the familiar refrain: 'Isn't an hour in the garden better than an hour in the queue?'

The Ministry of Agriculture made 'How to Dig' in 1941, again with a commentary by Roy Hay. This stupefyingly dull film was nevertheless extremely clear – and the digger was brilliant at his task. However, it is hard to imagine that it was popular with cinema audiences, who had no choice but to watch these public information films before the big feature was screened. Remarks like 'Thorough digging is essential to success in gardening' must have been enough to make their hearts sink.

However, there were obviously not enough gardeners doing their bit, because in 1942 the Ministry of Information released a perky cartoon entitled 'Filling the Gap'. It reminded viewers that twelve million hundredweight[51] of vegetables was imported before the war that could not now be imported, and continued: 'There are still too many lawns and flower gardens and vacant plots all over the country, which must be dug and must grow vegetables . . . Every bit of land must play its part or we shall go short . . . So put your garden on war service. If you haven't got a garden, go to your local council and ask for an allotment.' The film ended with the words, in block capitals, 'NEXT WINTER MAY BE A MATTER OF LIFE OR DEATH'. This shows how seriously the authorities viewed the impending food crisis of late 1942 and early 1943.

Often the short films were linked to published Ministry leaflets. One such was a cartoon entitled 'Blitz on Bugs', which featured a voiceover by C. H. Middleton: 'Tackle the pest, tackle him early. Dig for Victory leaflet no. 16 tells you how.'

One short film, entitled 'The Compost Heap', was made by a New Zealander, Margaret Thomson, who was the first female film director to work in Britain and who also made a number of educational films concerning children. 'The Compost Heap' was released in 1942, and showed very clearly how to make a four foot by three foot heap in the vegetable garden, as well as what to put on it and how to turn it.

Although cinemas were almost always urban places of entertainment, the regional offices of the Ministry of Information also arranged film showings in rural village halls and schoolrooms; where no electricity was available, a projector van could be hired, free of charge. What is more, a commercial concern, Plant Protection Ltd, which was owned by ICI and sold fertilisers and pesticides, commissioned a series of five silent, colour films on vegetable gardening which were offered free of charge to clubs, factories and offices, and came complete with screen, projector and someone to operate it. The series was entitled *A Garden Goes to War* with individual titles such as 'Spadework' and 'Odd Jobs in the Garden'. According to *The Gardeners' Chronicle*, 1,200 people – of what must have been a particularly captive audience – watched these films in an Ilford air-raid shelter at Christmas 1940.[52]

The National Allotments Society's annual report for 1941 congratulated the Ministry of Agriculture on their Dig for Victory campaign, which admittedly was nothing startling, since the Society did so without fail each year.

The Ministry of Agriculture and Fisheries have conducted this very successful campaign on 'two fronts' so to speak, firstly, that of publicity, and, secondly, that of practical advice.

Both branches of activity have been remarkably well done, so much so, that it has confounded the critics of Government methods.

The coloured posters and charts displayed have been so original and arresting as to arouse the interest of nearly every member of the community. The simplicity of their design, and the message and helpful advice which they convey, has struck the popular imagination and set the nation digging.[53]

The information poster certainly came into its own during the Second World War, becoming a powerful tool for disseminating advice, for motivating the population and for changing established habits of mind and action quickly and radically. A wartime poster's impact was immediate but fleeting, which meant it had to be clear, concise and unambiguous. On the other hand, by its nature, it lacked the wearisome verbosity of many of the information leaflets thought necessary by Ministries. And, particularly where subtle pictorial humour was deployed, as with Fougasse's seminal 'Careless Talk Costs Lives' posters, the results were images that lived on in the memory.

The Ministries of Agriculture, Food and Information, as well as the War Office, all engaged artists and graphic designers to design posters. Many of these turned out to be works of enduring quality and appeal. For artists, this war work was a life-saver. In late 1939, most were facing a crisis. Almost overnight people stopped buying paintings, since war conditions breed uncertainty and a loss of confidence on the part of those with the money to spend on art. Exhibitions became more difficult to stage and commercial art studios also suffered and were forced to lay off staff. Fortunately, artists found a champion in Sir Kenneth Clark,[54] who was Director of the National Gallery at the outbreak of war – as well as Director of the Film Division of the Ministry of Information. Gathering together old friends and colleagues, such as Paul Nash, Dame Laura Knight and Henry Moore, into a committee, Clark persuaded the Ministry of Information to fund the modest administration of what became known as the Central Institute of Art and Design, based at the National Gallery, whose task was to introduce potential artists to the appropriate ministry departments. The idea was that CIAD would 'act as a centre of information and as a clearing house on all matters relating to art and design and to diffuse such information in the interests of artists and designers'.[55] CIAD liaised with government committees, in particular the Ministry of Information's War Artists' Advisory Committee, ·also chaired by Clark. As it turned out, only a very few well-known artists, such as Edward Ardizzone and Sir Muirhead Bone, were given contracts and paid a salary. Most artists and cartoonists were only commissioned for specific projects.[56]

Without doubt, Abram Games was one of the most talented and successful of wartime poster artists. Of Polish-Jewish descent, he was born in the East End of London. After a brief period at art school, in 1932 he went to work for Askew Younge, a commercial art studio, but was sacked four years later for being unruly. He was told by his boss that he would never make a poster designer as he was not humble enough, to which Games replied: 'I am humble only before God.'[57] He became a freelance designer, eventually finding work from London Transport and the Co-operative Building Society. By the time he was conscripted in June 1940, at the age of twenty-six, twenty-four of his posters had been published.

Initially, Games was a private in the 54th Division, detailed to draw maps. However, in early 1941, his fortunes improved when the army decided it needed a professional designer to draw posters, and his name came first, alphabetically, on their list. He was interviewed by the public relations department at the War Office and made up to a corporal, and once he had retrieved his drawing instruments from the cellar of his bombed-out home in the East End, he set to work in an attic room at the War Office. By the end of the war he had designed one hundred information posters concerning many aspects of army life, from cleanliness to handling ordnance safely.

In 1942, he designed two posters with a horticultural theme, the aim being to inspire troops to grow vegetables in their camps. One shows a plot of cultivated land, with young green plants in rows, and a garden fork and spade standing upright holding up a table, above which they transform into a kitchen fork and knife. In between the cutlery is a plate of vegetables, a mug and an army cap. The caption reads: 'Every piece of available land must be cultivated. GROW YOUR OWN FOOD And supply your own cookhouse'. The other – 'Use Spades Not Ships – Grow Your Own Food' – depicts a gigantic oval garden spade above rows of greens on the left, joined with a ship's bow and funnel on the right, above a blue sea.

Games used unexpected colours and sharp lines to depict strange and memorable collisions of disparate ideas. His motto was 'maximum meaning, minimum means', and there is a clean spareness about his work which feels modern but which also harks back to Soviet Realism. He was particularly clever in his use of the mutation of forms, for example drawing a sword that gradually morphed into a paintbrush or indeed a spade turning into a ship's bow.

Games's daughter Naomi remembers him saying: 'I wind the spring and the public, in looking at the poster, will have that spring released in its mind. You have to involve the viewer in your thought processes. There will be an inevitable association between image and advertiser. Lettering, to be kept to the minimum, is never to be added as an afterthought.'[58] In 1948, Games wrote in the magazine *Art and Industry*, 'I felt strongly that the high purpose of the wartime posters was mainly responsible for their excellence.'[59] He continued to produce memorable images after the war, in particular the iconic Festival of Britain emblem.

Another poster artist, Hans Schleger, who worked under the name of Zéro, was also Jewish, but in this case a German refugee who had been naturalised in 1939. Two of his posters have a distinctly contemporary feel to them: one is a picture of potato rows with the word 'food' composed of vegetables and a large placard reading 'Grow Your Own'; the other shows a cabbage with a spoon and fork on top placed on a table, and the words 'Feed Right to Feel Right' printed as a heading on a newspaper close by.

More conventional in style, but no less memorable, is a poster devised by Peter Fraser of a smiling, pipe-smoking allotmenteer marching along a path with a garden fork over one shoulder, clutching vegetables in one hand and a trug of more vegetables in the other, with allotment sheds in the background. Since this poster was published late in the war, the slogan reads 'Dig on for Victory'. And who could resist the appeal of John Gilroy's grinning pig, with the strapline 'We Want Your Kitchen Waste', or Lewitt–Him's[60] poster advertising the 'Off the Ration' exhibition at London Zoo in October 1941, showing a kangaroo carrying carrots in one paw and a pig, a hen and a rabbit in her capacious pouch?

In April 1940, the artist Duncan Grant, who was a member of Kenneth Clark's committee, wrote to the Ministry of Information recommending that female artists should also be employed, on the grounds that they would give a different version of wartime life. He was pushing at an open door, because that month Evelyn Dunbar was commissioned to undertake six pictures of women's work, for a fee of fifty guineas.

Evelyn Dunbar was one of five women chosen by the War Artists' Advisory Committee (there were thirty men), but the only woman to be given six-month-long salaried commissions. She was born in 1906 in Rochester and studied at the Royal College of Art. She had developed an abiding interest in farming and gardening which served her well during the war, and made a modest name for herself in the 1930s, collaborating with others on a series of large-scale murals based on Aesop's fables at Brockley County School for Boys in Lewisham, London. She also illustrated *Gardeners' Choice*, a book describing forty garden plants, as well as the 1938 *Country Life* Gardeners' Diary.

From the start Dunbar made it clear to the MoI that she was particularly interested in agriculture and horticulture, so she spent much time recording the work of the Women's Land Army, in their many and various roles. Her pastoral pictures included *Milking Practice with Artificial Udders*, *Sprout Picking in Monmouthshire*, *Land Girls Pruning at East Malling* and *A Canning Demonstration*. This last depicted a group of ladies in hats, sitting in rows at one end of a cavernous village hall listening to a demonstrator explaining the finer points of fruit preservation. There is something both tender and wryly humorous in her treatment of the subject. Indeed, her images of a rural Britain at war have something of the neo-romanticism of Eric Ravilious or John Piper.

It was not only artists and graphic designers who were employed in recording and propaganda work; photographers were also considered vital for capturing the evanescent moment, whether it be Tommies making a brew in the Normandy *bocage* or a woman drinking tea amongst the rubble after a night of air raids. One of these was Cecil Beaton, the fashion and portrait photographer, whom the Ministry of Information employed from July 1940 as an official war photographer. He spent the war capturing images of the Home Front, as well as of troops in the Middle East, China, Burma and India.

In 1943, the MoI asked him to take pictures of the girls at work at the Waterperry School of Horticulture for Women (see Chapter Four). Although Beaton had worked for *Vogue* magazine before the war, he does not appear to want to make his subjects beautiful, but rather to capture something of their youthful earnestness, as well as a certain shy coquettishness, perhaps inevitable when sheltered young women found themselves under the keen scrutiny of an elegant and well-spoken man. Amongst the extant photographs is one of the Principal, Miss Beatrix Havergal, thinning glasshouse grapes with a forked twig and a pair of fine scissors, and another of her teaching her students to prune pear cordons on a wall. The image of the immaculate and productive kitchen garden, with its straight rows in strong diagonals, is almost painterly in its composition – and must have been the despair of any amateur allotmenteer who saw it. But the grimy hard work and grind is not glossed over: there are pictures of girls bent almost double as they 'thin' onions in a field and pick strawberries, or tackle the spraying of fruit trees without any kind of face or hand protection.

Undoubtedly the most famous horticultural image of the war was that of the left boot planted on the spade as it is just about to be pushed down into soil. This iconic picture, with its strong suggestion of Everyman, embodied in a tweedy leg ending in turn-ups and a stout and scruffy boot, under the words 'Dig for Victory', depends for its impact and appeal on its simplicity and purposefulness.

There are two separate stories concerning the origins of this image. For a long time it was thought that the boot belonged to a highly experienced and hard-working allotmenteer called William McKie, who was lauded in the *Acton Gazette* of 7 February 1941 under the headline 'The Man whose foot all the nation knows'.

However, there may be a stronger claimant to the boot, one Thomas Morgan Jones, who worked for Morgan–Wells, an advertising agency in Chancery Lane. He recalled sketching out a drawing for a photograph and then bringing tweed trousers, a pair of boots and a spade from his home in Sunbury-on-Thames, as well as some soil from nearby Lincoln's Inn Fields. The soil was placed on a board. A photographer called John Gill captured the image in the studio and added the sky later.[61] If you look closely at the image, you have a sense that the spade could not go further into the soil, or perhaps that is simply auto-suggestion. Whatever the truth of the origins of this image, it remains the most powerful visual symbol of the involvement of British gardeners in growing their own food in wartime.

CHAPTER SEVEN

THE OLD ORDER
CHANGETH

In the pages of *The Gardeners' Chronicle* for 6 January 1940, T. F. Tomalin, head gardener to the Earl of Bessborough at Stansted Park in Sussex, wrote – below a picture of a gent in a stiff collar, tie and a neat moustache – about the difficulties of growing indoor fruits in wartime: 'nearly all will try to carry on as best they can, and even though war-time crops may not reach peace-time perfection, *a work of national importance will have been achieved* [my italics] if our Vines and Fig trees, our Peaches and Cherries are maintained in health and vigour until normal conditions are re-established'.[1] As history was to show, this was the most wishful of thinking.[2]

The Gardeners' Chronicle gives us clues to the state of professional horticulture at the beginning of the war. Established in 1841, this weekly was traditionally where 'Situations Vacant' and 'Wanted' were advertised. The time-lag between requesting an advertisement and publication meant that in September 1939, readers were greeted with small ads like: 'G. T. W. Fitzwilliam, Esq., MFH, highly recommends his HEAD GARDENER. Life experience in all branches, glasshouses, flower gardens, kitchen gardens, lawns and pleasure grounds; also reconstructional work. Good controller and capable manager of large staffs . . .'[3] In those days, MFH was instantly recognisable as the acronym for Master of Foxhounds, indicating that this employer was a man of substance and respectability. There was nothing that pointed to G. T. W. Fitzwilliam, MFH, thinking that things would not go on much as they had done before.

But it was soon possible to see the impact of wider events both on organisations and on particular individuals. For example, in the 30 September edition, Lady Raphael of Hockley Sole, near Folkestone in Kent, announced that she was closing her estate and therefore recommending her forty-eight-year-old gardener for hire. On the advice of the government, Lady Raphael was leaving an area of the country later known as 'Bomb Alley'.

By the late September editions, there were classified advertisements from gardeners applying for jobs who were 'not liable for service in the Forces'. Such men would have been snapped up, since able-bodied gardeners in the Territorial Army and those between eighteen and twenty-one were eligible to be called up immediately, with journeymen, foremen and general hands 'reserved' only from the age of twenty-five. At the gardens at Ashburnham Place in Sussex, Harry Dodson,[4] a nineteen-year-old journeyman, remembered that several men did not arrive for work on Monday 4 September. He did not have long to wait himself; his own papers arrived in less than a fortnight.

Even those gardeners aged over twenty-five sometimes felt under moral pressure to join up immediately. A head gardener under whom I worked during the 1970s sourly recalled the first day of war when his employer told him that since all her sons had volunteered, she expected her gardeners to do so as well. In April 1940, the rules changed, with men required to register for service if they were aged anywhere between twenty and twenty-seven. Later that summer, even those actively involved in food production were eligible for call-up from the age of twenty-one.

If a gardener engaged in food production was particularly important to his employer, the latter could apply to the county War Ag committee for six months' postponement of the call-up while a replacement was found, and it was possible to go on applying every six months thereafter. In the case of well-connected employers, there was always the chance that 'pulling strings' might work. One correspondent to *The Times* in 1941 told how he persuaded the Westmorland War Ag that, as he had lifted all his roses and chrysanthemums and was growing vegetables and potatoes instead, together with tomatoes in his hothouses, and selling produce to fund his wife's knitting parties for the RAF, they should give him a certificate of reservation so that he could retain his gardener. He protested he used no 'influence' but the committee duly obliged.[5] However, in the end, most men under the age of forty-one, unless medically unfit for duty, were forced to leave their gardens. After all, although there was a good case for keeping home skilled men for efficient food production, especially of the all-important tomatoes,[6] making exceptions for them would not have gone down well with the general population.

Saying goodbye to someone who was off to join the services could be wrenching for both employer and employed. Captain W. E. Johns expressed what a lot of middle-aged employers who had been through 'the last show' must have felt:

George has gone to the war, cheerfully, but in his heart (I know) unwillingly. I was strangely moved as he walked down the road, for I know something of war,[7] and my imagination refused to visualize this boy, who tries not to tread on the worms when he digs, stabbing another man with a bayonet. It would be easier to imagine St Francis wringing the neck of a nightingale. Poor George. He doesn't even know what it's all about. He never will know, not even if he survives, for there is no hate in his heart and his thoughts run only in the drills and furrows that he makes in the soil. The fate of kings, of nations or empires means less to him than the well-being of his cabbages. Why should it? He has nothing to gain and all to lose in this senseless slaughter. Yet he has gone, gone with no more emotion than if he were going home from work – as he may be. For my conscience sake I must keep his garden tidy while he is away.[8]

Marjorie Williams ran a two-acre wartime market garden in Cornwall, selling her produce to a greengrocer in St Austell. She felt much like Johns when she finally said goodbye to her gardener, Ray Hawkridge, in May 1941. She had made a point of taking notes of all the jobs that they had done together, as well as how to maintain the Petter tractor engine.

Nevertheless my heart sank as the day drew near, and he became sadder and sadder. We shook hands in the evening outside the lower garage, and he walked away slowly, turning once before he rounded the bend. I confess I did then feel desolate, and as if, broad as my shoulders are, they were not broad enough for what they would now have to bear. I went into the empty garage, sat down with my head on the trestle table and wept.[9]

Fortunately, professional gardeners were accustomed to being shouted at, obeying orders without question, working in bad weather and filthy conditions, and living cheek by jowl with other young men. All of which must have made their transition to service life rather easier than for many an office-bred young man, straight from home.[10]

Meanwhile, the life they left behind in the mansion gardens, public parks and botanic gardens of Britain changed radically and almost instantaneously. The remaining gardeners had to parcel out the work in new ways, and a number of teenagers found themselves allocated tasks they would never have been allowed to do before the war. Percy Thrower's father, head gardener at Horwood House in Buckinghamshire, saw his labour force fall immediately from nineteen to three. On the last day of 1939, he died from a haemorrhage of the lungs, but his son believed that his death was caused as much by the heartbreak of seeing the gardens deteriorate rapidly in wartime.

The head gardener or parks superintendent had to hope that men who had recently retired would come back to offer their services, which in many instances they did. But practical horticulture takes its toll over a working lifetime, and a man of sixty-five or more could not be expected to have the strength or stamina of a young man of nineteen.

Some head gardeners were left to make their own decisions, if their employers went to live elsewhere. Those owners who stayed had to consider, together with their head gardeners, whether to register for food production. Deciding on this course meant that gardeners were obliged to devote 90 per cent of their time to the cultivation of foodstuffs, in particular high-value vegetables like lettuces and tomatoes, but it also meant a fuel allowance, and the materials to maintain and repair glasshouses. Professional men in private service, who had looked down on commercial operations all their working lives, believing their kind of gardening to be superior, soon found themselves planting out hundreds of tomato plants, where once there were orchids, and packing up produce once a week to be picked up by the lorries belonging to market gardening co-operatives.

In their mild distaste for commercialism, these gardeners found kindred spirits in their employers. When Muriel Green was undergoing her initial gardening training at Woodyates Manor in Wiltshire, she and the other girls were told to turn a rose garden into an onion plantation. 'We call it the "the onion bed",' she wrote, 'but Lady L[ucas] says it's to be known as "the old rose garden" to show what she has sacrificed I suppose.'[11]

Ann Gimson was aged seventeen in 1942 when she joined the Women's Land Army and went to work in the gardens belonging to the Earl of Radnor at Longford Castle, near Salisbury. The gardens were geared up for food production, but still seemed to exhibit many of the features of old pre-war estate gardening. In an interview long after the war,[12] she remembered vividly the uniform with which she was issued: brown breeches, green jersey, heavy brown shoes, an overcoat, dungarees, pale-coloured Aertex shirts, oilskin mackintosh, sou'wester, black Wellington boots and a green WLA armlet and hat, presented to her by the county Representative, Lady Hurd. She lodged with the other Land Girls in the village of Bodenham, and stayed there until the war ended. She felt she was badly paid; in particular she received no pay for overtime, despite long hours worked in the summer. At one point Lady Denman herself was forced to come from Sussex to arbitrate at a meeting between the employer and girls, where overtime rates were agreed.

The work was strenuous, and Miss Gimson was often wet and cold, but she enjoyed the variety unique to estate gardens.

> Sometimes [there were] days confined to the potting shed
> pricking out plants, potting and re-potting mature ones, wreath

making, washing pots or in the greenhouses tending tomato plants, disbudding chrysanthemums, pollinating peach trees, tying and thinning grape vines. And outside hoeing, layering strawberries, weeding and sorting onions, fruit picking with interminable hours of watering hundreds of potted plants both in the hot houses and outside . . .

We would often enjoy a luscious peach and nectarine and many an apple whilst gathering fruit for the Markets or for the Earl and Countess at The Castle, who, we felt sure, would forgive this naughtiness for they genuinely appeared to respect the work we Land Girls were doing in place of the menfolk. We were only once invited into the Castle, apart from our visits to present fruit and vegetables to the Butler in the kitchens, and this was to a Reception for all the workers after the second marriage of Lord Radnor . . .

It was strange to have Maize (Sweet Corn) growing in front of the Castle instead of the previous lawn and Italian Rose Garden. The Maize at this time was mainly to keep the American Troops happy who were stationed in the grounds before the English Boys.[13]

In September 1942, *The Gardeners' Chronicle* reported on the female gardeners' endeavours at the castle: 'Cabbages and Brussels sprouts are now growing in the centuries-old lawns and extensive herbaceous borders at Longford Castle, the Earl of Radnor's seat; five or six tons is the estimated yield of Onions planted in the famous sunken Italian garden near the Avon.'[14]

Apart from the move to food production, the other reason why the gardens changed so markedly and quickly was that, far more than was the case in the First World War, country houses were requisitioned by the authorities as bases for the services, as well as hospitals and convalescent homes. More than 3,000 establishments were taken over by the Ministry of Health alone. To avoid that fate, some owners invited evacuated boarding schools, or even businesses such as insurance companies, to occupy their premises. Rightly, it was thought that these would be less trouble. Boughton House in Northamptonshire hid treasures that belonged to the British Museum; part of the house at Ditchley Park became a nursery school for evacuees' children.

If a house was requisitioned by the government for use by the services, the professional gardeners that remained saw their precious lawns disappear under Nissen huts, conservatories shaded by temporary buildings, flower borders trampled and parkland trees cut down. They also had to put up with plenty of low-grade pilfering by the house's guests. On the other hand, they also sometimes acquired help from garden-minded soldiers or sailors, as well as a ready market for their produce. What is more, as many large gardens had been in all but name market garden operations before the war – because the houses had had large staffs and many visitors – the changeover to food production methods was not as dramatic as it might have been. And the gardeners did not lack for the skills required.

But it wasn't the same. How could it be? Harry Dodson, after he had been discharged from the army as medically unfit, worked at Leigh Park in Hampshire, which was a land naval base named HMS *Vernon*. He was 'second of six'[15] there, and his job was to produce fresh fruit and vegetables for the mess canteen. Because naval engineers tested mines in the pleasure grounds, these had to be kept in good condition, in case German spotter planes flew over; the garden needed to look like an ordinary private one, with bedding-out in front of the mansion, rose beds and mown lawns. In fact, a sharp-eyed German pilot might have found the manicured grounds suspicious. At other houses, gardeners grassed over the parterres, once colourful with annual flowers, so that enemy aircraft could not use them as markers. However, since they couldn't grass over the Big House, this seems more a symbolic than a useful gesture.

Professional gardeners were not slow to complain to the newspapers about the changes forced upon their precious gardens. One correspondent wrote to *The Gardeners' Chronicle* in July 1941:

. . . when one sees numbers of tents pitched and occupied by our troops, stretching almost throughout the whole length of some of our cherished herbaceous borders, one wishes that a larger number of our fighting men were plant lovers. Although the area in which these tents were pitched had been requisitioned, no intimation had been given that soldier-men were actually to live and sleep on masses of herbaceous and other plants. Nevertheless, one has to be philosophic and realize that this site was chosen because of the camouflage effect of the many shrubs and climbing Roses that form the background of the borders.[16]

The worst problems for the conscientious head gardener were undoubtedly the thoughtless damage and the shortage of labour, but there were plenty of other difficulties as well. Having to teach novices, and female novices at that, without extra remuneration for the training work they did was a sore point, as the letters page of *The Gardeners' Chronicle* bears witness.[17] And there was the problem of wages altogether. During the war, the agricultural labourer's wage rose by 90 per cent; gardeners were paid on the same scale. An under-gardener earned £1.14s. in 1939 and £3.10s. in 1945.[18] Yet head gardeners were often not given a rise but instead allowed by their employer to take commission on the sales of produce. This could be profitable, but it lacked the certainty of an uplift in basic salary.

More nebulous, but no less keenly felt by head gardeners, was the sense that standards were slipping badly. The rigorous and extended on-the-job training that they themselves had undergone could not be kept up in wartime. Gardeners were not slow to articulate their anxieties. As we saw in Chapter Three, they disliked the Ministry's first 'Food from the Garden' bulletin; behind their carefully worded letters to '*The Chron*' about it was a groan of pain. They were middle-aged men who had learned their craft from self-confident, opinionated Victorians, resplendent in frock coats and top hats. These men had impressed upon their apprentices the importance of constant care and attention to detail. Standards had inevitably declined during and just after the First World

War, but on some large country estates at least, 'the old ways', particularly in the kitchen garden, had been re-established by the early 1920s. Now, however, these professionals knew that things would change again, and probably this time for ever, but they still could not stop themselves from wanting the country to do 'a proper job'.

Ted Humphris felt the head gardener's burdens keenly. He worked at Aynhoe Park on the Northamptonshire/Oxfordshire border for thirty years from 1938, and is one of the few working gardeners to have left a published memoir of the time. The army took over part of the house, together with much of the pleasure grounds and parkland, so from 1 July 1940, at the instigation of his employer, Mr Cartwright, Humphris began to run the greenhouses and kitchen garden as a market garden, on his own account. For the first few months he had no help, except from his wife and his schoolboy son.

In the spring of 1941, Humphris managed to find a strong and willing teenage girl to help him, and 'during these difficult times she became invaluable to me'.[19] However, despite the extra pair of hands, he had to give up growing 'luxury' produce like asparagus and strawberries. The motor mower remained idle for lack of petrol, so only the grass immediately next to the house could be cut – with a hand mower. The rest was scythed twice a year. Even more irritating to him, 'the military were constantly erecting new buildings, and expanding their installations. Fruit trees were felled to make way for Nissen huts, flower borders and box hedges were swept away, and cook houses and petrol dumps took their place.'[20] The outer kitchen garden was staffed by military gardeners[21] to provide produce for their canteen, which must have been something of a relief to Humphris. On the other hand, the long lean-to greenhouse where he grew glasshouse fruit and tomatoes was constantly being broken into and the fruit stolen. So he removed the peach trees and invited the army personnel to grow their own (guarded) tomatoes.

His situation was not always to be pitied.

I found another market for my produce, supplying fruit and vegetables to the officers' and sergeants' messes whenever possible. In addition I often supplied boxes of fruit to soldiers who were going home on leave, and these were made up of grapes, peaches, nectarines, various coloured plums, as well as apples, pears, and tomatoes. I was assured that these parcels were most welcome, and I received many repeat orders.'[22]

He also sold produce to the general public on two evenings a week.

In 1945, when Harry Dodson left HMS *Vernon* and moved to Nuneham Park in Oxfordshire, the house there was still occupied by the Forces, and he had to think laterally to secure the maximum produce from the space available:

There was a very long peach house and the trees were planted *across* the house instead of in borders up the sides. This meant that the peach trees were smaller than conventionally planted ones would have been, but you did get a space of about 9ft between each tree and those spaces took first a crop of radishes, lettuce and carrots and, when these were cleared, tomatoes. You could get three rows of tomatoes, five plants to a row. They were treated as a cold house crop and came into bear in late July with a full crop during August and early September. The peaches were left there undisturbed and there was a ready market for both peaches and tomatoes in Oxford.[23]

All four of Nuneham's large vineries lost their vines, and were turned over entirely to tomato crops, but the gardeners somehow also managed to grow 1,000 autumn chrysanthemums, which were bought by Oxford colleges and the smart Randolph Hotel.[24]

At Lulworth Castle in Dorset, peaches, grapes and rhubarb were grown and 'almost any price was paid for them. I am afraid that, even here, [the] black market flourished, but has it not been going on since Adam was a gardener?'[25] A tantalising comment from Harry Fox, who did not elaborate further.[26]

Although the vast majority of estates went over to food production, abandoning most of their pre-war decorative work as a result, at Levens Hall in Westmorland, F. C. King was given a special allocation of petrol so that the famous topiary yews could be cut each year with petrol-driven hedge clippers. Since most of these eccentric trees had been in the garden since the very beginning of the eighteenth century, they were considered of national importance. On the other hand, he dug up the bowling green for food production, only to discover that it was so well drained, thanks to clinker at the base, that it did not grow good vegetables.

If one large country house exemplifies the enormous impact the war had on such establishments and their gardeners it is Ditchley Park in Oxfordshire (see Chapter One). Ditchley's honoured place in our wartime island story came about as the result of the political position of its owner, Ronald Tree, who was by then Parliamentary Private Secretary to the Minister of Information. In November 1940, Tree was summoned to meet Winston Churchill in his room in the House of Commons, where the Prime Minister invited himself to stay for weekends at Ditchley. This was to be, as he put it, 'when the moon is high', in other words when it was thought too dangerous for him to stay at Chequers in Buckinghamshire, in case the German bomber pilots knew the whereabouts of his country residence. Three days later, Churchill arrived with a platoon of soldiers as guards, and his staff. In all, he stayed at Ditchley Park on thirteen 'Fridays-to-Mondays' between November 1940 and September 1942. As a result, Ditchley Park and the Trees – already politically and socially well connected, with friends like Anthony Eden, Minister of War, and relatives like Nancy Astor, the first female MP in the House of Commons – found themselves right in the centre of the national struggle.

Much later, Nancy Tree recalled those days: 'Ditchley never skipped a beat with Winston there. He was a very easy guest. We still had our servants in the first year of the war, and the house was run as I always ran it. The schedule never changed.'[27] There are some remarkable photographs of that period, notably of Winston Churchill staring at a grass snake on the lawn, with the tripod mount for an ack-ack gun behind him; even more extraordinary is the picture of Air Marshal Sir Charles Portal standing in the Jellicoe parterre wearing a large floppy hat, with a hoe in his hand.[28] Truly a Churchillian moment, when affairs of state and gardening collided.[29] However, that very particular interlude only delayed at Ditchley what was happening everywhere else. In the later years of the war, the Trees lost their gardening staff to the forces, and had to rely instead on those too old or young to fight.

Youth is the reason why fourteen-year-old Harry Fox secured a job in 1941 as a garden boy in the old walled gardens at Lulworth Castle in Dorset. Years later he recalled:

> There were two walled gardens of an acre each and filled with long ranges of Peach Houses and Vineries. . . . The remnants of the past were everywhere . . . Bell cloches of every size, lantern handlights, copper fumigators, brass syringes, massively heavy cold frame lights with scores of little panes of glass in them and the old worm-eaten handles of the implements of torture, the spades worn down and still shiny, the hose worn to a thin piece of sharp steel and that very heavy oak wheelbarrow with no 'stop' over the wheel when it would come back over one's feet when one tipped it up too far . . . During the 2nd World War the old garden regime had passed quietly away, unnoticed, with the gentle dignity that gardening was made of. The lawns, once proud, were dug over and the 'taties' and Brassicas replaced them . . . We were not officially supposed to grow flowers where vegetables could be grown but we always managed a few pots of chrysanths for Christmas and in Springtime we raided the woods for bunches of Snowdrops and Lent Lilies.[30]

Although estate gardens were mainly staffed by adolescents, women and middle-aged or elderly men, conscientious objectors (otherwise known as 'pacifists' or, sneeringly, 'conchies') also sometimes filled the gaps made by conscription, since it was war work with which they could not possibly disagree. It is also likely that the authorities thought that they could not infect many others with their views if they were stuck in lonely, unpopulated places. A conscientious objector who responded to the Mass-Observation Directive on Rationing in 1943, wrote: 'My job as a market gardener is tolerable but I shall be glad when I can change to something quite different. It is healthy and interesting up to a point, but there is a lot of monotonous drudgery.'[31]

The Royal Horticultural Society's gardens at Wisley did not escape the changes. Most men, both gardeners and scientific advisers, were called up, and, as elsewhere, the shortfall was addressed by recruiting women and older men. The flower trials work, which had been a feature of the gardens at Wisley ever since they were given to the Society, was abandoned – apart from the long-term trials of shrubs – in favour of vegetables. The area known as Battleston Hill had been bought to extend the gardens in 1938 and was intended as a trial ground for rhododendrons, but potatoes also grew there throughout the war. The gardeners at Wisley also carried out seed germination tests on the seed imported from the US under the Lend-Lease agreement, on behalf of the Ministry of Agriculture.

Although the Royal Botanic Gardens at Kew closed its gates on the outbreak of war in order to construct air raid shelters and arrange for evacuating the most valuable of the botanical collections, they were opened again by the end of September, and remained open during the rest of the war, even after garden buildings sustained bomb damage. The entry fee was only 1d, so the Gardens' 300 acres were a particularly valued recreational space for hard-pressed Londoners. Indeed, visitor numbers went up during these years.

Mrs Waller, a Swanley-trained gardener who went to work at Kew early in 1941, recalled that the salary was 45s. a week, out of which she paid 25s. for her board and lodging. When she arrived, she was issued with a navy blue apron and leather clogs. 'These were very cumbersome as they had wooden soles and horseshoe-like metal attached to the soles.'[32] The stores at Kew were still issuing these clogs when I arrived as a student in 1976, and, like Mrs Waller, I found them invaluable in the hothouses, when 'damping down' with a hose, because they did not slip in the wet like Wellington boots. What is more, because they were wooden, they were warmer when one stood on a concrete floor to pot up plants.

These clogs received a mention in the *Journal of the Kew Guild*:

Women gardeners have come to Kew once more after an interval of nearly a quarter of a century, and though the costume has changed considerably, the fashion in clogs remains the same . . . They [women] are employed in the Propagating Pits, Decorative Department, Flower and Rock Gardens, and in certain sections of the Tropical Department, where they can each apply their own particular experience, and by endeavouring to set up a high standard of work, disprove the saying for all time that *Nepeta Mussinii*[catmint] is the only plant a woman can't kill.[33]

Presumably to take the sting out of his words, the correspondent went on magnanimously to concede: 'In fact, the Kew women gardeners are now part of the Kew landscape.'[34]

By 1942, many of the flower beds and hothouses were producing 'hundreds of tons'[35] of hardy and tender vegetables and fruit, and were mainly tended by female gardeners.

Because of Kew's vulnerable position in the south-west suburbs of London, bombs fell on the gardens from time to time. During the night of 24/25 September 1940, windows were shattered in the Herbarium and Library, and in 1941 a stick of bombs fell near the Pagoda but did no damage. By a rich irony, holes had already been drilled in each of the ten floors of the 163-foot-tall Pagoda so that designers from the Royal Aircraft Establishment nearby could study the flight of bombs that they dropped. One night, thirty high-explosive bombs broke a lot of glass in the Temperate House and Palm House. The Tropical Water Lily House was badly damaged, as was the stableman's house, although there were no serious injuries. '. . . one of the stokers . . . was stoking under the Palm House [where the heating boilers were] when bombs fell nearby and the crashing of broken glass was a horrendous noise above him'.[36] There are 700 panes of glass in the Palm House, and they are curved; it must have been the devil of a job to replace them.

In late 1940, Sir Arthur Hill, the Director of the Gardens, had taken the precaution of overseeing the evacuation of many of the valuable books in Kew's library to a store in the basement of the New Bodleian Library in Oxford. One third of the irreplaceable herbarium collection – dried specimens of plants from all over the world – also went to Oxford. Professor Osborn, the Sherardian Professor of Botany at the university, saw to it that Kew botanists could use rooms at Yardley Lodge, and one of these botanists, Dr Turrill, took care of the material. In January 1941, another third of the collection went to two houses in Gloucestershire – Colesbourne Park and Cliffordine House – but some specimens moved from Colesbourne to the rectory at nearby Daglingworth later in the year. The Wallich Herbarium and other collections were lodged for the duration in Tring Museum.

Meanwhile, the Director and his depleted staff in the Jodrell Laboratory, led by Dr Metcalfe, were busy on a variety of war-related research projects, most particularly focusing on nettles (see Chapter Twelve).

As we have already seen, parks superintendents had a very busy war: they sat on War Ag committees, created model allotments, liaised with local allotment societies, gave talks and demonstrations, and helped to organise Dig for Victory 'weeks' and exhibitions. They also sometimes oversaw cultural events in their parks, such as bandstand concerts, circuses and other summertime entertainments. Urban parks generally were well-used during the war since, for a variety of reasons, most people decided to spend their holidays at home. Open-air entertainments were popular: in Victoria Park in east London, Sadler's Wells Ballet gave eight performances in 1942 and there was open-air dancing on VE night.[37]

At the same time, parks superintendents had to try to ensure, despite a much reduced, often rather elderly labour force, that the open spaces, including golf courses, in their area were maintained properly or, alternatively, ploughed up for growing crops. Many men did sterling work in difficult circumstances, making sure, for example, that model allotments were manned at weekends to give the public expert information. According to the *Journal of Park Administration* in 1941, 'In Queen's Park, Manchester, a 120-foot long, 6 feet wide flower border changed to a salad bed, filled with chives, onions, spinach beet, Swiss chard and endive.'[38]

In the parks of large cities, superintendents also had to negotiate the installation of a range of military equipment, from air raid and trench shelters to barrage balloon sites and anti-aircraft batteries. If in the way, mature trees were cut down by park staff. In Victoria Park, the lido swimming pool was used to supply the Fire Service with 65,000 gallons of water.

Most parks lost their railings in 1943 to the Ministry of Supply, to be melted down for industrial purposes. In Battersea Park, for example, forty tons of railings were removed. This exacerbated the already thorny problem of night-time trespassers and sleepers, which had become an issue in many parks in 1940, after the decision was made that gates should remain unlocked so that parks could be sanctuaries in case of air raids. Damage to park buildings, benches, plantings – even wildlife – had resulted. The superintendent of Victoria Park in Portsmouth, who wrote for *The Gardeners' Chronicle* under the pseudonym Pompey, despaired: 'I sometimes wonder if the death-knell has not been rung on ornamental gardening in public parks . . . unless there is a great improvement in the behaviour of those who visit the parks, and for whom they are provided, it will not be possible to regain the high standard of floral displays to which we are accustomed.'[39]

A full year before the war started, the Ministry of Agriculture consulted the Bailiff of the Royal Parks in London, F. E. Carter, about the possibility of cultivating parts of the parks for growing food in the event of war. The Ministry considered that 'it should prove most valuable from the propaganda point of view, if it were possible for the Office of Works to arrange for tractor ploughs and cultivators to be at work in the parks immediately war is declared . . . It appears that Mr Carter has already drawn up a scheme under which the flower beds in the parks would be planted, say, with potatoes and the glass-houses devoted to tomato growing . . .'[40] This was only a continuation of what had happened during the First World War, of course, when food had been grown in large areas of the Royal Parks.

On 12 September 1939, the Office of Works gave the go-ahead for Bushy Park and Hampton Court Park to be ploughed up. The Ministry of Information film section was alerted, as were five newsreel companies, including Pathé and British Movietone News. Two Land Girls were recruited, and their travel expenses authorised, but in the end, film was only taken of the tractor-driver. History does not relate what happened to the Land Girls. A press release a month later was entitled 'Ploughing up Bushey [sic] Park. Land that has been Grass since Napoleon's Day.' The following summer, 120 acres of Hampton Court Park also went under the plough, for wheat, potatoes and vegetables.

Two innovations peculiar to wartime made an impact on the general population, and thus also on professional and amateur gardeners. One of these was 'double summer time', when the clocks were moved two hours ahead of Greenwich Mean Time. This had the effect of making evenings lighter for longer, achieved by not putting back the clocks an hour in the autumn of 1940. British Double Summer Time remained in place until 1945.

The other aspect of wartime conditions that affected gardeners and farmers particularly was the complete absence of weather forecasts, either on the radio or in the newspapers. Weather forecasts were cancelled abruptly on 5 September 1939, on the grounds that they might give aid to Britain's enemies; they were not reinstated until 2 April 1945. Radio gardeners like Mr Middleton had to be very careful what they said about the weather, and ordinary gardeners had to learn once more their forefathers' skill in reading the cloud formations, or otherwise rely on a number of unreliable folk sayings. It was just one more irritation about which they had to be stoical.

Whatever the tiresome exigencies under which professional gardeners laboured in wartime, none had such a hard time of it as the 600 British-born gardeners working in the 2,400 or so cemeteries which had been laid out by the Imperial War Graves Commission at the end of the First World War in France and Belgium. Indeed, many of these men had been combatants in the Great War and had stayed on to tend the graves of their comrades, often marrying local girls and settling down to spend, as they thought, their whole working lives on the Continent. Approximately eighty other IWGC staff, mostly office workers, were based in the two countries.

Sir Fabian Ware, the Vice-Chairman of the Imperial War Graves Commission, had persuaded the French authorities to give these gardeners special status as civilians, which meant that if war came to France, they would be entitled to French rations and could carry on working. Only one cemetery, close to the Maginot Line, was abandoned in 1939. This situation continued until the Blitzkrieg in May 1940 and the invasion of the Low Countries on 10 May. According to Philip Longworth, the historian of the Imperial War Graves Commission, 'Within a month the organization in France as well as Belgium had crumbled, the work of a generation abandoned to the enemy.'[41]

The Commission in London was slow to see the potential danger to their staff, and it was left to the men at the headquarters at Wimereux, near Boulogne in northern France, to activate what contingency plans were in place. The staff were told to stay where they were unless or until ordered to evacuate by the French civilian authorities. Meanwhile, Captain Haworth, who was in charge in Belgium, was ordered to gather together the men with their families and await transport to take them over the border, so that they could entrain for Cherbourg. On 18 May, about 200 people assembled in the yard of the British School in Ypres, but only one bus turned up, along with some cars, so those men without families were told to ride bicycles, and some of them managed to board a ship at Boulogne. The refugee train to Cherbourg did not materialise, so Haworth borrowed a couple of buses from the British Army, only for his charges to be dumped by the side of the road in St Omer when the army needed the buses back. Eventually, a lorry and some cars transported them to Calais, and on 23 May, now 240 strong, they boarded *The City of Christchurch*, bound for Southampton, as the port was shelled by German bombers.

Twice, on 16 and 17 May, Captain Melles at Arras in France had contacted the headquarters at Wimereux to ask for permission to evacuate all his staff, and twice he had been refused. He had been told to await the general order to evacuate, but there was by now so much confusion and panic in northern France that no such order was ever given. It was not until 21 May that the Commission in London thought the situation 'alarming'. Even on the 29th, they were assuming that 'a nucleus of staff' would continue to work in accessible cemeteries. Melles managed to get some men and their dependants away to Fougères, and thence to Cherbourg, and others made their way to a rendezvous in Rouen, and then on trains to the same port. Lone bids for safety were very difficult since the roads were jammed with refugees, there was often no available food and there was widespread rumour-driven panic. Some men left their dependants behind; others stayed at their posts and did not attempt to escape. The last ones arrived at Southampton on 6 June. Of the 540 Commission employees in France and Belgium in May 1940, 334 made it safely back to England.

The men and their families who arrived in England were exhausted, hungry, demoralised and mostly destitute, and the Commission had swiftly to summon up charitable help for them. In the next three weeks, the staff processed more than 400 men, women and children. The next task was to find the men paid horticultural work. This turned out to be relatively straightforward: the IWGC had a useful contact in Colonel Durham, Secretary of the Royal Horticultural Society, who had previously been Director of Works for the Commission; while the staff at the Royal Botanic Gardens, Kew, had for many years given expert advice to the Commission's Horticultural Director. The Commission also wrote to 200 town clerks, the National Farmers' Union, the Association of Cemetery Superintendents and a variety of landowners. Within two months most men had been offered gardening jobs. Indeed, four of them proved extremely useful in replacing conscripted gardeners at the RHS gardens at Wisley.

Not for a long time did the Commission discover what had happened to the 206 employees who failed to make it to England, but by March

1942 they had established that eleven men were dead or unaccounted for, 159 had been interned and there were thirty-six at liberty, mainly because they claimed citizenship of Eire, and were therefore neutral.[42] One Irishman, Robert Armstrong, a former Irish Guardsman who tended the cemetery in Valenciennes, helped a number of Allied POWs to escape from France, but was arrested by the Gestapo in 1943. Although his death sentence was commuted to fifteen years in prison, he died in Waldheim concentration camp in 1944. There is a memorial to him in the British war cemetery at Valenciennes.

Several gardeners died in European internment camps, and some internees expressed bitterness towards the Commission, which they held responsible for their parlous situation. However, others turned their captivity to good account, taking the opportunity to study for the Royal Horticultural Society's exams.

Professional gardeners, in both private establishments and commercial concerns, as well as the millions of amateurs, benefited from the work done in wartime by the horticultural research stations to find ways to increase yields of edible produce. One of the most distinguished of these establishments was the John Innes Horticultural Institution[43] (JIHI) in Merton, Surrey. The institution had been set up in this southern suburb of London in 1910 as a result of a legacy bequeathed by John Innes, a wealthy squire and businessman who lived at the Manor House, Merton Park. When he died in 1904, he left his house, land and money to found a public museum, research establishment or a school of horticulture.

When the Institution opened on 1 January 1910, its first Director was William Bateson, until then Professor of Biology at Cambridge. Bateson introduced Gregor Mendel's pioneering work on the principles of inheritance to Britain, and was the man who invented the term 'genetics'. The following year, a student gardener scheme was founded. The board of the JIHI interpreted its benefactor's wishes quite liberally and the Institution became well known for its pioneering work on both genetics and the study of plant cells (cytology), as well as the breeding of improved fruit varieties and the study of genetically controlled incompatibility mechanisms[44] between fruit varieties. A tetraploid[45] blackberry called 'John Innes' went on sale in 1934, while 'Merton Thornless' – which is still widely in cultivation today – was released in 1941. The Institution was led in wartime by a well-regarded cytologist, Cyril Darlington, who undertook pioneering work on cell structure, and became Director on the retirement of the agricultural scientist, Sir Daniel Hall,[46] in 1939.

For wartime gardeners and commercial growers, the most important research work to be conducted at the JIHI was on potting composts and was carried out during the 1930s by the remarkable W. J. C. Lawrence (see Chapter Five). Lawrence had begun his working career at Merton in 1913 as a fourteen-year-old boy when his doctor advised outdoor work, for the simple reason that his eyesight was too bad for office work. He started as an unpaid garden boy, worked his way up to sub-foreman, then moved to Kew as a student gardener. After the First World War, he came back to Merton to work as a technical assistant to Morley Crane, who carried out research on fruit breeding and also studied the genetics of colour pigmentation in dahlias. Rather unexpectedly, and not entirely to Lawrence's satisfaction, Sir Daniel Hall asked him to become the Institution's gardens curator in 1932, at a time when the gardens were rather neglected and in need of taking in hand. As a salve to Lawrence's pride, Hall promised him that he could continue working on the genetics of colour pigmentation in *Streptocarpus* (Cape primrose). He might be running the gardens, but he could not quite tear himself away from research.

As it turned out, Lawrence's greatest contribution to the war effort was initiated almost by chance. In 1933, some important genetics research work on *Primula sinensis* had to be entirely scrapped because three quarters of the seedlings died from wilt disease. This prompted Lawrence and his assistant, John Newell, to begin a series of trials on seed and potting compost mixtures, in order to try to discover whether they could find more reliable media in which to germinate and grow on seedlings.

When Lawrence became gardens curator, he had found a long list of potting composts suitable for particular plants stuck on a wall in the potting shed. Like so many other gardening establishments, the Institution used time-honoured but completely unscientific recipes for potting composts, which often succeeded because of the amenability of the plant being potted rather than from their intrinsic efficacy. These composts were based on a mixture of loam, leaf mould, sand and often also lime mortar rubble. The fertiliser added was usually bonemeal, but could be anything the head gardener had in the potting shed, so that the mixture was often unbalanced, and growth then was either too 'hard' or too 'soft'. The loam used was unsterilised, which meant that often two or three times as many seeds had to be sown as seedlings needed, because of the likelihood of death from 'damping-off' or another soil-borne disease. The composts also grew weeds.

At the same time, and in connection with this, Lawrence and Newell worked on methods of steam sterilisation to try to obviate these problems. They wanted to produce a standardised compost that would work better than any existing mixture.

It took several years of meticulous trialling before the two men developed formulae that they believed would reliably give optimum results. The biggest breakthrough came when Lawrence discovered that adding superphosphate to the compost would counter the nutrient deficiency caused by steam-sterilising the soil. They also discovered that only the loam needed sterilising, since sphagnum moss peat – which they preferred to leaf mould for its better porosity and water-retaining properties – is naturally sterile.

Lawrence wrote later that their experiments 'were made with no instruments other than a borrowed pH meter and a thermometer for measuring the temperature of soil while it was being sterilised. The appeal was to the plant. Did it grow better or worse? The answer was decisive. It grew best in the new composts!'[47]

By 1935, Lawrence had also worked out the optimum amount of fertiliser – sulphate of ammonia together with 'hoof and horn' – to add to the potting compost. At that point, he began to use one seed compost and one potting compost at the Institution; the results were a resounding success, at least as far as primulas were concerned.

He and Newell then experimented with growing other plant types in these composts. Detailed trialling revealed that the composts were suitable for at least 130 different kinds of plant, from alpines to tropical species. By 1938, they were able to publish formulae for a seed compost, which could also be used for striking softwood cuttings, together with three potting composts, distinguished from each other by a single, double or triple amount of the base fertiliser. The ratio of loam to peat to sand was 2:1:1 for the seed compost, and 7:3:2 for the potting composts – formulae that have remained the same to this day. The Institution did not patent the formulas. Fertiliser companies such as the stylishly named Ichthemic Guano Co.[48] manufactured the composts from 1939 onwards. They quickly became known simply as the John Innes composts, and they rapidly put an end to unstandardised, individual mixtures devised by gardeners, that had been at best wasteful and at worst disastrous.[49]

Neither Lawrence nor the John Innes Horticultural Institution made any money out of the discoveries, but they earned the gratitude of countless professional and amateur gardeners for decades to come. The composts were also important for the success of commercial plant production during the war, since they almost eliminated waste and the risk of failed crops. Moreover, they proved that it was necessary, rather than simply desirable, for horticultural practices to be tested scientifically. In the years after the war, when the labour force declined so rapidly, this was to prove crucial for what success commercial horticulture enjoyed.

The immediate impact of these composts might have been enough for many men, but not for the ever-enquiring Lawrence, who went on to conduct a number of other trials in pursuit of more efficient food production. For example, he investigated whether early 'pricking-out' resulted in better and faster growth, especially as far as tomatoes[50] were concerned. He discovered that early pricking-out produced sturdier, more precocious plants that fruited earlier. He also exploded the myth[51] that pot plants in glasshouses had to be planted into warm, rather than cold, soil or compost and watered with lukewarm, rather than cold, water, lest they suffer a check from the shock. He discovered that cold soil and water made absolutely no difference to the growth of pot plants.

However, even more important was his discovery in December 1943 that standard north–south-orientated glasshouses allowed in only 52 per cent of the available light from outside, but that this rose to 70 per cent if glasshouses were facing east–west, thereby also gaining in heat retention by 5 per cent. After the war had ended, these discoveries caused him to design glasshouses with larger panes of glass. He wrote an influential work, *Science and the Glasshouse*, on the subject, which was published in 1948.

When the blackout regulations were lifted completely in April 1945, Lawrence began investigating the possibilities of installing artificial lighting in glasshouses to promote or alter plant growth for commercial purposes. By switching on lamps attached to the rafters of the greenhouse for set periods of the night, it was found possible to manipulate the timing of flowering. This was to have great benefits for post-war chrysanthemum and poinsettia growers.

Perhaps because of his particular experience, Lawrence understood better than most the importance of disseminating the results of research work, and that included communicating with growers in a language they could understand. During the 1930s, the relationship between commercial concerns and the horticultural research stations was surprisingly remote and detached. Until the war, scientists rarely met nurserymen or vice versa. That situation was to change, albeit slowly, during the period of hostilities, as both sides recognised that increased food production required a much fuller exchange of ideas.

As a result, Lawrence regularly published his findings in popular horticultural journals such as *The Gardeners' Chronicle*. He was fully supported in this by the Institution's wartime director, Cyril Darlington, who encouraged him in the writing of a number of leaflets and bulletins, aimed at both professional growers and amateur gardeners, as well as writing some himself. All of these bulletins were based on articles originally published in scientific or horticultural journals, but simplified sufficiently to suit a wide audience. They were: 1. John Innes Composts; 2. Soil Sterilisation for Pot Plants; 3. The Soil Steriliser[52]; 4. The Fertility

Rules in Fruit Planting; 5. Growing Tomatoes out of Doors; 6. Soil Ingredients of the Composts.[53] The Fertility Rules in Fruit Planting took advantage of John Innes research into the genetics of incompatibility in fruit varieties, information that gardeners and commercial growers still use today when planning orchard plantings. Growing tomatoes out of doors was a subject dear to amateur gardeners' hearts that benefited from wartime research at Merton Park.

Sixty-two thousand leaflets were sold at 6d each during the course of the war, and they went through several editions. As Darlington said, in an interview conducted in 1979:[54]

> When war began, my immediate special interest was to publish
> the information that we had that would be an advantage to food
> production . . . The Ministry of Agriculture wouldn't publish
> [the leaflets] because, naturally really, the Ministry of Agriculture
> at that time was strongly averse to any research[55]. . . particularly
> anything outside itself . . . so we published it ourselves.[56]

Wartime exigencies had caused at least one research station to abandon its ivory tower, and find that it didn't miss it.

Young school leavers and female gardeners replaced those called up, and the Institution reduced the burden of garden work by substituting the growing of food crops for some of the experimental work. The geneticists worked instead on raising hybrid tomato and other seed that yielded well, as well as producing tomato and cucumber seed for Carter and Sons.

Of course, the John Innes Horticultural Institution was hardly immune from wartime measures, especially since Merton, on the south-western edge of London and home to the Lines Brothers factory, was an obvious target for German bombers. Lines Brothers had been a famous toy business, using the trademark Tri-ang, but had switched to munitions manufacture when the war started. Most of the scientists and gardeners who were able to stay at Merton inevitably became involved in air-raid precaution duties. Four shelters were built in the grounds, and those books in the library considered irreplaceable were sent to Lord Wandsworth School at Long Sutton in Hampshire, or to the RHS Gardens at Wisley.

That was just as well, for one bomb fell in the walled garden at Merton Park in May 1941 and, more seriously, there were a number of attacks by V-1 flying bombs – 'doodlebugs' – between 15 June and 27 August 1944, on which day twenty or so fell within a mile of the Manor House. The bomb that dropped on the afternoon of Sunday 20 August knocked down the garden wall, blew out the glass in the glasshouses and damaged the windows, roofs and ceilings of the main buildings. 'The general scene was one of appalling devastation.'[57] The entire *Antirrhinum* (snapdragon) crop, used for genetics research, was destroyed, and other crops grown for breeding work were also damaged. Only the books that were still in the library remained intact. So-called 'cloudy glass' was not available to reglaze the glasshouses until the following November.

In 1940, fear of potential bomb damage had led the Institution's Director to urge the Board of Trustees to make plans for temporary evacuation, if there was an emergency, with the idea that this might become a permanent move in time. Waterperry House outside Oxford, at that time leased to the Waterperry School of Horticulture for Women, was the chosen option. In early 1941, the JIHI began negotiations to secure the lease, for it looked to be a very attractive proposition, not least because of the link with Oxford University. Miss Havergal and Miss Sanders, the two Principals of the gardening school, took fright, not surprisingly, since the JIHI's Board of Trustees did not seem very alive to the difficult position into which they had been thrown, and the negotiations eventually foundered on the question of legal liabilities to the School of Horticulture.[58] So the Institution stayed at Merton until after the war. In 1949, it moved to Bayfordbury in Hertfordshire, where Lawrence designed state-of-the-art glasshouses. Waterperry continued to be a school that trained women gardeners until 1971.

Long Ashton Research Station in north Somerset was founded even earlier than the JIHI, in 1903. Because of its geographical position, and the interests of the local landowner, Robert Neville Grenville, who endowed it, Long Ashton was originally mainly concerned with research into commercial cider apple growing and making. This remit gradually widened to embrace hardy fruit generally, including the study of their pests and diseases.

In 1918, the research station set up a Domestic Preservation Section at Chipping Campden in Gloucestershire. This establishment did very important work on developing precise standards and procedures for bottling, canning and preserving fruit and vegetables, and transmitting this knowledge to the housewife with a succession of books and teaching courses. *Home Preservation of Fruit and Vegetables* was first published in 1929, and went through a number of editions and impressions up to 1982. Its usefulness in wartime, both to the housewife and to Women's Institute organisers and speakers, can scarcely be overstated.

In the years before the war, the Long Ashton scientists invented 'Ribena' (see Chapter Twelve), made great strides in the visual diagnosis of nutrient deficiencies and excesses in fruit, and also investigated and tested effective pesticides. For example, the discovery that 'leaf scorch' in fruit trees was caused by a deficiency of potassium had a far-reaching impact on commercial fruit production, and the scientists also carried out highly influential work on which soils were most suitable for fruit growing. The station undertook research into plant nutrition of farm crops and vegetables as well as fruit, and the entomologists investigated ways of dealing with wireworm, which was a scourge when grassland was turned to plough – and lawns to vegetables – so had a direct bearing on both agriculture and horticulture in wartime. Much of this research had just reached the practical application stage when war broke out.

Other important work carried out at Long Ashton during the war centred on plant hormones and the development of artificial growth substances, in particular 'hormone rooting powder', used to stimulate rooting in cuttings. The scientists also investigated, in tandem with East Malling research station, 'reversion' in blackcurrants. Long Ashton discovered that this disease was caused by a virus, while East Malling concluded that 'reversion' virus was transmitted from bush to bush by the 'big bud mite'. The beneficial effect of all this research work on both gardeners and horticultural commercial concerns in wartime and after is incalculable but substantial.

In late December 1944, when the war was won but not yet over, *The Gardeners' Chronicle* printed a slightly sour leader which began:

> Farmers have received unstinted praise for their magnificent contributions to the national food supply during wartime, and deservedly so. Allotment holders have also had a good press, and their work has been lauded by Ministries and in every newspaper throughout the land. But professional gardeners have received scant praise and little encouragement from the powers that be, although the latter have not hesitated to seek the advisory services of the former, mostly without pay.[59]

The writer then computed the annual contribution in vegetables from allotments at something less than £10 a plot, and therefore £17,250,000 as an estimate of the total value of food produced by allotmenteers per annum in wartime. However, continued the leader, professional gardeners were probably cultivating three times as much land as allotment holders, and because they were trained gardeners, their output was probably twice as high. In other words, professional gardeners might well have produced six times as much for the national larder as allotmenteers – and deserved national recognition for it. Even if the calculations are impossible to verify, it is equally impossible to quarrel with that conclusion. Curiously, the leader did not mention the contribution of commercial operations, especially flower nurseries and long-established market gardens, but as we shall see, that was also substantial and sometimes achieved at great personal cost.

CHAPTER EIGHT

FAR MESSIER AND DIFFERENT

One morning [19 October 1939] Bunyard[1] said to me that we would deal with library business in the afternoon. He never came back which was not surprising. When on Air Raid Precautions this early morning someone showed me a newly arrived newspaper reporting the death of a noted rosarian, E. A. Bunyard. 'Did I know him?'

I went up to the R.H.S. and unfortunately it was true. He did *not* normally carry a revolver but kept it in a drawer except when he went out to his orchard to shoot bullfinches, those lovely pests of fruit trees in bloom. Evidently he had brought it to London with a set purpose. He went to the Royal Societies Club and there shot himself.[2]

E. A. Bunyard was not the only nurseryman to feel bleak about his future at the outbreak of war, and probably not the only one to take his own life. But he was a particularly important loss to horticulture: his knowledge of fruits and roses was encyclopaedic, he was a highly skilled communicator and, before he developed money troubles, had given much time freely to help the Royal Horticultural Society. He exemplified the best, most public-spirited kind of nurseryman, the sort who would have an important part to play in wartime, sitting on the County War Agricultural Executive Committees and giving expert, disinterested advice.

Bunyard had known from his experience of the First World War that commercial nurseries do badly when wars are fought, however much amateur gardeners wish to continue to cultivate their gardens in peacetime ways. At the beginning of the Second World War, nurseries tried to continue business as usual, but most soon saw the necessity of moving over to food production, or were forced by the county War Ag to do so. In the process, they lost much rare and valuable stock, and usually money as well, since decorative plants could be sold for more than vegetables.

The gardening writer Stephen Cheveley visited a local nurseryman just a week after war was declared:

> There we were, surrounded by his gardens, full of autumn flowers, and he puzzling as to what crops he should grow to keep the place alive during the war. The greenhouses must go for tomatoes. The land would have to carry onions, salad crops, and perhaps cauliflowers and other brassicas. But the big problem was that the place was not laid out on a sufficiently large scale to permit using horses, and the necessary implements, even if he had them. All the work was done by hand and it would not pay to produce vegetables entirely by hand labour.
>
> He was so cheerful and philosophical about the whole business that I came away feeling much better about things in general and rather virtuous in having made a start by uprooting my own flowers.[3]

If the nurseryman was cheerful, he was probably in a minority, for few can have had illusions about what was to come.

In many counties, the War Ags established horticultural subcommittees to oversee the transfer from growing ornamental stock to food production. Initially, the government allowed nurseries to retain up to 75 per cent of their pre-war area under glass for non-bulb flowers and 50 per cent outside, but there was to be no new planting of perennials or nursery stock,[4] and what nursery stock there was should only take up 10 per cent of the acreage. For those nurseries which boasted a list of thousands of different species and cultivars, such as Woods of

Woodbridge in Suffolk,[5] that was a disaster. Five of the seven glasshouses, which once contained a range of indoor decorative plants, were converted to tomato houses.[6] Only two glasshouses were retained for the propagation of decorative plants, and the cold frames were used to grow cucumbers. Those employees that remained would have to be retrained to grow vegetables. True, there was some help available in this change-over: at the beginning of the war, the distance-learning specialists at the Horticultural Correspondence College in Winchester prepared a non-examination course in commercial fruit and vegetable production, which was suitable for nursery workers. The college also produced a leaflet entitled 'The Professional Gardener at War'.

A number of nurseries specialised entirely in roses, the most popular of all shrubs grown in the garden. Harry Wheatcroft, the rose-grower and breeder from Nottinghamshire, famous for his handlebar moustaches and loud-checked suits, expressed the nurseryman's predicament very well:

We put the plough through a field of some hundred thousand [rose] trees – a heartbreaking job.[7] We tore from the greenhouses the bushes that were to give us blooms for the spring flower shows, and so made room for the more urgent bodily needs of the nation.

Pigs now wander about where our Polyantha roses bloomed. There's wheat and barley where acres of Hybrid Teas coloured the land – even the humble cabbage stands where standard roses once held majestic sway. The odour of our glasshouses has changed too. Here half a million onion plants have taken the place of the roses. They, in turn, will be succeeded by tomato plants and fruit; then lettuce, while the light still holds, and afterwards the humble mustard and cress . . .

All nurserymen in every county are making these drastic changes; much beauty has been destroyed and there's no need to pretend that it hasn't meant a heavy financial loss. Carnations, roses, flowering plants, trees and shrubs yield a good deal more in cash per acre than the crops and vegetables I've mentioned.

However, our actions today can't be measured by money, and perhaps we should be proud that our business has found us in charge of a small piece of British soil that we can now use for the country's good.[8]

This destruction, he wrote after the war, had cost the business over £100,000.[9]

Cheals of Crawley was a large, family-run nursery concern that had been founded in the 1860s at Lowfields, close to where Gatwick Airport now sprawls. It had a varied clientele, including some of the largest country estate owners in the south of England, and even had a thriving garden design service department, which laid out the Italian Garden at Hever Castle, amongst others. The nursery staff worked with the greatest of the pre-war landscape architects: Thomas Mawson, Sylvia Crowe[10], Brenda Colvin and Geoffrey Jellicoe. The Cheal family were Quakers and their business practices were predicated on a strong community ethic.

The war caused a considerable interruption to their business, especially in the garden design department. Cheals no longer had the opportunities to advertise their wares and speak to potential customers at the big flower shows like Chelsea, which was where they had wooed the pre-war amateur gardener. Perhaps influenced by their Quaker ideals, the company refused to allow the quality to decline: there was 'still a Cheals way of doing things'.[11] But maintaining standards was well-nigh impossible with staff numbers so much reduced. The company switched to food production, but was permitted to keep its large stock of fruit trees, which were gradually sold during the five years of war. The staff also lifted, and presumably destroyed, many trees and shrubs from the fields, to free up land to grow cereals, including oats to feed the five horses that were retained for carting, since petrol was so hard to come by.

An analysis of the value of stock and crops shows starkly how much ornamental nurseries lost financially when they switched to food production. In 1941, the Cheals nursery stock was worth £15,500, while food crops brought them a mere £400. In 1942, the stock value had fallen to £12,700 while food crops went up to £1,600. The nursery grew potatoes, which netted £6 a ton, sugar beet at £4 a ton, and sweetcorn, which was sold to the Canadian troops stationed around Crawley.

The glasshouse space, as in most nurseries, was filled with tomato plants. Tomatoes were the most profitable food crop by some distance, even though their cultivation required considerable modifications to the dahlia greenhouses. In 1942, Cheals produced – indoors at Lowfields and outdoors on the lighter land at their nursery at Pulborough – ten and a half tons of tomatoes, which sold for £90 a ton.

Early in the war, Cheals was also designated the local ARP headquarters, so time had to be spent filling sandbags and equipping the offices with special telephones and first-aid supplies. In early 1944, the head ARP warden, who was also the Cheals chief clerk, was cycling home after an air raid when a delayed-action incendiary bomb detonated as he rode past and killed him. That summer, substantial damage was sustained when a local ack-ack gunner brought down a V-1 flying bomb, which damaged glasshouses and buildings and narrowly avoided harming some of the workers. These occasional, but very real, dangers were the lot of all nurseries based in the south-east of England.

Sunningdale Nurseries in Berkshire was a smaller concern than Cheals and its wartime problems were proportionately greater. Apart from the rhododendron wood, which did not require much maintenance, the rest of the nursery was 'a sea of weeds and scrub. The propagating was confined to a few bell jars, the larger beds overgrown and overrun by weeds, and there were no frames or greenhouses.'[12] This was a nursery whose infrastructure was already neglected, but the war vastly exacerbated the problem. However, as so often happened at the time, a keen plantsman saved the day: in this case, Louis Gray, the manager, who 'kept his eye on the numerous special forms and seedlings that amounted to so much of the basic material in rhododendron collections through this long period and indeed is still unsurpassed'.[13]

As time went on, the restrictions on nurseries grew steadily tighter; so much so that by 1942, only 10 per cent of glasshouse space could be allocated to permanent flower crops, and only a quarter of open land could be used for raising flowers. This order hit bulb nurseries very hard, and therefore particular areas of the country, such as Cornwall and Lincolnshire, where the daffodil growers were clustered together. That year, Mr E. Watts of Devoran, Cornwall, told a radio audience:

> Next week I'm hiring in a tractor to plough . . . under daffodil bulbs in fields which will be carrying a corn crop this summer, followed by cabbages next winter. Ploughing under these bulbs means a *tremendous* loss to me. We flower farmers have been a lifetime building up our stock of daffodils, and the bulbs represent much of our capital. I've already ploughed out practically half what I had, and you can quite imagine how I feel towards this utter destruction. The bulbs have to lie out in heaps to rot. But that doesn't count much in wartime.[14]

Some nurserymen went further than was strictly required by the War Ags. Angus Wilson, a well-known iris breeder, was one of these. A fellow nursery owner, Olive Murrell of The Orpington Nurseries, wrote to the artist Cedric Morris, who bred irises as well as painting them, bemoaning the fact that Wilson had ploughed in all his irises for potatoes.

> In fact I feel so dreadfully upset . . . that I have not replied [to him] for fear I say too much and get him on the raw and he tells me to mind my own business!!! As he had seven acres surely he could have kept the cream of them in one acre and given the rest to Potatoes. I really think he must have quite lost all proportion. I know how difficult it was to keep quite sane at the beginning of the War, but after all his years of work and the fine collection he had amassed it does seem quite mad to destroy the whole lot for <u>Potatoes</u>.[15]

For nurserymen specialising in large nursery stock – magnolias, rhododendrons and camellias, which were the staples of woodland gardens, for example – a decade might pass before plants were big enough for sale, so this switch to food production was especially damaging. It really was small wonder that some nurserymen gave up the struggle and preferred to sell their nurseries – usually for a knockdown price. The number of notices advertising the sale of nurseries in the specialist press rose sharply during the war.

Glasshouses were a particular liability for nurserymen and market gardeners during the war, as they became harder or even impossible to heat, especially after stringent fuel restrictions were introduced. Even when 'cold', they still needed to be repaired, and both glass and timber were in progressively shorter supply. There were many acres of glasshouse along the southern coastal strip – where sunshine hours are highest – and these were especially vulnerable to damage from bombs, especially 'doodlebugs', which often ran out of fuel and plummeted before they reached their target, London.

Not all nurseries and market gardens were situated in the countryside; a number were near or even in big cities, and here bombers naturally also caused problems, for greenhouses in particular. Gordon Veitch, who owned a market garden in Birmingham, had to contend with forty bombs falling within 400 yards of his property during the war, and much of his time was taken up replacing glass in the greenhouses. One Sunday, his entire family spent the day picking pieces of glass out of a chrysanthemum crop.

Commercial operations were closely overseen by the paid War Ag advisers, whose tasks ranged from detailing every holding and plotting the fields on a map, to discussing with growers the niceties of crop rotation and notifying the authorities of derelict land that could be brought back into cultivation. These advisers also had to enforce the often unpopular regulations. For example, Hubert Taylor, who oversaw 4,000 horticultural growers in one area of Hampshire, had the unenviable job of telling sweet violet nurserymen that all their stock had to be thrown away in favour of a more useful crop.[16] Strawberry growers too were to get rid of most or all of their stock and instead grow potatoes, runner beans, ridge cucumbers for pickles, and tomatoes, since the Ministry of Agriculture considered strawberries to be a 'luxury'. As the operation's profits would usually decline substantially as a result, the adviser's job required a good deal of sensitivity. Nor would everybody toe the line: one grower in Somerset was fined £10 plus costs in the magistrates' court in February 1941 for cultivating strawberries instead of cabbages on a quarter-acre of land.

In the early days, the government did not sufficiently appreciate just how short of imported fruit the nation would become and, at least initially, orchard fruits were no more favoured than strawberries, especially because many commercial orchards were neglected during the 1930s and it would take time, money and skilled labour to bring them back to optimum fruiting. The Ministry ordered that derelict orchards be grubbed up and potatoes grown there instead, and no new fruit trees were to be planted unless authorised by the War Ags. Where existing fruit orchards did survive – as in Kent and Herefordshire particularly – the fruit had often to be picked by city dwellers who heeded the call to 'Lend a Hand on the Land' and spent their summer holidays in the country. (They also helped get the harvest in.)

In the case of derelict or abandoned land, advisers, such as Ron Sidwell of Worcestershire, would generally recommend that a local grower take it over after the War Ag had sent its Machinery Unit to clear the trees and scrub, and Land Girls had done the initial manual cultivation. Sidwell's tasks also included lecturing growers new to vegetable crops on pest control together with other vital cultural information.

Sidwell recalled after the war that nurserymen who had turned to growing vegetables from flowers could be devious. They would cultivate pelargoniums amongst their lettuces and cabbages, so that it was very difficult for him to estimate what acreage there was under flower cultivation, and whether it was more than the 10 per cent allowed.[17] This kind of deception was strongly deprecated by the authorities.

These horticultural advisers, especially the younger women 'straight out of college', did not always impress the people they went to see, among them Harry Fox at Lulworth Castle. No doubt he took his tone from his superiors: 'Some days quite unexpectedly a young woman from County Hall in Dorchester would make an unannounced visit to see if all the available ground was cultivated and planted up. These "advisers" were well meaning [but] knew almost nothing about the "land" and its seasons. They had been hurriedly trained, had never used a spade or a pair of secateurs and were thoroughly unpractical.'[18] This seems harsh, but such a judgement may have to do with the fact that this adviser wanted Harry's boss to plant tomatoes in the vinery, when he knew that the vine leaves would make it too shady for them to thrive. When the adviser came again and saw thin, etiolated plants, she accused the head gardener of not feeding them enough. Perhaps in that case, Harry Fox had a point.

Generally, the changeover to food production was easier for the workers in market gardens and nurseries, used to large-scale growing, than for those who had worked in country houses and suburban mansions before the war. In September 1941, when Muriel Green became an under-gardener on a large estate in Suffolk that had been taken over by the army, she complained that, after what she had experienced in a private garden, 'the work is far messier and different in a commercial garden. I prefer the neat particular methods I was trained to.'[19] Inevitably, most private estates were becoming messy and different, especially if they had turned more or less completely to food production.

Commercial nurseries and market gardens were just as badly hit by the compulsory conscription of young men as farms were, perhaps even more so since it was sometimes possible for a farmer to persuade the county War Ag to reserve one son at least to continue to work at home. So market gardens came to be largely staffed by girls of the Women's Land Army. On the whole, these girls took to the work since, unlike on many small farms, there were often a number of like-minded, or at least like-aged, girls to befriend, and fun could be found in the strangest places. And the work varied through the year, even if certain jobs were loathed. The most unpopular was undoubtedly the picking of Brussels sprouts, since it had to be done in all weathers in winter, and the girls could not wear gloves since these became wet and then froze. It was all right once the feeling had entirely left the hands, but many a Land Girl could have wept as her hands thawed out at dinner time.

Beryl Robe joined the Women's Land Army in December 1941, just before her eighteenth birthday, and was sent to a large and well-known market garden in Milford, Surrey, owned by F. A. Secrett,[20] who was sufficiently well-regarded to be asked to give advice to the RHS and MAF for their bulletins. The market garden was over 100 acres in size, and Beryl worked in the company of about twenty other girls of a similar age. She recalled later that 'vanners' – horses that pulled carts – were still used, although tractors were increasingly replacing them.

The work could be extremely heavy, in particular the lifting and moving of Dutch lights over frames of lettuce seedlings, which would later be planted out in the fields. There were at least a dozen banks of frames, each one over a cricket wicket[21] in length, with forty or fifty Dutch lights. Lettuces were one of Secrett's main crops. 'I can remember very long, hot summer days spent cutting many hundreds, going down lines of lettuce feeling each heart with the back of my knuckles to make sure it was firm enough and ready to be cut for market.'[22] She also cut up rhubarb crowns and left them outdoors in boxes to catch the frost, before planting them out in rows in the field. This was to force them into precocious growth, so that they would command a higher price in the shops.

The girls picked beans and peas on a piecework basis, paid by each 28 lb box. They would stay at the Land Army hostel at the weekends to gather these crops, earning almost as much in a couple of days as they did in the rest of the week.

For the owners of commercial operations, however, the new workforce could pose problems. Willie Barker, a market gardener from Walton-on-Thames, had to depend on a very motley labour force, about which he complained: Land Girls, Romany gipsy women camped nearby, recuperating Welsh Guardsmen from nearby Sandown Park, and volunteers from the Surrey Land Club, who were mainly office girls who liked to help out at weekends. These girls were very willing but inexperienced, and did not always know the difference between a weed and a young carrot.

Market gardens like Secrett's and Willie Barker's sent their produce to Covent Garden. Barker took to driving there in the daylight during the Blitz, rather than before dawn, but the journey was often made very fraught and circuitous by recent bomb damage. Smaller or more remote operations tried to sell their crops locally, if they possibly could, to avoid the difficulties and expense of long journeys. For example, before the war there had been a Waterperry stall at Swindon market; in wartime this was switched to Oxford, because it was much nearer to Waterperry. This stall became famous in the area for the quality of the fresh fruit and vegetables sold there, as well as the cut flowers, plants and certificated virus-free raspberry canes. All this produce had to be dug up, counted, tied and put in the marketing shed the day before, ready to be placed on the van early in the morning. Ursula Maddy, a student at Waterperry during the war, recalled:

> Anyone who has been involved in the marketing of vegetables, or bunching flowers or tying up bundles of raspberry canes will know how important it is to be able to count . . . If asked for example to pull four dozen bunches of baby beetroot – the dozen still reigned supreme at that time – the marketer would first cut forty-eight 'strings', short lengths to be used for tying the bunches, not too long as that would be wasteful of string, and not so short as to be fiddly and time-consuming. The 'strings' were then tucked into the belt and the marketer stood astride the row of beet, pulled the six largest within reach, tied them neatly and always with two turns round the necks, and dropped the bunch at the side of the row . . . The bunches were then picked up, counted and packed neatly into the wooden bushel boxes, all of which were marked with the school's name; the produce was finally hauled up through the gardens on flat trolleys to be washed in the marketing shed sink.[23]

Upwey Nurseries, near Weymouth, sold its produce directly from the glasshouses. Mrs B. M. E. Male joined the Land Army in February 1943 and was sent there to help grow tomatoes. The tomato seed was sown in old wooden fish boxes (a feature of living near the coast) and put in a propagating house; seedlings were then potted on into five-inch pots and either sold to amateur gardeners to grow on or planted out in the two other houses.

The workers sold tomato fruits to the public every Tuesday and Thursday morning at 6.30 a.m., having picked them the previous day and weighed them into 1 lb bags. The price was fixed – regardless of whether the tomatoes were grown under glass or in the open – by the Ministry of Food, at 1s.8d per bag. Even at that time of the morning there was always a queue of people already waiting when the staff arrived for work, and they would sell 600 to 700 lbs a day.

One year at Upwey, the glasshouse tomato plants developed a disease early in the season, so Mrs Male's superior planted cucumbers in the glasshouses instead. 'Of course my Boss had to go to court as he had broken the law but he was only fined a small amount. He made quite a packet from his "mistake", well worth while and the people enjoyed the cucumbers.'[24] This illustrates the insouciance with which generally law-abiding people often broke emergency wartime regulations, and how they viewed being 'had up' for it. That is perhaps not to be wondered at, since people's lives were circumscribed by so many regulations, often applied in an infuriatingly bureaucratic, if not actively draconian, manner. Indeed, the rise in crime figures in the early years of the war was largely the result of there being so many more laws to break.

Commercial market gardens tended to be one-site operations and often highly individual in their approach. Not so the Land Settlement Association, which was run co-operatively, with a number of small-holders based on one of several sites. The tenants of the LSA more than repaid the government's faith in them, although this may have much to do with the fact that all new smallholders appointed in wartime were men with existing horticultural or agricultural skills. In a debate on 'post-war work' in the House of Lords in February 1944, the Earl of Elgin and Kincardine recounted to the House the results of a survey of 550 LSA tenants. He told their Lordships that after wages, rents, taxes and other costs had been deducted, each

I was front-page news

a year ago . . . more precious than gold
to those lucky enough to get a pound of me. That was
because you relied on having me brought to you from
abroad. Yet, if women and older children, as well as
men, are sensible enough to Dig for Victory now, you
can have me ALL THE YEAR ROUND for only the
cost of a packet of seeds . . .

YOU SEE, I AM ONE OF THOSE CROPS YOU CAN STORE

DIG FOR VICTORY NOW!

★ ★ ★ *If you haven't a garden, ask your Local Council for an allotment. Send
NOW for Free pictorial leaflets "HOW TO DIG" and "HOW TO CROP" to
Dept. A.105, Ministry of Agriculture, Hotel London, St. Annes-on-Sea, Lancs.*

ISSUED BY THE MINISTRY OF AGRICULTURE

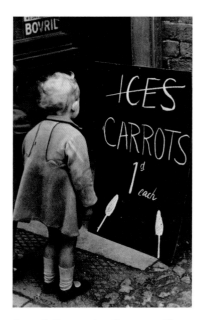

Before the war, 90% of onions were imported so they quickly became the scarcest vegetable in shops. Throughout the conflict, the Ministry of Agriculture produced many of these kinds of advertisements for newspapers and magazines; they were cheap to create and could respond to changing circumstances.

Carrot lollies were heavily promoted by the Ministry of Food, since ice creams and other sweets were scarce, but it is unlikely that these children thought them an adequate substitute, especially as they cost the same amount as the real thing.

Schoolboys from the Drury Falls Council School at Hornchurch in Essex arrive at their allotment in October 1941. They ran a shop where they sold their produce.

The best known of all Dig for Victory images, the foot on the spade was also used as a small logo on many other government posters. It is likely that this image was 'manufactured' in a studio.

C. H. Middleton, the most successful wartime radio gardener, discusses produce grown in Nottingham's parks with a Ministry of Agriculture official at the city's WAEC ('War Ag') show in September 1944.

The team from 'Radio Allotment' in action in Park Crescent near Broadcasting House in February 1942. Wynford Vaughan Thomas, Raymond Glendenning and Henry Riddell do the double digging, while Michael Standing commentates with Roy Hay at his shoulder.

Above left: The designer of this innovative wartime poster was Hans Schleger, also known as Zéro. A German Jewish refugee, who had previously worked in Berlin and New York, he was influenced in his graphic designs by Modernism.

Above right: Soldiers help clear debris from the blitzed Bank underground station in the City of London on 14 January 1941. In the background stands the Royal Exchange, used as a banner site. The message that day was singularly appropriate.

Right: Abram Games frequently designed information posters aimed at the armed services, with this one intended to encourage them to grow food on their bases. His motto was 'maximum meaning, minimum means' and he became famous for his ability to layer ideas, images and message into a single iconic design, as here.

Above left: A gardener tending his allotment close to the Albert Memorial in Kensington Gardens. This was one of the most high profile (and photogenic) of public green spaces in London turned over to vegetable growing as part of the Dig for Victory campaign.

Above right: Well-organised allotments cultivated by the firemen of Redcross Street Fire Station, within sight of St Paul's Cathedral, captured in late June 1942. This image shows clearly the effect of the Blitz on the City of London.

Left: April 1943: National Fire Service officers, seen here rounding up pigs on the bomb-damaged site of the Museum of the Royal College of Surgeons in London, would probably have been members of a pig club.

As with so much of the output of the Ministry of Agriculture's publicity division, this poster is folksy but sensible and clear in its directions on how to make a compost heap. Compost was vital to the home gardener, since there were few other bulky soil improvers available.

The Ministry of Agriculture's cropping plan for vegetables was designed to encourage gardeners, novice and experienced, to maximise production from their plots. It was admirably clear but required close attention (see below).

Even the Royal Family were pressed into service by the Ministry of Agriculture in its quest to get gardeners growing vegetables. In what must rank as one of the most eccentric publicity shots taken in wartime, the teenage Princesses, Elizabeth and Margaret Rose, dressed identically but unsuitably, study the Ministry's cropping plan in the Windsor Castle garden in 1943.

RAF personnel contemplate the vegetables they have grown on land surplus to service requirements at a show in September 1945.

Evelyn Dunbar was a war artist who painted pictures of women in the countryside. 'A Canning Demonstration' depicts a cavernous village hall in which the instructor, surrounded by her materials and watched over by a bossy organiser, is listened to by a group of village ladies. One of them has to sit near the door to welcome latecomers. There is both understanding and gentle humour in the portrayal of the women.

Members of the Mereworth Women's Institute in Kent make jam in an orderly and purposeful manner in August 1943. By this point they had already produced more than 5,000 lbs of jam from fruit grown locally that would otherwise have gone to waste.

Rose hips collected by children and women are milled and processed at the Farm Ice Creamery works in Acton, west London, to make rose hip syrup, a substitute source of vitamin C in place of imported citrus fruits.

May 1941: Land Army girls receive horticultural training in the 'frame-yard' at the Somerset Agricultural Institute at Cannington. They wore a distinctive uniform of fawn breeches or dungarees, fawn shirt, a green tie, green V-neck jersey, thick woollen socks, Wellington boots or stout shoes, oilskin mac, slouch hat and arm band.

Female students work in the beautifully ordered walled garden of Waterperry School of Horticulture for Women, Oxfordshire. Cecil Beaton, who worked as a war photographer for the Ministry of Information, captured this image in the summer of 1943.

Miss Beatrix Havergal, inspiration for Miss Trunchbull in Roald Dahl's *Matilda*, teaches the students how to prune pear cordons in the walled garden at Waterperry. In the foreground are staked tomatoes.

tenant made an average profit of £418 a year, equivalent to more than £16,000 today.

The LSA's output of important produce climbed substantially between 1939 and 1943. For example, in that period receipts from the sale of pigs, poultry, eggs and crops nearly doubled. Between 1940 and 1943, sales of tomatoes and lettuces rose more than five times, and those of onions twelve times. Even taking into account the increase in prices of vegetables during that period, these were still substantial gains in productivity.[25] This is impressive considering that the smallholdings were only five acres in size, although the tenants had the advantage of being part of a large co-operative.

Back garden and allotment growing could only ever augment the efficient commercial growing and distribution of vegetables and fruit, especially for the urban population. Commercial gardening operations had access to fuel to heat glasshouses, stronger insecticides and greater supplies of fertilisers. The varieties of vegetables grown were often not the same as those employed by amateurs, since yield took precedence over taste, and neither were cultivation methods or machinery.

This was one reason why there were a number of large-scale seed houses – Suttons, Carters, Thompson and Morgan, and Webbs being the best known – which catered specifically for the amateur market. These concerns sold their seed through both horticultural sundries shops – of which there was at least one in every town – and hardware shops, as well as by mail order. Cuthbert's sold much of their seed through the high street retailer Woolworth's at 1d a packet. Other wartime seedsmen which, like Cuthbert's, no longer exist included Dobbie's of Edinburgh,[26] Sowerbutts of Ashton-under-Lyne, Alfred Dawkins of Chelsea and Ryder and Son of St Albans.

The larger seed firms such as Suttons sent out coloured brochures or catalogues each year, mainly in late autumn, so that gardeners could choose what they wanted during the slack period in winter. (Head gardeners often tackled this task on Boxing Day.) These brochures became very thin during the war, and what illustrations survived to illuminate the text were in black and white. In 1943, the government insisted that catalogues should only be sent out to customers who specifically requested them, in order to try to cut down on waste paper. Vegetable seed catalogues were free, but flower ones cost 1d.

Suttons sold most of its seed by mail order, but also some through retail outlets such as Barrow's Stores in Birmingham and Messrs E. Dingle in Plymouth, as well as the Suttons office and shop at 69 Piccadilly in central London. The company could call itself the 'Royal Seedsmen' because it was 'by appointment' to George VI. In the autumn of 1941, the foreword to the main catalogue for 1942[27] was entitled 'Food for Thought – Thought for Food', and was accompanied by a picture of broccoli being harvested in a field, with horses pulling a cart – and a formation of Spitfires flying overhead, just in case the point was missed. The foreword began:

> During the past year this island has been a fortress – a fortress which stands firm today notwithstanding the fact that the enemy has violated so many of the laws of war in his efforts to break the spirit of our people. It may truthfully be said that the spirit of England has never been more sure and steadfast than at this hour of destiny. While our brave men do battle with the enemy and the dwellers in our great cities stand up to attack, it is the bounden duty of those who have the smallest space to cultivate, to do so intensively, in order that the brave may be fed and that the life line of the Atlantic may not be unduly strained. 'I vow to thee my country all earthly things above Entire and whole and perfect, the service of my love.'[28]

The use of the words 'bounden duty', a phrase from the Anglican Book of Common Prayer, together with the quotation from a well-known hymn, gives a pointer to the religious convictions of the Suttons in the business: 'Mr Phil' Sutton, his son, Owen,[29] and two nephews, Martin and Noel.

A study of the 1942 Suttons catalogue reveals that a number of seed varieties which were popular then are still widely grown by gardeners today: parsnip 'Tender and True', radish 'French Breakfast', perpetual spinach, turnip 'Early Snowball', tomato 'Sutton's Abundance', carrot 'Sutton's Champion Scarlet Horn', cucumber 'Sutton's Improved Telegraph' and cabbage 'Improved Winnigstadt'. If a particular strain of a cultivar had been bred by the Suttons plant breeders, the firm was bound to add the fact to the vegetable's name. The firm sold vegetable seed collections at a variety of prices, depending on the number of cultivars, from 8s.6d (6s. for the small garden) up to 42s. It also sold asparagus crowns, sea kale roots, strawberry plants, like 'Royal Sovereign' and 'Cambridge Early', Jerusalem artichokes, pot and sweet herbs, and seed potatoes, such as 'Arran Pilot', 'Majestic', and 'King Edward VII'.

Flowers were relegated to the back of the catalogue but still consisted of an extensive variety of annuals, both hardy and half-hardy, as well as alpines and perennials. The gardener could also buy a collection suitable for an unheated greenhouse. Gardeners were advised to plant half-hardy annual seed in the ground late in the spring, on the assumption that they would have no opportunity to germinate it under glass.

Suttons also sold flower bulbs and perennial plants. Fifteen shillings would buy twelve 'Good varieties, our selection' of delphiniums, while 27s.6d bought twelve 'Better varieties, our selection' and 54s. 'Newer varieties, our selection'. It is tempting to think that customers were throwing good money away by buying the 'Good varieties, our selection'.

Suttons were substantial grass seed merchants as well, even providing a 'Cumberland-turf mixture' – highly recommended for golf courses – which the catalogue assured the customer would produce 'a sward similar in character to sea-washed turf'. For the home gardener, they advertised a mixture suitable for tennis and croquet lawns.

The list of horticultural sundries is intensely appealing to any keen gardener: serge aprons for 12s.6d while best shalloon cost 13s.6d, both requiring three clothing coupons; bamboo canes; trug baskets; metal foil bird scarers; birch and palm besom brooms; galvanised buckets; glass cloches; three types of glove (Ladies' Gauntlet, Ladies' Chamois and Men's Hedgers); hydrangea colorant; wall nails; garden nets; seed sowers; wasp and fly traps, and Haws' galvanised watering cans in three-, four-, six- or eight-quart sizes, all with both a fine and a coarse 'rose'. It was even possible to buy sterilised potting soil at 3s.6d a bushel. However, I suspect the most helpful equipment for the urban gardener was the Universal Pump sprayer, with four feet of rubber hose, two feet of brass lance, and a spray nozzle and jet, advertised as 'Very useful also in case of Air Raid fire'.[30]

Like Cheals, Suttons boasted a garden design and construction department. 'Customers are offered practical service of the highest standard and we cordially invite inquiries for making new gardens or for re-designing present ones to suit war conditions.'[31]

As with so many other horticultural operations, these seedsmen became heavily dependent on female labour. One employee was Lillian Harbard, a city girl who had worked for the matchmakers Bryant and May in Bow, east London; this unpleasant occupation was made much more so by the bombing of the East End. In early 1942 she joined the Land Army, since, understandably, she wanted to leave London to work in the country. She was sent to work for Suttons Seeds at their Slough trial grounds, growing vegetable plants for seed. (She put on three stone in weight and was much healthier as a result.) The gardeners harvested the plants in the autumn, using billhooks, then laid them out to dry. They threshed the bigger seed with a small machine in the field, and the small with old-fashioned flails in the barn. Then they bagged the seed up and sent it to the Reading headquarters, where there were cleaning machines. They also grew flowers on the trial grounds and collected the seed, but only enough to keep the strains going until the war was over.

In order to try to minimise the damage bombing might do to the company's site, Suttons had a number of contingencies in place before the war started. By May 1939, twenty-four volunteer firemen, sixteen air-raid wardens, eight decontamination officials and sixteen first-aiders had been recruited from the workforce. In this regard, Suttons was very similar to thousands of other medium-sized businesses situated in provincial towns. The firm's patriotism extended to storing 1,000 tons of coal for the Ministry of Fuel on part of the company's sports ground, between the bowling green and the workers' allotments. When Reading town centre was bombed on 10 February 1943, a secret radio station was damaged. Ten days later it was transmitting again from a small room in the glasshouse complex at the Suttons trial grounds.

Because the Chelsea Flower Show was cancelled during the war, there were none of the magnificent displays of flowers and vegetables that had so distinguished the company in the pre-war era.[32] Despite that, shortage of labour meant that Suttons was forced to try to get the seed testing done earlier in the year, so that there was not too much rush in the busy autumn and winter selling period.

By the summer of 1942, seed itself was in short supply. Before the war, a large percentage of that sold had been imported from countries like North Africa and Italy, which had a better and more reliable climate for seed growing. British winters made it impossible, for example, to produce cauliflower seed because the heads died in cold weather. However, by the third year of the war, those countries were in the thick of the fighting. By early March 1942, Suttons had already sold out of runner bean, onion, leek, early potato and cress seed, and deliveries of other seeds to customers were taking three weeks. It was not a happy situation. However, only in the following autumn did the exigencies of trading in wartime surface openly, in the 1943 brochure: 'Orders will be fulfilled from first-class stocks, but under present conditions we cannot undertake to handpick seed to the standard which has been customary in the past.' For a company that began trading in the 1860s and took pride in being the Royal Seedsmen, that must have been very difficult to admit.

The larger items, such as seed potatoes, were sent to customers in jute or hessian bags, but these became so scarce that by 1942 the customer was paying a deposit of a few pence on them: 'It is of National Importance that sacks and bags be returned to us, when the Deposit Charge for same will be credited.'[33] By the time of the next annual catalogue, the customer was reminded of this 'Under the conditions of The Control of Textile Bags (No. 1) Order, 1943 . . .' an example of Whitehall micro-management if ever there was one.

North Americans were very generous in sending seed to Britain to augment depleted stocks at home. Unlike plants, seed did not present any phytosanitary challenge, and was also easy to transport in bulk. By January 1943, ninety tons of American-raised seed had been distributed to members of the National Allotments Society. Seeds came in collections in boxes, and included the name and address of the donor, which often initiated thank-you letters from grateful recipients. Some of the seed was unfamiliar to British gardeners, and some, like sweetcorn, did not grow very well in a cooler climate. Seed also arrived from the Dominions, including Australia, New Zealand and Canada, and in this case it was channelled through the Royal Horticultural Society to prisoner-of-war camps in Europe (see Chapter Ten).

The success of food production in market gardening and commercial horticultural enterprises can, at least to some extent, be gauged by the size of acreage devoted to it during the war. Between 1936 and 1938, more than a quarter of a million acres on average were under vegetables, but this had almost doubled to just over half a million acres in 1945. The potato acreage of 600,000 acres also doubled. On the other hand, the amount of fruit grown hardly changed in the six years of war. The worst affected nurserymen were those specialising in ornamental stock. Flowers and nursery stock declined from a high of 25,000 acres in 1939 to 18,000 in 1940, 14,000 in 1941, 12,000 in 1942, and 9,000 in 1943 and 1944. In other words, the overall ornamental acreage in 1942 was less than half its pre-war level.[34] This was almost all as a result of the increasingly restrictive regulations issued by the Ministry of Agriculture.

Only in 1945 did the acreage begin to climb slowly once more. By then, commercial nurserymen and seedsmen were aware that they would have to make further major adjustments, this time to peacetime conditions. But at least, after the Battle of El Alamein was won and the tide of war turned, so that the prospect of a victorious peace took on a more discernible shape, they could begin to expand, knowing that gardeners would once more be clamouring to improve the look of their flower gardens.

CHAPTER NINE

A REFRESHMENT OF THE SPIRIT
OF MAN

> Yet shall the garden with the state of war
> Aptly contrast, a miniature endeavour
> To hold the graces and the courtesies
> Against a horrid wilderness. The civil
> Ever opposed the rude, as centuries'
> Slow progress laboured forward, then the check
> Advance, relapse, advance, relapse, advance,
> Regular as the measure of a dance;
> So does the gardener in little way
> Maintain the bastion of his opposition
> And by a symbol keep civility;
> So does the brave man strive
> To keep enjoyment in his breast alive
> When all is dark and even in the heart
> Of beauty feeds the pallid worm of death.[1]

Vita Sackville-West tried her best to keep enjoyment in her breast alive at Sissinghurst Castle in Kent, although its vulnerable position alarmed her deeply at times. Begun in 1939, her poem, 'The Garden', was the sequel to the award-winning 'The Land' (1926), and in it she expressed the love that she and her husband, Harold Nicolson, felt for the garden, which they were in the process of making. Nicolson was a Member of Parliament, freelance journalist and official in the Ministry of Information for much of the war, yet he found time to write a daily diary in which he chronicled his weekends at Sissinghurst as well as his working weeks in London. He received almost daily letters full of garden news from Vita, who was also a county Representative for the Women's Land Army, about which she wrote a book in 1944. Together the Nicolsons constitute one of the most extraordinary – and best-documented – examples of a couple who managed to maintain an interest in gardening for its own sake, while still being thoroughly involved in the war.

Kent was under very real threat of invasion in 1940, and the Battle of Britain was fought in the skies above the Tudor tower of Sissinghurst Castle. The house also stood on the path that the German army would take to London, after Admiral Raeder had persuaded Hitler to confine the proposed invasion to the coast between Folkestone and Bognor Regis. So worried were the Nicolsons in 1940 that Harold procured cyanide pills for them both from his doctor, so that they could commit suicide rather than be captured by the Germans. He had been a very vocal opponent of the Munich settlement, and suspected that he was on a German hit list. Although the invasion never happened, German bombers flew over Sissinghurst on the way to bomb London and other southern cities and occasionally crashed nearby.

Yet despite the deadly seriousness of the times, as well as the personal danger, the Nicolsons continued to develop a garden of such quality that it is, even now, considered one of the finest in England.[2] Nicolson peppered his diary accounts and letters to his wife with reflections about it.

11th August, 1940. A lovely clear morning but rather cold. I bathe nonetheless. A great heron flaps away from the lake. The cottage garden is ablaze with yellow and orange and red. A real triumph of gardening. Viti, who is so wise and calm, asks the unspoken question which is in all our minds, 'How can we possibly win?'[3]

2nd September, 1940. Sissinghurst. There is a tremendous raid in the morning and the whole upper air buzzes and zooms

with the noise of aeroplanes. There are many fights over our
sunlit fields. We go up to see Gwen [his sister] at Horserace and
suggest improvements in her garden.[4]

17th August, 1941. Do my *Spectator* article. In the afternoon
we go on pleaching the limes.[5] It rains dreadfully and we are
anxious about the harvest.[6]

On 24 September 1942, Harold Nicolson wrote to his wife at a time
when they were able to employ just one young gardener, who was
exempted from war service on medical grounds, as well as a Land Girl.

We can't hope to make [the garden] *look* very nice except for
May, June and July. There is no hope of us being able to make an
August or autumn garden. But I think we can struggle along to
make it the framework of the perfect garden. I think we should
concentrate on increasing what does well. More elaboration of
our own stock. Now, all annuals and even biennials involve more
work than we, with our present resources, can perform. Cut
them out. Away with antirrhinums. But we can legislate for 1946,
grow seeds and take cuttings. More forsythia, more magnolia,
more kerrya, more fuchsia – all the things that entail
comparatively slight trouble and mean beauty in 1946.[7]

The garden at Sissinghurst owed a great deal more in its design to
the theories of Miss Gertrude Jekyll and William Robinson than to those
of Christopher Tunnard. It was unashamedly backward-looking, harking
back to a more innocent, secure age before the First World War spoiled
everybody's peace of mind. Vita used the sumptuous colours of old roses,
which she planted lavishly in very large beds bounded by sheltering yew
hedges, put in bright spring bulbs under homely pleached limes and
made a cottage-type garden in 'sunset colours'. It was all beautifully and
carefully done.

Their close friend Leonard Woolf, husband of Virginia, who lived in
Sussex, also tried his best to forget the war when he could. One day,

Virginia called to him in the garden to say that Hitler was on the wireless, but he stayed outside planting his irises, declaring that they would be 'flowering long after [Hitler] is dead'.[8]

Margery Allingham was as famous a writer in her day as Vita Sackville-West, and a keen gardener, although not in the Nicolson class. Her garden was certainly a consolation to her. In her memoir of the first two years of the war, *The Oaken Heart*, she wrote about the day war broke out: 'I spent much of my childhood alone in a garden, and I have never lost the habit of hanging about in one in times of stress, waiting for a comforting thought. I do not mean anything fancified, of course . . . but I do expect to get in that sanctuary a momentary clarity of mind which will give me a definite lead at least as to the next step in whatever I may be about.'[9]

The idea of the garden as a sanctuary against what Vita Sackville-West called 'a horrid wilderness' is a very ancient one, dating from a time when gardens with high walls were actual physical refuges from attack from humans or wild animals. The notion of a garden as a metaphorical or psychological sanctuary was one that enjoyed widespread currency during the war.

Ironically for Margery Allingham and her husband Philip Youngman Carter, living within sight of the Essex coast, the physically protective qualities of the garden were fragile indeed. Yet it still had a part to play in their personal drama. On 10 May 1940, the couple went out into their garden to make plans in case there was an invasion. Pip had been called up and would shortly be leaving home, so they decided that if Margery were ordered to evacuate, she would put a note to say where she was going under the sundial, 'if it was still there . . .'[10] After he left, she pottered around the garden. 'The situation made me feel self-conscious. I could not pick a few flowers for the house without wondering if it was a waste of time, or, worse, a gesture.'[11] Later that month, when invasion really seemed imminent, she recalled how everyone seemed to be working even harder than usual; 'indeed, it seemed to get more important every day that one should get on with one's normal routine. Things like doing the washing up and weeding the vegetables and making the beds and cleaning the house seemed vital. It appeared urgent that the meals should be to time and the clocks wound up and even the flowers kept fresh . . . It was *the thing to do* for the emergency.'[12] Doing the washing up had an immediate effect, but weeding the vegetables required the weeder to continue to live in hope that the skies would not come crashing in.

Margery Allingham and Vita Sackville-West lived in parts of the country that were highly vulnerable to attack – at least until June 1941, when the threat of invasion receded after Germany invaded Russia. So the snatched moments of distraction in the garden must have had a particularly strong savour. But gardening and the garden also proved a powerful and salutary diversion for many others who were not so badly placed. For Mrs Clara Milburn, living in a village a few miles outside Coventry, the garden was where she went for solace and absorption when anxieties threatened to get the better of her. In the early days of June 1940, while waiting to hear whether her 'missing' son had survived the Dunkirk evacuation, she went into the garden to work. And when she heard the news on 21 March 1941 that her nephew had been badly injured and his wife killed when a bomb hit their house in Putney, she turned again to her garden. 'All the afternoon I worked in the garden,' she wrote, 'sowing seeds and digging – one just had to be *doing*.'[13] Practical gardening is a constant theme running through her diaries: her almost daily reports of enemy losses and Allied successes are interspersed with accounts of 'sticking' the peas or weeding the borders.

On 15 February 1941 she wrote: 'This is another of Hitler's "invasion" dates, but up till 9 p.m. he has not arrived . . . Jack [her husband] sprayed the fruit trees with a cleansing wash and I did another yard or two of pear tree border.'[14] And on 1 June that year: 'I . . . put in the rest of the snaps [snapdragons] after raking out the rest of the tulips in the dining-room bed. I kill all the wireworms, calling them first Hitler, then Goering, Goebbels, Ribbentrop and Himmler. One by one they are destroyed, having eaten the life out of some living thing, and so they pay the penalty.'[15] There is no doubt that for Clara Milburn, gardening was an extremely important release valve for the tensions she felt, especially when, during nights in 1941, she and her husband had to try to sleep in the air raid shelter in their orchard as the German bombers passed over the house on the way to Coventry and Birmingham.

Clara Milburn was a regular churchgoer, and the following diary entry, for Sunday 6 October 1940, shows how she conflated her religious and horticultural life together to develop what we would now call a coping strategy. She had been very depressed about her son Alan's capture and incarceration in a German prisoner-of-war camp, but after she had attended church, she felt better and made a conscious effort to count her blessings:

> And then one's spirits just had to rise in the garden and one thought of the queer things one was thankful for personally – such varied things as the five tall cypresses on the lawn, so handsome; the bronze green of the yew hedge in the fading light, the *colour* of colours; a new thumbnail just grown to perfection after nearly a year; the feel of newly-cut hair and the blessing of a permanent wave; one's good bed; the rain and the sun; autumn colouring; good garden tools and a wickerwork barrow . . . And then for one's good friends and most of all for the nearest and dearest – and home.[16]

Her son, Alan, was imprisoned for nearly five years in camps in Germany and Poland (see Chapter Ten), and the care with which she committed those parts of his letters which dealt with his burgeoning interest in, and commitment to, vegetable gardening in her diary signifies that the fact was a consolation to her. Mother and son might be forced apart, but they had a common interest to help sustain them.

Further north, in Barrow-in-Furness, Nella Last, the unhappily married wife of a master carpenter, and one of the most assiduous and engaging of all Mass-Observation diarists, described how she tried to keep her anxieties at bay in May 1940. After she had heard the news that France had fallen, she sniffed sal volatile[17], splashed her face with water, put on a flower-patterned dress and some make-up and went out into the garden to pick roses to put on the tea table. The effort revived her. She regained her composure and had tea laid by the time her husband came home.

Nella Last was a member of the 'respectable' working class, living in a northern industrial town that was very likely to be bombed. She was not aristocratic like Vita Sackville-West, nor was she literary like Margery Allingham or moneyed and confident like Clara Milburn, but she had a particular gift for simply expressing the kind of comforting domestic thoughts that helped get her, and probably millions of other women like her, through the worst days. And her garden definitely helped. On 14 March 1941, the day after Barrow, which was a shipyard town, came under sustained attack from German bombers, she wrote in her diary:

My table had boiled eggs [from her own hens], wholemeal bread, damson jam and a little cake cut in small pieces and spread out to look more – all home-made and simple, but my gaily embroidered cloth and bowl garden made it festive. My 'garden' is a bowl of moss and ferns off a sheltered wall. Today I stuck four yellow and two white crocuses in the damp moss. The warmth of the room opened them, and they looked like gold and white stars against the deep green moss.[18]

At the height of what came to be known as the Barrow Blitz, on 2 May that year, she wrote:

The garden is wakening rapidly, and I can see signs of blossom buds on my three little apple-trees. I put a lot of water round the roots as last year, in the drought, the blossom withered without setting. I'm keeping my rockery plants alive with constant watering for the sake of the bees, since I want them to come constantly now there are signs of blossom. A blackbird seems to be building nearby – she has been busy with straw all day today – and now the old tree at the bottom of the next-door garden shows buds against the blue sky.

My husband had a night off from work and said he really must get another row of peas and potatoes in, so I got some mending and ironing done . . .[19]

Late the following winter, when prospects still seemed bleak, Nella Last's reflections echoed those which comforted Clara Milburn:

Today [Sunday 1 March 1942], when I went down the garden path for a bit of green for my hens, I suddenly saw a little clump of snowdrops, as they shone snow-white from a patch of dirty-grey melting snow. I felt I could have knelt on the wet path in ecstasy to admire their frail brave beauty. There is always such a feeling of a miracle in the first flower or budding tree, and after this dreadful winter, it seemed like a promise to see the wee white things nodding in the wind. Whatever troubles we have to face in the near future will be easier if there is life around. Somehow God and his Goodness seem nearer if there are flowers and leafed trees.[20]

In the late 1930s, Britain was a predominantly Christian country and about a third of the population attended church or chapel on a regular basis. There they would have been exposed, in sermons and lessons from the Bible, to a host of garden, gardening and flower images: the garden of Eden, Paradise as a garden, the invocation not to be anxious – 'Consider the lilies of the field' – the garden of Gethsemane, the garden where Jesus was laid in the tomb. On Armistice Day every year, the clergy would remember the fallen of the last war lying in the beautiful flowery gardens laid out by the Imperial War Graves Commission, and the way that poppies bloomed in Flanders Field. Taking advantage of this, the Ministry of Agriculture even suggested that clergymen preach on Digging for Victory, 'enclosing a list of suggested texts with headings on which to base the sermons.'[21]

Although the grimly serious and practical gardening contributors to the daily and weekly newspapers rarely wrote in such elevated terms, or expressed themselves so lyrically, they still loved their flowers deeply, and yearned to keep something of the pre-war atmosphere in their gardens.

Early in the war, *The Gardeners' Chronicle* made its view plain. The issue of 23 September 1939 began with the by then customary encouraging, patriotic editorial leader:

> . . . we are fighting to preserve a way of life which already
> has succeeded in making the world a happier place for many,
> and will, if preserved, succeed yet more in bringing
> happiness to everybody capable of enjoying it. It is wise,
> moreover, to go on not only doing all we can to bring
> victory nearer, but also to do all we can between while to
> forget about the war – let the captains and the Kings depart
> for a little while and the tumult and the shouting die!. . .
> Therefore next week and onwards we shall continue to write
> about things of gardening interest in the hope that they may
> divert the reader from a too constant concentration on war
> work, for now, more than ever, is the garden 'a refreshment
> of the spirit of man'.[22]

This was to prove a frequent and enduring theme throughout the war: that gardening offered a valid, respectable, even necessary escape from the anxiety, bone-tiredness and stress which dogged many civilian lives.

All through the war, contributors to *The Gardeners' Chronicle,* such as T. F. Tomalin of Stansted Park and B. Hills of Exbury, continued to submit their effusions on growing indoor grapes or *Phalaenopsis* orchids, capable to a quite remarkable extent of ignoring the world outside their own small and enclosed domain.

The 'Correspondent' who wrote *The Times* gardening column on a Saturday likewise managed always to include something about the flower garden. In October 1941 he wrote:

In southern gardens the decline into winter . . . has been gradual and almost ideal. The days have been mostly calm and the earth has been warm and dry. Autumn flowers have been gayer than usual, and the second display of hybrid roses has made up for the more meagre blooming of the first.

Now that shrubs that need little attention are doubly precious, growers should concentrate on those roses that make the bravest show in September and October. General McArthur, Ophelia, and Mrs Sam. McGredy, are only three of these, but the others are well known.'[23]

He could not then resist shaking his head over the dangers of weeds, like the dreaded willowherb, seeding in the unattended gardens of vacant houses and blowing their seeds hither and thither.

The pages of the *Journal of the Royal Horticultural Society* tell the same story of individuals doing their best both to gain comfort from their gardens and forget the war for a while by writing a well-researched article on a nineteenth-century plant hunter, a monograph of a plant genus, a report of a trial of border carnations, or a description of a Scottish garden.

Those who lectured to Fellows of the Society also sought to divert their attention away from the war. Dr H. V. Taylor, the Horticultural Commissioner to the Ministry of Agriculture, might have been an architect of the Dig for Victory campaign, but in March 1940 he declared: '. . . for the present let the flowerbeds and the lawns continue to give their pleasure. There is little to be had elsewhere. Every work of beauty has been covered up and every street disfigured with horrid sandbags, so everywhere ugliness abounds. The lawns and flowers are needed to correct our perspective and maintain our morale.'[24] This must have been music to the Fellows' ears.

Against all odds, in 1940 Sir Daniel Hall's magnum opus, *The Genus Tulipa*, was published. We have met this polymath before, since he was Director of the John Innes Horticultural Institution until 1939, and the RHS's Editor and Librarian after E. A. Bunyard's suicide, but he was also a fanatical tulip lover, and this monograph was the result of a life-time's study.

Other RHS-sponsored monographs did not fare so well, having to be shelved due to a shortage of paper and printing ink until the war was over. To ease the frustration that this caused, a number were published, at least in part, in monthly instalments in the *Journal*. Sir Frederick Stern's study of the genus *Paeonia* (peony) was treated in this way, with a synopsis published in successive months in 1943. It is salutary to reflect that Stern was carefully noting the botanical characteristics of the flowering peonies in his garden, Highdown, which was situated in an old chalk quarry only a few miles from the barbed-wired entanglements along the beach at Worthing, as the 'little ships' prepared to sail across the Channel to rescue troops off the Dunkirk beaches in late May 1940.

Another fist shaken at Fate was the publication during the war of the Horticultural Colour Chart. Its indispensability to plant breeders and selectors resided in the fact that it allowed them correctly and definitively to designate the colour of a flower, for the benefit of nurserymen when describing them in catalogues, and gardeners when deciding whether to buy them. It had a print run of 5,000.

In its New Year issue of 6 January 1940, *The Gardeners' Chronicle* praised the Royal Horticultural Society when reminiscing about the previous year's Autumn Show at Vincent Square:

Horticulturists will remember the old year because of the
wonderfully bountiful crops of Apples harvested . . . and they
will not soon forget that joyous meeting at Westminster when
the Royal Horticultural Society held a fine exhibition of flowers,
fruits and vegetables. This show, arranged after hostilities created
conditions, which led to a cessation of the Society's activities
with regard to public exhibitions and meetings, came as a very
welcome surprise. Welcome because it carried an implication of
defiance against the pomp and circumstance of war; a demand
for peaceful conditions wherein to foster and encourage the
science and art of gardening; and a demonstration of the skill

and earnestness of cultivators, for both halls were filled with produce of the highest class brought from considerable distances and under many difficulties of time, labour and transport. Because of these things the show was a great surprise to those who were unaware of the patience and quiet determination of gardeners . . . It did everyone good to be there, and probably nothing the RHS has done during recent years has given so much pleasure and brought the Council so many congratulations.[25]

A number of smaller shows were held at Vincent Square whenever there was a cessation in the bombing campaign. For example, in 1943 there were two fruit and vegetable shows, one in July and the other in October. There were also four other meetings; these were usually half a day long and included, as a draw to visitors, a lecture given by an eminent horticulturist. Constance Spry talked on 'Flower Decoration in War-Time' in April, and Miss K. Noble from the Ministry of Food on 'Fruit Bottling and Vegetable Cooking' in July. The Fellowship were encouraged to bring along plants from their gardens to these shows and to enter them in competitive classes. The shows were poor things by pre-war standards, but they showed the Fellows that there was some point in continuing to pay their four guineas to the Society.

The *Journal* was at its slimmest, and without proper covers, from May 1942 and through 1943, but it still included notices of events, awards given to plants, enthusiastic descriptions of plants flowering that month at Wisley, as well as learned scientific articles, descriptions of large gardens, especially those containing rare trees and shrubs, short accounts of parts of the Society's history and practical information on growing vegetables. Despite the obvious limitations, the continuing quality of the *Journal* in wartime owed much to the care and hard work of Sir Daniel Hall and Roy Hay, as well as the enthusiasm of knowledgeable Fellows.

What was true of newspapers and journals was equally true of the wireless. Right at the beginning of the war, on 5 September 1939, C. H. Middleton wrote to George Barnes, Director of Talks at the

BBC, requesting permission to mention flowers from time to time. As a lover of flowers himself, Middleton was obviously anxious on his own account, but he was also under pressure particularly from nurserymen and gardeners – even such grand ones as Lionel de Rothschild, who owned a much-admired 'woodland' garden at Exbury in Hampshire – not to abandon flowers entirely. Barnes was content, provided that flower gardening did not interfere with information about food production.

Middleton also did what he could to encourage towns and villages to found or revive gardening societies. He was an enthusiastic public advocate of the local gardening group, not only because it gave its members the chance to buy cheap seed and fertilisers, bought in bulk at a discount, and often brought local land into allotment cultivation, but also for the community and charitable spirit it fostered at monthly meetings and annual flower shows. These shows, sometimes called 'Victory Shows', reminded people of the homely way of life before the war and gave them the potentially morale-boosting benefits of collective effort. Middleton was not content simply to talk about it; in 1940 he helped to found the Weston and Weedon Horticultural Society in his old home village. This society held monthly meetings in the village hall 'which included talks, discussion, coffee and biscuits, and sometimes even a song or two . . .' [26] In December 1941, Middleton devoted a broadcast to an account of the flower show organised by the society that September, the first one in the village for more than forty years.

Some thought it wrong and a waste of time to hold a show in war-time. I wonder how you feel about it? Personally, I think that so long as a show is run on sensible lines in the right spirit, and at the right time, there is everything to be said for it. Gardeners as a class are good wholesome people, they love to get together and discuss their triumphs and their failures . . . They like to brag and show each other what they can do, and go one better than somebody else. The show is a great occasion for a gathering of the clans, a day of reminiscences. It brings a bit of light and pleasure to what otherwise is rather a drab routine.'[27]

The show was held in the grounds of 'the local mansion', presumably Weston Hall, where Middleton's father had worked. It was obviously a rip-roaring success, helped by the presence of the BBC, who broadcast an interview with Middleton by Wynford Vaughan-Thomas. The Home Guard provided the band, the WI made the teas, there was a souvenir programme, and at the end of an exhausting but thoroughly enjoyable day, the society sent £120[28] to the Red Cross Agricultural Fund and a lorryload of vegetables to a local army base. Rather sweetly Middleton said: 'I was merely one of the helpers who hung around and did as he was told.'[29] Perhaps, but he was the reason that they sold 1,000 programmes and the enormous marquee was packed with produce.

Despite energetic efforts by many people to retain something of the pre-war atmosphere in their gardens and horticultural societies, it was inevitable that the changed conditions that war brought should obtrude in unlooked-for ways, even for those trying very hard to forget it. For example, gardens surrounded by iron gates and fences found that the authorities came and removed them, unless the owners could persuade them that they were of particular historical importance. In 1943, Lt Col. R. R. B. Orlebar of Hinwick House in Northamptonshire wrote indignantly to his newspaper to complain about the threatened removal of his garden gates, which would make the flower gardens 'practically unchanged since 1710' 'prey to any invaders', by which he meant straying cattle. Apparently the lady from the Ministry was quite unmoved when he told her that for the past three years some of the flower beds had been turned over to vegetables.[30]

A protective insularity is a great boon in bad times, but that exhibited by Lt Col. Orlebar, and indeed many other very keen gardeners, did not always go down well in the wider world, particularly when there was also more than a frisson of class envy in the mix. In January 1941, the Duke of Westminster, one of the richest and most powerful land-owners in the country, brought a libel suit against the left-leaning workers' newspaper the *Daily Mirror*, and its famous columnist 'Cassandra'. In an article, Cassandra had juxtaposed the information that 643 children had been killed during October 1940 as a result of air raids with the fact that, just at that time, the Duke's collection of orchids had arrived in Florida in fifteen packing cases, to be cared for by an expert gardener until the end of hostilities. The clear implication was that the Duke was spending money sending luxury hothouse plants to America while poor parents could not afford to evacuate their children across the Atlantic to escape the bombs. The particular mischief of these statements was that Lord Haw-Haw[31] repeated them for German propaganda purposes.

The Duke's legal counsel told the court that he had 'been at great pains to cut down his expenditure on his hothouses and flower gardens to an absolute minimum, and to use them only in a way which would assist the national effort to produce food. He had sold orchid plants of great value and a number of those had been resold to America, which produced American currency for this country . . .'[32] Once these facts were known, the newspaper apologised and agreed to pay costs and a sum in settlement to the Duke, which he promised to give to a charity concerned with children who were air-raid victims.

The Duke was lucky that he had managed to find a market and place of safety for his orchids. Generally, ordinary gardeners who loved their greenhouse plants, especially orchids and other tropical species, fared badly, especially after the government introduced heating fuel restrictions under the Control of Fuel (No. 3) Order, in force from 15 January 1943. This prohibited the use of fuel in glasshouses in private gardens for ornamental plants or glasshouse fruits without a permit from the Minister or a regional fuel controller. Before the directive was due to come into effect, Lord Aberconway, the stalwart President of the Royal Horticultural Society, exchanged stiff letters with Gwilym Lloyd George, the Minister of Fuel and Power, who asserted rather obviously that 'private luxuries must give way to national necessities'.[33] Aberconway responded that the large anthracite coal that was burned in greenhouse boilers was not used in domestic properties, so there was no conflict, but this cut no ice with the Minister. The RHS fought hard to save a few of the finest collections of glasshouse plants, which they could persuade the authorities were of national importance, but the vast majority of those belonging to amateur enthusiasts perished.

So ordinary gardeners had to fall back on cultivating hardy species, if they wanted to nurture plants that were not edible, as well as those that were. They did as much as they could within the constraints of having little to choose from in nursery and seed catalogues, and less space available in their gardens. Gardeners continued to grow Michaelmas daisies, so that they had something colourful to put round the font in church for Harvest Festival, tended pelargoniums in the cold greenhouse, weeded the rockery, and picked sweet peas grown against the fence for the house. And they looked for brightness and cheering colour in the contents of a 6d packet of hardy annual seed.

The desire to be cheered up by flowers and to cheer others is encapsulated in this contribution by a gardener from Middlesex in *The Gardeners' Chronicle*: 'Orange Marigolds, Scarlet Pelargoniums, pink and red Impatiens, golden *Spartium junceum*[34] and mauve Heliotrope. What a mixture! I don't care one little bit so long as the colour and perfume please old ladies, young children and the lassies from the factories and first aid posts, and even the stalwart fellows from the ARP and AFS [Auxiliary Fire Service] posts − so there!'[35]

People did not even always need to go to those lengths, since provided there was time to keep the weeds at bay, established gardens still blossomed and flourished each year with peonies and irises, phlox and lupins, indeed all the richness and variety of perennial plants that came up every year without fail, not to mention shrubby cotoneasters, hybrid tea roses, scented philadelphus, climbing *Clematis montana* and winter jasmine. It is certain that these continued to give pleasure all through the war years, even if they had to rise above a green carpet of ground elder.

The home garden also played an important part in the holiday plans of Britons. Holidays abroad were obviously impossible, but even those in Britain were difficult to organise, since many seaside hotels had been requisitioned by government departments, taken over by commercial companies or, in the case of the Isle of Man, turned into internment camps. In any event, public transport in wartime could be severely disrupted without warning by enemy action or troop movements.

How best to spend any holiday on offer was something that exercised everyone on the Home Front. At a time when use of the motor car was severely curtailed by petrol rationing[36], spare time almost inevitably had to be spent mostly at home, and very often in the garden, unless civilians heeded the call to spend their free time in agricultural work camps. General interest magazines encouraged their readers to live in the open air wherever possible – walking in the countryside, picnicking with their children, listening to concerts in the park, playing competitive sports or garden games like croquet or clock golf, and gardening. Advertisements reinforced the message. In 1941, Ryders, the seedsmen, produced the following didactic advertisement:

Flowers can play a far more important part in our lives in war-time than you may first imagine. Not only do they brighten our homes by providing colour and harmony, for table and interior decoration, but they do something more – they stimulate and brighten our mental outlook too!

Remember also, that the tending and growing of flowers soothe mind and nerves as nothing else can in times of stress and strain.[37]

This theme of how gardens could ease the worst effects of 'nervous strain' or illness influenced the requisitioning of 'rest-break houses' by the government. In 1944, for example, a large modern house in Walton-on-the-Hill was taken over for the purpose; there is a charming photograph in the Imperial War Museum archives of women sitting on the (unmown) grass and working amongst the the lupins in the border. The Women's Land Army also had the use of three rest-break houses, which were funded by labour groups in the United States via the British War Relief Society of America. One was in Torquay in Devon, where twenty-five women could be accommodated, another at Llandudno for fifteen, and another in Edinburgh. No doubt they were thoroughly appreciated by anyone lucky enough to be sent there, but the numbers accommodated were necessarily small. Mostly, the only holiday that a Land Girl got was a week a year back at home with Mother and Father, sitting in a deckchair in the garden. But in an era when foreign holidays even in peacetime were only for the rich, this was as good as it got.

CHAPTER TEN

GARDENING BEHIND THE WIRE

I f many Britons saw their gardens as refuges from the dreary or fright-
ening realities of their daily life, and gardening as one of the principal
activities that reassured them that a pleasant, peaceful, hopeful normality
was possible, how much more must gardening have meant to the unwillingly incarcerated – those in prisoner-of-war and internment camps,
both in Great Britain and abroad. Certainly there is evidence that,
wherever imprisoned men and women were allowed to till a bit of
garden, they did so, often in circumstances where Nature, as well as
Man, was thoroughly against them.

Incarceration, especially over a long period and when the future
is uncertain, takes a heavy toll on human beings, both physically and
psychologically. It is almost guaranteed to cause stress, anxiety, even
depression. Unlike criminals, service personnel do not deserve punish-
ment, and worse still, their sentence is indeterminate. During the
First World War, a German doctor, A. L. Vischer, coined the phrase
'barbed-wire disease' for the syndrome from which many prisoners
of war suffered. The thorny strands of barbed wire entangled the
prisoners; they could see beyond them to the outside world but were
forbidden from taking part in it. Moreover, since most prisoner-of-
war and internment camps were uncomfortable and overcrowded,
had only rudimentary sanitation, afforded little or no privacy, were
mostly sited in very dreary, isolated places, and were guarded by a
(usually) extremely hostile enemy, it is not surprising that the inmates
were prone to bouts of irritability, short temper, lethargy and
melancholy.

The greatest number of British service personnel captured at any one time were taken prisoner in northern France in May and June 1940, and the men were made to kick their heels for five years in north European camps, usually in Germany or Poland. Servicemen were also taken prisoner in north Africa and Italy, in which case they ended up in Italian POW camps.[1]

For most British servicemen in European camps intense boredom and frustration were the main enemies, and they tried hard to find any distraction to pass the time. As it turned out, wherever they could, at least some used gardening as a welcome diversion, as well as a means of supplementing their rations and an outlet for their youthful energy and competitive spirit. Adding to the rations was important: prisoners of war and internees in Germany received food to the value of approximately 1,500 calories a day, which meant that, although not actually starved, they were certainly malnourished. Moreover, even where the food was adequate, it was deadly monotonous.

Of course, in all military camps, of whatever kind, prisoners were at the mercy of the sternness and caprice of their captors. But one or two of the more enlightened German commandants actively promoted gardening, in officers' camps at least.[2] In May 1940, the German OKW (Oberkommando der Wehrmacht, or Supreme Command of the Armed Forces) granted prisoners permission to make gardens, with the costs of the necessary supplies to be part of the camp budget. As a result, the commandant of Oflag 8B in Silberberg, Poland, published the following camp standing order: 'For the improvement of the meals and the health of *all* Ps.o.W. through extra vitamins, gardens inside the camp are placed at the disposal of Ps.o.W. and will be managed by them.'[3] The work was to be carried out under the direction of a British officer, and unauthorised gathering of vegetables would be punished as theft. The commandant went on to say that he intended to increase the gardening area substantially, and advised prisoners to send home for seeds without delay.

That was made possible by a stipulation in the 1929 Geneva Convention (to which Germany was a signatory) that prisoners be allowed to receive post and parcels from their families and from the Red Cross. Not surprisingly, the men treasured these parcels; their arrival was always a red-letter day. During the First World War, the Royal Horticultural Society had organised the sending of flower and vegetable seeds to internees and prisoners of war, especially those in the Ruhleben internment camp in Berlin, so it was not difficult to get such a scheme going once more.

The first RHS meeting concerned with the dispatch of seeds was held in May 1941, with a Red Cross official present. The committee agreed that plain seed envelopes should be sent, with only the name of the seed, some cultural instructions and the name and address of the Society written on them. This was to ensure that the seeds did not contravene any prison regulations and risk being destroyed as a result. The Red Cross official promised to provide books for instruction if the RHS recommended a list. The Society's representatives agreed to ask commercial companies to provide seed, and put a notice in the *Journal* to encourage amateurs to donate small flower bulbs.[4]

As a result, during the year 1942–3, the RHS dispatched 793 parcels of seeds to prisoners of war and internees in Germany, Italy and France. These were largely the gift of the leading British commercial seedsmen, but packets of seeds, or the money to purchase them, were also received by the RHS from horticultural organisations and the Red Cross in Canada, Australia and South Africa. Although largely forgotten now, this was one of the most worthwhile contributions that the RHS made to the war effort.

A letter received by the RHS in April 1943 is typical of the prisoners' response to these parcels, and bears reproducing in full:

> Central Library,
> Stalag XXA
> 14th April, 1943

On behalf of the men of this Stalag I would like to offer our sincere thanks for the many parcels of seeds we have received from you for this season.

They are in great demand by our central and isolated detachments and you have enabled us to satisfy all demands. The men have been amazed at the large variety we have been able to offer them; their praise of the work that is being done for we [*sic*] prisoners of war, and the amount of hard work they put into the proposed garden sites, is proof that they are appreciative.

All are primarily interested in the vegetable seeds, but the flower seeds have also been in great demand, particularly by our hospital, which has quite a large flower garden. It is not hard to imagine the comfort and solace which your efforts bring to our sick who have so many idle hours in which their thoughts naturally turn to home.

Once again this year I am organising a Gardening Competition and I will be pleased to forward you an account of it in due course.

You may find satisfaction in knowing that whenever we see fresh flowers on the table or we are eating our vegetable garden produce, each of us thinks again of the good work done by the Royal Horticultural Society.

Yours sincerely,

(Sgt) W. O. Wright,

Head Librarian.[5]

The RHS made sure that horticultural textbooks were among those books sent out by the Red Cross Society's Educational Books Section to prisoner-of-war camps in Germany and Italy.[6] As a result, prisoners began to study for RHS examinations. The first nine 'other rank' candidates sat them in July 1942, invigilated by their sergeants. In 1943, a Sergeant A. W. J. Souster gained a medal, being equal first with a candidate in Britain in the first class of the RHS National Certificate in Elementary Horticultural Practice. Another successful candidate in the National Diploma of Horticulture 'will take the practical examination on returning to this country'.[7] These exams continued to be taken in camps until the war ended, and those who had studied for them but not yet sat the exams were given two years in which to do so after the war, without any charge being made. Fifty candidates took the opportunity to do so.

2nd Lieutenant Alan Milburn, of the 7th Battalion, Royal Warwickshire Regiment, who was wounded and captured at Dunkirk, undoubtedly benefited from Red Cross parcels of seed. As we have seen, his mother, Clara, wrote a diary throughout the war, and she included snippets from his letters in them. Here is a typical entry, dated 16 July 1942: '*A letter from Alan, dated 19.6.42*, telling of the first results of their gardening efforts – a dish of fresh greens, turnip tops, for their evening meal. He also says horses are very popular in the camp now! Their hut is beside the road and they get first pick!'[8] By January 1944, he was in Oflag VIIB near Eichstätt in Bavaria: 'Gardening is occupying a lot of his time and for serious reading he has studied The Beveridge Report[9] – Alan! Gosh!!'[10]

Alan Milburn had plainly become very involved in gardening, for on 10 July that year, he wrote to his parents: 'My news is, of course, all onions – 6,000 planted so far and about 19,000 to plant . . . one morning last week I had a trip to the nursery in town where the tomato plants and onion seedlings are being raised.'[11] A letter written in October 1944 shows how hopeful he was of release in the near future: 'Next month we shall start digging, and so it will go on until we are told "You can go home now".'[12] Clara Milburn continued: 'He tells of progress of the onions, tomatoes and beetroot, the runner beans – with black fly, which were then disposed of by ladybirds . . .' By January 1945, he had been detailed to work as a gardener in the town each day. He finally arrived back in England on 10 May, two days after VE Day.

The soils in some camps were atrocious, but that did not necessarily put off the committed. The going was particularly hard at Stalag Luft III, as the camp had been built in a recently felled pine forest, and the soil was extremely acidic and infertile as a result. While imprisoned there, Squadron Leader C. I. Rolfe kept a garden diary, and in 1944 he described the garden, even including a plan. It 'consisted of small strips of "home made" soil dug in and amongst the typical pine needle strewn sand on which the camp was built. In 1942 Polish officers occupied this room[13], and they it appears dug into the sand every available scrap of refuse. In 1943 this decayed matter enabled the room to reap quite a good crop of onions, tomatoes, marrows, radishes etc.'[14] The problem was that the gardens suffered from the depredations of hares, which must somehow have got through the wire. The prisoners set a trap for these but only succeeded in catching the Padré's cat.

That must have been frustrating, but gardening in a prisoner-of-war camp could sometimes seem downright pointless. Brian Filliter, a British flying officer, had problems knowing what to say in his letters home: 'you write, and you don't want them to worry about you at home, so you say, "we're busy making a garden". Gardens! What a farce! Nothing grew, and people walked all over it. But the folks at home are sending you gardening books.'[15] That must have been a common experience in those desolate northern European camps.

Where camp gardens existed and flourished, they proved to be a potent reminder to service personnel of their homes. They probably also gave them back a sense of the seasons passing, and connected them once more with the soil. It is highly likely that being in charge of a garden allowed them to feel a little more in control. The vegetables they grew improved their diet and the flowers convinced them that there was still beauty and homeliness to be found in a distinctly ugly and alien environment. And, crucially, caring for a garden did much simply to pass the time. Prison camp gardens were, in the best sense, 'defiant', the word that Kenneth I. Helphand used in the title of his important book on the subject. As he puts it: 'As a creative, purposeful activity, gardens engaged all aspects of a person, with an aesthetic as well as a practical result.'[16]

Of course, gardening was only one of many leisure activities in POW camps,[17] but it served another purpose, besides providing something to do and some much-needed variety and vitamins in food. As combatants, many, if not most, young men felt that they had a duty to try to break for freedom and get home to join their units once more, or at the very least harry and occupy the enemy. They spent long hours ingeniously planning and trying to effect their escape, and gardening activities could be a very useful subterfuge while tunnels were dug. Prisoners in Stalag Luft III,[18] a camp for those British and American servicemen who had tried to break out from other camps in the past, dug three tunnels simultaneously – named 'Tom' 'Dick' and 'Harry'. However, they encountered a serious problem in getting rid of the tunnelled soil because it was lighter in colour than the topsoil. Their solution was to mix it up surreptitiously with the soil in the prisoners' vegetable gardens. This was done by prisoners nicknamed 'penguins', who carried bags full of soil hanging down inside their baggy trouser legs and attached to a string round their neck. When they pulled the string, the bag emptied the soil on to the ground and they scuffed it in with feet or tools. An almost unbelievable 100 tons of soil was disposed of in this way.[19]

Lieutenant van Kyrke, a naval officer imprisoned in an officers' camp near Bremen, was also responsible for getting rid of tunnel soil. According to David James, in his book *A Prisoner's Progress*, van Kyrke took a great interest in ullage[20] pits. 'A base of sand, covered with tea leaves and potato peelings, may not make the finest garden manure, but it does get rid of a lot of embarrassing soil.'[21]

Helphand wrote on the subject of the psychology of prisoners that 'In defiant situations, humans display a surprising resourcefulness in design and function, in formal arrangement, and in the appropriation of, gathering, and use of materials. Recognition of our own creativity under adverse conditions heightens our satisfaction in being in such a garden.'[22] Nowhere was this truer than in the POW camps under Japanese control in the Far East. When Japan entered the war, they had no prisoner-of-war camps at all – since they did not expect to imprison anyone – so the first ones were makeshift in the extreme. And since Japan was not a signatory to the Geneva Convention, almost all prisoners were subjected to a very harsh regime of hard labour. Perhaps the worst off were those service personnel who were captured by the Japanese after the fall of Singapore or during the Burma campaign and forced into slave labour, many of them helping to build the Burma Railway.[23] The daily food ration was only 500 to 600 calories in Japanese POW camps (and 1,000 in civilian internment camps), so the inmates slowly starved and were prey to terrible diseases such as beri-beri, which were the result of poor nutrition.[24]

Some productive gardens were made in officer camps although rather fewer in those for enlisted men, but they were on nothing like the scale found in European ones.[25] The biggest was probably on Changi island, where vegetable gardens were established using POW labour, with as many as 1,000 men employed. It is tragically ironic that the camps where the need for extra vitamins was greatest were the ones least likely to have gardens.

Servicemen know that there is a risk of being captured and imprisoned when they take part in armed conflict, but civilians do not normally expect such a fate when they take up a job in a foreign country. Yet some found themselves interned simply because they were in the wrong place at the wrong time. This happened particularly when Belgium, Holland and France were invaded in May 1940, when Manila was overrun after the Japanese attack on Pearl Harbor in December 1941, and after Singapore fell to the Japanese in February 1942.

Internment camps in the Far East – in countries as disparate as Indonesia and Japan itself – housed mainly expatriates who had been working in civil service jobs, medical facilities, universities or Christian missions. These people were often married with children. In all, there were 75,000 internees, mainly British, American and Dutch. There were many camps, but the best-documented as far as gardening is concerned, are probably the old gaol on the small island of Changi, which had been the British army base in Singapore, together with Stanley in Hong Kong, and the campus of the University of Santo Tomas in Manila.

Before the war, a number of these internees had been accustomed to employ servants to do the heavy work in house and garden. Yet many stories have emerged of their courage and resourcefulness; in particular, a number of internees made vegetable patches where it could not be imagined that plants would ever grow. In Stanley camp in Hong Kong, one internee, Jean Gittins, made a hand tool from a piece of wood about six inches long, with half a dozen nails banged through it. She and some friends laid out their garden on a flat roof, so that they could guard it more easily from pilferers. There they grew shallots and mint to improve the taste of the rice on which they mainly lived. Others began to follow their example, and the thieving ceased. In 1943 they also grew tomatoes, lettuce, root crops, peas and celery, adding beans, cucumbers, pumpkins and peanuts the following year. They collected seeds from their rations and from the plants they grew, and stored them in labelled packets. In the autumn of 1944 the Japanese cut the water main, so they had to haul all the water for the gardens from previously disused wells. William Sewell, a Quaker university professor, said that the gardening in the Stanley camp reminded him of subsistence farming on the hills of Chungking. He realised that 'so many of the things which we had thought of as typically Chinese were merely the normal results of human endeavour in the presence of need and the absence of money and tools'.[26]

A distinguished British botanist, Dr G. A. C. Herklots – until the war Reader in Biology at the University of Hong Kong – was also interned at Stanley. According to *The Gardeners' Chronicle*, which announced his internment, he was 'a man of wide interests, being an able botanist, an all-round naturalist and an enthusiastic horticulturist'.[27] He was remembered by fellow internees as someone who taught them about the wild fruits and roots that they could, or could not, safely eat. In a book published after the war, he described how 'In 1941 the first edition of "Vegetable Cultivation in Hong Kong" was written in a hurry under conditions far from ideal. It was inevitably scrappy and full of errors. During 43 months of internment at Stanley, Hong Kong there was ample opportunity to prepare a second edition which was published in 1947. This edition also contained inaccuracies.'[28] Twenty years later, he used the information in his book *Vegetable Cultivation in South-East Asia*, which covered a wider field than simply Hong Kong, and corrected the inaccuracies, though it still contained many of the pen-and-ink drawings that he had done while interned in Stanley.

Herklots also described what he called the 'Stanley compost', which he developed during the war.

The method of making compost employed by me at the internment camp at Stanley during 1942–1945 is simple and was extremely successful. The only available source of organic nitrogen was human urine; this is perfectly safe to use for this purpose as it is free from the eggs of parasitic worms and is free from harmful bacteria such as those that cause dysentery. (Night soil, which may be contaminated by dangerous parasites should not be so used unless it has matured in a covered tank for at least three weeks.) Narrow trenches were dug in succession along the foot of a barbed wire fence some nine feet high and the excavated laterite-soil wheeled away and discarded. At the bottom of the trench was placed a thick layer of dried rubbish, chiefly grass, and on this was placed a generous layer of ashes from the kitchen fire of grass (occasionally of wood, bark and sawdust). Half a can or a can of fresh urine was poured on top of this and the mixture covered with a thick layer of topsoil carried in from the local hillside; this was well trodden down. The process was repeated once or twice, depending on the depth of the trench, the final level of the soil being three or four inches above the original level. Into this top layer of soil more ashes were raked and the bed well watered. Seeds of Chinese green cucumber and of Yates' Crystal Apple cucumber were subsequently sown in these beds; the plants grew well and in 1942 yielded 140 cucumbers which were greatly appreciated.[29]

Cucumbers the internees were familiar with, but they often had the added difficulty of not knowing how to grow tropical vegetables. However, sheer necessity taught them how to cultivate the staple, sweet potatoes, as well as a number of other exotic vegetables, such as amaranth, kangkong – a semi-aquatic relative of morning glory, which grew very well – tapioca, eggplant (aubergine), chillies, beans and Ceylon (Malabar) spinach.

If anything, the camp at Santo Tomas in Manila seems to have been the most horticulturally advanced of them all. It was an enormous place, housing perhaps 5,000 civilian internees, of whom 900 were British or Empire citizens. A seven-acre area in the north-east corner was cleared of junk and made into gardens, under the supervision of a committee of experts. The gardeners grew a range of edible plants, both likely and unlikely, including many local staples such as yams and talinum. They grew kangkong, as the internees at Stanley also did, along with pechay, upo, chayotes, gabi, concomas and mongo beans. They planted papaya trees, which grew very quickly, and boiled the unripe fruits to make them edible. They also grew hedges of cassava. In April 1942 they harvested nine baskets of talinum, which was enough for everyone in the camp to eat something. Later that year, they discovered an enormous water tank, and rigged up an irrigation system to the vegetable gardens. This was destroyed in a bad flood in November 1943, but they found the will and strength to remake it. Only once during the war did they receive Red Cross parcels – just before Christmas 1943. As the war wore on, and the Allies began to put pressure on the Japanese, the situation worsened and food rations declined still further. The internees were forced to eat weeds, even lily bulbs. The average weight loss for a male internee over the period of incarceration was 53 lb, or nearly four stone. It is impossible to put a dietary value on the vegetables grown, but their value for raising morale cannot be doubted.

In the first two years of the war, there were no camps for foreign combatants in Britain, since the threat of invasion meant that any captured service personnel were sent across the Atlantic to the United States and Canada instead. Italian prisoners from north Africa were not shipped to England from the Mediterranean until July 1941, because of the continuing conflict there. However, once the threat of invasion by Germany had completely receded that summer, the numbers detained grew rapidly. By the end of the war, there were more than 600 camps or hostels housing POWs in Britain.

Many prisoners volunteered to work on farms and market gardens rather than spend their days in stupefying idleness. The prisoners were paid a small amount for their work, under the Geneva Convention. They wore a distinctive uniform of British army khaki, which had been dyed a purple-brown colour. There were circular lighter-coloured or red patches on their backs, and diamond-shaped patches on their trousers, so that any man who tried to escape was highly conspicuous. Not that escaping was a realistic option in an island of hostile foreigners. From January 1942, 'good conduct' prisoners even lived on farms, rather than returning to camp each night. By the end of the war, there were 58,000 POWs working on farms or in commercial gardening operations.

Wilfrid Cheal, owner of the large nursery Cheals of Crawley (see Chapter Eight), recalled:

A prisoner-of-war camp was set up a few miles away at Norwood Hill, and in the early days we had some very lively times with the Italians sent to us, who proved to be extremely volatile and unreliable. Many were the fights that took place with agricultural weapons, so that we had to demand their withdrawal. Later the Germans were much more useful, and finally the eastern European displaced persons proved to be a great asset, and very grateful for the opportunity to work.[30]

The eastern Europeans were mainly Russian, Polish and Czech refugees.[31]

German prisoners of war were not employed in farming or market gardening operations until the autumn of 1944. All had to live in camps, and they were not allowed to work in the same gangs as Italians, since it was thought that there were a lot of dangerous Nazis amongst them. On the whole, though, the Germans seem to have been good workers. A. G. Street wrote in *The Farmer's Weekly*: 'from the little I have seen of the work of the German POW to date, he seems to be worth three average Italians; since the way in which many of the latter cycle and laze around the countryside is little short of offensive'.[32] Dorothy Pembridge remembered barrowing hundreds of lettuces that were to be sold while the Italian POWs sat in the sun watching her and the other girls work. Such righteous indignation is understandable, but it is hard to see why the Italians *should* have worked any harder than was absolutely necessary to justify their rations. Employers paid the War Ags for these workers; the POWs themselves received £1 a week.

Prisoners of war even found themselves working in mansion gardens. For example, Italians helped to clear out the hundred acres of badly overgrown pleasure grounds beyond the formal gardens at Ditchley Park. For the Trees, prisoners proved to be useful replacement labour for their British gardeners away on active service. And at Nuneham Park in 1945, Harry Dodson worked alongside German POWs. 'I had no feeling against them,' he said. 'Two or three of them had worked in botanic gardens and parks in Germany in pre-war days and one of them especially was very interesting to talk to. He used to tell me the name of a plant in German and I'd tell him what it was in English.'[33] However, harmony could be fragile. One under-gardener at Nuneham had been imprisoned in Germany: 'One morning I suppose the poor chap flipped at seeing these Germans working in the same area as him. He came up through the frame yard in a terrible rage, swinging a rope round with a noose on the end – and if he could get hold of one of them he was going to string him up.'[34] The head gardener's wife and Harry rushed to calm him down, but it was a nasty moment.

In 1939, there were 80,000 civilian German or Austrian nationals living in Britain, as well as many Italians – bakers, restaurateurs and ice cream sellers in the main. Six hundred of these nationals were considered to be dangerous, and were immediately interned. Another 9,000 were restricted in where they went and with whom they associated. The others, many of them Jews who had arrived in Britain after Hitler's rise to power in 1933, were extremely grateful for the shelter and protection they had been offered, and were free to go where they liked. However, after France fell in May 1940, all aliens, friendly or otherwise, who had not taken out naturalisation papers were interned in camps. Men and women, even married couples, were separated. One camp was situated on York racecourse, another at Huyton near Liverpool, but most were on the Isle of Man. Many of these were comprised of a collection of seaside boarding houses surrounded by barbed wire, so there were little or no opportunities to make a garden.

A number of the internees were immensely distinguished people – scientists, musicians, artists and the like – and when the threat of German invasion lessened substantially, most were set free, beginning in early 1941. One such was an elderly German Jew called Sophus Coutinho, a cactus expert who had been employed at the Hamburg Botanic Gardens before he escaped from Germany. He spent the latter part of the war working in the Cactus House at Kew.[35]

Amongst those Britons interned as enemies of the state, Sir Oswald Mosley, the head of the British Union of Fascists, was the most notorious. He was imprisoned at the beginning of the war, under Defence Regulation 18B. His wife, Diana,[36] was also incarcerated, in Holloway Prison in London. In December 1941, Winston Churchill agreed that the pair might be united. Thereafter they lived in a small house inside the prison walls, and grew vegetables, including cabbages and aubergines, as well as wood strawberries, in a vegetable plot. After the war, Lady Mosley said, in a typically teasing Mitford way, that she had never since grown *fraises des bois* that tasted as good as the ones she grew in prison.

CHAPTER ELEVEN

ANIMALS IN THE BACK GARDEN

When war broke out, the majority of amateur gardeners had little or no experience of looking after livestock. This was partly because, with the coming of motorised transport in the early years of the century, self-sufficiency – even in the country – was no longer so important. But it was also because householders were not encouraged to keep animals; indeed, quite the reverse. In 1940, however, after meat was put 'on ration', the government told local councils to lift all restrictions on people keeping livestock in gardens, in order that they might provide their families with cheap sources of protein.[1] Both bacon and eggs had been imported in large quantities from Denmark before the war, but that country was occupied by Germany in April 1940. Bacon was included in the first tranche of rationed foods in January 1940, although eggs remained off ration until June 1941.

Few things were likely to keep civilians more happily occupied than the everyday care of domestic animals, and happy occupation is what the authorities thought would see the population through the dark days. So, just as with the 'Dig for Victory' campaign, there was much more than a whiff of morale-boosting about this exercise in promoting domestic food production.

MAF concentrated its efforts on convincing the population of the value of keeping hens, ducks, geese, goats, rabbits, pigs and bees, and on teaching them to do it in ways that did not endanger the health of either the animals or their keepers. As with vegetable growing, they set about developing a substantial education campaign. Leaflets with titles such as 'Rabbits for food, fur and profit' were available for a small sum, while posters with slogans like 'To save your bacon save your scraps' were commonplace. There was even a radio programme on the subject of 'back-yard' livestock keeping, entitled *Backs to the Land* (see Chapter Six).

Those who heeded the call to keep poultry were encouraged to ask for advice from the Domestic Poultry Keepers' Council, which could point them to legitimate sources of supply, while specialist magazines like *Poultry Farmer, Feathered World* and *The Smallholder* published advertisements from reputable suppliers that had been passed by the Poultry Advertisement Control Board. If it had not existed, it would be impossible to invent such a body, but the PACB was just one more example of central government's desire to direct almost every aspect of civilian life. For advice about rearing pigs there was the Small Pig Keepers' Council, set up by the National Pig Breeders' Association and the Ministry of Agriculture. This was probably most useful to amateur swineherds when they had to deal with their animals' carcasses.

There was much discussion in newspapers as to which livestock was the most appropriate for a garden situation. Most seemed to agree that poultry for meat and eggs was easiest, since a few hens could be looked after in quite confined conditions, and though prone to some ills, they were generally hardy, sturdy and cheap to buy. Novice poultry keepers were advised to buy one chicken per person in the house, with one for luck.

Eggs were also the source of protein that was likely to be rationed most severely. At the beginning of the war, chicken farmers had to cut the size of their flocks drastically, by about 30 per cent, when dairy cattle became the top priority for the limited supplies of cereal feed. What is more, beer, which was never rationed, required 600,000 tons of barley a year, which would have fed 36 million hens.[2] As a result, in 1941 there were only 12 million hens in the country, which was a sixth of the pre-war number. That is why, from June 1941, shell eggs (as opposed to powdered egg, remembered without affection for turning a greenish colour when scrambled)[3] were rationed to just one per adult per week.

Thousands of people took up the challenge of keeping chickens, building hen coops and runs on their back lawns, and even learning how to incubate eggs and rear chicks, if they had tolerant neighbours who did not mind being woken up by a cockerel's crow in the morning – although allotmenteers had to apply to their landlord for permission if they wanted to keep a cockerel. Many people plumped for buying day-old chicks, which had been 'sexed', to avoid the nuisance and waste involved in rearing cockerels. Pullets, which were eight-week-old chickens, were sold by hatcheries and arrived in labelled cardboard boxes at the local railway station.

According to Alan Thompson, the editor of *Feathered World*, and columnist for the *Daily Herald*: 'The hen's egg is the finest concentrated food known to man. It is produced by a humble, and slightly ridiculous, creature whose remarkable qualities have never been justly appreciated.'[4] So wrote a genuine enthusiast. Certainly, as well as being full of protein, eggs were a necessary ingredient in many recipes, and when a hen's laying days were over, she made a good, if rather tough, Sunday roast. In those days, the practice of boiling up kitchen scraps to feed to chickens was positively encouraged, and it was possible to keep two or three hens without much expenditure.[5] From 1941 on, in return for coupons so that they could buy meal for hens – at 4 lb per month per hen – poultry keepers waived their right to an egg ration. They would still have been better off, however, since a hen might lay 250 to 300 eggs a year. The problem was that the daily allowance of two ounces of 'Balancer meal' per chicken was not really enough for a bird to lay well, especially as there was no mixed corn available to supplement it, unless the gardener grew his own maize. The authorities recognised this and put the allowance up by a quarter in June 1943.

Poultry keepers were also encouraged to feed hens crushed dried acorns and beech mast as well as fish waste, stale bread and dried grass mowings. Those who were also gardeners grew Jerusalem artichokes, lucerne, linseed, mangolds, sunflowers and buckwheat as well, or their neighbours did it for them in exchange for eggs. Most seed merchants sold some or all of these as seed.

C. H. Middleton had nothing but praise for hens: he declared that they would keep down the grass in orchards, clean up the fruit cage of insect pests and fallen fruit in autumn and provide invaluable, strong manure. Chicken manure was especially good for adding to the compost heap because, being high in nitrogen, it accelerated decay. A virtuous circle could be established, if the compost was put on the vegetable garden, where food for the hens was grown. Middleton was of the opinion that the manure from a dozen hens was enough for a 'fair-sized' vegetable plot, although it is doubtful that many garden owners had room for twelve chickens.

At a time when domestic refrigerators were the exception rather than the rule, surplus eggs would not keep long, unless they were submerged in 'waterglass', when they would last at least six months. Waterglass was a solution of sodium silicate, usually made up in a bucket or earthenware crock. Preserving in waterglass was a popular way of providing eggs for cooking in the winter, when the hens were not laying so prolifically. Surplus eggs and chickens were also given as presents or as barter for other foodstuffs, clothing coupons and so on. In September 1943, for example, Mrs Milburn exchanged a basket of pears and apples from her fecund orchard for a fat cockerel and some blackberries.

So, for a variety of reasons, the number of hens that were kept in back gardens more than doubled during the war to 11.5 million, and by the end of the war these hens were producing a quarter of the eggs consumed in the United Kingdom. And all of this despite the fact that domestic egg production per bird declined in the war years.

For more adventurous spirits or those with bigger gardens and ponds, ducks were a possible alternative. Khaki Campbells were always recommended for their eggs, since they would lay almost every day of the year, while Aylesburys were the first choice for meat. Experts advised that, although ducks puddled the ground terribly with their webbed feet, they did not require a coop, at least in 'unfoxed areas',[6] a distinct advantage considering the general shortage of timber and chicken wire.

Geese were highly recommended by professionals for their meat as they grew so quickly and could be killed at sixteen weeks, by which time they already weighed over 10 lb. They also lived entirely on grass. But they were not popular with 'back-yarders', since goose meat was usually considered too rich and fatty to be palatable, and geese generated copious quantities of droppings so were genuinely not suitable for small gardens. However, in rural areas they did make very good 'watchdogs', and they could not fail to amuse their owners. Margery Allingham tried looking after a pair in Tolleshunt D'Arcy: 'The two geese we acquired last winter [1940] are still wandering round the front meadow like highbrows at a private view, honking at anything which displeases them.'[7]

Goats, whilst providing unrationed milk, butter and even meat, were also not very popular since they were far from straightforward to look after. They needed both night quarters and space for grazing in the daytime, and it was advisable to tether them securely rather than let them range unfettered, when they would give a whole new meaning to the word 'omnivorous'. As a correspondent to *The Gardeners' Chronicle* warned: 'There would be no difficulty in finding something the goat would eat, but there might be trouble in keeping it from consuming much that was not intended for its food.'[8] C. H. Middleton also had something pungent and to the point to say about this particular animal. When asked by a listener what was the correct food for goats, he replied that his neighbour had some which seemed to thrive on waste paper, woollen socks, lilac and delphiniums. But he rather thought this was not the orthodox diet.

One of the undoubted success stories of livestock keeping during the war was the proliferation of 'pig clubs'. These were usually co-operatives, whereby a group of local people looked after a pig or pigs, collecting swill for their feed and receiving some part of the pig in return once it was slaughtered, as well as a proportion of strong manure for the garden. This swill was kitchen food waste, boiled for an hour to make sure that there was no danger of any disease being passed on to the pigs.

Belonging to a pig club entitled its members to a ration of precious imported meal. Oddly, this ration was rather more per pig than that which commercial pig keepers received. The professionals could be forgiven for feeling aggrieved, since they were the ones with the experience of pig rearing, yet it was their livelihoods that were affected adversely by the government's almost messianic desire to keep the civilian population usefully occupied.

The social benefits of keeping pigs were frequently stressed. In December 1940, *The Times* carried an editorial singing the praises of pig clubs, not only for the meat they produced but for their capacity to cheer up their keepers: 'for those who have little time to spare and sometimes feel harassed by the rush of these days a pen of pigs, especially after they have enjoyed a meal of kitchen waste, presents a restful picture and an antidote to worry'.[9]

In 1942, by which time there were 4,000 registered pig clubs, it was estimated that amateur pig keepers produced five million pounds of pork products in a year. In Paddington, London, there was a municipal piggery on a recreation ground where, between 1941 and 1943, more than 3,300 pigs were raised. Tottenham, also in London, was famous for its pig club, which was founded by sixty-eight members of its borough cleansing department. These dustbin men owned a hundred pigs at a time and kept special buckets on their lorries for vegetable waste. Miss Violet Hudson, sister of the Minister of Agriculture, opened the first ARP pig club in June 1940; it was based in Wandsworth.

Councils bought special equipment to boil pig swill, and municipal swill bins became a common sight in urban streets. Posters enjoined the public not to put in anything that might harm the pigs, such as tea or rhubarb leaves. The resulting concentrated pig food was sold to pig clubs.

In 1942, the County Garden Produce Central Committee issued guidelines about the gathering of acorns to give to pigs. Schoolchildren were encouraged to collect them for pig keepers, and 5s. to 7s.6d per hundredweight was thought a fair price for them. At the same time, livestock keepers were urged to ask local farmers whether they could glean their fields, after harvest, for grain to give to both pigs and poultry. Gleaning was not something that had been seen in the countryside since the agricultural depressions of Victorian times, and it speaks volumes about the shortage of suitable forage for these animals.

As time went on, it became clear that there was insufficient meal left for the needs of commercial pig farmers, so the Ministry halved the ration available to pig clubs, and required them to make available half of any slaughtered pig for distribution, or else give up their bacon ration.

It was also permissible to look after pigs in your own back garden, and a household was allowed to kill two pigs a year, although they had to employ a professional slaughterer to do the deed. Half a side of meat could be sold to the local butcher at wholesale prices. Tuition was available from instructors, such as those trained by the National Federation of Women's Institutes, on how to carve up a pig into cuts, preserve these in salt (usually in the bath), make sausages and bacon, and cook the various parts of the pig thriftily and successfully.

Pig keepers were notably stalwart, considering the inherent difficulties of collecting good-quality swill without foreign bodies in it, housing pigs when building materials were short, sending a much-admired animal to be slaughtered and having to deal with the cutting up and curing of carcasses. It says much for the population's attachment to the full English breakfast that so much effort was put into acquiring it.

Lady Addle had something pertinent to say in the pages of *Punch* about rearing pigs at her large country home, Bengers:

Indeed, Addle [her husband] is himself a considerable pig expert, having for many years personally reared our own special breed, the Bedsocks White. 'Treat pigs and butlers well and they will never let you down,' he has often said, and I must say, except for one butler who drank his Napoleon brandy and one pig who ate his wrist watch, it has proved completely true. Addle frequently supervises the mixing of the pig food himself, so as to be certain it is rightly managed. He won't even trust me to put aside the remains of some of my tastiest dishes, unless he knows just what are the ingredients. 'That's all right for your evacuees but not for my pigs,' he sometimes says . . . [10]

Where there was no room for larger animals, the other obvious 'livestock' for amateurs to keep were honeybees, which could quite easily be kept in hives in town gardens, although they were more usually to be found in cottage gardens in the country. Of course honey was a substitute for pure sugar, and therefore much in demand after January 1940, when sugar was rationed to eight ounces a week, but its antibacterial healing properties were also valued. In larger country establishments and commercial orchards, bees also pollinated fruit trees. At Broughton Hall in Staffordshire, Land Girl Sibyl van Praet sometimes helped to look after several hives in the kitchen garden. Years later, she recalled that 'Late one sultry afternoon a swarm formed in an apple tree. I held a laundry-basket high above the garden wall somewhat precariously whilst Mr Lowe [the head gardener] struggled to bring down the heaving, seething, buzzing mass – in one brown ball – safely gathered, a new colony and very precious.'[11]

An ex-Swanley girl, Mrs Rachel Thorpe, who worked on an erstwhile fruit and strawberry farm at Wisbech, which in wartime was predominantly given over to vegetables, helped look after bee hives and remembered that the honey was pink because the bees would fly to the Chivers jam factory close by and lick up the jam.

More popular than bees, and probably more appealing, were rabbits, which were reasonably easy to accommodate in a back garden, although their care required quite a commitment on the part of their keepers. The does had to be mated, the young looked after, the adults killed on a regular basis and a number of hutches maintained, since buck rabbits fought one another if kept together.[12] Skinning and curing the pelts also took a certain level of skill.

The great advantage of rabbits was that they were the only species of livestock which could be reared just as easily in the city as the countryside. On 20 September 1941, the Duke of Norfolk visited Bethnal Green to see the Bethnal Green Bombed Sites Association allotments, but he also looked in on several back yards to inspect chickens and rabbits, and there are photographs extant of the genial Premier Duke of England sharing a joke with a Cockney in front of vertical tiers of rabbit hutches.

It was said that a single domesticated rabbit provided 2½ lb of meat at little cost, because rabbits could live on food that would otherwise be wasted, and because they were big enough to be killed and eaten when only four months old. (Provided, that was, the children of the rabbit keeper let him do it.) A buck and three does would provide fifty-five young a year, enough for one meat dish for the family each week.

The only rabbit food that owners could buy – provided they were registered with the Ministry of Agriculture Rationing Division – was bran, at a rate of 7 lb per quarter for each doe. If you owned four does or fewer, you could only purchase bran through a domestic rabbit club. Fortunately, rabbits would eat any amount of raw vegetables, pea haulms, carrot tops and non-poisonous weeds like dandelions, as well as cooked potatoes, lawn mowings, kipper skins, tea leaves and cheese rinds. To see their rabbits healthily through the winter, gardeners were advised to grow a number of strange-sounding brassicas, such as gap kale, marrow stem kale, kohlrabi, perpetual kale and thousand-headed kale, as well as cattle carrots, swedes, sugar beet and chicory. Rabbit droppings were the return: they are rich in the major nutrient elements and could be used as a manure, either fresh or after they had rotted down in the compost heap.

Rabbits also provided fur pelts. The best rabbit types for this were chinchilla, sable and rex, whose fur felt like plush. Rabbit fur was in the best condition to make pelts between October and April, and the rabbits were killed when they were six months or more. A full-length fur coat required about forty skins.

The Prime Minister's wife, Clementine, had an interest in rabbit pelts as the chairman of 'Mrs Churchill's Red Cross Aid to Russia' campaign that began in 1941. In 1943, the National Federation of Women's Institutes agreed to support this initiative. One WI member recalled: 'We were urged to keep rabbits, eating the meat to supplement our meagre rations and curing the skins which were then to be made into fur jackets, hats and gloves. Classes on "The Curing of Rabbit Skins" and on glove making were held, whilst other skins were sent to National Headquarters for further processing.'[13] In two and a half years, the Red Cross sent 2,071[14] fur-lined garments to the Soviet Union, and Mrs Churchill's fund raised over £8 million.

As the war wore on, keeping back-yard animals became harder, although resourcefulness and ingenuity sometimes made up for the lack of proper materials. One rabbit keeper, Ken Allen, could not get 1-inch wire for his hutch, so he used the mesh from a Morrison table shelter.[15] And domestic animals were kept in some strange places: 'Admiral Lundy', the manager of the Savoy Cinema in Brighton, kept both ducks and rabbits on the roof of his flat above the cinema, many feet above street level.

Despite all the encouragement of the authorities, however, keeping livestock never became truly popular. Taken all in all, that is hardly surprising, since most gardens were not really suitable to become small-holdings. A Wartime Social Survey of May 1945 set out to discover, amongst other things, how many private households kept livestock, and the number turned out to be a very modest 14 per cent. Of these, 72 per cent had hens, so only 10 per cent of all households; 30 per cent owned rabbits, 10 per cent kept ducks, 3 per cent geese, 6 per cent pigs, 1 per cent goats and 3 per cent bees. The average number of hens kept was seven and of rabbits five. It is particularly surprising how few households kept bees, when honey was such a longed-for sugar substitute. The answer must lie in both the initial outlay required, and the knowledge that had to be acquired to make a success of beekeeping.

The subject of domesticated livestock starkly pointed up the divide between the country and the town. Country people had always kept small animals – usually poultry and pigs – in their gardens, to a greater or lesser extent. Even if enthusiasm had declined in the immediate pre-war years, most country people remembered their mothers salting bacon for the winter, and making a meal out of every part of the animal except the squeak. And country people had a tradition of bartering eggs for other goods with their neighbours. Urban keepers might have access to the many Dig for Victory exhibitions mounted in towns and cities, where animal experts stood ready alongside the gardeners to answer questions, but that can never have been the same as living next door to an expert livestock keeper.

Country people also had the opportunity to eat wild animals, as well as plants. Villagers could easily acquire a couple of wild rabbits or a brace of pigeon, for a favour done for someone who had permission to shoot on a farm or landowner's estate. With so many gamekeepers away at the war, these animals, classed as vermin, were numerous. Even game birds were given away: Muriel Green recorded in her diary in October 1939 that her family had been given three partridges by the local baronet.[16] Her mother ran the village garage, so perhaps a little extra petrol had gone the baronet's way. Who knows? And there was plenty of fishing to be had in brooks and trout streams, for anyone with the leisure to fish them.

These were all ways of varying the diet which were not usually open to town dwellers. It is small wonder that many believed country people 'had it easy'. It also seemed to them unfair that the rural population could take the opportunity to buy fresh vegetables at source from market and mansion gardens, rather than having to wait until they appeared in shops, and have such easy access to farmhouse butter or duck eggs. Country people could also pick their own apples and pears, while children could be sent blackberrying in the hedgerows in autumn and to pick dandelion leaves in spring for salads and nettles for nettle soup. Muriel Green wrote excitedly, after a trip to the local woods in March 1941: 'We have found an onion ersatz. Garlic! Wild garlic! . . . it was as good as any onion.'[17]

Country people, on the other hand, were quick to complain that they could not take advantage of eating in British Restaurants[18] or works canteens, where the food was cheap and nutritious, and that by the time they arrived in their local town on an erratic bus service on a Saturday afternoon, there was nothing left worth buying in the shops.

Not surprisingly, many people happy to grow vegetables thought keeping livestock was a step too far. It was (or could be) a substantial commitment of both time and money, initially at least. Nor did the population in general feel happy about dispatching live creatures when required. According to a disgusted Alan Thompson, some would not even take the trouble to save kitchen waste for other people's livestock:

'There are plenty of people too busily occupied, or maybe some too lazy and unpatriotic to exert themselves and undertake any work of national importance.'[19] That seems a bit harsh in the circumstances, but certainly livestock keeping never became anything more than a minority interest in wartime, even if a strong folk memory of it remains to this day.

CHAPTER TWELVE

FIERCELY STIRRING CAULDRONS

The other side of the coin of the government's concern to get civilians to grow food and keep animals to supplement their rations was to encourage them to do something useful, healthy and thrifty[1] with what they produced. Not only did the authorities think that people were ignorant of gardening techniques, but they also believed they would need a good deal of help in understanding what different foods offered them in the way of nutritional values, how to stretch their rations in the most efficient way and how to cook food properly. 'The people' became the target for a concerted campaign by the Ministry of Food, whose remit was the supply and distribution of food as well as – in conjunction with the Ministry of Agriculture – the provision of information and education. For a brand-new ministry, these were major challenges. Fortunately, cometh the hour, cometh the man.

A strong case can be made that Frederick Marquis, the first Baron Woolton,[2] was one of the great heroes of the Second World War. As Minister of Food, he oversaw a department whose task was nothing less than ensuring that what food there was found its way equitably to all civilians, as well as the armed forces, and that no one in Britain starved.[3]

Lord Woolton was not a politician. He was first a social scientist, with a pronounced interest in the poor,[4] then a journalist, a civil servant during the First World War concerned with procuring clothing for the army, and finally a shopkeeper on a very large scale, rising through the ranks at Lewis's department store in Liverpool to become chairman of the company in 1936. In 1939, he was elevated to the peerage. At the start of the war, he had sufficiently caught the eye of politicians to be recruited for the job of Director-General of the Ministry of Supply, but was then swiftly promoted by Neville Chamberlain to be the non-partisan Minister of Food, succeeding William Morrison in April 1940. Once Lord Woolton had learned how to deal with politicians and civil servants – no easy task for a successful, independent-minded businessman – he set about making sure that the population had enough of the right kind and amount of food both to survive and to have the strength to do the duties required of them.

Lord Woolton was tall and striking-looking, with a humorous smile and an unassuming, courteous manner; indeed, he was known colloquially as 'Uncle Fred'. His origins were modest – his father had been a Salford saddler – but he was well educated, having attended first Manchester Grammar School and then the University of Manchester, where he read combined sciences. His natural empathy and 'common touch' served him, and the Ministry, extremely well on a number of fraught occasions, but he combined those virtues with a ferocious work ethic. For example, his frequent twelve-and-a-half-minute radio broadcasts rarely took him less than eight hours to prepare, and he studied hard to ensure that his delivery on air was natural and engaging.

Looking back some years after the war was over, Lord Woolton wrote:

As a nation, it was broadly true to say [in 1939] that we were indifferent to both our agriculture and our horticulture. We could get cheap food abroad . . . There was, in fact, little except potatoes that we grew in this country that somebody else could not produce either cheaper or earlier . . . Those of us who had been through the First World War knew how nearly we had lost it by being starved out by the submarines . . . When war began we were importing 29.3 million tons of food, which was rather more than half of our total consumption.[5]

Rationing had already been in place for three months when Woolton took over at the Ministry of Food, and he continued the established policy, namely never rationing any foodstuff that could not be continuously supplied, in however small an amount, to the entire population. Meat had been put on ration on 11 March 1940, in this instance by value rather than weight, to take account of the many kinds of cuts there were, some cheaper than others. The move was very unpopular, since all classes ate meat and there were few vegetarians. The fuss over meat rationing was the reason why Woolton waited until the following July before he ordered the rationing of tea, cooking fats and margarine.

His watchword was 'Fair shares all round' and it was this simply expressed, fair-minded attitude which earned him the respect, even affection, of the population. Considering what an extremely dull diet was imposed on people, this was some achievement. Those items for which the Ministry could not guarantee a continuous supply were put on 'points': the scarcer the product – say, tinned salmon – the greater the number of points needed to acquire it. This was a flexible system: the points could be varied, depending on supply. Potatoes and bread were never rationed at all in wartime, since Lord Woolton considered them vital 'fillers': sufficient of these would ensure that people did not actually starve. Even if the gritty wheatmeal National Loaf was unpopular with a people firmly attached to white bread, at least it was nutritious and satisfying.

In his memoirs, published in 1959, the (by then) Earl of Woolton wrote:

By the time the war ended we were importing less than one-third of the amount of food, measured by weight, that we brought to this country in 1939, but that did not mean that we only had available these drastically reduced food values – otherwise we should have been in desperate straits: the scientific assessment of our needs, coupled with much ingenuity in securing concentration of the foods we bought, helped us to get through . . .[6]

There was particular pressure brought on me to reorganize the sale and distribution of vegetables. I had some prejudgement in

this matter; as a retailer I had been anxious to bring down prices
of vegetables. I knew there was a consensus of public opinion,
much encouraged by the market-gardeners and the farmers, that
there was no justification for the prices of lettuces or cabbages or
apples sold in the shops being so much higher than the prices that
were paid to the grower . . . The truth is that the cabbage in the
field is not very much use to anyone except the farmer, and by
the time it has found its way, amidst all the jostling of other
cabbages, to arrive at the ultimate reason for its existence, it has
travelled through many commercially dangerous processes.[7]

The public disquiet at what *The Times* called the 'long-standing scandal'[8]
concerning the disparity between the price paid to growers and that
paid by consumers turned out to be a most intractable one in wartime.
There were too many intermediaries and Covent Garden in London was
far and away the biggest distribution centre in England, so transport
costs could be high. It is small wonder that Woolton was as keen as
Robert Hudson that householders should grow their own fresh produce.

An important initiative of Woolton's was the singling out of particular
groups to receive food supplements not available to the general population. Farm workers received an extra ration of cheese, while workers
in heavy industry, such as mining, enjoyed a larger meat allowance. As
a result of the Lend-Lease agreement with the United States, both orange
juice and cod-liver oil were imported in sufficient quantities for children
under five to be given both free, while they and expectant mothers –
and later older children, adolescents and invalids – also received a larger
ration of milk than the two pints a week standard for adults. This enterprise was called the Welfare Foods Scheme, and it came into being in
December 1941. Lord Woolton wrote later:

. . . we worked out a diet for the nation that would supply all
the calories and all the vitamins that were needed for the
different age groups, for the fighting services, for the heavy
manual workers, for the ordinary housewife, for the babies and

the children, and for pregnant and nursing mothers. That was large-scale and all-embracing planning, and I determined to use the powers I possessed to stamp out the diseases that arose from malnutrition, especially those among children, such as rickets. The health of the children of to-day is the reward of that policy.[9]

This initiative convinced the public that the government cared about the nation's most vulnerable citizens. It is just a pity that the take-up was not as good as it should have been. In August 1942, a survey disclosed the shameful fact that only 38 per cent of mothers gave their entitled children cod-liver oil, and only 54 per cent the orange juice.[10]

Lord Woolton said that he soon learned that the way to get the public's co-operation was not by preaching at them, but by telling them which foods were valuable, and providing them with recipes to use those foods successfully. He fully understood the importance of publicity and educa- tion, but he also knew that it had to be done in a way that would stick in the minds of a harassed, distracted population.

He thought it useful to harness humour to get a serious idea across and enlisted the help of a couple of jolly cartoon characters, Potato Pete and Dr Carrot, to be used in 'Food Flashes' and other material published in newspapers or shown in cinemas. Potato Pete was usually portrayed with a stalk of wheat sticking out of his mouth, and wearing clothes and a hat. One cartoon of him bore the legend: 'Good taste demands I keep my jacket on'. Dr Carrot was carrot-shaped, bright orange, bespectacled, and carried a top hat and a case emblazoned with the words 'VIT A'. Lord Woolton even sent a telegram to Walt Disney in Hollywood asking him to create cartoon carrot characters, which Disney did by return: Carroty George, Pop Carrot and Clara Carrot.[11]

Both potatoes and carrots could be grown in great quantities on British farms and in market gardens; indeed from time to time there were substantial gluts of them, which prompted frenetic publicity campaigns intended to cut the surplus. Outrageously, the public was also told that eating a lot of carrots was the reason why RAF personnel such as Group Captain John 'Cats Eyes' Cunningham were so successful as night fighter pilots; in this way the government hoped to hide from the Germans the fact that a sophisticated airborne radar system had already been developed. Lord Woolton was fond of saying that 'A carrot a day keeps the blackout at bay.'

These two vegetables were promoted vigorously quite as much for their versatility as their food value. Cooked, mashed, dried potatoes could be used in recipes instead of flour[12], while carrots were an adequate substitute for sugar in a number of sweet dishes and even carrot jam. Whether children ever ate carrots on sticks to make up for the lack of ice lollies, except when posing for publicity photographs, is a moot point.

The Ministry of Food's propaganda efforts concentrated partly on the output of a five-minute wireless programme, *The Kitchen Front*,[13] which was broadcast at 8.15 a.m. six times a week from June 1940 until the end of the war. This often light-hearted programme was aimed principally at housewives, and was transmitted at a suitable time before they went out to shop. It consisted of a mixture of seasonal recipes, nutritional facts and rationing information, delivered by broadcasters like Freddie Grisewood and S. P. B. Mais[14]; cookery writers such as Marguerite Patten and Ambrose Heath; Mavis Constanduros, who played a charwoman, 'Mrs Buggins', and 'Gert' and 'Daisy', a comic double act by two sisters, Elsie and Doris Waters.[15] Mrs Buggins' humour relied partly on that old comedy standby the malapropism, as in: 'Well, if you don't care about the nice recipes I bring you, I might as well go to Russia and fish for surgeons in the vodka!'[16]

The programmes were popular, attracting 15 per cent of the available audience, with an average of five million listeners. This number always went up on the one day in the week when the Radio Doctor – Charles Hill – was on the air. He would describe special diets for invalids, or talk about the harm that too much sugar could do; one Boxing Day he discussed indigestion.[17] Fifty-five per cent of housewives listened to *The Kitchen Front*, and unlike many other worthy radio programmes, this one attracted working-class women. Grisewood was particularly popular when he developed the persona of amiable incompetence as 'A Man in the Kitchen', presumably because he reminded so many housewives of their husbands.

Since meat was so strictly rationed, *The Kitchen Front* not unnaturally emphasised the value of vegetable dishes. The most prominently plugged of these was 'Woolton Pie', created by the chef at the Savoy Hotel in the spring of 1941. This dish consisted of diced root vegetables, such as swedes and carrots, together with spring onions and a small amount of oatmeal and vegetable extract, put together with potato as a pie crust, and baked in the oven. A friend of Lord Woolton referred to it as 'steak and kidney pie without the steak and kidney'.[18]

The ingenuity of both professional and amateur cooks was impressive; in addition to Woolton Pie, they invented a number of 'mock' recipes, such as 'mock goose', which used lentils, 'mock oyster soup' – with fish trimmings and Jerusalem artichokes – 'mock venison', which used cold mutton, and 'mock apricot flan', which mixed carrots and almond essence to approximate to the flavour of apricot. 'Mock cream' was made with cornflour, milk and margarine.

The Kitchen Front strongly encouraged the preserving of fruit and vegetables. Housewives were taught how to bottle fruit without sugar, dry apple rings, salt runner beans for winter and make pickles, chutneys and even rose-hip syrup. Wasting any kind of food was portrayed, at least subliminally, as unpatriotic. A popular poem of the time ran:

> Those who have the will to win,
> Cook potatoes in their skin,
> Knowing that the sight of peelings,
> Deeply hurts Lord Woolton's feelings.

The programme lasted for more than a thousand editions, and its audience size increased rather than diminished as the war went on. The Ministry of Food retained a substantial influence on the programme's contents. All the recipes were tested in the kitchens at the Ministry offices in Portman Square. There was a running battle between the Ministry of Food and the BBC over who should have most control, the Ministry frequently overstepping the bounds that the BBC Talks Department thought appropriate, especially over the matter of the drafting of speakers' scripts.[19] That said, when the Ministry of Food withdrew in January 1945 and left the programme to the BBC, the Director of Talks had to admit that the Ministry scriptwriters had been masters of the skill of getting over enough information in five minutes. Despite the programme's popularity, there may not be much concrete evidence that *The Kitchen Front* itself substantially changed the way the nation ate; rationing self-evidently had already done that. In the opinion of Siân Nicholas, 'the programme's capacity to influence behaviour was immaterial to its success; its simple willingness to be helpful was probably its greatest asset to morale'.[20]

Reinforcing what was said on the wireless, food advice centres in every town provided information to citizens on both rationing and cooking. Food facts were published in newspapers every week and longer articles could be found in women's magazines and the weekly *The Listener*. Leaflets were printed on subjects such as 'How to Eat Wisely in Wartime', with phrases like 'The greener the leaf, the greater the food value', or the less than tempting 'Salads can be the principal part of a meal'.

Cinemas[21] also played their part, screening information films and 'Food Flashes', devised by the Ministry of Food. The Food Flash[22] was fifteen seconds long and made a single, unequivocal point. For example, one Food Flash consisted of a shot of a civilian tucking into potatoes with apparent relish, with a snappy voiceover: 'There's plenty of potatoes around at the moment. And at pre-war prices too.' (The camera panned to a pile of potatoes at a greengrocer's, with the legend '9d for 7 lb'.) 'That's the boy. Have a second helping. Here's spud in your eye.'

These Food Flashes were meant to work as a 'carrot', but Lord Woolton did not shrink from also carrying a big stick. He issued statutory orders dealing with waste, and those found to be wastrels were prosecuted with severity. The prohibition against putting usable food waste in rubbish bins was a great impetus to householders to put it in pig swill bins instead (see Chapter Eleven). 'We had created a moral atmosphere,' Woolton wrote after the war, 'but we had also shown people how they could use their food to the best advantage, and even how they could use waste food by arranging for it to be collected and subsequently made into food for pigs and poultry.'[23] He also made sure that there were stringent penalties for anyone caught selling food on the black market.

Lord Woolton did not get everything right. In particular, he – and Winston Churchill – underestimated the effect that their requests to the American government would have on the US economy. Lend-Lease had been introduced in 1941, the first goods arriving at the end of May. This was the way America 'loaned' military materiel, food and other supplies to Britain, and other allies, at a time when Britain had few dollars to spend. The loan was to be paid back after the war. Lend-Lease introduced British children to the delights of Spam and powdered egg but the fifteen million tons of food imports annually asked for put a strain on farmers, and caused bad feeling between food officials in the United States and their counterparts in Britain.

Wartime surveys on the subject of the impact of government food information made quite depressing reading, for both the officials of the Ministry of Food and the BBC. Three years into the war, one investigation revealed that most of the respondents did not understand which were the most important foods for health. The great majority of housewives served green vegetables 'regularly', but that was defined as at least once a fortnight in season.[24] It seems that, despite all the exhortation, encouragement and information, a great many cooks fell short of the ideal – or so the Ministry thought. Woolton's Parliamentary Secretary, Mr William Mabane, announced at the launch of the 1943 Dig for Victory campaign: 'Fundamentally men are better cooks than women, but this is no reason why women should cook as badly as they do. Many people in this country have never really tasted vegetables. All they know is the sodden pap produced by over-boiling unprotesting vegetables in a bath of water.'[25] He urged people to study the Ministry of Food recipes to improve their cooking, although he may not have chosen the best words to achieve that. Robert Hudson, the Minister of Agriculture, then piled in by saying that, while spending a weekend in a pub in Lincolnshire, he had had to send back his plate heaped with vegetables as they were too badly cooked to be edible.

Women also criticised other women. As Constance Spry put it in *Come into the Garden, Cook*, published in 1942:

> Vegetables can be food for the gods, though you may think this
> an over-statement if you have just had a spell of pot-luck in
> provincial hotels up and down the country, or if, perversely, you
> throw your mind back to train dining-cars or to the smell that
> hit you as you passed the open door of a seaside boarding house
> at lunch time one summer's day. I cannot think how even
> experienced cooks find it possible to turn nice material into
> such nasty food.[26]

Nevertheless, despite the less than total co-operation of the population, and their inability always to learn the lessons so assiduously taught, the Ministry of Food's achievements were substantial. It is generally agreed that the population was healthier during the war than before it. In particular, the health of the poor benefited from both the equitable nature of rationing and the restraint provided by price controls.

On 12 August 1942, Clara Milburn wrote in her diary:

> An American professor visiting England is amazed at the
> health of the people after three years of war, and says the
> children are splendid. The health of the nation is better than
> before the war, says our Ministry of Health. There is no
> malnutrition. We shall probably have to tighten our belts a bit
> more this winter, but it is wonderful what has been done in
> the way of food-growing.[27]

That was the achievement of Robert Hudson and Lord Woolton.

As we have seen, Lord Woolton certainly understood the value of food and food production for boosting civilian morale, and in the members of the Women's Institute he found willing allies, whose good-heartedness and practical common sense could generally be relied upon. In 1940, he granted the National Federation money[28] to organise a network of fruit preservation centres in villages; these would make surplus fruit and vegetables into jam or chutney, as another means of boosting home food production. There had been such a scheme in the First World War, but this time it was on an altogether bigger scale. The result of this activity was to identify Women's Institutes for ever after as champion jam-makers,[29] something they have found it difficult to leave behind in more peaceful times.

In the late summer of 1940, there was a substantial glut of plums in country gardens, which threatened to go to waste since plums are notoriously liable to spoil in transit, because of the juiciness of their flesh and the thinness of their skins. This overproduction plainly had to be dealt with locally so, in a matter of weeks, 2,600 fruit preserva-tion centres were set up in village halls and other public buildings. The WI members dealt with only that fruit that could not be trans-ported to a jam factory or used in the kitchen; they received a fixed price for their collected fruit but were not paid anything to make it into jam.

According to the historian of the WI, Cicely McCall:

Here was the longed-for piece of war service . . . Jam. It seemed the perfect solution. Jam-making was constructive and non-militant . . . It accorded with the best Quaker traditions of feeding blockaded nations. For those dietetically minded, jam contained all the most highly prized vitamins . . . And for the belligerent, what could be more satisfying than fiercely stirring cauldrons of boiling jam and feeling that every pound took us one step further towards defeating Hitler.[30]

A professional gardener and WI inspector, Miss Viola Williams, recalled:

A lot of what I would call the non-Ladies of the Manor came into their own with the jam centres, because they were the ones who knew how to make jam. You would start at the crack of dawn, probably on primus stoves, and go on all day with great cauldrons of jam, and then bottle it. It was like a small factory.

I was inspecting. I had to check on cleanliness, on packaging, on labelling, and although we weren't in a position to (because we didn't have saccharimeters), we were supposed to check on sugar content, too. A 'selling jam' has to have 60% sugar in it . . . and this is one of the things we had to check out. You can work it out by quantities: if you knew how much sugar was available to make into a jam, then you could work out – almost to an ounce – how much jam should have been produced with a 60% sugar content. The reason for checking was that we were given the sugar on trust. There was utter and complete honesty, but it was a temptation to siphon away the sugar and use it for yourself during those days of high rationing. I think people did used to go home with a saucer full of scum, which is almost as good as jam but which you couldn't possibly have put into the bottles. But I would say that there was almost 100% honesty in those jam centres.[31]

In 1940, 1,631 tons of fruit and vegetables were preserved or canned[32] in the fruit preservation centres, calling forth a letter of congratulation from Lord Woolton himself to Lady Denman on 31 December 1940:

I have been greatly impressed both by the quantity of preserves made and by the enthusiasm and determination with which the members of these centres . . . undertook the formidable task of saving the exceptionally heavy plum crop . . . This was work of national importance, demanding administrative ability of a high order at the Headquarters of your organization, and local initiative and co-operation which are a fine example of democratic action at its best . . .[33]

It is perhaps hard for us now to appreciate just how important jam was to the morale of a nation with a notable sweet tooth – a nation that had eaten prodigious quantities of cakes and biscuits before the war – at a time when all sugar products were severely rationed, and when there was much less emphasis than now on the harm sugar can do to teeth.

The Ministry of Food left the administration of the scheme to the NFWI headquarters, in particular to Miss Edith Walker, the Agricultural Secretary. She recalled years later that:

> People [by which she meant country housewives] felt that in the larger War effort they were of no use to anybody and were not important. The number of WIs decreased. It was in this situation that the Preservation Scheme was particularly important in boosting morale in the countryside. The foundations of this had been laid from the earliest days, and WI [market] stalls and Village Shows provided a nucleus for it. Most County Federations had always had an Agricultural Sub-Committee . . . The Scheme undoubtedly helped to keep the WIs going during the War. One of the advantages they had was a Literature Department, which could provide labels, leaflets and recipe books. The Scheme also gave a great boost to the Markets.[34]

One useful facet of the Women's Institute movement was that it had worldwide connections, so when the National Federation executive approached the Americans for help, through the agency of the Associated Country Women of the World, the result was a delivery of 500 Dixie canning machines and a complete fruit preservation unit. These made it possible for some WI teams to go from village to village, canning the produce that had been collected locally, in village halls, farm kitchens or private houses. In east Kent, canning machines were hired out for three shillings a day. The resulting produce was taken to wholesale depots, sold to local shops or bought by the women who made it.

Surely the most heroic Women's Institute was the one in Hawkinge, a Kent coastal village which was badly hit by bombs, since it was close to an RAF station. So many people were evacuated that the Women's Institute was reduced from 108 to five members, yet they still managed to produce 784 lb of jam in September 1940 and 14 cwt in 1941. A hundredweight (cwt) is 112 lb, which makes that 1,568 lb. Mention should also be made of the WI in Rosedale, on the North York Moors, whose members made over 3½ tons of jam during the war in the village reading room, which had no water supply, electricity or gas. The water had to be brought in buckets from a quarter of a mile away.

In March 1941, Blisworth WI in Northamptonshire passed a resolution that it would form a centre for fruit preservation 'in response to an appeal by His Majesty's Government', and in June, £6 was loaned from WI funds to help set it up, as well as £5 from Mrs Clinch, who was Madam President of the Blisworth WI all through the war.[35] In that year, 333 lb of jam were made and sold. The fruit preservation centre was opened again in the village the following year, but as no surplus fruit had been handed in, it did not operate. Perhaps a late frost did for the blossom?

Marguerite Patten, the cookery writer, who was an adviser to the Ministry of Food, recalled being responsible for a food advice centre in Ipswich and overseeing jam-making sessions in fruit preservation centres.

The sessions were not entirely peaceful, for most ladies were experienced housewives, with their own very definite ideas on how jams should be made; some wanted to use their own recipes and addressed me firmly. 'Young woman, I was making jam before you were born' – quite right – but my job was to ensure that every completed pot of jam contained 60% sugar and was carefully sealed to ensure it really would keep well under all conditions, so I had to stand firm.[36]

Four and half thousand fruit preservation centres were open in 1941, which meant that three-quarters of the 5,700 WIs had volunteered for the scheme. Housewives were encouraged to take their fruit to these centres, as that year there wasn't any sugar available for home preserving. There were mutterings from some countrywomen that they were not allowed to buy the jam that they had made that year at wholesale prices, as jam rationing had been introduced; moreover, the price they received for any fruit they collected was not generous. As a result, some were not inclined to help out in the preservation centres.

This discontent came to the ears of Lord Woolton, who roundly ticked countrywomen off in a radio broadcast in June, reminding them somewhat tactlessly of the rather greater sacrifices made by their urban sisters. Miss Walker was summoned by Sir Henry French, Woolton's Permanent Secretary, to explain, but she told him that whatever was being said, the WIs were getting on with the work and producing the jam.

The editor of the WI magazine, *Home and Country*, wrote that autumn that the 'momentary confusion' had resulted from the fact that the centres were worried about their solvency if they could not sell their produce immediately, as they had done the year before. The incident was all rather embarrassing. However, this was the only time that the countrywomen's patriotism was ever remotely called into question.

Despite the rumblings of discontent, more than 1,100 tons of fruit made 1,630 tons of preserves that year. The Queen – who was a member of the Sandringham Women's Institute – made 'surprise' visits to a number of fruit preservation centres in Buckinghamshire in July, and Mrs Roosevelt, the American President's wife, also visited a centre.[37] 'The Women's Institutes help to make the wheels go round,' she is reported as saying afterwards.[38] As evidence that the quarrel between the NFWI and the Ministry had been patched up, Miss Walker received an OBE in recognition of her achievements.

The grants from the Ministry of Food and Ministry of Agriculture – £5,125 for the fruit preservation scheme and £3,800 for the produce guilds in 1942 – increased steadily during the war, a firm indicator that the Ministry continued to think the work useful. In 1944, there were 1,174 fruit preservation centres open, even though there were four consecutive nights of sharp frost in May, which damaged every kind of fruit crop in many parts of the country. It was only in 1945, when a late spring frost again damaged blossom, and war weariness overtook even the spirited women of the WI, that the numbers of centres dropped very sharply and the Ministries of Agriculture and Food were refunded some of their grants. The scheme, as overseen by the Ministry of Food, came to an end that year.

Between 1940 and 1945, more than 5,300 tons (about 12 million lb) of fruit was preserved, which was the equivalent, according to Sir Henry French, of a year's jam ration[39] for more than half a million people.[40] When he announced this to an audience of 300 WI delegates, I have no doubt that his speech was met with hearty applause, since that sounds a great deal. However, in fact, all that hard work achieved less than half of one per cent of the national requirement for (rationed) jam in wartime, so the effort was largely symbolic. It was probably just as well that those five stout-hearted women of Hawkinge, hot and flustered from making jam in the boiling-hot weather of September 1940, with the Battle of Britain raging over their heads, did not know that.

In popular mythology, jam has threatened to obscure the true value of the Women's Institutes during the war, which was their equally strong attachment to building 'Jerusalem' in England's green and pleasant land. The making of jam was only one of many activities in which country-women used their organisational skills and their appetite for selfless hard work to further the war effort. It was the Institute member's determination not to let her sword sleep in her hand that earned her the nation's gratitude and respect.

Inevitably, the jam-making campaign was gently satirised in the pages of *Punch*, most notably by Mary Dunn, through her fictional creation, Lady Addle.

Nowadays people seem too apprehensive about wasting sugar to experiment, and hence some splendid ingredients wither in the fields and hedgerows for want of plucking. The common burr for instance, soaked overnight and well stewed, makes an unusual jelly with a sweetish taste not unlike plate[41] powder. Acorns, boiled to a pulp, will help to eke out your quinces if they are scarce. Then potato jam, with a little cochineal and some very fine grass seed for pips, with a raspberry jam label on the jar, does splendidly for people who have, either temporarily or permanently, lost their taste. I find my evacuees always demand raspberry or strawberry jam, so I have been reduced to innocent little ruses such as I quote above, or sometimes to boiling up a pound jar of one of them with a pint of conker stock, which sets into two or three jars of a kind of jelly-ish jam, or perhaps more accurately, a jam-ish jelly.

I must stress the importance of your jelly cloth. Most cookery books recommend flannel for straining. I go further and say that old flannel is the best, especially some personal belonging such as an old flannel hot-water bottle cover or a beloved dog's blanket, which seems in some strange way to give the jelly a very poignant flavour.[42]

An attachment to the home-made, the thrifty and the honest was admired even by sophisticates like Constance Spry. In *Come into the Garden, Cook* she wrote,

It is a good thing to live at the heart of an empire that rules the seas. It has been good to share the luxuries of other countries, but it is not good to neglect what we have ourselves, to lean back in a lazy dependence, or to forget the lore of the past.

Before the war, when luxury shops might fill their shelves with flavours and spices from the Orient, with rare honeys and exotic jams, tribute was still paid to the home-made. It would seem that the housewife continues to have something up her sleeve, which cannot be quite copied in a wholesale manner. Now we must depend on what is home-made to a degree that would have come perhaps more easily to our grandmothers.[43]

Abundant nature certainly provided ingenious cooks with ingredients which would not have been countenanced in kitchens before the war. But necessity was the spur. Fanny Cradock, who made her name as a television cook after the war, usually wearing a Norman Hartnell ballgown, recalled: 'Our cooking used to amaze our friends. They thought we had black market supplies from Fortnum's . . . Bracken shoots were asparagus and I used liquid paraffin for my pastry. We caught and cooked sparrows from the garden and often ate baked hedgehogs (rather like frogs' legs).'[44]

A widely travelled Frenchman, le vicomte de Mauduit, was the great expert on this kind of natural scavenging. He had written a number of conventional cookery books before the war but, in 1940, he published a book about what could be harvested in the countryside, with a foreword by no less a personage than Lloyd George himself. 'During the war,' de Mauduit wrote, 'it [searching for food in the countryside] will serve to relieve some of the strain on the nation's food supply and will teach those of us who will turn to the countryside for immunity from direct war destruction how to maintain life in the case of difficulties with regard to the carriage and distribution of food.'[45] Directing his remarks at rural dwellers, campers, caravanners, hikers and what he called 'the necessitous', he predicted that, armed with this book, they could live in comfort, plenty and health even if all banks, shops and markets closed for indefinite periods. This

book would have been particularly helpful if Britain had been successfully invaded, and guerrilla bands formed, since he instructed his
readers which wild birds' eggs could be eaten, how to prepare a
hedgehog, grill a squirrel, stew a starling, find an edible frog, dry fish,
and use fennel stalks for fuel. He recommended soapwort as a substitute for soap for washing linens, which must have been very useful,
since soap was hard to find in shops; this could be the reason why this
rampant nuisance is still to be found in many country gardens. In order
to cheer his readers, he also gave recipes for gorse wine, red beet port
and hop beer. And if they should suffer from minor ills, there were
instructions on how to make a parsley-water eye-bath for a bloodshot
eye, or an infusion of dried red roses, violets, borage and anchusa
flowers 'for a sad heart'.

This story does not have a happy ending. Le vicomte travelled back
to his homeland when war broke out, was captured by the Germans
after the fall of France and died in Dachau concentration camp on 2
February 1945.[46] This was a tragic end for a man with a curious mind,
a cultivated palate and an obvious *joie de vivre*.

Scavenging for food in the countryside was on the whole a private
preoccupation; searching out native drug plants, on the other hand,
became institutionalised. Many medicinal drugs and nutritional supplements had been imported from abroad before the war and had
therefore become scarce or even, as in the case of some tropical
plant drugs like quinine, unobtainable. However, a surprising number
of imported drugs were derived from plants also native to Britain.
The obvious solution to any shortage, therefore, was to gather
native-grown drug plants or suitable substitutes, and to this end the
Ministry of Health assembled a Vegetable Drugs Committee. On it
served a number of civil servants and experts, including a pair of
scientists from the Royal Botanic Gardens, Kew, Dr Metcalfe and Dr
Melville.

There were four main areas of interest to this committee. One was
the necessity to find native red seaweeds, which might be suitable for
making agar, a jelly used in bacteriological research in the laboratory as

well as an emulsifying agent, a food additive and a treatment for consti-
pation. Before the war, it had been almost entirely imported from Japan,
around the coasts of which *Gelidium amansii* and related red seaweeds
grow. By 1941, this source was threatening to dry up, and did so entirely
after Japan entered the war in early December. Algologists were therefore
dispatched around the British coastline to study the various kinds of
native seaweeds and discover whether any were suitable alternatives to
Japanese seaweeds. Boy Scouts were encouraged to help, in what must
have been a rather unenviable task. The scientists working in the Jodrell
Laboratory at Kew did much of the research work on potential substitutes, in particular 'Irish moss', *Chondrus crispus*, which was already used
as an emulsifier in cod-liver oil. It was thought that, if mixed with
another seaweed, *Gigartina mamillosa*, it might make a suitable alternative
to agar jelly. As things turned out, this was not the case, but the scientists
did discover that this mixture made an admirable substitute for gelatine
in food products like tinned tongue. Meanwhile, algologists at the Scottish
Marine Biological Association station at Millport on the river Clyde
discovered that there were British species of *Gelidium*, as well as another
red seaweed, *Ahnfeldtia*, which were good enough to be used as agar
substitutes. These were only available in small quantities, but that was
better than nothing.[47]

The second area of research 'of national importance' was aimed at
expanding the range of nutritional supplements. At the beginning of
the war, there was already in production one syrup which was high
in vitamin C. During the 1930s, as a result of a need to do something
with periodic commercial fruit gluts, scientists at Long Ashton, led
by Dr Vernon Charley, had investigated the possibilities of making
syrups and juices for flavouring milk shakes. When the Bristol soda
and mineral water manufacturer, H. W. Carter, showed an interest in
the blackcurrant syrup, Charley authorised its trialling in the factory,
with a Long Ashton technician in attendance. As a result, in 1936
H. W. Carter launched the syrup commercially, under the name
'Ribena', a word derived from the botanical name for blackcurrant,
Ribes nigrum.[48]

Once the war started, the Ministry of Food considered that a palatable and ready source of vitamin C was particularly important for infants and small children, who would not eat enough green vegetables to receive the necessary daily intake of the vitamin. The distribution of Ribena was authorised for children, expectant mothers and others in particular need of vitamin C, although the Ribena trade name was abandoned for the duration. Lord Woolton believed its production to be so important that two 'shadow factories' were fitted out elsewhere, since Bristol was a likely target for air raids. Almost the entire national commercial crop of blackcurrants went into the manufacture of this syrup. Indeed, the quantity of fruit needed was so great that it could not all be processed in the short harvest period, so the Campden Research Station arranged for much of it to be canned at various canning centres, for processing later.

After a meeting of the Vegetable Drugs Committee in June 1941,[49] Dr Melville wrote: 'As the Ministry of Health has found it necessary to arrange for the preparation of a syrup from black currants for use as a Vitamin C concentrate, it may be worth while to consider the possibility of using wild rose hips in a similar manner as they are richer in ascorbic acid than blackcurrants.'[50] Rosehips have a good flavour, like a quality plum or a guava, and also contain vitamin A, which children need to help prevent 'night blindness'. So Dr Melville began to work on research into rose hips in collaboration with Dr Magnus Pyke, chief scientist at the research laboratories of Vitamins Ltd in Hammersmith.[51] They soon discovered that there were two major difficulties: palatability and collection.

In September 1941, the Ministry of Health asked Dr Vernon Charley and his colleagues at Long Ashton to help. Rose hips turned out to be more problematic than blackcurrants, because of the prickly, irritant hairs that surround the seeds in the hip. The call from the Ministry came a mere three weeks before the picking season began; nevertheless, Dr Charley and his team set to work, using a number of unlikely bits of machinery, including domestic laundry mangles and lawn rollers, to extract the juice. They discovered that the best method was to mill the hips quite finely and put the resulting mash into boiling water to stop all enzyme activity immediately.

Collection was also going to be a problem, with the adult population otherwise occupied, so the Director of Kew, Sir Arthur Hill, led a concerted campaign in September to encourage Boy Scouts, Girl Guides, schoolchildren and WIs (as well as the Scottish Rural Institutes and Scottish WVS) to go out and collect hips. The idea was that the Women's Institutes' County Herb Committees would act as local organisers, since collection needed to be orderly and swift, with only a limited time between picking and processing. The advice from Kew was that the hips 'should be weighed, invoiced and sent to your central depot where payment will be made for weight at the rate of 2/- per stone, with an additional 6d per stone for incidental expenses'.[52] Scouts and other youth organisations supplemented their funds in this way, and war charities also benefited.

By experimentation, Dr Charley later discovered that wild rose hips had the highest concentration of vitamin C when they were just beginning to colour up but were still hard; and that the best hips, from the nutritional point of view, were to be found in hedgerows in the Lake District and county Durham northwards. They were therefore best collected in early August, which fortuitously coincided with the school holidays.

The Vegetable Drugs Committee wrote to the County Herb Committees, saying that the target figure was 1,500 tons; in other words, an enormous amount. It can have been no surprise that those hard-working children only managed to collect 220 tons in 1941. Nevertheless, rose hip syrup went on sale in chemists on 1 February 1942.

In 1942, 333 tons of hips were collected and in 1943, 492 tons. It was a great deal, but only a third of what could have been processed. All this highlighted the difficulties in wartime of mobilising a sufficiently large but partly juvenile volunteer force, whose effectiveness was often determined by the enthusiasm, or lack of it, of particular local education authorities. There was no doubting children's willingness, but the scale of the task was simply beyond them. It is interesting to note that the northern collectors did best, probably because they had both *Rosa canina* and the later-ripening, downy-leaved *Rosa mollis* to choose from, so there was a longer season for collection.

The third area of interest to Sir Arthur Hill and his scientists at Kew was the quest for potential substitutes for rubber, the traditional source of which was cut off completely when the Japanese overran Malaya in 1942. The scientists tested the efficacy of a Russian species of dandelion, bizarrely, but nothing much came of it.

Kew was much more successful with the humble perennial nettle, which could be used for the industrial extraction of the green pigment, chlorophyll. The value of chlorophyll resided in its use as a colouring in fats and soaps, as well as camouflage paint. The stems of nettles could be made into high-class paper, and experiments were also attempted to see if nettle fabric was useful in the construction of aircraft. Yet again youthful collectors, together with the Women's Institutes, were involved, gathering nettle leaves and drying them. Guidance to the Boy Scouts included the advice: 'Unless the collector is more than usually resistant to nettle stings, leather gloves should be worn.'[53] 'Stingers' were a fact of life to country children, but it would be surprising if many of them could cheerfully do without gloves.

As far as medicinal drugs were concerned, the most sought after were the leaves and seed of foxglove, belladonna leaves, dandelion roots, stinging nettles, colchicum corms,[54] broom flower tops, male fern, valerian and thorn apple. Also valuable were sphagnum moss – a very absorbent material used as a dressing for wounds – and the conkers of horse chestnut trees, which were used for making the glucose-rich pick-me-up Lucozade, as well as a treatment for varicose veins and other inflammatory conditions. Ordinary culinary herbs were also required, but these were mainly grown in gardens and nurseries, for ease of collection.

In 1941, the wholesale drug company, Brome and Schimmer, published an explanatory booklet entitled 'Herb Gathering'. Two herbalists, Barbara Keen and Jean Armstrong of the Valeswood Herb Farm, wrote the text.

In it were descriptions of all the many and various wild flowers, roots and herbs that were needed by the Ministry of Health, and, crucially, how they should be treated and dried. Fortunately, it included drawings from *Illustrations from the British Flora*, so it is to be hoped that no one mixed up their belladonna with their broom.

The booklet was badly needed, because that year the collection of medicinal herbs by amateurs turned out to be rather haphazard and experimental. The minutes of the meeting of the Vegetable Drugs Committee on 17 December 1941 certainly indicate this: 'It has been found that although enthusiasm was great, and interest widespread, throughout the country, there was serious lack of co-ordination and technical knowledge on the subject of drying the herbs collected. Nevertheless, medicinal herbs to the value of approximately £2,000 were collected, dried and marketed.'[55]

In order to encourage the opening of local drying centres to process the material in preparation for sending it to the pharmaceutical companies, the Vegetable Drugs Committee recommended that small loans be given to the WI County Herb Committees so that they could set up drying rooms in village halls and the like, and then recoup the cost of the loan by selling the dried material. Once dried, herbs were taken to the County Federation central collecting depots – where a trained person was needed to ensure that the drying had been done properly – whence they were mainly dispatched to Messrs Brome and Schimmer in Southwark. Brome and Schimmer paid for these culinary and medicinal herbs on a sliding rate according to their rarity and utility.

Each year, after consultation between the Vegetable Drugs Committee and the pharmaceutical companies, the list of genera required changed to some extent. Miss Elizabeth Hess, who sat on this committee for part of the war, recalled later that the government was very anxious that those people collecting poisonous plants should know exactly what they were doing.[56] Children were not allowed to collect belladonna, for example. To try to limit the amount of misidentification of herbs, Kew also organised the distribution of forty sets of cigarette cards[57] with colour illustrations of wild flowers; these were given to the volunteers from pharmacy colleges whose job it was to instruct WI members and other volunteers. There were short broadcast talks on the subject, as well as talks and demonstrations round the country by members of a panel of experts.

Miss Hess's expertise as a trained horticulturist made her a very useful collector. In the spring of 1942 she was given the task of finding a ton of broom flowering tops. She knew that the native broom (*Cytisus scoparius*), which yields sparteine sulphate, grew in a particular ten-acre plantation near Brandon in Suffolk. She could not find any of the usual volunteers, so she made a personal approach to the senior pupils of the two Thetford grammar schools. Thirty teenagers agreed to give their time over the Easter weekend. They worked in teams, which became predictably competitive with each other, and in four days managed to pick and stack four tons of broom tops, earning themselves five shillings per hundredweight, or £20.[58] Mr Allen of Stafford Allen, which processed the drugs, had written to the Acting Director[59] at Kew in December 1941, saying that he did not have a great deal of faith in Boy Scouts and Women's Institutes – in other words amateurs – as collectors. On this occasion, at least, he must have had to eat his words.[60]

A few potentially poisonous or unusual native plants – aconitum, belladonna, foxglove, henbane and thorn apple – could never be supplied in sufficient quantity by wild collection, so were specifically grown for pharmaceutical use in scientific institutions such as Kew and the John Innes Horticultural Institution, as well as in large private gardens like Exbury, which were overseen by expert owners and experienced gardeners.

The collection of herbs, both culinary and medicinal, continued throughout the war and just beyond, although the urgency diminished in the later years as foreign countries came back once more into Allied hands. Sir Arthur Hill had seriously overestimated the capacities of mainly amateur and untried volunteers, in particular to pick the right parts of the right plants, often in remote places that were difficult to get to, and to dry them efficiently in less than ideal circumstances. The sheer number of different plants required,[61] some of them, like meadow saffron (*Colchicum*), quite local in their distribution, added to the collectors' difficulties. Nevertheless, worthwhile work was done at a time of great need, and participation in such an obviously useful activity remained a source of pride to those involved; however young, they had contributed something valuable to the war effort, and they never forgot it.

CHAPTER THIRTEEN

KEEPING ON KEEPING ON

The two years that followed VJ[1] Day on 15 August 1945 were, in a number of significant ways, a dreadful time for Britons. True, victory meant peace at last after six weary years, but the demobilisation of the forces was a slow and piecemeal affair, and when they finally got home, service personnel found a very changed physical and economic landscape.

Britain's blitzed towns and cities required a great deal of reconstruction. Three quarters of a million houses had been badly damaged or destroyed. Many historic buildings had also been reduced to rubble, or were finished off by demolition squads. Materials to repair blitzed dwellings or build new ones were in very short supply. Concrete bunkers, barbed-wire entanglements and forbidding notices disfigured the coastline, city parks and the countryside.

The civilian population was shabby, grey, thin and very tired. There was not much to cheer them up, since there was little to buy in the shops, even if they had money and coupons to spare. The abrupt end of Lend-Lease in August 1945 meant that factories were forced to produce goods for export rather than home consumption in order to generate foreign exchange and pay back the Americans.

There was also precious little for anyone to do in their leisure time and few places to go. Even the weather conspired against them, for January and February 1947 was the snowiest and coldest winter for many years. Matters were made worse because all fuels were severely rationed. People remember feeling everlastingly cold. Only the gradual implementation, between 1944 and 1948, of what came to be known as the Welfare State brightened the prospects for a population that had so enthusiastically embraced its foreshadowing, the Beveridge Report, in 1942.

To add to the communal misery, bread and potatoes were rationed for the first time in 1947. (How Lord Woolton must have disapproved.) Other food supplies were also tight, the shortages exacerbated by the need to try to provide help for shattered European countries. As a result, in August 1946, the Central Office of Information[2] sent the BBC a memorandum, prompted by the Ministry of Agriculture and Fisheries' 'Dig for Victory — Over Want' campaign, the name given to the post-war push to keep gardeners producing fresh vegetables and fruit.

According to the COI, the 1946/47 campaign would have two main objects:

(i) To ensure the continued cultivation of vegetable production on existing allotments and, so far as is practicable, to ensure that further allotments are taken up.
(ii) To secure, by more efficient production methods, an increased output from allotments and gardens, especially during the winter months.[3]

There was a world shortage of bread grains, so farmers had been asked to cultivate a further half a million acres for arable crops, both to provide bread flour and to feed livestock. These were acres which had, partly at least, grown vegetables during the war. So, just at the moment when kitchen gardeners thought they could lay down their hoes, they were told that the need was more urgent than ever.

The memorandum went on:

Since the end of hostilities the production of vegetables by private enterprise has declined and the proposed campaign is intended to re-awaken the public to the gravity of the food situation in relation to vegetables; to stimulate those who have continued to cultivate their allotments and gardens and to encourage those who have, with the conclusion of hostilities, devoted their energies to re-designing their gardens for the growth of flowers, etc., to renew their efforts in the cultivation of vegetables.[4]

This was probably a pious hope, particularly as the monthly magazine that the Ministry of Agriculture was proposing to issue in order to support the campaign would cost gardeners 6d, and had to be sent away for. The memorandum proposed 'Dig for Victory – Over Want' weeks, and announced that there would be film publicity as well as advertisements in newspapers. The BBC was asked to help with broadcasts. However, the anticipated cost of the enterprise was only £30,000, so it was plainly a much scaled-down affair. Apart from Fred Streeter mentioning the campaign once a month in his 'Fruit and Vegetables' wireless talk, the BBC does not seem to have been much inclined to promote the government's efforts. It was hardly surprising. In the slang of the time, everyone was thoroughly 'browned off'.

Despite that, the Defence Regulations that empowered local authorities to let land for allotments, together with the suspension of restrictions on keeping pigs, hens and rabbits, survived the expiry of the Emergency Powers (Defence) Acts in February 1946. Indeed, they were not allowed to lapse until 1951 because of the pressing need to maintain food production at as high a level as possible.

The figure of three million allotments that Robert Hudson had so optimistically envisaged early in the war had never been anything like achieved. Indeed, it was never much more than half that number, and even that began to decline as peace beckoned, despite the pious intentions of 96 per cent of allotmenteers and 86 per cent of private gardeners who responded to an MAF survey in 1942[5] to continue food production after the war.

Approximately half a million allotments had disappeared or ceased to be cultivated by 1947. This was mainly due to the rush by local authorities to reclaim the 'non-statutory' sites, so that they could build much-needed houses on them, and not just in the big cities that had been bombarded. But there was something else at work here: the allotment seemed intimately associated with the war, upon which most people understandably wished to turn their backs. As the wartime community spirit, born of adversity and a compelling common purpose, gradually seeped away, allotments became almost exclusively the province of older men, who had rediscovered their misogyny now that no one was telling them that everyone had to pull together. By the 1950s, women were far less commonly seen on allotments. As for children, many of them could not wait to give up picking caterpillars off the brassicas. Allotments were associated with 'make do and mend' – many an Anderson shelter found its way to an allotment site to be used as a makeshift tool shed – monotonous diets and austerity. More and more allotments became neglected and unkempt, making them progressively less attractive to the disengaged. And there were other factors. Frozen food, for example, was playing an increasingly important role for the housewife: if you could buy peas which, when defrosted and cooked, were as good as, if not better than, those you picked from your allotment, there was less inclination to go on battling with pea moth and greenfly. By 1955, there were only 800,000 allotments; all the wartime gains and more had been lost. School gardens likewise declined after the war, in some places made back into playing fields immediately, in others continued with for a few years yet.

So much for amateurs, who had the choice whether to cultivate a garden or not. The position of established (and would-be) professional gardeners was uncertain and anxiety about future employment widespread. On 6 April 1944, the government had announced plans to provide training for fit men and women released from war service, and this was targeted at agriculture and horticulture as well as other types of industrial employment. A game of 'pass the parcel' then ensued between the Ministry of Agriculture and the Ministry of Labour as to who should arrange this training. In the end, the Ministry of Agriculture took on the responsibility and a conference was organised in March 1945, which included the usual interested parties.[6]

This conference attempted to look into the future prospects for professional gardening. The members estimated that there were about 80,000 full-time gardeners in post before the war, and anticipated that, in future, rather fewer would be needed for private gardens and estates but that there would be 'a steady increase in the demand for gardeners in public parks, sports grounds of institutions . . . and cemeteries'.[7]

As far as training was concerned, Wisley, Kew and the Royal Botanic Gardens, Edinburgh, agreed to instruct men with some previous experience, Kew and Wisley suspending their student gardenership scheme until the supply of government trainees was exhausted – although they did take back those former students whose studies had been interrupted by the war. The conference decided that most training of demobbed novices would have to be done in twelve-month placements at carefully selected horticultural establishments and gardens, with the funding split between state (40 per cent) and employer (60 per cent). The RHS put a notice in the July 1945 issue of the *Journal*, giving a brief outline of the Ministry's scheme, and asking Fellows in England and Wales to offer suitable placements if they could. In the event, the Society was more proactive in this matter than were parks administrators, who had to be chivvied. The government scheme started in March 1946. However, it is doubtful whether this initiative made a great deal of difference to the number of trained gardeners.

In 1944, the Ministry of Agriculture had also sought advice, separately, from the Horticultural Education Association about the training of ex-service personnel as 'jobbing' gardeners, i.e. men (and they were mostly men) who worked part-time in a number of gardens. The Association was keen to make clear to the Ministry that gardening was not some kind of soft option – 'Gardening is not light work unless the jobs are specially chosen – the light jobs are few in number and in most cases the employers of jobbing gardeners do the light work themselves' – and it recommended a minimum of a year's instruction in a public park or garden, or in a commercial firm which specialised in jobbing gardening and landscaping work.

In a conclusion which shows a lively appreciation of the difficulties, the Association's Secretary, a Mr G. C. Johnson, wrote:

HEA council hopes that if a scheme is initiated, possible trainees will not be given an unduly optimistic impression of the prospects of jobbing gardening. War-time demands and wages can be no guide to what can be earned in the post-war years. Persons judged to be unsuitable for other jobs by reason of low intelligence, or poor physique should not be encouraged to take up this type of work.

Though sensible, this was bound to be a vain aspiration. He continued: 'Lastly, to make a success of jobbing gardening demands initiative, a good general knowledge of gardening operations coupled with hard work, and ability and willingness to humour the whims of their prospective employers, who often need help, but not guidance.'[8] How right he was, but such pessimism did not augur well for a successful initiative.

At the end of hostilities, the prospects for Land Girls and other female gardeners were even less promising, since many had to give way to returning male employees, especially in commercial operations, and they were not included in any post-war retraining scheme. To add insult to injury, Land Girls were given neither a medal nor any kind of official recognition, or indeed any of the post-war benefits such as resettlement grants to which even civilian auxiliary workers were entitled. Post-war benefits for the WLA were something for which Robert Hudson had fought in Cabinet, but he had come up against the adamantine opposition of Winston Churchill, amongst others.

The Land Girls were not impressed. As one of them wrote: 'I joined in June 1939. I have lost my pre-war office job . . . my sole souvenir of five and a half years' loyal service is a rather battered scarlet armlet – not even a discharge badge.'[9] The shabby treatment of Land Girls prompted Lady Denman to resign from her position as Director of the WLA in protest, much to her colleagues' consternation, since she was the public face, and driving force, behind the organisation. In the end, after questions in Parliament, and lobbying, Land Girls were allowed to keep their greatcoats and the government contributed to their benevolent fund. That was all. The WLA was disbanded in

November 1950. In 1951, when Lady Denman was invested with the Grand Cross of the British Empire, the King told her, 'We always thought that the Land Girls were not well treated.'[10] It was not until many years later, in 2008, that the 30,000 surviving Land Girls and members of the Timber Corps received a specially designed commemorative badge and certificate.

At one point during the war, Lady Denman had been called down to Longford Castle in Wiltshire to arbitrate in a dispute over wages between Land Girls working on food production for the Earl and Countess of Radnor. Some years after the war, the Dowager Countess wrote:

> I remember standing beside our beacon fire on VE night in
> 1945. We were telling ourselves that the miracle had happened;
> we were all alive, the house had not been bombed, the troops in
> it were British and not German, we had won the war!
> Nevertheless, in all the rejoicing my husband, speaking as the
> owner of a country house, said to me 'Now our personal
> problems begin.'[11]

The Radnors were by no means alone in feeling a sense of chill foreboding. The country houses and their gardens and parks which had been requisitioned by the government for wartime duties had fared extremely badly. Even those not substantially damaged by heavy war machinery and careless servicemen had not had anything spent on their fabric for six years. Without the kind of maintenance that was routine in peacetime, these estates degenerated very quickly. Those parts of gardens no longer used for food production became hopelessly overgrown even more quickly than the wallpaper curled or the plaster fell. As the garden historian Miles Hadfield put it: 'The largest, most magnificent house can, with central heating and little else, remain uninhabited with little harm for many months. But an untouched, even merely unmown garden, can become an almost irrevocable wilderness in weeks.'[12] That may be a little melodramatic, but the general point is a good one. For some gardens, the point of no return had arrived even before VJ Day was celebrated. For many others, it was only a few short years away.

The owners of requisitioned country houses could ask for government reparations for damage actively caused, or which had come about as a result of lack of maintenance, but that did not solve the real problem, which was the disappearance of the workforce. Servants never returned in pre-war numbers, partly due to rising wages, which made them often unaffordable, and partly because of their own widened horizons. Wages had risen by 50 per cent during the war, while prices had only increased by 33 per cent. Farm rents were low, so land was not generating much wealth; meanwhile this was a time of dizzying hikes in death duties and other taxes. By 1947, supertax on the wealthy had reached 90 per cent. The landowning classes were broke and getting broker. The last thing they wanted was unsustainably large wage bills to perpetuate a way of life that, even to many who were born to it, seemed increasingly anachronistic.

In the largest houses, with the largest gardens, the shortage of skilled gardening labour showed very quickly. A system that had previously demanded such high standards meant that any falling-away was highly visible. The decorative parts of gardens were choked with aggressive perennial weeds from six years of neglect. Moss had spread like a green stain on gravel paths that had once been raked weekly on a Friday afternoon, while shrubs outgrew their space and hedges became unkempt, swiftly shooting up into trees. Tender bedding plants no longer filled the parterres, leaving empty beds to be colonised with weeds. Only the real survivors of the plant world – daffodils and snowdrops, rhubarb, apple trees, bergenias, water irises – continued to flourish year after year. With their boilers cold and pipes furred, the greenhouses were emptied of their dead plants, often leaving only a 'Black Hamburgh' grape, its rampant shoots finding their way through the broken panes of the hand-made curved-edged glass. The bothy, where the unmarried gardeners had lived, stood empty or was rented out, while the door of the potting shed hung off its hinges. Inside, the unwanted clay pots lay in their hundreds in rows on the wooden shelving, never to be filled again, while rusting garden tools hung from hooks, no rough hands left to grasp their smooth handles. The hand-made red bricks in the kitchen garden walls crumbled, while algae grew thick in the central pond and the cankered branches of apple trees sloughed their bark. Wanton vandalism often wrecked what decay had not.

At Longford Castle, the Dowager Countess opined:

The flower-garden round the house, lawns, paths and even the gravel in the front and the yard at the back are almost like the rooms you live in; keep them orderly and maintained and they are a pleasure to all, but once they deteriorate they are a depressing burden. As in the house you can reduce them in size, simplify, mechanize, yet it is inevitable that they will remain too big for the owners to do them for themselves. I remember in the war that one hardly noticed the weedy paths between the beds of onions in the rose-garden. After the war it seemed as important to get back good lawns, straight verges and clean gravel as to have flowers again. Lack of order and maintenance can wreck morale both indoors and out.[13]

That demoralisation was widespread; it took owners of a very particular and unusual stamp not to yield to it.

One garden that had brought in modern machinery during the war to make up for the lack of labour was Levens Hall in Westmorland. But this, predictably, caused a different problem. The head gardener, F. C. King, in answer to an article by G. Copley in *The Gardeners' Chronicle*, wrote that his employer now only needed to employ four men, rather than the ten required before the war, if King used new technology to the full:

It would seem to me that I have a tractor which works about four weeks a year, a clipping machine which works five, a sterilizer one, and at least four young gardeners looking for other employment, for I can hardly recommend my employer to retain both them and the machinery. If my experience be duplicated, where does Mr Copley suggest the lads who come back should look for employment, or does he suggest I should get rid of the tools in favour of the lads?[14]

It was a difficulty, and one all employers had to deal with sooner or later. Most chose the tools.

Ted Humphris and his employer, Mr Cartwright, at Aynhoe Park did not see the end of the army occupation until 1947. The troops left a legacy of concrete emplacements and Nissen huts, although it must be said that the concrete slabs came in useful for laying out a new terrace. Humphris substantially simplified the garden. He mourned the loss of so many fine trees, but managed to get the lawns back in order in a couple of years, grass being such an amenable medium, if mowed frequently. A fierce storm in early 1947 damaged the glasshouses; the peach house was pulled down, its timbers and glass used to repair others and build a new one.

Humphris also began to use machinery. 'Reluctantly many of the pre-war practices in the kitchen garden had to be abandoned for labour saving reasons. One major change was the use of a motor plough and cultivators instead of spade and rake.'[15] But some garden tasks could not be mechanised. 'The many varied fruit trees trained along the garden walls, which for over a hundred years had provided an abundance of succulent fruit, were torn out of the ground, for no better reason than shortage of labour to attend to their many needs. The war years had certainly hastened the end of the old methods of cultivating and running a garden.'[16]

As for Ditchley Park, the reign of the Trees did not long survive the war. The couple divorced in 1947, and Nancy married Colonel C. G. Lancaster and moved to Kelmarsh Hall in Northamptonshire. In any event, the times were out of joint. The servants who left by 1942 never came back in the same numbers in 1945, and without them, the very particular charm and attraction of Ditchley Park – grand yet luxuriously comfortable – could not survive. Geoffrey Jellicoe, designer of the Italianate parterre, wrote:

> After the war Ronald Tree tried to adapt the house to the new economic conditions, but this was not to be. The final decision to leave England came after he had purchased a splendid set of wrought iron gates and stone pillars for the entrance forecourt and was unable to get a permit for their erection (I remember the costs of the material involved was a few pounds and I remember, too, seeing the stonework lying disconsolately on the ground). After this he sold Ditchley[17] and retired to Barbados, where I built him a Palladian mansion out of coral, entrance gates and all.[18]

Although Ditchley Park has survived and flourished as the home of the Ditchley Foundation, the great west parterre has been grassed over.

In 1951, Nancy Lancaster divorced her second husband and in 1954 moved to Haseley Court in Oxfordshire. She retained the famous 'chess set' topiary garden that Mr Shepherd, one of her predecessor's gardeners, had continued to clip, without payment, all through the war years. In the walled garden, she laid out a charming garden in the Sissinghurst style, with the help of the designer Vernon Russell-Smith. After a fire in the big house, she moved into the converted coach house in its grounds, while still somehow retaining control over the walled garden. When I went to work for her in the summer of 1974, there were only two gardeners: Mr Clayton, the Northumbrian head gardener, and a retired farm worker called Tom Chalk. Mr Clayton thought it his duty to teach me the 'old ways', as if I were a journeyman improver from fifty years before, so I caught just a last, fleeting glimpse of the system first established in Georgian times.[19]

It is possible to argue that post-war exigencies ended once and for all the servitude experienced by both indoor and outdoor staff in great houses. Never again would substantial numbers of gardeners be at the beck and call of capricious mistresses and mean masters, trapped in a severely hierarchical system from which it was difficult to escape, even their homes tied to the job, and so lost if the job was lost. But it is also possible to argue that never again would horticulture reach such a high standard of excellence, and that most of those gardeners took enormous pride in their skills and knowledge and did not often feel that their shackles chafed. There may have been more of the latter at the war's end, but the system had had its day. All that was left on many estates were the ghosts of aproned gardeners carefully closing wooden doors in garden walls against the rabbits at the end of a long day.

There were precious few high-profile champions for these houses and gardens after the war, with the exception of the National Trust and, to a lesser extent, the Ministry of Works, the forerunner of English Heritage. During the war, the National Trust had accepted into its care a number of very fine houses, most usually left or given because of the financial difficulties of the owners, or their conviction that circumstances were going to be so different after the war that hanging on to these heritage pieces was pointless. Among these gifts were Killerton in Devon, Wallington in Northumberland, West Wycombe Park in Buckinghamshire, Charlecote Park in Warwickshire, Blickling Hall in Norfolk, Polesden Lacey in Surrey and Stourhead in Wiltshire. All had very notable parks or gardens surrounding them.

Even someone who did not know what had happened to estate gardens during the war could infer from the substantial number of large country houses that were either sold or allowed to become ruinous and/or demolished in the years after 1945 that the situation was critical. In 1974, it was estimated by the organisers of the Victoria and Albert Museum's first exhibition on the subject, *The Destruction of the Country House*, that about 250 houses 'of architectural and historic importance' had been lost in the thirty years since 1945. In 2011, John Martin Robinson put the number of English country houses demolished between 1945 and 1955 at nearly 1,000.[20] Even if not all of those were of particular architectural and historic importance, that still represents a great loss to the country's cultural heritage.

Of course, Britain was comprehensively bust in 1945, and the socialist government under Clement Attlee's premiership was mainly uninterested in underwriting the renovation and renewal of large houses belonging to the aristocracy that his party so heartily disliked. The particularly large number of Victorian houses demolished in the 1950s pricked the conscience of thoughtful people like John Betjeman, who could see their historical, cultural and aesthetic value, but it was an architectural style that was comprehensively out of fashion. The Victorian Society was founded in 1958, to champion the cause of many properties in trouble, but by then it was too late for dozens of them.

After a house's sale or demolition, the pictures, furniture and books might find other careful owners, but the gardens, being so much more changeable and dynamic, could not be preserved, and the memory of most is now only enclosed in leather-bound albums of monochrome photographs, stuck in the basements of county records offices. Even houses that survived, if they changed their use, lost the gardens they once had. For example, Hewell Grange in Worcestershire, which once had immensely elaborate formal gardens, became a borstal in 1946. The gardens are still tended by prisoners at Her Majesty's Pleasure, but they would be scarcely recognisable to the Windsor-Clive family who owned them before the war.

There were also a number of gardens famous or noteworthy in their own right which were in need of saving. These gardens the National Trust was very reluctant to consider, since suitable capital endowments were unlikely to come with them.

It was thanks in large part to the purposefulness and vision of the RHS President, Lord Aberconway, as well as that of the National Trust luminary, James Lees-Milne, that a dedicated NT and RHS Gardens Committee was brought into being, with the aim of administering and raising money for the maintenance of a small number of the best gardens in England that could be given to the National Trust. In late 1947, Lord Aberconway called a meeting with Lees-Milne, as well as Dr George Taylor of Kew and the King's brother-in-law, Major David Bowes-Lyon, who was to be Aberconway's successor as President of the RHS. They proposed setting up a Gardens Fund. James Lees-Milne was of the opinion that 'There are thousands of English people who love gardens even more than buildings, and would willingly subscribe to such a fund.'[21] This initiative was immensely important as a first step towards creating a climate of interest in, and care for, historic gardens.

Lord Aberconway told the Fellows of the RHS at the Society's annual general meeting in 1948 that 'only gardens of great beauty, gardens of outstanding design or historic interest would be considered . . . and those having collections of plants or trees of value to the nation either botanically, horticulturally or scientifically'.[22] As it happened, there would be far more gardens with those characteristics to save than the money and will to save them.

Nevertheless, Lord Aberconway mobilised the gardening aristocracy as best he could. Vita Sackville-West made a radio broadcast appeal for donations to the newly formed Gardens Fund. She also suggested that the National Trust approach the Queen's Institute of District Nursing, which raised money to help retired or sick district nurses. Since 1927, this charity had been supported by grand garden owners when they opened their gardens once a year to visitors, under what was called the Gardens of England and Wales Scheme.[23] The Queen's Institute agreed that, from 1949, a share of the proceeds would go to the Gardens Fund, in return for the Trust actively supporting the Scheme. The arrangement has lasted to this day.

In 1948, the National Trust took on its first garden, Hidcote Manor in Gloucestershire, which had been developed thirty years earlier by an American, Lawrence Johnston.[24] There was no endowment, and in the early years after opening, the costs far outweighed the visitor receipts. In 1949, the garden might see as few as seven visitors in a day, while the bill for gardeners' wages was £20 10s. a week.[25] By 2011, however, the number of visitors had reached 177,000 a year. Lord Aberconway's own garden, Bodnant, passed to the National Trust with an endowment in 1949. In 1954, another great garden also came to the Trust: Nymans in Sussex.

Acquired gardens provided many different and complex challenges to the National Trust, in particular how to retain the very personal and specific atmosphere created by a garden owner, whilst taking account of plant growth and change over time, as well as the need to provide appropriate public access.[26] But from the point of view of conservation and as a spur to garden historians,[27] this burden was crucial.

In 1946, to his credit, Hugh Dalton, the Labour Chancellor of the Exchequer, established a fund designed to help save important houses or landscape for the nation, as a memorial to those killed in the Second World War. This fund – £50 million a year initially – saved a few grand country houses and, with them, their gardens, but it was cut to £10 million in 1957. The 1950 Report of the Gowers[28] Committee on Houses of Outstanding Historic or Architectural Interest, which found that the main reason that the great houses were falling into ruin was the 'burden of taxation', emphasised the need to preserve both house and setting if estates were to be given to the nation in lieu of death duties. Nevertheless, no one in 1950 could possibly have predicted the renaissance of so many houses that did survive in private hands, thanks to the courage, drive and optimism of their owners, especially the 'stately home as public leisure ground' pioneers like the Duke of Bedford, the Duke of Devonshire and the Marquess of Bath.[29] Not until the early 1980s was their task eased by a more sympathetic tax regime combined with low inflation.

In 1974, the architectural historian John Harris wrote:

There can be no plea for a continuance of the aristocratic
tradition, and there can be no government help for any owner
who wishes to live an aristocratic way of life. Fortunately most
owners of houses open to the public are hard-working and
dedicated to the new life for their houses. We can all participate
in this life with a sense of national pride in one of the greatest
artistic achievements of western civilization. It is surely of
immense consequence that this achievement can give pleasure

and happiness to millions, who at will can move from noisy
dusty cities to enjoy the country house in its park and estate,
that perfect union of art with nature.[30]

This may seem self-evident now, but it certainly did not in the years
after the war.

So much for the big houses and their gardens, but the future of
gardening in England no longer lay with them. Harry Roberts, a pres-
cient contributor to a book of essays about England published in 1945,
wrote:

> In the present century Britain has been engaged in two great
> wars, conducted on novel lines, with novel weapons; the total
> effect of which on gardening in this country is bound to be
> immense. Already one sees a great reduction in the number of
> large gardens in private hands. The cultivation of flowers except
> on the smallest scale is discouraged, and large estates all over
> the country are being split up for building development. After
> the war, nearly all gardens in private hands will be essentially
> villa gardens or cottage gardens. We shall then see who among
> us are real gardeners.[31]

As it turned out, there *were* some real gardeners, and with the decline
or disappearance of many country estates, it was time for plantsmen to
take a more important role in the horticultural life of the nation. These
were the owners of village manor houses and old rectories, often bought
for a song after the war and filled with furniture bought equally cheaply
at provincial auctions. These houses possessed smaller gardens than those
that surrounded stately homes, and the employed help might be only
that provided by a steel worker or farm labourer supplementing his
wages on a Saturday morning, or a semi-retired professional gardener.
The results might possibly be a Sissinghurst; they would never again be
a Chatsworth. Nevertheless, they could be very appealing and were to
become attractions to visitors in their own right.

Lionel Fortescue, for example, retired from his career as a 'beak' at Eton College in 1945, and moved to the West Country, as it had a kinder climate for gardening than Berkshire. The garden he made around The Garden House, Buckland Monachorum, in Devon, was to become one of the brightest jewels of post-war gardening, and is now administered by a charitable trust and regularly open to the public.

Close in age to Fortescue was Sir David Scott, who retired as head of the Consular Service in the Foreign Office in 1947 to live in one wing of Boughton House in Northamptonshire, which he rented from his cousin, the Duke of Buccleuch and Queensberry. There, with his wife, Dorothy, he made, out of a 'vast thicket', an informal tree and shrub garden, which became famous amongst gardeners for the quality and rarity of its plants. This garden was created by two people grieving for the loss of their only child, a son killed in North Africa in 1941. They were one couple amongst many to discover the healing qualities of gardening after the war. In 1970, after Sir David's wife had died, he married Valerie Finnis, head of the alpine department at the Waterperry School of Horticulture, and one of Miss Havergal's students there during the war. Together, the Scotts continued to develop one of the most highly regarded plantsman's gardens of the post-war era, a powerful draw for keen gardeners when it opened twice a year for the National Gardens Scheme.

An acquaintance of the Scotts, Maurice Mason, a Norfolk farmer who grew sugar beet and corn in a big way during the war, developed a garden that contained ten glasshouses, including several tropical 'stove' houses. He is commemorated in a widely grown begonia that he bred called *Begonia x masoniana*.

Amongst wartime combatants, Peter Healing of the Priory, Kemerton, in Worcestershire, had used the time he had been forced to spend in a German POW camp to good effect. He recalled later:

By the end of the war I found myself in Germany with only one book, William Robinson's [*The*] *English Flower Garden*,[32] perhaps one of the best gardening books ever written, and it was

through him that I pictured the form that the borders must take
. . . The main border, some 150 feet long and now eight feet
wide, was planned to start with grey foliage through white,
cream and pink to pale yellow, working up by strong yellows to
a crescendo of reds, maroon and bronze. From there it would
fade gradually in the reverse order down to whites and greys in
the far distance.

The second border was to be whites and creams, with pale
pinks and lavender, while the cross-border under the ruin would
be every shade of red. It would never become garish or too
strong as there are so many really dark reds and bronze flowers
and foliage to choose from and these would absorb the heat of
the scarlets.

Such ideas were translated into yards of planting plans and
proudly transported home at the end of the war. Little was it
realized that not only were very few of the plants or seed
available but that these quantities would involve much
propagation.[33]

Although William Robinson is the name on the spine of *The English
Flower Garden*, the chapter on colour was in fact written by Miss Gertrude
Jekyll. In it she explained her theory of colour and the way it should
progress in a border, from the very palest at the end to the hottest
colours in the middle, and then gradually pale again. What Peter Healing
created at Kemerton was a classic Jekyllian herbaceous border, and one
that became famous in the 1980s, when garden photography really began
to do justice to the quality of colourist plantings.

Existing gardens happily rescued from neglect after the war, to become
appealing destinations for garden visitors, also included Ralph Dutton's
garden at Hinton Ampner House in Hampshire. This garden had been
abandoned in wartime to 'that rough gardener – Mother Nature'.[34]

At last the sad years of war ended, and in July 1945 I was back
in my house gazing out onto the chaos of what had once been a

well-kept garden. The wide terrace had been given up to rough grass, trodden by the two hundred little feet of the children who had inhabited the house during the war. We had no machine to do the work, nor petrol had we possessed one, but I was lucky in finding two elderly men expert in the use of the scythe. Thus during the long summer evenings they spent many hours rhythmically mowing the rough herbage – a Millet scene – till the terrace had once again some semblance of a lawn.[35]

Another contemporary, the Dowager Marchioness of Cholmondeley, remembered in 2001 what it was like when she and her husband, Hugh, moved to Cholmondeley Castle in 1949. 'When friends came to stay for the weekend, we gave them an axe and a saw, and told them to set to. There was thick scrub of laurel and *Rhododendron ponticum* everywhere, and clearing took years. Things were funny after the war – petrol was rationed, it was hard to get help, and making a garden was practically unheard of.'[36] All these people still employed gardeners, but not on anything like the scale that had been commonplace amongst their class before the war.

In more modest and, of course, far more populous gardens, the process of reclamation could happen much more quickly. Gardeners often could scarcely wait to put back their lawns, take the tomatoes out of the herbaceous border and hide the vegetables once more behind the rustic trelliswork. Nella Last in Barrow-in-Furness wasted no time in getting rid of her poultry and reinstating the lawn. A month before VJ Day, she wrote about wanting to get home from an outing in order to cut and roll the lawn: 'It was just as lovely in the garden, and work was a pleasure. As the sun cooled, people started to come out to cut the lawn and water seedlings; the music from "Music Hall" drifted out through open casements . . . When I looked out of the back-bedroom window, I could *not* realise that I'd had an untidy hen-run so recently.'[37]

Wartime measures might be happily abandoned, but on a Sunday afternoon in the second half of the 1940s, there was precious little else that the householder could do except some kind of gardening. Shops were closed, there were no spectator sports like cricket or horse-racing, and few people had access to what limited television there was. Little wonder, therefore, that gardening flourished, especially the specialisms like rock gardening or rose growing, once the nurserymen had recovered their poise and were sending out plants once more.

At the annual general meeting of the RHS in 1948, Lord Aberconway remarked – to laughter – that somebody had suggested to him that the marked increase in membership of the Society was as a result of austerity and the absence of petrol, so that there was little else to live for. The audience might have thought that comment funny, but it contained a great deal of truth.[38]

There was no denying that the war had changed private gardening, making it a more communal experience. After the conflict, it gradually became more inward-looking once more, mirroring the increasing intro-spection of a population which gradually, through the 1950s and 60s, traded many of its former public pleasures for the private delights of the television. Gardening was no longer so obviously a shared activity, where vegetables and cultivation tips were exchanged across the garden fence. In the post-war years, gardens were places where amateur enthusiasts grew perfect blooms of chrysanthemums, dahlias or hybrid tea roses, often for exhibiting in the local flower show, but there to prove individual skills rather than the grower's attachment to national solidarity or a defiant fist shaken at Adolf Hitler.

One definite boost to gardening, especially commercial growing, was the revival of the Chelsea Flower Show in 1947, much encouraged by the horticulturally sophisticated King George VI. The nurserymen were initially very dubious about whether it was possible, and the show was certainly rather smaller than the pre-war exhibitions. However, Lord Aberconway averred that it was 'as full of artistry . . . and of interest . . . The exhibitors thought they could not do it, but they rose to the occasion wonderfully and they did it.'[39] The Chelsea Flower Show continued to be an important event in the annual 'London Season'; in those years it was smart to be seen there, since it was not yet the seething mass of humanity that it became in the 1970s.

In the same year, 1947, the RHS published *The Fruit Garden Displayed*. Like its companion, *The Vegetable Garden Displayed*, this book remained in print for decades. The Royal Horticultural Society had had 'a good war', and peacetime would consolidate its pre-eminence as the main adviser to keen amateur gardeners, in England at least.

Those nurseries which exhibited at Chelsea were facing a very different world. Some embraced the opportunities, while others faltered. For Cheals, an old-fashioned family concern that had prided itself on its high standards of cultivation and its exalted clientele before the war, the winds of change were very cold. Many country estates were broken up, the houses frequently sold for institutional use or carved up into flats, if not demolished, and much land in the south-east of England was sold for housing development. Garden design commissions, which of course had had such a beneficial effect on their nursery plant sales, became decidedly more modest.

Worse still, there was hardly any plant stock left at the end of the war – it had either been sold and not replaced, or had grown too big to be easily sellable – so although there was a sudden substantial demand from gardeners, many nurseries could not meet it. Customers had to order in spring for an autumn delivery, and even had to pay in advance. In desperation, Cheals turned to the Dutch to provide wholesale trees and shrubs, because the wonderfully fertile soil at Boskoop meant that they grew more quickly there.

At Sunningdale Nurseries, which had been in such a sorry state during the war, the future was brighter. James (Jim) Russell set about reclaiming the nurseries, and laid out roads, lawns, show borders and a propagation unit. He also had the sense to employ Graham Stuart Thomas, who was to become the pre-eminent expert on shrub roses, as his manager in 1956.

Generally, the nurseries that recovered best were those that catered for the massed ranks of modest gardeners. Harry Wheatcroft, with his brother, discovered that they had sustained grievous losses amongst rose varieties during the war. He particularly mourned the disappearance of a rose he had bred called 'Peter Pan', never to be resurrected. Nevertheless, their nursery recovered quickly, Wheatcroft believed because of the loyalty of pre-war customers, and was soon winning prizes again, notably at the 1949 National Rose Society's autumn show. The nursery staff also helped to lay out a new trial ground for the National Rose Society, near St Albans. This Society achieved its largest membership in the 1950s. Everybody could grow roses in their gardens, and most people wanted to. Indeed, roses positively thrived in industrial cities before the Clean Air Act of 1956, because the sulphur in the atmosphere kept 'blackspot' fungus at bay.

Wheatcroft's fortunes were also boosted by something that happened at the beginning of the war. As France was about to be overrun, François Meilland, a young rose grower in the south of France, managed to smuggle out – via the American consulate in Lyons – a small package of budded rootstocks of a new hybrid tea rose that had impressed rosarians at a conference in France in the summer of 1939. This rose was remarkable for its healthy and strong growth, and the size and shape of its golden-yellow flowers, with their distinctive and, to my mind, rather dispiriting pink edge. After the war, it was named 'Peace', in the English-speaking world at least. Harry Wheatcroft initially bought 10,000 'eyes' (to 'bud' onto rootstocks), but the rose's popularity grew so rapidly that in the end he sold far more than that. 'Peace' captured the public imagination, and it was planted in most post-war rose gardens, often no doubt where the wartime vegetables had once grown.

Suttons of Reading, the seedsmen, also recovered relatively quickly. The firm had a stroke of luck in September 1945, when the Dutch somehow managed to export 5,000 tons of bulbs to the United Kingdom, which meant that Suttons could fulfil that autumn's bulb order after all. The company's garden construction department also thrived; it collaborated with a firm of garden architects, Messrs Milner Son and White, and sent its own workmen to carry out the Milner plans for herbaceous and shrub borders, lily ponds and rock gardens, terracing and hedging. A 1950s advertisement read: 'Character, simplicity, charm and restfulness are the keynotes of a garden designed by SUTTON'S of READING.'[40]

Those people living without gardens in towns and cities saw their main pleasure grounds, the public parks, regain much of their pre-war attraction, with the return of the brilliantly colourful bedding schemes of old and the grassing over of utilitarian model allotments. Parks were definitely the beneficiaries of the move of ambitious trained gardeners away from private service, since public authorities could offer more advantageous terms and conditions, and did not require such a level of old-fashioned deference from their employees.

However, the question of wilful and accidental damage in parks was still an issue: 'to practice horticulture as we knew it in pre-war days in fenceless parks is not only heart-breaking but a waste of time, money and labour', wrote a gloomy park superintendent in 1948.[41] Even after the railings were put back in many parks, the vandalism continued. It was not as widespread as in the war years, but it never again disappeared entirely.

To make way for returning demobbed male gardeners, as well as refugees from country house gardens, not to mention new machinery, women mainly lost their jobs in parks and public gardens. The fifty girl gardeners at Kew had been reduced to six by 1946. In any event, many Land Girls married straight after the war and left market gardening or farm work for good. Not until 1975 did those few female gardeners who remained in horticulture achieve equal pay with men. Today, in very changed circumstances in the labour market, there are probably more women in managerial positions in horticulture, both professional and commercial, than there have been at any time since the very particular conditions of wartime.

The research stations that had contributed markedly to the success of wartime commercial horticulture were brought under the control of the Ministry of Agriculture after the war. One regretted consequence of this was the ending of the student trainee-ship scheme at the John Innes Horticultural Institution. However, with their public reputations enhanced, the stations expanded in both size and number, most notably with the foundation of the Glasshouse Crops Research Institute in Littlehampton and the National Vegetable Research Station at Wellesbourne.

The country's gratitude to agriculture and horticulture for the part they played in feeding the nation ensured a fair wind for reforms in the immediate post-war years. Sir Daniel Hall's blueprint for the future, *Reconstruction and the Land*, formed the basis of the 1947 Agriculture Act. This provided guaranteed prices and subsidies to farmers and promoted the rapid mechanisation of agriculture, which had begun in wartime, thus ensuring a more efficient industry at a time of rapidly increasing population and expectations.

One of the Act's effects was to encourage the use of pesticides, in the interests of cost savings and productivity. Gardeners were not slow to follow farmers, and for a generation, they sprayed lavishly. However, in the 1970s, as the evidence of damage to land and wildlife gathered strength – and public opinion gradually turned against chemicals – the organic gardening movement, spearheaded by Lawrence Hills and his Henry Doubleday Research Association,[42] expanded. The leading lights of this movement readily acknowledged their debt to the pioneers of thirty years before, in particular Sir Albert Howard, Lady Eve Balfour and the other founders of the Soil Association.

In *A Green and Pleasant Land*, I have attempted to bring to the reader's attention those gardeners who particularly deserve to be remembered for their contributions to the war effort. These were the parks superintendents, who abandoned their much loved floral displays to teach urban novices how to grow Brussels sprouts, together with the massed ranks of unmarried women – Miss Elizabeth Hess, Miss Viola Williams, Miss Edith Walker, Miss Dorothy Hinchcliffe, Miss Beatrix Havergal amongst them – who, unencumbered by husband or children, worked tirelessly on county horticultural committees and in horticultural colleges, or drove around the countryside in the pitch black to teach other ladies in draughty village halls how to sow peas or collect medicinal herbs. As important were the middle-aged nurserymen and older professional gardeners, as well as the girls of the Women's Land Army, who together grew the vegetable produce that really made a difference to the nation's health. These people showed an impressive devotion to duty, which could probably only be sustained while there was a pressing external threat to life and livelihood.

As for amateur gardeners, their horticultural efforts had been a significant feature of their war, bringing them together with others and giving them a sense of common purpose. Their hours of patient gardening became part of the accumulated shared memories of civilian life, especially each spring when thoughts turned once more to sowing seeds and spending weekend afternoons with neighbours and children on the allotment. The success of the Dig for Victory campaign might have been more apparent than real – the result of a collusion between government, press and professional gardeners – but its very existence and persistence enhanced the self-image and morale of gardeners and even of those who never dug up their gardens or rented an allotment but knew somebody who did. In short, 'growing your own' became a shared and positive national experience, sufficiently strong and pervasive to survive to this day.

For those people still alive who went through the war, there is satisfaction and pride in the memory of how they and their contemporaries thoroughly confounded the politicians, the military hierarchy and, most particularly, the psychiatrists by their behaviour. With insignificant exceptions, those battling on the Home Front showed themselves equal to the tasks required of them. They refused to buckle under the pressure brought about by restrictions, shortages, overwork, lack of money and security, strain, danger and demoralisation. The growing of, and delight in, vegetables, fruit and flowers helped a significant number of them to do that. Those of us who came afterwards have much upon which to reflect, and for which to be grateful.

SELECT BIBLIOGRAPHY

Primary Sources

BBC Written Archives Centre, Caversham (BBC WAC)
British Library Newspaper Reading Room, Colindale (BL)
Imperial War Museum Archives, Kennington (IWM)
John Innes Centre, Norwich (JIC)
Mass-Observation Archive, University of Sussex, Brighton (MOA)
Museum of English Rural Life, Reading (MERL)
National Allotments Society, Corby (NSALG)
The National Archives, Kew (TNA)
Northamptonshire Record Office, Wootton (NRO)
Royal Botanic Gardens, Kew (RBGK)
Royal Horticultural Society's Lindley Library, Westminster (RHS)
Women's Library, London Metropolitan University, Whitechapel (WL)

Country Life
Daily Express
Daily Telegraph
Evening Standard (London)
Extracts from the Proceedings of the Royal Horticultural Society
The Field
The Gardeners' Chronicle
Home and Country
Journal of the Kew Guild
Journal of the Royal Horticultural Society
The Listener
My Garden
The Times

Books

There are very few books that deal specifically with the subject of gardening during the Second World War. They are: *The Wartime Kitchen and Garden* by Jennifer Davies (BBC Books, 1993), which accompanied the television series of the same name; *Digging for Victory: Gardens and Gardening in Wartime Britain* by Twigs Way and Mike Brown (Sabrestorm, 2010); *The Spade as Mighty as the Sword* by Daniel Smith (Aurum, 2011); and *The Ministry of Food* by Jane Fearnley-Whittingstall (Hodder and Stoughton, 2010). All tell different aspects of the story and all are worth reading.

Allingham, Margery, *The Oaken Heart* (Michael Joseph, 1941 and Hutchinson, 1959)

Artiss, Percy, *Market Gardening: A Practical Guide to the Commercial Cultivation of Flowers and Vegetables* (Collingridge, 1948)

Becker, Robert, *Nancy Lancaster: Her Life, Her World, Her Art* (Knopf 1996)

Bedford, Sarah, *George VI* (Penguin, 2011)

Benton, Alison, *Cheals of Crawley: The Family Firm at Lowfield Nurseries 1860s to 1960s* (Moira Publications, 2002)

Brickhill, Paul, *The Great Escape* (Sheridan Book Company, 1995)

Briggs, Asa, *The War of Words* (OUP, 1970)

Broad, Richard and Fleming, Suzie (eds.), *Nella Last's War: The Second World War Diaries of Housewife, 49* (Profile Books, 2006)

Brown, Jane, *A Garden of Our Own: A History of Girton College Garden* (Friends of Girton Garden, 1999)

Calder, Angus, *The People's War: 1939–45* (Jonathan Cape, 1969)

Central Statistical Office, *Statistical Digest of the War* (HMSO and Kraus, 1975)

Chamberlain, Joanne, *Trench Warfare: A Study of 'Dig for Victory' in Brighton and Hove During World War Two* (unpublished dissertation, University of Sussex, 2001)

Chamberlin, E. R., *Life in Wartime Britain* (Batsford, 1972)

Cheveley, Stephen, *A Garden Goes to War* (J. Miles, 1940)

Clarke, Gill, *The Women's Land Army: A Portrait* (Sansom, 2008)

Collingham, Lizzie, *The Taste of War: World War Two and the Battle for Food* (Penguin, 2012)

Conford, Philip, *The Origins of the Organic Movement* (Floris Books, 2001)

Cowell, Cyril and Adams, Morley, *Adam the Gardener: A Pictorial Guide to Each Week's Work* (Chatto and Windus, 2011)

Croall, Jonathan, *Don't You Know There's a War On?: Voices from the Home Front* (Sutton, 2005)

Crouch, David and Ward, Colin, *The Allotment: Its Landscape and Culture* (Faber and Faber, 1988)

Donnelly, Peter (ed.), *Mrs Milburn's Diaries: An Englishwoman's Everyday Reflections 1939–45* (Harrap, 1979 and Abacus, 1995)

Dudgeon, Piers, *Village Voices: A Portrait of Change in England's Green and Pleasant Land 1915–1990* (Sidgwick and Jackson, 1989)

Dunn, Mary, *The World of Lady Addle* (Robin Clark, 1985)

Earley Local History Group, *Suttons Seeds: A History 1806–2006* (Earley Local History Group, 2006)

Elliott, Brent, *The Royal Horticultural Society: A History 1804–2004* (Phillimore, 2004)

Ender, Peter, *Up the Garden Path* (Herbert Jenkins, 1944)

Foreman, Susan, *Loaves and Fishes: an Illustrated History of the Ministry of Agriculture, Fisheries and Food 1889–1989* (HMSO, 1989)

Games, Naomi, Moriarty, Catherine, and Rose, June, *Abram Games: His Life and Work* (Princeton, 2003)

Gardiner, Juliet, *Wartime: Britain 1939–1945* (Headline Review, 2005)

Garfield, Simon, *Private Battles: How the War Almost Defeated Us* (Ebury Press, 2007)

Garfield, Simon, *We are at War* (Ebury Press, 2009)

Garner, Gwen, *Extra Ordinary Women: A History of the Women's Institutes* (WI Books, 1995)

Gibson, Trish, *Brenda Colvin: A Career in Landscape* (Frances Lincoln, 2011)

Gillies, Midge, *The Barbed-Wire University; The Real Lives of Prisoners of War in the Second World War* (Aurum, 2011)

Goodall, Felicity, *Voices from the Home Front: Personal Experiences of Wartime Britain 1939–45* (David and Charles, 2004)

Goodchild, Claude and Thompson, Alan, *Keeping Poultry and Rabbits on Scraps* (Penguin, 1941)

Graham, E., *Gardening in War-time* (Peter Davies, 1940)

Hall, Sir Daniel, *Agriculture in the Twentieth Century — Essays on Research, Practice, and Organization to be presented to Sir Daniel Hall* (Clarendon, 1939)

Harris, Alexandra, *Romantic Moderns: English Writers, Artists and the Imagination from Virginia Woolf to John Piper* (Thames and Hudson, 2010)

Harrisson, Tom and Madge, Charles (eds.) *War Begins at Home* (Chatto and Windus, 1940)

Hay, Roy, *Gardener's Chance: From War Production to Peace Possibilities* (Putnam, 1946)

Hayes, Nick and Hill, Jeff, *Millions Like Us?* (Liverpool University Press, 1999)

Hellyer, A.G., *Your New Garden* (Collingridge, 1937)

Helphand, Kenneth I., *Defiant Gardens; Making Gardens in Wartime* (Trinity University Press, 2006)

Herklots, G. A. C., *Vegetables in South-East Asia* (George Allen and Unwin, 1972)

Horwood, Catherine, *Gardening Women: Their Stories from 1600 to the Present* (Virago, 2010)

Howard, Sir Albert, *An Agricultural Testament* (OUP, 1940)

Humphris, Ted, *Garden Glory: From Garden Boy to Head Gardener at Aynhoe Park* (Collins, 1988)

Huxley, Gervas, *Lady Denman GBE* (Chatto and Windus, 1961)

Jeffery, Philip, *Harvest of the Spade* (Longmans, Green, 1944)

Jenkins, Inez, *The History of the Women's Institute Movement of England and Wales* (OUP, 1953)

Keen, Barbara and Armstrong, Jean, *Herb Gathering* (Brome and Schimmer, 1941)

King, Peter, *Women Rule the Plot* (Duckworth, 1999)

Kitchen, Penny (ed.), *For Home and Country: War, Peace and Rural Life as Seen Through the Pages of the WI Magazine 1919–1959* (Ebury Press, 1990)

Koa Wing, Sandra (ed.), *Our Longest Days: A People's History of the Second World War* (Profile Books, 2008)

Kynaston, David, *A World to Build: Austerity Britain 1945–48* (Bloomsbury, 2007)

Lawrence, W. J. C., *Catch the Tide: Adventures in Horticultural Research* (Grower Books, 1980)

Lawrence, W. J. C., (ed.), *The Fruit, the Seed and the Soil: Collected Edition of the John Innes Leaflets Numbers 1 to 9* (Oliver and Boyd, 1954)

Lees-Milne, Alvilde and Verey, Rosemary (eds.), *The Englishman's Garden* (Allen Lane, 1982)

Lees-Milne, James, *Caves of Ice* (Chatto and Windus, 1983)

Longmate, Norman, *The Way We Lived Then* (Hutchinson, 1971)

Longmate, Norman, *The Home Front* (Chatto and Windus, 1981)

Longworth, Philip, *The Unending Vigil: A History of the Commonwealth War Graves Commission 1917–1984* (Leo Cooper in association with Secker and Warburg, 1985)

Mackay, Robert, *Half the Battle: Civilian Morale in Britain during the Second World War* (Manchester University Press, 2002)

Maddy, Ursula, *Waterperry: A Dream Fulfilled* (Merlin Books, 1990)

Mauduit, Vicomte de, *They Can't Ration These* (Michael Joseph, 1940)

McCall, Cicely, *Women's Institutes* (Collins, 1943)

McCooey, Chris (ed.), *Despatches from the Home Front: The War Diaries of Joan Strange 1939–1945* (Monarch, 1989 and JAK Books, 1994)

McLaine, Ian, *Ministry of Morale: Home Front Morale and the Ministry of Information in World War II* (Allen and Unwin, 1979)

Middleton, C. H., *Digging for Victory: Wartime Gardening with Mr Middleton* (Aurum, 2008)

Middleton, C. H., *Mr Middleton Suggests* (Ward Lock, 1939)

Nicholas, Siân, *The Echo of War: Home Front Propaganda and the Wartime BBC, 1939–1945* (Manchester University Press, 1996)

Nicolson, Nigel (ed.), *Harold Nicolson Diaries and Letters 1939–45* (Fontana, 1970)

Patten, Marguerite, *Victory Cookbook: Nostalgic Food and Facts from 1940–1954* (Chancellor Press, 2002)

Purcell, Jennifer, *Domestic Soldiers: Six Women's Lives in the Second World War* (Constable, 2010)

Richardson, Tim, *English Gardens in the Twentieth Century* (Aurum, 2005)

Rix, Martyn and Alison, *Garden Open Today* (Viking, 1987)

Robinson, Jane, *A Force to be Reckoned With: A History of the Women's Institute* (Virago, 2011)

Robinson, John Martin, *Felling the Ancient Oaks: How England Lost its Great Country Estates* (Aurum, 2011)

Robinson, William, *The English Flower Garden* (John Murray, 1898 edn.)

Rohde, Eleanour Sinclair, *Vegetable Cultivation and Cooking* (Medici Society, 1958)

Sackville-West, Vita, *The Land* (William Heinemann, 1926)

Sackville-West, Vita, *The Garden* (Michael Joseph, 1946)

Sackville-West, Vita, *The Women's Land Army* (Imperial War Museum, 1993)

Searle, Adrian, *Isle of Wight at War 1939–45* (The Dovecote Press, 1990)

Spry, Constance, *Come into the Garden, Cook* (J M Dent, 1942)

Stent, Ronald, *A Bespattered Page?: The Internment of 'His Majesty's Most Loyal Enemy Aliens'* (André Deutsch, 1980)

Stewart, Sheila, *Lifting the Latch: A Life on the Land* (Day Books, 2002)

Strong, Roy, Binney, Marcus and Harris, John, *The Destruction of the Country House 1875–1975* (Thames and Hudson, 1974)

Summer, Julie, *Remembered: The History of the Commonwealth War Graves Commission* (Merrell, 2007)

Taylor, James, *Careless Talk Costs Lives: Fougasse and the Art of Public Information* (Conway, 2010)

Thrower, Percy, *My Lifetime of Gardening* (Hamlyn, 1977)

Titmuss, R. M., *Problems of Social Policy* (HMSO, 1950)

Tree, Ronald, *When the Moon was High: Memoirs of Peace and War 1897–1942* (Macmillan, 1975)

Tunnard, Christopher, *Gardens in the Modern Landscape* (Architectural Press, 1938)

Turner, W. J. (ed.), *The Englishman's Country* (Collins, 1945)

Tyrer, Nicola, *They Fought in the Fields* (Tempus, 2007)

Verrill-Rhys, Leigh and Beddo, Deirdre (eds.), *Parachutes and Petticoats: Welsh Women Writing on the Second World War* (Honno, 1992)

Wade, John Reed, *War-time Gardening* (Pearson, 1940)

Wallace, T. and Marsh, R. W., *Science and Fruit: Commemorating the Jubilee of the Long Ashton Research Station, 1903–53* (University of Bristol, 1953)

Waller, Margaret, *London 1945: Life in the Debris of War* (John Murray, 2004)

Ward, Sadie, *War in the Countryside: 1939–45* (Cameron Books in association with David and Charles, 1988)

Waterson, Merlin, *The National Trust: The First Hundred Years* (BBC Books and National Trust, 1994)

Way, Twigs, *Allotments* (Shire, 2010)

Way, Twigs (ed.) *Allotment and Garden Guide* (Sabrestorm, 2009)

Webber, Ronald, *Market Gardening: The History of Commercial Flower, Fruit and Vegetable Growing* (David and Charles, 1972)

Wheatcroft, Harry, *My Life with Roses* (Odhams, 1959)

Wheatcroft, Harry, *The Root of the Matter* (Golden Eagle, 1974)

Williams, Marjorie, (ed. Cassandra Phillips), *Letters from Lamledra: Cornwall 1914–1918* (Truran, 2007)

Williams, Tom, *Digging for Britain* (Hutchinson, 1965)

Wilson, Edward (ed.), *The Downright Epicure: Essays on Edward Bunyard* (Prospect Books, 2007)

Wood, Martin, *Nancy Lancaster: English Country House Style* (Frances Lincoln, 2005)

Woolf, Leonard, *Downhill All the Way: An Autobiography of the Years 1919–1939* (Hogarth Press, 1967)

Woolton, Lord, *Memoirs of the Rt Hon. The Earl of Woolton C.H., P. C., D. L., Ll.D.* (Cassell, 1959)

Articles and Pamphlets

Agriculture and Fisheries, Ministry of, *Growmore Bulletin No. I: Food From the Garden* (HMSO, 1941)

Agriculture and Fisheries, Ministry of, *Dig for Victory Leaflets 1–26*, (HMSO, 1941–45)

Conway, Hazel, 'Everyday landscapes: public parks from 1930–2000' in *Garden History* vol. 28, no.1

Elliott, Brent, 'Bedding Schemes' in *The Regeneration of Public Parks* eds. Jan Woudstra and Ken Fieldhouse (Spon, 2001)

Games, Abram in *Art and Industry* vol. 45, July 1948

Haynes, Barbara, 'The Society at War' in *Journal of the Royal Horticultural Society*, Vol. 129, November 2004

Hess, Elizabeth, 'Collecting Broom' in *The Chemist and Druggist,* 18 April 1942.

Howkins, Alun, 'A Country at War: Mass-Observation and Rural England 1939–45' in *Rural History,* vol. 9, no. 1

Jellicoe, Sir Geoffrey, 'Ronald Tree and the gardens of Ditchley Park: The human face of history' in *Garden History* vol. 10, no.1

Stamper, Anne, *Countrywomen in war time — Women's Institutes 1938–1945*, paper delivered to the Second International Conference on the History of Voluntary Action, held at Roehampton Institute, University of Surrey, September 2003 (www.thewi.org.uk)

Thorpe, Andrew, in *The Civilian at War: The Home Front in Europe, Japan and the USA in World War II* (ed. Jeremy Noakes) (University of Exeter Press, 1992)

Websites

www.bbc.co.uk/history/ww2peopleswar
www.bbc.co.uk/historyatthebbc
www.carrotmuseum.co.uk
http://hansard.millbanksystems.com
www.iwm.org.uk
www.nationalarchives.gov.uk
www.oxforddnb.com
www.thewi.org.uk

Introduction

1   NSALG, Annual report of the National Allotments Society for year ending 31 May 1939, p.6.

Chapter One: The Scene is Set

1   TNA: PRO RG 23/26

2   In the nineteenth century, the expanding petit bourgeoisie in towns took pleasure in renting 'guinea gardens' in suburbs, for productive gardening and leisure. Many of these had become allotments by 1900.

3   *The Times*, 1 January 1940.

4   A. G. Hellyer, *Your New Garden*, Collingridge, 1937 edn, pp.11–12.

5   Arthur Hellyer became a highly respected and influential post-war writer, contributing for many years to the *Financial Times*, as well as editing *Amateur Gardening*.

6   VMH stands for Victoria Medal of Honour, the highest accolade awarded by the Royal Horticultural Society.

7   *Journal of the Royal Horticultural Society*, March 1940, p.89.

8   Christopher Tunnard, *Gardens in the Modern Landscape*, Architectural Press, 1938, p.79.

9   This described a man who had served his apprenticeship but still had some way to go to get to the top. Literally, it meant someone paid by the day, or *journée*.

10 Percy Thrower, *My Lifetime of Gardening*, Hamlyn, 1977, pp.39–40.

11 Page was one of the great post-war landscape gardeners. He worked mainly on the Continent, but is known to thoughtful gardeners in Britain because of his seminal work, *The Education of a Gardener*.

12 According to Robert Becker, *Nancy Lancaster: Her Life, Her World, Her Art*, Knopf, 1996, p. 231.

13 Hazel Conway, 'Everyday landscapes: public parks from 1930–2000', *Garden History*, vol. 28, no. 1, p.122.

14 Coincidentally the month that Adolf Hitler came to power in Germany.

[15] There were 242,000 allotments officially recorded in England in 1873. Twigs Way, *Allotments*, Shire, 2010, p. 12.

[16] These calculations should be treated with the utmost caution; since most allotment holders would not have weighed or recorded their crops, it is impossible to extrapolate accurately.

[17] Under the Allotments Act of 1925.

[18] The Munich crisis was precipitated by German troops marching into the Sudetenland, a border region of Czechoslovakia mainly peopled by ethnic Germans. On 30 September 1938, Germany, Italy, France and the United Kingdom signed the Munich Agreement, thus letting down Czechoslovakia but averting the immediate threat of European war.

[19] NSALG, Annual report of the National Allotments Society for year ending 31 May 1939, p.4.

[20] Ibid.

[21] The Society of Friends, otherwise known as the Quakers.

[22] A prominent member of the Society of Friends, and also a Vice-President of the NAS.

[23] Figures from *Statistical Digest of the War*, first published by the Central Statistical Office, 1951; published with amendments by HMSO and Kraus, 1975.

[24] Jennifer Davies, *The Wartime Kitchen and Garden*, BBC Books, 1993, p.13.

[25] Wooden glazed frames placed over young plants, either to protect them from the cold weather or, as in this case, to force vegetables into early growth, to achieve higher prices.

[26] Chris McCooey (ed.), *Despatches from the Home Front: The War Diaries of Joan Strange 1939–1945*, JAK Books, 1994, p.12.

[27] F1 hybrids are created by controlled cross-pollination. As the seedlings all have the same parents, they are much more uniform than those varieties which are the result of 'open pollination', and in the case of vegetables they tend to mature at the same time. F1 hybrids became widely used in commercial horticulture after the war, because of these obvious advantages.

[28] Where it is still held each May.

[29] They are now at Brogdale in Kent.

[30] Grey squirrels are not native to Britain, and seriously damage the prospects of the smaller, native red squirrel. This was an early, sadly unsuccessful, foray by the RHS into wildlife conservation.

[31] Reginald Farrer (1880–1920) wrote the standard work on rock gardening,

the two-volume *The English Rock Garden*, as well as the popular *My Rock Garden*, amongst others.

32 The National Vegetable Society was not founded until 1960.

33 From 1927 the British Broadcasting Corporation.

34 Marion Cran is forgotten now, but she was a popular author of discursive gardening books such as *The Garden of Ignorance* and *The Garden of Experience*.

35 A scientist working at the East Malling research station in Kent, who became the Ministry of Agriculture's Horticultural Commissioner in wartime.

36 Everybody referred to him thus.

37 Siân Nicholas, *The Echo of War*, Manchester University Press, 1996, p.14–15.

38 E. R. Chamberlin, *Life in Wartime Britain*, Batsford, 1972, p.30.

39 Rambling roses.

40 Quoted in Simon Garfield, *We Are At War*, Ebury Press, 2009, p.112.

Chapter Two: What Happens Now?

1 Margery Allingham, *The Oaken Heart*, Michael Joseph, 1941, pp.86–7.

2 Harold Nicolson, *Diaries and Letters 1939–45* (ed. Nigel Nicolson), Fontana, 1970, p.25.

3 A gross overestimate. It is unlikely to have been even a tenth of that number.

4 Quoted in Robert Mackay, *Half the Battle: Civilian Morale in Britain during the Second World War*, Manchester University Press, 2002, p.20.

5 The Air Ministry came to the same conclusion the following year, estimating that in the first sixty days of the war it was possible that there might be 600,000 dead and 1,200,000 injured by German bombing raids.

6 E. R. Chamberlin, *Life in Wartime Britain*, Batsford, 1972, p.9.

7 Not everybody initially; gas helmets for babies and masks for young children were not available until 1939.

8 R. M. Titmuss, *Problems of Social Policy*, HMSO, 1950, p.20.

9 Quoted in Norman Longmate, *The Way We Lived Then*, Hutchinson, 1971, p.122.

10 Andrew Thorpe, in *The Civilian in War: The Home Front in Europe, Japan and the USA in World War II* (ed. Jeremy Noakes), University of Exeter Press, 1992, p.21.

[11] Mass-Observation was (and is) a social research organisation founded by an anthropologist (Tom Harrisson), a poet (Charles Madge) and a progressive film-maker (Humphrey Jennings) in 1937. The aims of the organisation were to examine aspects of British life using volunteers who answered questions on subjects such as rationing and leisure activities. During the war, some 500 volunteer diarists wrote accounts of their daily lives, constantly or sporadically. Although the contributors were self-selecting (many answered an advertisement in the *New Statesman*), their testimony is invaluable to the researcher, because it is contemporaneous and thus not distorted by hindsight. For about a year at the beginning of the war, Mass-Observation was commissioned by the Ministry of Information's Home Intelligence Division to monitor civilian morale, amongst other things.

[12] MOA, FR 606 Portsmouth, 'Reaction to the Blitz', March 1941, quoted in *Half the Battle*, op. cit. p. 2.

[13] MOA, *War Begins at Home*, ed. Tom Harrisson and Charles Madge, Chatto and Windus, 1940, p.413.

[14] Richard Broad and Suzie Fleming (eds.), *Nella Last's War: The Second World War Diaries of Housewife, 49*, Profile, 2006, p.127.

[15] A child's toy.

[16] Allingham, *The Oaken Heart*, op. cit., p.137.

[17] An Irishman of modest background, Bracken was the most successful wartime Minister of Information, partly because of his energy and partly because he had a much sharper intuition about people's moods and reactions than his more patrician and high-minded predecessors.

[18] Hansard, House of Commons, 10 June 1941, vol. 372, col. 152.

[19] Siân Nicholas, *The Echo of War*, Manchester University Press, 1996, p.70.

[20] Robert Hudson replaced Dorman-Smith in May 1940, when Neville Chamberlain resigned and Winston Churchill became Prime Minister. Lord Woolton had replaced the unpopular Morrison the month before.

[21] In fact, the demarcation lines were by no means always clear, and there was much collaborative effort.

[22] *Daily Express*, 21 November 1939.

[23] *The Gardeners' Chronicle*, 9 September 1939, p.189.

[24] Farmers were paid £2 an acre for ploughing up grassland before the end of December 1939.

[25] Quoted in Juliet Gardiner, *Wartime: Britain 1939–1945*, Headline Review, 2005, p.174.

[26] TNA: PRO MAF 48/732.

[27] Ibid.

[28] Hansard, House of Lords, 28 September 1939, vol. 114, col. 1208.

[29] There was some hostile action, notably at sea, as well as limited Luftwaffe raids on Scottish targets, before the German invasion of Denmark and Norway in April 1940.

[30] The blackout was not lifted until September 1944, and then only partially.

[31] Air Raid Precautions. ARP wardens were the first line of civil defence.

[32] 'Vegetable and Fruit Growing in an Emergency', presented to the Council of the Royal Horticultural Society on 25 October 1938.

[33] The New and Old Halls were used by the GPO for sorting Christmas post each December.

[34] Extracts from the Proceedings of the Royal Horticultural Society, vol. LXVIII (1943), p.i.

[35] The Gardeners' Chronicle, 2 September 1939, p.186.

[36] Ibid., p. viii

[37] Ibid., 9 September 1939, p.189.

[38] Ibid., p.190.

[39] Before nurserymen developed the modern practice of 'containerisation' – when plants are potted up and can be sold and planted at any time of year, provided the soil conditions are right – most plants were sent out from nurseries during the dormant season between November and March. This required nursery workers to go into the fields and dig up ordered plants, pack them in freezing-cold packing sheds and put them on carrier lorries. It also meant sending out catalogues and brochures in good time, which required forward planning and a clear idea of present and future stock.

[40] The Gardeners' Chronicle, 30 September 1939, p. v.

[41] Journal of the Royal Horticultural Society, December 1939, p.546.

[42] Ibid., p.549.

Chapter Three: Dig for Victory!

[1] Daniel Smith makes a good case for the anonymous leader writer being Michael Foot in The Spade as Mighty as the Sword, Aurum, 2011, pp.43–5.

[2] Evening Standard, 6 September 1939.

[3] Frankly, it does sound very alarming. But to put it into context, during April 1941, nearly 700,000 tons of shipping was lost.

4 *Evening Standard*, 12 September 1939.

5 *The Times*, 4 October 1939.

6 The slogan even turned up from time to time as the answer to a newspaper crossword clue.

7 Cultivation of Lands (Allotments) Order, 1939.

8 Local authorities already had powers under the Land Settlement (Facilities) Act of 1919 to provide seeds and equipment at cost price to allotmenteers where there was currently no allotment society or co-operative in place.

9 Hansard, House of Lords, 28 September 1939, vol. 114, col. 1206.

10 TNA: PRO MAF 48/732.

11 *The Times*, 24 February 1940.

12 Jennifer Purcell, *Domestic Soldiers: Six Women's Lives in the Second World War*, Constable, 2010, p.29.

13 Stephen Cheveley, *A Garden Goes to War*, J. Miles, 1940, Foreword.

14 Ibid., p.17.

15 Lt Col. W. L. Julyan, 'Tomato production in the army', *The Field*, 3 October 1942, p.362.

16 Quoted in *The Times*, 1 January 1940.

17 Auberon Waugh, son of the novelist Evelyn Waugh, recalled that his mother finally procured a banana for each of her three children, with special banana coupons, just after the war ended. '… the great day arrived when my mother came home with three bananas. All were put on my father's plate, and before the anguished eyes of his children, he poured on cream, which was almost unprocurable, and sugar, which was heavily rationed, and ate all three.' Auberon Waugh, *Will This Do?*, Century 1991, p.67.

18 Philip Jeffery, *Harvest of the Spade*, Longmans, Green, 1944, p.18.

19 Before 1940 this was known as the GPO Film Unit.

20 Scotland was served by a separate Department of Agriculture but it worked very closely with MAF.

21 *The Gardeners' Chronicle*, 6 January 1940, p.11

22 'Food from the Garden', 'Growmore' Bulletin No. 1, HMSO, 1941, Foreword.

23 BBC WAC, RCONT1 – Middleton C H – Talks File 2, 20 January 1940.

24 Other slogans included 'An Hour in the Garden Saves One in the Queue', which was such nonsense that it did not catch the public imagination to anything like the same degree. 'Dig for Victory and Dig for Dear Life' fared no better.

[25] The London Blitz began on 7 September 1940 and continued for fifty-seven consecutive nights.

[26] Roy Hay, *Gardener's Chance: From War Production to Peace Possibilities*, Putnam, 1946, p.13.

[27] Quoted in Twigs Way and Mike Brown, *Digging for Victory: Gardens and Gardening in Wartime Britain,* Sabrestorm, 2010, p.63.

[28] BBC WAC, R30/2179/1 29 September 1941.

[29] *The Times*, 3 August 1940.

[30] IWM, BBC Wartime Kitchen and Garden Interviews 171 (2627).

[31] *The Gardeners' Chronicle*, 16 May 1942, p.203.

[32] Ibid., 23 December 1944, p.233.

[33] *The Listener*, 11 June 1942, p.759.

[34] Ibid.

[35] Ibid.

[36] BBC WAC, RCONT1 – Hay, Roy – Talks File 1 – 1939–1949, 15 September 1941.

[37] Bill Deedes, the model for William Boot in Evelyn Waugh's *Scoop*, was a journalist who became an MP and editor of the *Daily Telegraph*.

[38] Letter to *The Times*, 30 June 1943, p.5.

[39] Within a few years of being returned to grass after the war, these lawns had given the lie to the old story that it took 300 years to produce such perfect swards. In fact lawns are the better for being dug up and resown from time to time.

[40] Jane Brown, *A Garden of Our Own: A History of Girton College Garden*, Friends of Girton Garden, 1999, p.32.

[41] Leigh Verrill-Rhys and Deirdre Beddo (eds.), *Parachutes and Petticoats: Welsh Women Writing on the Second World War*, Honno, 1992, p.55.

[42] Quoted in Smith, *The Spade as Mighty as the Sword*, op. cit., p.94.

[43] Representatives of the Ministry of Agriculture and the Ministry of Food, as well as voluntary organisations like the NAS, National Federation of Women's Institutes and advisers from the county agricultural education authorities, sat on these committees.

[44] Members of the VPAs paid a small affiliation fee to the County Garden Produce Committees and thereby tapped into their bulk-buying capacities, the loan of machinery and the advice of experts. These clubs were open not only to gardeners but also to keepers of domestic livestock and beekeepers, the idea being that gardeners could help provide food for livestock, while livestock keepers could supply local manure.

[45] Hansard, House of Commons, 11 March 1941, vol. 369, col. 1158W.

[46] Hansard, House of Lords, 1 July 1941, vol. 119, cols. 587–96.

[47] *The Times*, 13 December 1941.

[48] Hansard, House of Commons, 14 July 1943, vol. 391, cols. 327–8.

[49] A perch is the same as a rod or a pole, about 30 sq yds.

[50] MOA, Diarist 5098, diary for 26 October 1940.

[51] Ibid., diary for 11 January 1945.

[52] Quoted in Smith, *The Spade as Mighty as the Sword*, op. cit., p.54.

[53] Quoted in Jennifer Davies, *The Wartime Kitchen and Garden*, BBC Books, 1993, p.111.

[54] Quoted in Joanne Chamberlain, *Trench Warfare: A Study of 'Dig for Victory' in Brighton and Hove During World War Two*, unpublished dissertation, University of Sussex, 2001, p.20.

[55] TNA: PRO MAF 48/744. In 1943, Southern Railway was estimated to have 13,790 allotments on 606 acres. At the same time, London Transport had 3,300 plots for employees and non-employees on 95 acres; Great Western had 19,307 allotments on 984 acres; while LNER had 24,510 allotments on 1,443 acres. In Scotland LNER had 2,370 plots with an area of 118 acres, so the total for LNER was 26,880 on 1,561 acres. London Midland and Scottish had 20,607 in England and Wales, with an acreage of 1,269, although the company does not seem to have had any allotments in Scotland. In October 1945, the total number of railway-leased allotments was 82,290, with an acreage of 4,417, which was not dissimilar to the 1943 figures.

[56] Chamberlain, *Trench Warfare*, op. cit., p.23.

[57] BBC WAC, R34/642, 14 August 1943.

[58] About £6,250,000 in today's money.

[59] Ministry of Agriculture, 'Allotment and Garden Guide', vol. 1, no. 4, April 1945, reproduced in edition by Twigs Way, Sabrestorm, 2009, p. 67.

[60] 1,267 allotment holders, 1,240 gardeners and 475 cultivators of both allotments and gardens.

[61] Which was included in this particular survey, even though the work was carried out by the Ministry of Agriculture rather than Scotland's Department of Agriculture.

[62] Only 10 per cent of those surveyed said that they used the Ministry cropping plan as their main guide, and only another 15 per cent used it partially.

[63] TNA: PRO RG 23/26. In a review of a film in the Dig for Victory series,

entitled 'Garden Tools', *The Gardeners' Chronicle* (5 June 1943, p.223) could not resist joking about New Victory Diggers: 'Give us the job, and we'll finish the tools.'

[64] TNA: PRO RG23/26, 8.3.

[65] TNA: PRO RG23/26, 8.1.

[66] *Daily Express*, 24 September 1942.

[67] TNA: PRO MAF 156/375.

[68] TNA: PRO MAF 156/375, table 1.

[69] Ibid.

[70] TNA: PRO MAF 156/375, table 4.

[71] TNA: PRO MAF 156/375.

[72] Certainly the success of the campaign to get people to lend the government money to pursue the war effort by buying National Savings and Defence Bonds can be accurately measured, and it was impressive. In 1943, small savings stood at £719 million, up from £62 million in 1939, while public issues reached £1,176 million in 1945, up from £10 million in 1939.

[73] TNA: PRO MAF 156/375.

[74] *The Gardeners' Chronicle,* 11 October 1941, p.126.

[75] Peter Ender, *Up the Garden Path*, Herbert Jenkins, 1944, p.7.

[76] Ibid., p.25.

[77] Mary Dunn, *The World of Lady Addle*, Robin Clark, 1985, pp.229–30.

Chapter Four: Women and Children Go to It

[1] *The Gardeners' Chronicle*, 30 December 1939, p.394.

[2] Quoted in Twigs Way and Mike Brown, *Digging for Victory: Gardens and Gardening in Wartime Britain*, Sabrestorm, 2010, p.161.

[3] Ibid.

[4] In the same year, the Scottish Women's Rural Institutes came into being; although the SWRI always remained separate from the National Federation of Women's Institutes, it had well-nigh identical aims and organisation.

[5] Quoted in Gervas Huxley, *Lady Denman GBE*, Chatto and Windus, 1961, p.67.

[6] Mont Abbott of Enstone, Oxfordshire, recalled how much his mother and her female neighbours of all classes benefited from the founding of the Women's Institute in the village just after the First World War. Sheila Stewart, *Lifting the Latch: A Life on the Land*, Day Books, 2002, pp.82–3.

[7] There were 318,000 members at the time of the organisation's twenty-first birthday in 1937, and 331,612 enrolled in 5,720 local Institutes in 1939. The annual subscription was two shillings.

[8] The Representation of the People Act of 1918 gave the vote to women over thirty who owned property.

[9] Founded in 1938 and headed by the Dowager Marchioness of Reading, the WVS was 843,000 strong by February 1941, and the largest women's organisation in the country. As well as ARP duties, WVS volunteers ran day nurseries, canteens and rest centres for those bombed out of their homes as well as organising salvage collections and 'rural pie schemes' for agricultural workers.

[10] The Women's Institute magazine, *Home and Country*, July 1938, p.283. Some small Institutes did fold or cease their activities in wartime.

[11] WL, 5FWI/A/3/73, 1 September 1939.

[12] WL, ibid., 5 June 1940.

[13] Ibid.

[14] A speaker, presumably, on the RHS list.

[15] IWM, the papers of Miss Elizabeth Hess, 14035.

[16] Ibid.

[17] The collections contained two kinds of pea, broad beans, runner beans, long or globe beet, Brussels sprouts, purple sprouting broccoli, Savoy cabbage, summer cabbage, carrot, leek, lettuce, perpetual spinach, onion, turnip and parsnip.

[18] BBC *WW2 People's War*, A4304125, 29 June 2005.

[19] TNA: PRO RG 23/26.

[20] *The Gardeners' Chronicle*, 3 June 1944, pp.223–4.

[21] Chris McCooey (ed.), *Despatches From the Home Front: The War Diaries of Joan Strange 1939–1945*, JAK Books, 1994, pp.61–2.

[22] Quoted in Way and Brown, *Digging for Victory*, op. cit., pp. 164.

[23] IWM, BBC Wartime Kitchen and Garden Interviews, Miscellaneous 171 (2627).

[24] The WLA had a forerunner: the Women's National Land Service Corps, founded in 1916.

[25] Vita Sackville-West, *The Women's Land Army*, Imperial War Museum, 1993, p.10.

[26] Ibid., p.14. Vita Sackville-West was not above finding a lady gardener for a friend, even though he was not engaged in food production. Joan Chapman recalled of her work for an elderly general that 'Nothing we

grew was ever sold or went to help the war effort. At the time it worried me terribly. I spent my days picking raspberries for dinner parties, pruning espalier fruit trees – instead of growing food for a country at war.' Quoted in Nicola Tyrer, *They Fought in the Fields,* Tempus, 2007, p.94.

27 Trish Gibson, *Brenda Colvin: A Career in Landscape*, Frances Lincoln, 2011, pp.115–16.

28 Quoted in Peter King, *Women Rule the Plot*, Duckworth, 1999, p.118.

29 MOA, D 5324, diary for 23 March 1941.

30 Hot and cold running water; obviously enough of a luxury for Muriel Green to think it deserved a mention.

31 MOA, D5324., diary for 28 April 1941.

32 MOA, ibid., diary for 19 April 1941.

33 Auxiliary Territorial Service, which supported the British army.

34 MOA, D5324., diary for January 1942.

35 IWM, BBC Wartime Kitchen and Garden Interviews, Miscellaneous 171 (2627).

36 Interview by Elizabeth Grice, *Daily Telegraph*, 12 August 2012.

37 MERL, FR STU, Studley College Archive.

38 She is reputed to have been the model – in appearance at least – for Miss Trunchbull in Roald Dahl's *Matilda*. Dahl certainly visited the gardens from time to time, when living at Great Missenden. Personal communication with Valerie Finnis, *c*.2000.

39 Quoted in Ursula Maddy, *Waterperry: A Dream Fulfilled*, Merlin Books, 1990, p.152.

40 From 7 a.m. to 12 noon and 1 p.m. until 5 p.m., and a good half-day on Saturdays.

Chapter Five: Groundwork

1 In all this outpouring of helpful information, the government did not forget completely those would-be gardeners without access to any land at all. The Ministry of Agriculture published a 'Dig for Victory' leaflet entitled 'Roof and Window-box Gardening', which dealt with difficulties such as wind, drought and the need to choose the right containers in which to grow plants, not to mention the right varieties of dwarf vegetables. It was pretty half-hearted advice, but may well have been useful to the many town-dwellers without the time or strength to rent an allotment.

[2] TNA: PRO RG 23/69. The least favoured vegetables (if amounts grown is a guide), according to a survey of gardens carried out in England and Wales in September 1944, were haricot beans, spinach and spinach beet, kale and celery.

[3] Even if the fruits did not ripen before the autumn, they could be used in pickles and chutneys.

[4] This technology, first developed by the Americans and the Japanese in the 1940s and 50s, revolutionised the growing of vegetable crops in developed countries. F1 hybrid seed has a number of advantages over open-pollinated seed, in particular vigour, uniformity, earliness, long shelf life and resistance to disease. But the offspring of F1 plants do not come 'true' from seed, and F1 seed is more expensive than open-pollinated.

[5] Parsnips and carrots are biennials and run up to flower the following spring, when the roots become woody and inedible.

[6] Peter Donnelly (ed.), *Mrs Milburn's Diaries: An Englishwoman's Everyday Reflections 1939–45*, Harrap, 1979. The answer to Mrs Milburn's question is 'no'. As it was June, she had left the potatoes far too long in the clamp, and sunlight filtering through would have encouraged them to sprout. In the process, they would have shrivelled.

[7] WL, 5/FWI/A/3/73, WI Wiltshire Supplement, October 1939.

[8] Marjorie Williams, *Letters from Lamledra* (ed. Cassandra Phillips), Truran, 2007, p.146.

[9] *The Times*, 8 March 1940.

[10] E. Graham, *Gardening in War-time*, Peter Davies, 1940, pp.50–1.

[11] IWM, BBC Wartime Kitchen and Garden Interviews, Miscellaneous 171 (2627).

[12] Levens Hall is most famous for its 300-year-old yew topiary. It is open to the public.

[13] A large proportion of the available chemical fertilisers were manufactured or sold by Plant Protection Ltd of Yalding, Kent, a subsidiary of ICI.

[14] 'Sixties' were 3″ in diameter, 'fifty-fours' were 4″, 'forty-eights' were 4½″ and so on. The most famous pottery for clay pots was Sankey's of Nottingham, which continued to make them until 1976, when the firm changed to manufacturing plastic pots.

[15] Leaflets advised: 'Keep the hoe going. What feeds a weed will feed a cabbage to feed you.'

[16] *The Land* by Vita Sackville-West (William Heinemann, 1926), p. 35.

[17] 'Biological control' is the phrase used for control of pests or diseases using other living organisms. It was in its infancy in the 1940s but is now very well established, in gardens as well as nurseries.

[18] Constance Spry, *Come into the Garden, Cook*, J. M. Dent, 1942, pp.84–5.

[19] W. J. C. Lawrence, *Catch the Tide: Adventures in Horticultural Research*, Grower Books, 1980, pp.11–12.

[20] The dilution rate was one ounce to twelve gallons of water.

[21] *The Gardeners' Chronicle*, 13 January 1940, p.15.

[22] Quoted in Adrian Searle, *Isle of Wight at War 1939–45*, The Dovecote Press, 1990, p.152.

[23] 'Dig for Victory' leaflet no. 17.

[24] The house in Worcestershire to which the King and Queen were to be evacuated, should London become too dangerous for them.

[25] IWM, BBC Wartime Kitchen and Garden Interviews, Miscellaneous 171 (2627).

[26] Spry, *Come into the Garden, Cook*, op. cit., p.11.

[27] Quoted in Twigs Way and Mike Brown, *Digging for Victory: Gardens and Gardening in Wartime Britain*, Sabrestorm, 2010, p.167.

Chapter Six: Talking of Scarlet-Veinèd Beet

[1] Professor Joad, the best-known of the BBC *Brains Trust* team.

[2] Anon, *Punch*, 17 May 1944, pp.82–3. No apologies, seemingly, to John Keats.

[3] The family's main seat was Renishaw in Derbyshire.

[4] Quoted in www.bbc.co.uk/historyofthebbc/resources/in-depth/gardening.

[5] *Catholic Herald*, 27 September 1935, p. 13.

[6] Quoted in Daniel Smith, *The Spade as Mighty as the Sword*, Aurum, 2011, p.48.

[7] Asa Briggs, *The War of Words*, OUP, 1970, p.301. *The Kitchen Front* had an average listenership in 1940 of 5,400,000, while the most popular programme of all was *Saturday Night Variety*, with 10,700,000 listeners.

[8] By which he meant weeds.

[9] Broadcast reproduced in *The Listener*, 4 January 1940, p.33.

[10] *The Listener*, 18 January 1940, p.137.

[11] Ibid., 9 May 1940, p.939.

[12] Quoted in Smith, *The Spade as Mighty as the Sword*, op. cit., p.47.

[13] How right he was! See Chapter Three.

[14] *The Listener*, 1 February 1940, p.228.

[15] Ibid., 9 May 1940, p.940.

[16] He was sent a copy of Ministry of Agriculture guidance notes in advance of publication, so that he did not diverge from official policy.

[17] Recalled by John Green, of the BBC Talks Department, and quoted in Briggs, *The War of Words*, op. cit., p.45.

[18] At the beginning of the war, the BBC output was largely educational in nature, since it was still very much under the influence of its founder, Sir John Reith. The war inevitably changed that, at least to some extent, when the BBC discovered that variety and dance band programmes, not to mention Tommy Handley's *It's That Man Again* (*ITMA*), were most popular with listeners.

[19] Nick Hayes and Jeff Hill, *Millions Like Us?*, Liverpool University Press, 1999, p.77.

[20] Only the News and Talks departments stayed in London throughout the war.

[21] Quoted in Smith, *The Spade as Mighty as the Sword*, op. cit., p.142.

[22] BBC WAC, RCONT1 – Middleton, C H – Talks File 2 – 1939, letter from A. H. Manktelow (MAF) to George Barnes, head of BBC Talks Department, 5 September 1939.

[23] BBC WAC, RCONT1 – Middleton, C H – Talks File 3 – 1940, Internal Memo, 5 March 1940.

[24] *The Brains Trust* was a wireless programme broadcast on the Forces service from January 1941. A panel of three men – a philosopher, Cyril Joad, a scientist, Julian Huxley, and a retired naval officer, Commander A. B. Campbell – answered questions put to them by members of the public. They were joined occasionally by guests. The discussion was chaired by Donald McCullough.

[25] BBC WAC, RCONT1 - Middleton C H - Talks File 4 - 1941–6.

[26] Briggs, *The War of Words*, op. cit., pp.218–19.

[27] On 1 September 1939 he recorded a five-minute talk on 'The Wartime Garden', which was transmitted a few days later.

[28] BBC WAC, RCONT1 - Middleton C H - Talks File 4 - 1941–6.

[29] Roy Hay was away in the British Sector in Germany, teaching food production.

[30] Roy Hay, *Gardener's Chance: From War Production to Peace Possibilities*, Putnam, 1946, p.55.

[31] BBC WAC, R30/2179/1.

[32] Hay received six guineas a programme for his pains; this rose to eight guineas in 1944.

[33] BBC WAC, R30/2179/1.

[34] BBC WAC, R30/2 179/1. On 21 January 1942, Michael Standing wrote to a colleague: 'We're treating this little enterprise comparatively seriously, and we don't want even to hint to listeners that we're approaching the subject in a frivolous frame of mind.' Which suggested strongly that they were.

[35] Hay, *Gardener's Chance*, op. cit., p.56.

[36] BBC WAC, R30/2179, Listener Research Bulletin 149.

[37] Garden historian and nurserywoman.

[38] Gary Dexter, 'Alternative Reading', *The Spectator*, 3 December 2005.

[39] TNA: PRO RG/23/26 An inquiry into the effects of the 'Dig for Victory' campaign made for the Ministry of Agriculture in August and September 1942. Of the sample, only 0.6 per cent gathered their information from *The Gardeners' Chronicle*, which, if they had known it, would have been galling to those hard-working, public-spirited head gardener contributors.

[40] Ibid.

[41] *Daily Express*, 13 April 1940.

[42] Ibid., 17 January 1942.

[43] Raymond W. B. Keene, *Over the Garden Fence: Old-Timer Talks About Flowers*, Staples Press, 1946, p.11.

[44] She wrote a weekly column in *The Observer* from 1947 until her death in 1962.

[45] Navy, Army and Air Force Institutes, which provided canteens and other amenities for the troops.

[46] *Journal of the Royal Horticultural Society*, February 1943, pp.38–9.

[47] *The Times*, 3 February 1943.

[48] Quick-maturing crops like salads sown between rows of slower-growing vegetables.

[49] John Reed Wade, *War-time Gardening*, Pearson, 1940, p.v.

[50] In 1945, thirty million cinema tickets were bought every week.

[51] There are twenty hundredweight (cwt) in an imperial ton.

[52] Quoted in Jennifer Davies, *The Wartime Kitchen and Garden*, BBC Books, 1993, p.48.

[53] NSALG, Annual report of the National Allotments Society for year ending 31 December 1941, p.1.

[54] In the 1960s, Lord Clark wrote and presented *Civilisation*, a ground-breaking television series on art history; the satirical magazine *Private Eye* forever after referred to him as Lord Clark of Civilisation.

[55] TNA: PRO INF 1/232.

[56] Cartoonists often earned 10s.6d for a rough drawing and two and a half guineas for a complete cartoon, while an artist might get five guineas for a rough drawing of a poster and twenty-five guineas for the finished product.

[57] Quoted in Naomi Games, Catherine Moriarty and June Rose, *Abram Games: His Life and Work*, Princeton, 2003, p.18.

[58] Ibid, p. 15.

[59] Abram Games, *Art and Industry*, vol. 45, July 1948, p.24.

[60] Lewitt (Jan Le Witt) and George Him were Polish-born artists who came to England in 1937 and worked for the Ministry of Information designing posters in the early years of the war.

[61] The story is told in Smith, *The Spade as Mighty as the Sword*, op. cit., pp.134–5.

Chapter Seven: The Old Order Changeth

[1] *The Gardeners' Chronicle*, 6 January 1940, p.4.

[2] In 1940, a shot-up German plane crashed near Stansted Park and the bombs it was carrying caused damage to both the gardens and the nearby church.

[3] *The Gardeners' Chronicle*, 2 September 1939, p.ix.

[4] In later life, Harry Dodson found fame as the expert gardener presenting the BBC series *The Victorian Kitchen Garden* (1987), *The Victorian Flower Garden* (1991) and *The Wartime Kitchen and Garden* (1993).

[5] *The Times*, 3 March 1941.

[6] A case made eloquently by Lord Bingley in the House of Lords in February 1941.

[7] During the First World War, Captain Johns fought at Gallipoli, then joined the newly formed Royal Flying Corps and trained as a bomber pilot. He was shot down and taken prisoner by the Germans in September 1918, two months before the Armistice.

[8] Captain W. E. Johns, 'The Passing Show', *My Garden*, vol. 18, November 1939, p.301.

[9] Marjorie Williams, *Letters from Lamledra*, (ed. Cassandra Phillips), Truran, 2007, p.152.

[10] Some gardeners went on to have very successful military careers, none more so than John Hudson, a trained horticulturalist, who became a celebrated bomb disposal expert, winning the George Medal and bar. He also had a distinguished post-war career as Professor of Horticulture at Nottingham University and then director of Long Ashton Research Station.

[11] MOA, D 5324, diary for 25 April 1941.

[12] IWM, Papers of Miss A. L. Gimson 86/6/1 (1916).

[13] Ibid.

[14] *The Gardeners' Chronicle*, 26 September 1942, p.106.

[15] That meant he was the second-highest-ranked gardener of the six employed.

[16] *The Gardeners' Chronicle*, 5 July 1941, p.6.

[17] See, for example, ibid., 25 October 1941, p.149.

[18] When wages were raised at Madresfield, Dorothy Pembridge and the other Land Girls lost their vegetable allowance.

[19] Ted Humphris, *Garden Glory: From Garden Boy to Head Gardener at Aynhoe Park*, Collins, 1988, p.161.

[20] Ibid.

[21] Almost certainly under the 'soldier-gardener' scheme.

[22] Humphris, *Garden Glory*, op. cit., p.161.

[23] Quoted in Jennifer Davies, *The Wartime Kitchen and Garden*, BBC Books, 1993, p.114.

[24] IWM, BBC Wartime Kitchen and Garden Interviews, Miscellaneous 171 (2627).

[25] Ibid.

[26] Vegetables and fruit were not rationed, and so were not a target for organised black marketers, but (though the evidence is understandably scant) it seems likely that professional gardeners did sometimes sell their scarce produce above the fixed price or in greater quantity than was allowed to favoured customers.

[27] Quoted in Robert Becker, *Nancy Lancaster: Her Life, Her World, Her Art*, Knopf, 1996, p.249.

[28] Sir Charles (later Viscount) Portal, Chief of the Air Staff, was a keen gardener.

[29] The Trees also played host to important Americans like Averell Harriman and Harry Hopkins, Roosevelt's special envoys.

[30] IWM, BBC Wartime Kitchen and Garden Interviews, Miscellaneous 171 (2627).

[31] Quoted in Alun Howkins, 'A Country at War: Mass-Observation and Rural England 1939–45', *Rural History*, vol. 9, no. 1, p.91.

[32] IWM, BBC Wartime Kitchen and Garden Interviews, Miscellaneous 171 (2627).

[33] *Journal of the Kew Guild 1939–1940*, p.854.

[34] In 1941, a parody of Rudyard Kipling's 'The Glory of the Garden' appeared in the *Journal of the Kew Guild*: 'Now Adam was a gardener, and God who made him sees/That half a gardener's proper work is done upon his knees;/But with Adam gone to fight the foe and only home on leave/The proper one to kneel and plant and grow our food is – EVE!' Quoted in Catherine Horwood, *Gardening Women*, Virago, 2010, p.327.

[35] Quoted in ibid., p.332.

[36] IWM, BBC Wartime Kitchen and Garden Interviews, Miscellaneous 171 (2627).

[37] Hazel Conway, 'Everyday landscapes: public parks from 1930–2000', *Garden History*, vol. 28, no. 1, p.124.

[38] Quoted in ibid, p. 123.

[39] Quoted in Brent Elliott, 'Bedding Schemes', in Jan Woudstra and Ken Fieldhouse (eds.), *The Regeneration of Public Parks*, Spon, 2001, p.117.

[40] TNA:PRO MAF 48/725.

[41] Philip Longworth, *The Unending Vigil: A History of the Commonwealth War Graves Commission 1917–1984*, Leo Cooper in association with Secker and Warburg, 1985, p.161.

[42] In the First World War, the entire island of Ireland was part of the United Kingdom, and Irishmen from what is now Eire, as well as Ulster, fought on the Allied side.

[43] After 1960, the John Innes Institute.

[44] Fruit varieties that are incompatible cannot cross-fertilise each other's flowers to produce fruit.

[45] i.e. with four sets of chromosomes.

[46] Librarian of the Royal Horticultural Society in his retirement, author of a monograph on tulips and one of the architects of post-war agriculture in Britain.

[47] W. J. C. Lawrence, *Catch the Tide: Adventures in Horticultural Research*, Grower Books, 1980, p.56.

[48] Later called Fisons.

[49] Although soil-less 'multipurpose' composts began to replace John Innes composts in the 1980s, gardeners still consider that there is a place for

the latter for plants in permanent pots, and where stability is required, since loam-based composts are heavier than soil-less ones. It is highly unlikely, in this author's opinion, that the garden centre revolution in the 1960s would have been possible without John Innes composts, since retailers needed to have flowering plants growing in neat pots to sell, rather than dormant and messy bare-rooted ones dug up out of the field.

[50] There was much emphasis on tomato research at JIHI, since tomatoes were such an important glasshouse crop, in peace and war.

[51] A myth, incidentally, which was still popular with professional gardeners when I trained in the 1970s.

[52] Lawrence and Newell designed a low-pressure, low-cost steriliser and published the specifications, so that growers could make it themselves.

[53] Lawrence, *Catch the Tide*, op. cit., p.106.

[54] JIC, interview by B. J. Harrison in 1979, published on www.jic.ac.uk website.

[55] A tantalising comment.

[56] Although the Ministry of Agriculture provided a grant to the JIHI from 1935, the latter was still largely a private charitable institution.

[57] JIC, annual report of the John Innes Horticultural Institution, 1944, p.1.

[58] Embarrassingly, the JIHI's annual report for 1941 was printed when it was confidently assumed that this negotiation would be successful, and an erratum slip had to be included to say that it was not.

[59] *The Gardeners' Chronicle*, 23 December 1944, p.233.

Chapter Eight: Far Messier and Different

[1] The Keeper of the RHS Lindley Library.

[2] Personal communication dated 19 January 2001 from Dr William Stearn (Librarian of the Lindley Library) to Edward Wilson, quoted in Edward Wilson (ed.), *The Downright Epicure: Essays on Edward Bunyard*, Prospect Books, 2007, p.66–7.

On Bunyard's death, Sir Daniel Hall became Editor and Librarian, and Roy Hay was recruited as Associate Editor. So useful was Hay to the Dig for Victory campaign that both the RHS and MAF made a concerted effort to get him exempted from his special constable duties, and from being called up for military service.

[3] Stephen Cheveley, *A Garden Goes to War*, John Miles, 1940, p.18.

[4] 'Nursery stock' means hardy woody plants, that is, trees and shrubs.

[5] This nursery was later to become Notcutts, one of the most famous of the post-war tree and shrub nurseries, which also early became involved with the garden centre movement. It is now John Woods Nurseries.

[6] In 1938, 143,000 tons of tomatoes were imported into Britain, and only 60,000 tons grown at home.

[7] Elsewhere he wrote: 'I stayed at home that day. I just couldn't face the prospect of seeing a life's work destroyed.' Harry Wheatcroft, *The Root of the Matter*, Golden Eagle, 1974, p.109.

[8] Quoted in Sadie Ward, *War in the Countryside*, Cameron Books with David and Charles, 1988, p.13.

[9] £4 million in today's money.

[10] Sylvia Crowe advised the Road Beautifying Association. This organisation was founded in the late 1920s by Dr Wilfrid Fox with the aim of giving work to the unemployed and enhancing the landscape by planting trees and shrubs along highways being built to accommodate the increasing numbers of motorised vehicles. Cheals Nurseries planted choice trees on both sides of the Crawley bypass, only to see them badly damaged by tank movements during the war.

[11] Alison Benton, *Cheals of Crawley: The Family Firm at Lowfield Nurseries 1860s to 1960s*, Moira Publications, 2002, p.274.

[12] Anon, *The Gardeners' Chronicle*, 2 August 1967, p.17.

[13] Ibid.

[14] Quoted in Ward, *War in the Countryside*, op. cit, pp. 13–14.

[15] Letter dated 28 December 1942. Personal communication to author from Sarah Cook, 27 April 2012.

[16] IWM, the papers of Hubert Taylor, 14042/2/1–2.

[17] IWM, BBC Wartime Kitchen and Garden Interviews, Miscellaneous 171 (2627).

[18] Ibid.

[19] MOA, D 5324, diary for 13 September 1941.

[20] This company is still going (2012), having been founded in 1908.

[21] Twenty-two yards.

[22] IWM, BBC Wartime Kitchen and Garden Interviews, Miscellaneous 171 (2627).

[23] Ursula Maddy, *Waterperry: A Dream Fulfilled*, Merlin Books, 1990, pp.62–3.

[24] IWM, BBC Wartime Kitchen and Garden Interviews, Miscellaneous 171

(2627). In general, cucumbers were not thought by the War Ags nutritious enough to be candidates for wartime food production.

[25] Hansard, House of Lords, 15 February 1944, vol. 130, cols. 790–1.

[26] Dobbie's is still in business (2012), but as a chain of garden centres rather than a seed firm.

[27] Suttons also produced a catalogue specifically for small gardens, with a more limited choice of generally more compact-growing vegetable varieties.

[28] MERL, TR SUT P2/A350.

[29] Owen joined the Royal Navy in June 1943, leaving his cousins and father to take on his nursery duties.

[30] MERL, TR SUT P2/A350.

[31] MERL, TR SUT P2/A458.

[32] They were started again after the war, only to be given up as too expensive in the mid 1960s.

[33] MERL, TR SUT P2/A458.

[34] Figures from *Statistical Digest of the War*, first published by Central Statistical Office, 1951; published with amendments by HMSO and Kraus, 1975.

Chapter Nine: A Refreshment of the Spirit of Man

[1] '*The Garden*', a poem by Vita Sackville-West, begun in 1939 and published by Michael Joseph in 1946, pp. 14–15. It won the Heinemann Prize that year, and Vita received £100, which she spent on azaleas for the garden.

[2] It is now in the care of the National Trust.

[3] Harold Nicolson, *Diaries and Letters 1939–45*, ed. Nigel Nicolson, Fontana, 1970, p. 102.

[4] Ibid., p. 107.

[5] The limes he was pleaching (pruning and training to make a tall, narrow, straight hedge) were in the Lime Walk, which connects the Rose Garden and the Nuttery, and is particularly beautiful in spring, since the trees are thickly underplanted with bulbs.

[6] Nicolson, *Diaries and Letters*, op. cit., p. 183.

[7] Ibid., p. 242. Vita Sackville West herself did a great deal of the gardening, while Harold Nicolson confined his efforts to the Lime Walk. It is interesting that in 1942 he thought that the war would last at least until 1945.

[8] Leonard Woolf, *Downhill All the Way: An Autobiography of the Years 1919–1939*, Hogarth Press, 1967, p.254.

[9] Margery Allingham, *The Oaken Heart,* Michael Joseph, 1941, p.87.

[10] Ibid., p.180.

[11] Ibid., p.181.

[12] Ibid., p.191.

[13] Peter Donnelly (ed.), *Mrs Milburn's Diaries: An Englishwoman's Everyday Reflections 1939–45*, Harrap 1979, p.86.

[14] Ibid., p.83.

[15] Ibid., p.99.

[16] Ibid., p.59.

[17] Ammonium carbonate, an old-fashioned remedy for use by those in danger of fainting.

[18] Richard Broad and Suzie Fleming (eds.), *Nella Last's War: The Second World War Diaries of Housewife, 49*, Profile, 2006, p.109.

[19] Ibid., p.129.

[20] Ibid., p.185.

[21] Quoted in E. R. Chamberlin, *Life in Wartime Britain*, Batsford, 1972, p. 95.

[22] *The Gardener's Chronicle*, 23 September 1939, p.211. There is an echo here of Francis Bacon's essay *Of Gardens*: 'It is the greatest refreshment to the spirits of man', which is itself an echo of 1 Corinthians 16:18: 'For they have refreshed my spirit and yours …'

[23] *The Times*, 18 October 1941.

[24] Quoted in the *Journal of the Royal Horticultural Society*, June 1940, pp. 149–50.

[25] *The Gardeners' Chronicle*, 6 January 1940, p.1.

[26] C. H. Middleton, *Digging for Victory: Wartime Gardening with Mr Middleton*, Aurum, 2008, p.75.

[27] Ibid., pp.75–6.

[28] About £5,000 in today's money.

[29] Middleton, *Digging for Victory*, op. cit., p.77.

[30] *The Times*, 17 April 1943.

[31] This was the nickname for William Joyce, a Fascist who broadcast from Germany for most of the war and was hanged by the British for treason in 1946.

[32] *The Times*, 28 January 1941.

[33] RHS, Council Minutes Book, 1940–3, letter dated 19 December 1942.

[34] Spanish broom.

[35] Quoted in Twigs Way and Mike Brown, *Digging for Victory: Gardens and Gardening in Wartime Britain*, Sabrestorm, 2010, p.212.

[36] The 'basic ration' was abolished altogether in March 1942.

[37] Quoted in *Digging for Victory,* op. cit., p. 209.

Chapter Ten: Gardening Behind the Wire

[1] On 8 September 1943 the Italians signed an armistice and effectively laid down their weapons. The camps were usually taken over by German units.

[2] It seems that commandants in officers' camps in Germany, called Oflags, were more inclined to allow, even encourage, gardens than those overseeing camps housing NCOs (non-commissioned officers) and enlisted men, which were called Stalags. Confusingly, a camp housing RAF officers was called a Stalag Luft, as in the famous Stalag Luft III.

[3] Quoted in Kenneth I. Helphand, *Defiant Gardens*, Trinity University Press, 2006, p.130.

[4] RHS, Council Minutes, May 1941.

[5] *Journal of the Royal Horticultural Society*, August 1943, p. 219.

[6] This is almost certainly how Peter Healing managed to get hold of a copy of *The English Flower Garden* by William Robinson: see Chapter Thirteen.

[7] *Journal of the Royal Horticultural Society*, September 1943, p.287.

[8] Peter Donnelly (ed.), *Mrs Milburn's Diaries: An Englishwoman's Everyday Reflections 1939–45*, Harrap 1979, p.146.

[9] The Beveridge Report (The Report of the Inter-Departmental Committee on Social Insurance and Allied Services) was the work of an Oxford economist, William Beveridge. It served as the basis of the welfare state legislation after the war. Its publication in 1942 met with warm approval from the British public.

[10] Donnelly, *Mrs Milburn's Diaries*, op. cit., p.198.

[11] Ibid., p.226.

[12] Ibid., p.253.

[13] The hut where prisoners lived and slept.

[14] Helphand, *Defiant Gardens*, op. cit., p.132.

[15] Ibid., p.133.

[16] Ibid., p.148.

[17] See Midge Gillies, *The Barbed-Wire University*, Aurum, 2011.

[18] Near Sagan in Poland.

[19] Seventy-six prisoners eventually escaped through 'Harry' in 1944, but all but three were recaptured and fifty were shot. This event is universally known as 'The Great Escape', and a Hollywood film, loosely based on the book by Paul Brickhill, was made in 1963 starring Steve McQueen and Richard Attenborough.

[20] A strange word in the context, presumably meaning compost.

[21] Quoted in Helphand, *Defiant Gardens*, op. cit., p.134.

[22] Ibid., p.6.

[23] By the end of the war, the Germans had 248 camps in Germany, France, Poland, Italy and Austria, and were guarding 225,996 British and North American troops. 132,000 Allied troops were imprisoned in the Far East.

[24] Beri-beri results from a deficiency of vitamin B1 or thiamine.

[25] Red Cross parcels were a rarity in Far Eastern camps.

[26] Quoted in Helphand, *Defiant Gardens*, op. cit., p.139.

[27] *The Gardeners' Chronicle*, 16 May 1942, p.202. In 1975 I met Dr Herklots occasionally when he came to look at plants he had introduced that were growing in the tropical glasshouses at Wisley, where I was working. He was a charming man, but even if I had known of his wartime experiences, I would have hesitated to ask him about them.

[28] G. A. C. Herklots, *Vegetables in South-East Asia*, George Allen and Unwin, 1972, p.xi.

[29] Ibid., p.59.

[30] Quoted in Alison Benton, *Cheals of Crawley – The Family Firm at Lowfield Nurseries, 1860s to 1960s*, Moira Publications, 2002, p. 280.

[31] It was thought politic to keep the Russians apart from the other ethnic groups, to avoid trouble as a result of the treatment of eastern European countries by the USSR.

[32] Quoted in Sadie Ward, *War in the Countryside*, Cameron Books with David and Charles, 1988, p.47.

[33] Quoted in Jennifer Davies, *The Wartime Kitchen and Garden*, BBC Books, 1993, p.91.

[34] Ibid.

[35] IWM, BBC Wartime Kitchen and Garden Interviews, Miscellaneous 171 (2627).

[36] She was one of the famous Mitford sisters.

Chapter Eleven: Animals in the Back Garden

[1] Poultry had been widely kept in town and country in the last years of the 1914–18, so older people had memories of doing that at least.

[2] Lord Arnold raised this anomaly in the House of Lords on 10 June 1941, but to no avail. It was not thought good for morale for the British working man to be denied his pint of beer, even if it was watered down.

[3] Powdered egg was made by dehydrating shell eggs in an industrial process. Much of it came from the United States. It had the advantage of storing well for long periods and could be used in a variety of ways. Most people have unhappy memories of it, especially when rehydrated, though it was fine for baking.

[4] Claude Goodchild and Alan Thompson, *Keeping Poultry and Rabbits on Scraps*, Penguin 1941, p.1.

[5] Sir Reginald Dorman-Smith announced on 4 September 1939: 'Poultry kept in small numbers in city and suburban gardens or allotments can be fed almost entirely on all forms of household waste', a statement more likely to confuse than enlighten.

[6] Seventy years later, there is no such thing as an 'unfoxed area' in country or town, since fox numbers are no longer controlled to anything like the same extent that they were before and during the war.

[7] Margery Allingham, *The Oaken Heart*, Hutchinson, 1959, p.249.

[8] *The Gardeners' Chronicle*, 13 January 1940, p.24.

[9] *The Times*, 10 December 1940.

[10] Mary Dunn, *The World of Lady Addle*, Robin Clark, 1985, p.163.

[11] IWM, BBC Wartime Kitchen and Garden Interviews, Miscellaneous 171 (2627).

[12] Often rabbit-keeping neighbours got round this problem by sharing the care of one buck between them.

[13] Quoted in Piers Dudgeon, *Village Voices: A Portrait of Change in England's Green and Pleasant Land 1915–1990*, Sidgwick and Jackson, 1989, p.94.

[14] Considering the enormous population of Russia, however, this looks more of a symbolic gesture than a really useful initiative. The money will have been much more useful.

[15] IWM, BBC Wartime Kitchen and Garden Interviews, Miscellaneous 171 (2627).

[16] MOA, D 5324, diary for 23 October 1939.

[17] Ibid., March 1941.

[18] These non-profit-making canteens were run by local authorities in halls or schools in towns and cities, providing cheap meals for workers and those bombed out of their homes.

[19] Goodchild and Thompson, *Keeping Poultry and Rabbits on Scraps*, op. cit., pp.142–3.

Chapter Twelve: Fiercely Stirring Cauldrons

[1] Thrifty particularly in the use of cooking fuels, both gas and electricity.

[2] He was made the Earl of Woolton in 1956.

[3] Lord Woolton was ably advised by experts like Professor Jack Drummond, a scientific nutritionist, and Professor John Raeburn, an agricultural economist and statistician.

[4] He had been profoundly affected as a young man living in Liverpool by the death from starvation of his next-door neighbour in 1908. *Memoirs of the Rt Hon. the Earl of Woolton, C.H., P.C., D.L., Ll.D.,* Cassell, 1959, p.1.

[5] Ibid., pp.192–3.

[6] Ibid., p.194.

[7] Ibid., p.215.

[8] *The Times*, 5 June 1942.

[9] *Memoirs*, op. cit., p.193.

[10] TNA: PRO RG 23/9A.

[11] Reported in the *New York Times*, 11 January 1942.

[12] Which was very important in 1943 when bread flour became particularly scarce.

[13] Originally called *Food Talk*.

[14] A prolific journalist and author, who wrote more than 200 books, many of them about the countryside.

[15] Their brother was Jack Warner, famous for his portrayal of the eponymous hero of *Dixon of Dock Green*, a long-running post-war police drama set in the East End of London.

[16] Quoted in Jennifer Davies, *The Wartime Kitchen and Garden*, BBC Books, 1993, p.46.

[17] Siân Nicholas, *The Echo of War*, Manchester University Press, 1996, p.81.

[18] *Memoirs*, op. cit., p.248.

[19] In this regard, *The Kitchen Front* was no different from a number of other wireless programmes that had a public information role.

[20] Nicholas, *The Echo of War*, op. cit., p.82.

[21] 19 million people went to the cinema each week, many of them more than once.

[22] Food Flashes were also broadcast on the wireless.

[23] *Memoirs*, op. cit., p.248.

[24] TNA: PRO RG 23/9A.

[25] Reported in *The Times*, 9 February 1943.

[26] Constance Spry, *Come into the Garden, Cook*, J. M. Dent, 1942, p.15.

[27] Peter Donnelly (ed.), *Mrs Milburn's Diary: An Englishwoman's Everyday Reflections 1939–45*, Abacus, 1995, p. 149.

[28] The Ministry of Food provided quite generous grants to pay for the organisation and running costs, as well as loans for capital outlay.

[29] So much so that 'Jam and Jerusalem' is inevitably the strapline for any article written about the Women's Institute, even now. 'Jerusalem' (words by William Blake, tune by Sir Hubert Parry) was, and is, the hymn that WI members sing before the start of every monthly meeting.

[30] Quoted in Piers Dudgeon, *Village Voices: A Portrait of Change in England's Green and Pleasant Land 1915–1990*, Sidgwick and Jackson, 1989, p.91.

[31] Quoted in ibid., pp.91–2.

[32] Only acid fruits were canned, because of the risk of the spread of botulism.

[33] Quoted in Penny Kitchen (ed.), *For Home and Country: War, Peace and Rural Life as Seen Through the Pages of the WI Magazine 1919–1959*, Ebury Press, 1990, p.57.

[34] WL, 5/FWI/A/3/73, interview with Miss Edith Walker by V. Royds, 15 July 1977.

[35] NRO, NFWI/69 Blisworth Women's Institute record book 1938–43. Mrs Clinch lived at Blisworth House, where she hosted many WI activities, including an annual garden party.

[36] Marguerite Patten, *Victory Cookbook: Nostalgic Food and Facts from 1940–1954*, Chancellor Press, 2002, p.2.

[37] WL, 5/FWI/A/3/73, interview with Miss Edith Walker by V. Royds, 15 July 1977. Miss Walker left the NFWI in late 1943, recruited by Lord Woolton to be head of the Food Advice Division of the Ministry of Food.

[38] WL, 5/FWI/A/3/73, Annual Report of NFWI for 1942.

[39] Each adult was rationed to one pound of preserves every two months.

[40] Anne Stamper, 'Countrywomen in War-time – Women's Institutes 1938–1945, *Home and Country*, June 1945', p.84.

[41] Nasty-smelling silver polish.

[42] Dunn, *The World of Lady Addle*, op. cit., p.246.

[43] Spry, *Come into the Garden, Cook*, op. cit., p.244.

[44] *Daily Telegraph*, Fanny Cradock obituary, 29 December 1994.

[45] Vicomte de Mauduit, *They Can't Ration These*, Michael Joseph, 1940, p.7.

[46] Reported in *The Times*, 22 November 1945.

[47] RBGK, 1/MUS/25/3.

[48] H. W. Carter was later taken over by Beechams, who then became part of GlaxoSmithKline. Ribena is still produced in the factory at Coleford to which H. W. Carter moved soon after the war.

[49] The Committee came under the auspices of the Ministry of Supply in early 1942.

[50] RBGK, 1/MUS/28/6. Rose hips were three to four times richer in ascorbic acid than blackcurrants.

[51] After the war, Dr Magnus Pyke became a popular television personality, capable of explaining complex scientific facts to a broad audience and famous for waving his hands about in an excited manner while doing so.

[52] RBGK, 1/MUS/28/6.

[53] RBGK, QX 95–00161/7, 'Collection of Drug Plants by Boy Scouts', April 1941.

[54] From which colchicine was derived. Horticultural scientists used colchicine to induce polyploidy in plants. It also had medicinal uses, in particular the treatment of gout.

[55] TNA: PRO MH 58/387.

[56] IWM, the papers of Miss Elizabeth Hess, 14035/3.

[57] Cigarette cards were found in cartons of cigarettes and featured a variety of subjects: they were prized by children, who swapped duplicates to obtain full sets of the various subjects.

[58] Elizabeth Hess, 'Collecting Broom', *The Chemist and Druggist*, 18 April 1942.

[59] Sir Arthur Hill was killed in a riding accident in November 1941.

[60] RBGK, 1/MUS/25/5/4.

[61] Each WI county committee was given a list of ten plant species to find, but even that limited amount could be very taxing to collect.

Chapter Thirteen: Keeping On Keeping On

1 Victory over Japan Day, when the Second World War was truly over.
2 This replaced the Ministry of Information in March 1946.
3 BBC WAC, R/34/642.
4 Ibid.
5 TNA: PRO RG 23/26.
6 Representatives from Scotland's Department of Agriculture, the Horticultural Trades Association, the RHS, the Royal Botanic Gardens at Kew, the Institute of Park Administration and the Women's Farm and Garden Association, under the chairmanship of the Ministry's Horticulture Commissioner, Dr H. V. Taylor.
7 TNA; PRO MAF 33/430.
8 Ibid.
9 Quoted in Gervas Huxley, *Lady Denman GBE*, Chatto and Windus, 1961, p.177.
10 Ibid., p.179.
11 Quoted in Roy Strong, Marcus Binney and John Harris (eds.), *The Destruction of the Country House*, Thames and Hudson, 1974, p.172.
12 Ibid., p.132.
13 Ibid., p.173.
14 *The Gardeners' Chronicle*, 3 June 1944, p.231.
15 Ted Humphris, *Garden Glory: From Garden Boy to Head Gardener at Aynhoe Park*, Collins, 1988, p.164.
16 Ibid.
17 Ditchley Park was sold first to Lord Wilton, from whom it was purchased in 1953 by Sir David Wills. Wills donated it to the Ditchley Foundation in 1958.
18 Sir Geoffrey Jellicoe, 'Ronald Tree and the gardens of Ditchley Park: The human face of history', *Garden History*, vol. 10, no. 1 (Spring 1982), p.89.
19 Nancy Lancaster lived on, elegantly, in the Coach House until her death in 1994, aged ninety-six.
20 John Martin Robinson, *Felling the Ancient Oaks: How England Lost its Great Country Estates*, Aurum, 2011, p.36.
21 James Lees-Milne, *Caves of Ice*, Chatto and Windus, 1983, p.249.
22 *Extracts from the Proceedings of the Royal Horticultural Society*, 1948, p.xxxiv.
23 Now the National Gardens Scheme of England and Wales. To their credit,

some garden owners had even continued to open to the public during the war.

[24] He also owned a garden called Serre de la Madone in Menton, southern France, from where he had to escape in a hurry in 1940 when France fell.

[25] There was a head gardener and four under-gardeners.

[26] A circle the National Trust has never been able satisfactorily to square.

[27] The Garden History Society was founded in 1965 and is now consulted in all planning inquiries concerning historic landscapes. English Heritage started to 'list' parks and gardens in 1983. The Register of Historic Parks and Gardens of Special Historic Interest in England now has more than 1,600 sites of national importance on it.

[28] Sir Ernest Gowers is probably best known these days for his *Plain Words: A Guide to the Use of English*.

[29] Owners of, respectively, Woburn Abbey, Chatsworth and Longleat.

[30] Strong, Binney and Harris (eds.), *The Destruction of the Country House*, op. cit., p.100.

[31] W. J. Turner (ed.), *The Englishman's Country*, Collins, 1945, p.202.

[32] Almost certainly it was sent to his camp by the Red Cross Society's Educational Books Section (see Chapter Ten).

[33] Alvilde Lees-Milne and Rosemary Verey (eds.), *The Englishman's Garden*, Allen Lane, 1982, p.72.

[34] Ibid., p.53.

[35] Ibid.

[36] Quoted in Stephen Lacey, 'Unforgettable fire', *Daily Telegraph*, 31 December 2001.

[37] Richard Broad and Suzie Fleming (eds.), *Nella Last's War: The Second World War Diaries of Housewife, 49*, Profile, 2006, p. 286.

[38] WI membership also went up sharply once the war was over and monthly meetings could be held once more in the evenings. For the WI, the spirit of educational betterment, co-operation and purposefulness of the war years continued, exemplified by the opening of Denman College in 1948.

[39] *Journal of the Royal Horticultural Society*, April 1948, p.xxxiv.

[40] Quoted in Earley Local History Group, *Suttons Seeds: A History 1806–2006*, ELHG, 2006.

[41] *The Gardeners' Chronicle*, 31 January 1948, p.38.

[42] Now known as Garden Organic.

ACKNOWLEDGEMENTS

A book of this nature is impossible without the willing help and advice of the librarians and archivists who look after primary source material in this country. I should particularly like to thank those at the National Archives at Kew; the Imperial War Museum at Kennington; the Museum of English Rural Life, University of Reading; the Lindley Library of the Royal Horticultural Society at Westminster; the John Innes Foundation Historical Collections at Norwich; the Women's Library at London Metropolitan University; the British Museum's Newspaper Reading Room at Colindale; the Mass-Observation Archive Reading Room, University of Sussex; the BBC's Written Archives Centre at Caversham; the National Society of Allotment and Leisure Gardeners at Corby, and the Northamptonshire Record Office at Wootton.

For secondary sources, I have been extremely fortunate to have access to books in the University Library, Cambridge, and I am most grateful to the Librarian and staff there.

The individuals who have helped me with invaluable advice, hospitality, the loan of books, the reading of parts of the manuscript, the taking on of other responsibilities so that I could concentrate on the book, or simply by keeping up my morale, include Adam and Anne Begley, Jane Brown, Amanda Buchan, Isabel Buchanan, John Coleman, Pauline Davidson, Dr Brent Elliott, Caroline Knox, Michael Neuberger, Anna Pavord, Cynthia Ogilvie, Tim Richardson, Emily and Will Thomas, Tom Wide, Rosalind Wild and Dr Sarah Wilmot. As ever, my husband, Charlie, has been a model of understanding and cheerful enthusiasm.

I should also like to thank my literary agent, Felicity Bryan, as well as the team at Hutchinson, in particular Sarah Rigby, Caroline Gascoigne, Jocasta Hamilton, Emma Finnigan, Charlie Mundy, Paulette Hearn, Amy Mitchell and Phil Brown, all of whom have helped to make the production of this book an unalloyed pleasure.

Every effort has been made to contact all copyright holders. If notified, the publisher will be pleased to rectify any errors or omissions at the earliest opportunity. The author and publisher would like to thank the following for permission to reproduce material:

Extracts from *The Oaken Heart* by Margery Allingham reprinted by permission of Peters, Fraser & Dunlop (www.petersfraserdunlop.com) on behalf of Peters, Fraser & Dunlop, Drury House, 34–43 Russell Street, London, WC2B 5HA Tel:020 7344 1000 Fax:020 7836 9539; BBC Copyright material and BBC Wartime Kitchen and Garden Interviews reproduced courtesy of BBC Written Archives Centre; extracts from Blisworth Women's Institute record book 1938–43 (NFWI/69) reproduced by permission of the Northamptonshire Record Office; "Trench Warfare', a study of 'Dig for Victory' in Brighton and Hove during World War Two', (unpublished dissertation, University of Sussex 2001), reproduced by kind permission of the author, Joanne Chamberlain; Crown Copyright material: contains public sector information licensed under the Open Government Licence v1.0; letter from Sir Wyndam Deedes reproduced by kind permission of the Estate of Sir Wyndam Deedes; extracts from the *Express* reproduced courtesy of *Express* Newspapers; extracts from *The Gardeners' Chronicle* reproduced courtesy of *Horticulture Week*, Haymarket Media Group; material by Roy Hay reproduced by kind permission of the author's estate; material reproduced from the Imperial War Museum archives: every effort has been made to trace copyright holders and the author and the Imperial War Museum would be grateful for any information which might help to trace those whose identities or addresses are not currently known; material from the John Innes archives reproduced courtesy of the John Innes Foundation; material from the Kew archives reproduced with the kind permission of the Board of Trustees of the Royal Botanic Gardens, Kew; material from the Lindley Library and Royal Horticultural Society archives reproduced courtesy of the Royal Horticultural Society; material from the Mass Observation Archive reproduced with permission of Curtis Brown Group Ltd, London on behalf of The Trustees of the Mass Observation Archive. Copyright © The Trustees of the Mass Observation Archive; extracts from *Mrs Milburn's Diaries: An Englishwoman's Everyday Reflections 1939–45* reproduced by kind permission of the author's estate; material from the Museum of English Rural Life reproduced courtesy of the Museum of English Rural Life, University of Reading; material from the National Allotments Society Archive reproduced courtesy of the National Society of Allotment and Leisure Gardeners; material by Harold Nicholson copyright of the Harold Nicolson Literary Estate; letter by Lt Col. R. R. B. Orlebar reproduced by kind permission of the author's estate; material by Marguerite Patten reproduced by kind permission of the author; extracts from *Punch* reproduced with permission of Punch Limited; material by Vita Sackville-West reproduced with permission of Curtis Brown Group Ltd, London on behalf of the Estate of Vita Sackville-West: *The Land* © Vita Sackville West 1926; *The Garden* © Vita Sackville-West 1946; material from *Countrywomen in war time – Women's Institutes 1938–1945* by Anne Stamper reproduced courtesy of the NFWI, as extracted in *Home and Country*, June 1945; letter from William Stearn reproduced by kind permission of Mrs Ruth Stearn; extracts from *Despatches from the Home Front: The War Diaries of Joan Strange 1939–1945* reproduced courtesy of Chris McCooey, JAK Books; material from the Studley College Archive reproduced courtesy of the Trustees of the Studley College Trust; extracts from the *Daily Telegraph* reproduced courtesy of the Telegraph Media Group Limited (TMG); extracts from *The Times* reproduced courtesy of *The Times*/NI Syndication; material from The Women's Library reproduced courtesy of The Women's Library, London Metropolitan University; extracts from *Letters from Lamledra* by Marjorie Williams reproduced courtesy of Truran Books.

INDEX